COUTURE
SEWING
TECHNIQUES

COUTURE
SEWING

TECHNIQUES

CLAIRE B. SHAEFFER

The Taunton Press

Front cover photo: This jacket, designed by Elsa Schiaparelli in 1938, features elaborate embroidery, molded-plastic locust buttons and fanciful pockets. (Photo by Susan Kahn. Metropolitan Museum of Art. Gift of Mrs. J. R. Keagy, 1974.)

Back cover photos by Susan Kahn (top) and Cathy Carver (bottom)

 The Taunton Press
Inspiration for hands-on living®

© 2001 by Claire B. Shaeffer
All rights reserved.

Printed in the United States of America
10 9 8 7 6 5 4 3

Couture Sewing Techniques was originally published
in hardcover in 1993 by The Taunton Press, Inc.

The Taunton Press, 63 South Main Street, P.O. Box 5506,
Newtown, CT 06470-5506
e-mail: tp@taunton.com

Library of Congress Cataloging-in-Publication Data
Shaeffer, Claire B.
    Couture sewing techniques / Claire B. Shaeffer.
        p.   cm.
    Includes bibliographical references and index.
    ISBN 0-942391-88-8 hardcover
    ISBN 1-56158-497-5 paperback
    1. Dressmaking.   2. Tailoring (Women's)   I. Title.
TT515.S483   1993   93-5680
646.4'04—dc20   CIP

ACKNOWLEDGMENTS

A book of this kind cannot be written without much help and cooperation. I am greatly indebted to the couture industry, which helped me enormously with the research for this book. My thanks in particular go to the *Chambre syndicale de la couture parisienne*, the governing body in Paris of the couture industry, and its members; the couture houses of Hardy Amies, Victor Edelstein, Hartnell and Lachasse in London; Scaasi in New York; and Valentino in Rome.

Special thanks as well go to Marika Genty, archivist at Christian Dior; Jon Moore, couturier at Hardy Amies; and Kim Fink, Coordinator for Study Storage at The Costume Institute of the Metropolitan Museum of Art, for their invaluable help the many times I asked. And thanks, too, to Didier Lecoanet, who permitted me to visit his design studio at Lecoanet Hemant; and to Mme Marguérite Carré for her personal memories of the techniques used at Christian Dior from 1947 to the late 1970s, when she was the *"première de premières."*

I'm deeply grateful to the other couture houses, bespoke tailors, embroiderers and custom shirtmakers who permitted me to visit their workrooms: Balmain, Chez Ninon, Christian Dior, Christian Lacroix, Frank Foster, Gieves and Hawkes, Givenchy, Hanae Mori, Huntsman, Lesage, S. Lock Ltd., Jean Patou, Henry Poole and Co. Ltd., Joseph Rudee & Sons, and Yves Saint Laurent.

And to the heads of the couture workrooms who patiently answered my many questions, my boundless thanks (the names here are those by which they're known in their workrooms): Alan, M. Claude, Mme Elianne, Mme Elisabeth, Erik, Mme Estelle, Mme Faure, Mme Geneviève, M. Gilles, Mme Joanine, Mme Juliette, Miss Lillian, Miss Margaret, Mr. Michael, Mme Odette, Miss Peggy, Peter, Pino, Mme Raymonde, Miss Rita and Wendy.

I also want to thank the curators and assistants of the museums that I visited for their kindness and help: Jean Hildreth, Arizona Costume Institute of the Phoenix Art Museum; Elizabeth Ann Coleman, The Brooklyn Museum; Laura Sinderbrand, Harold Koda, Ellen Shanley, Fred Dennis and Don Petrillo, The Fashion Institute of Technology; Melissa Leventon, Fine Arts Museums of San Francisco; the late Peggy Gilroy, Indianapolis Museum of Art; June Mohler, Kent State University Museum; Jean Druesedow and Kim Fink, Metropolitan Museum of Art; Charles Kleibacker, The Ohio State University; Barbara Dickstein, Smithsonian Institution; Santina Levey, Rosemary Harden and Jennifer Wearden, Victoria & Albert Museum; and Marielle Gierard and Florence Müller, Union française des arts du costume (UFAC).

For initially introducing me years ago to the fascinating world of haute couture, I'm especially grateful to Adeline Giuntini and the late Jessie Scarpa, who were my teachers at the Peralta Community College in Oakland, California.

For the magnificent photographs and illustrations in this book, I'm particularly grateful to Balenciaga Archives, Steve Buchanan, Butterick Marketing Co., Cathy Carver, David Coffin, Courrèges, Dior Archives, D-R, Louis Féraud, Deborah Fillion, Givenchy, Françoise Hugier, Susan Kahn, Lecoanet Hemant, François Lesage, Marc Martin, Hanae Mori, Deborah Newton, Yves Saint Laurent, Irving Solero and UFAC.

Although there's not room to mention every one of the many people and businesses who helped me in my research, I do want to thank Ghislaine Bregé, Britex Fabrics, Louise Brodie, Jan Burke, Elizabeth Corbett, Victor Costa, Sally Cotton, Lydia Cresswell-Jones, Peter Lewis Crown, Véronique de Moussac, Jean de Mouy, Laure du Pavillon, Denise Dubois, Stanley Garfinkel, Robert J.W. Gieve, Romy Godwin, Roy Gonzales, Max Michel Grand, Greenberg & Hammer, Colin Hammick, Joy Henderiks, Ann Hyde, Marie-Andrée Jouve, Betty Kirke, Deborah Kops, Eleanor Lambert, Linton Tweeds Ltd., Grazia Martino, Pamela Lamotte, Marylou Luther, Chez Ninon, Michael Novarese, Emilio Pucci, Elizabeth Rhodes, Hemant Sagar, Olga Saurat, Scarlett's, Imogene Schubert, Florence Schÿler, Barbara Tanner, Alexandra Tchernoff, Antoinette Verspoor and Wilmer Weiss.

I'm particularly grateful to The Taunton Press for undertaking such a challenging project and to its staff whose skills and enthusiasm helped to transform my dreams into reality. I especially want to thank Chris Timmons, my editor, for her invaluable guidance and never-ending patience; Catherine Cassidy, book designer and layout artist, for creating the elegant design; and Pam Purrone, copy/production editor, for her enthusiasm and efficiency.

And last, but not least, my thanks to my husband, Charlie Shaeffer, whose interest and encouragement have made it all possible.

This book is dedicated to home sewers everywhere who appreciate fine workmanship and take pleasure in creating beautiful garments.

CONTENTS

INTRODUCTION

What makes haute couture garments so special that some cost as much as luxury cars and small houses? What construction techniques are used for these garments? Are they really different from those used in home sewing and in the ready-to-wear industry? If so, how are they different? And can home sewers duplicate them?

These are some of the many questions that prompted me 12 years ago to begin thinking seriously about writing a book on couture sewing techniques. I had learned the basics of couture construction in college in the mid-1960s, but I was still unclear about how these techniques fit into the overall couture method of creating a garment. I was determined to figure this out and began my research in earnest.

In the early years, this research was limited to examining garments in museum collections. Even though this was, and continues to be, an invaluable source of information, there are limits on such research because the garments often have linings that hide many of their secrets. To solve this problem, I purchased a few couture pieces from resale shops, thrift stores and antique dealers so that I could rip out the linings to see what lay beneath and take the garments apart if I wanted. Ideally, I would have ordered my own couture design to learn more about the construction process, but, alas, my budget did not permit it.

About six years into my research, I had two unexpected opportunities: The first was to study with American couturier Charles Kleibacker, who taught me how to drape and sew bias-cut dresses. He also helped me update my basic couture skills, but more importantly, he helped me to understand more fully the relationship of the individual techniques to the larger couture method. The second opportunity was to work in luxury ready-to-wear designer Michael Novarese's factory in Los Angeles. Since Novarese combines many couture and ready-to-wear techniques to create his custom-made garments, this experience was also extremely useful for my research.

In the mid-1980s, I expanded my research to include visiting workrooms at couture houses, bespoke (custom) tailors and custom shirtmakers. Sometimes my visit lasted only an hour or a day, but occasionally I stayed a week. I've returned to a few of these workrooms again and again, and I've always learned something new.

By the time I actually began writing this book in early 1990, I had amassed dozens of notebooks and thousands of study photographs. I had interviewed couturiers, luxury ready-to-wear designers, tailors, shirtmakers, the heads of couture workrooms and their staff, the directors of couture salons and their sales staff, archivists, collectors, museum curators and even clients. I had enough information to write several books. Then the problem became an excruciating one: choosing what to include and what to leave out of the book I had in mind.

I decided, first, to describe couture techniques as practiced in couture workrooms rather than adapting these techniques for the home sewer, the approach I and other writers had always taken before. My reasons for this decision were twofold: I wanted to document at least a few of these techniques for future generations, since I fear that couture is a dying craft. And more importantly for home sewers, I feel strongly that grasping the principles used in sewing haute couture will help them better understand garment construction, and in turn help solve many of the problems they periodically encounter. An important benefit of deciding on this organizing principle was that it allowed me to set aside all my notes on luxury ready-to-wear techniques for a future book.

My second decision was to focus on construction techniques themselves, even though elements like draping and design, proportion and balance, fit and fabric are equally important. In choosing which techniques to include, I've concentrated on classic ones that can be applied to a variety of designs and fabrics and offer the most value to the greatest number of home sewers. I also decided to select, whenever possible, techniques that had not been described in print before and to exclude those similar to well-known home-sewing techniques described in many sewing books.

Although none of these editing decisions was easy, one was particularly difficult: I had originally intended to include alternative methods for many of the couture construction processes because in couture there are many means to arrive at the same end. In fact, I can think of no situation in couture where a single method is used universally. But the limits of space made it impossible to include all but the occasional alternative method for a given procedure. And in the end I relied on my observations as a teacher to select the methods that would enable home sewers to achieve the best results in the easiest way.

Also among my decisions was whether to photograph garments or samples. In the end, I decided to photograph both, and I chose garments that, unlike those selected for museum exhibits, are not always historically important nor necessarily the best example of a particular couturier's work. I rejected garments that had undergone major alterations since it's often difficult to determine what had been sewn in the original workroom. The pieces I finally selected all have specific construction details that home sewers can both duplicate and apply to the kinds of garments they're most likely to sew.

No matter what your sewing expertise, I hope you'll find this book a practical guide to the fine construction techniques of haute couture. While some of the techniques are less suitable than others for beginners and some are impractical for everyday sewing, most will be of value to the average sewer and can be used on a wide range of garments and fabrics. I hope you'll experiment with these techniques and look for new ways to apply them whenever you sew. And I hope you'll return again and again to this book, using it as a resource from which to draw, whether you limit your couture sewing to a detail here and there or decide to make an entire garment from beginning to end with couture techniques.

The book itself is divided into two sections. The first five chapters are designed to introduce you to the world of haute couture and familiarize you with the basic skills and essential techniques of couture. The last six chapters focus on the application of couture techniques to garments. My instincts as a teacher compel me to suggest that you read or closely peruse the first section before proceeding to the second.

The measurements used throughout the book are only guidelines, and although they may be appropriate for many fabrics, they might not be exactly right for the fabric you're using. For this reason, I suggest that you always purchase an additional ¼ yd. of fabric when you start a project so that you have extra material to make samples before sewing the actual garment. This allows you to fine-tune the dimensions for a particular fabric and practice your skills before working on the garment itself. Should you be unfamiliar with a particular technique or term, you'll find both a glossary and an index at the back of the book to help you.

With regard to the drawings in this book, note that the right side of the fabric is always shown shaded, and where a drawing has several steps, they are numbered sequentially. For the sake of clarity, thread tracing has been included in the drawings only where it's important to the information being conveyed. For the same reason, seam allowances appear narrow and consistent in width in the drawings, even though in couture, as explained in the text, they are inconsistent in width and quite wide.

I find sewing by hand and with couture techniques extremely rewarding. The pleasure of both making and wearing beautifully constructed garments far exceeds the time and effort required to complete them. I hope this book will help you develop these same skills and perfect old ones, and in turn, reward you with years of pleasure—and a closet full of beautifully made garments.

PART I

~

THE BASICS OF
COUTURE SEWING

CHAPTER 1

~

INSIDE THE WORLD OF
HAUTE COUTURE

When I left for Paris in January of 1991 for a week of press previews of the haute couture collections, the Gulf War had just begun and the weather was brutally cold. Though I'd visited the workrooms of many couture houses over the years, this would be the first time I would see the week of runway shows of the collections, and I was unsure of what to expect.

I soon found that each show was as different from the next as the designs it presented. But all were extravagant and exhilarating to watch. Photographers were everywhere, positioning themselves on both sides of the runway before the show and busily snapping pictures of important guests for the society pages of their newspapers. Once the show began there was no commentary, only music, from rock to opera, depending on the designer's preference or the show's theme. The designs themselves were magnificent, although some were outlandish and not really intended to be worn off the runway. Many, however, would appear in the next edition of major newspapers around the globe, and some would set the next season's fashion trends across the economic spectrum.

Literally translated, the French phrase *haute couture* means "sewing at a high level," but a better translation might be the "finest high-fashion sewing." Although the haute couture designs shown on runways in Paris, Rome, London and New York are too expensive for most pocketbooks, their influence on styles, colors and accessories echoes throughout the women's clothing industry worldwide. For the home sewer, haute couture designs have a special relevance. Custom-sewn for a select group of women who can afford them, couture garments are simply the most beautifully made in the world, and many of the techniques used in couture workrooms can be duplicated at home.

Originating in mid-19th-century Paris with the designs of an Englishman named Charles Frederick Worth (see the historical sidebar starting on p. 16), haute couture represents an archaic tradition of creating garments by hand with painstaking care and precision. In an elaborate process that's very much the same today as it was in the 1850s, each couture garment is custom cut, fitted and even frequently redesigned to suit a particular individual. The process involves numerous steps and people with specialized skills, from the *couturier*, or designer (traditionally, though not always, a man), who creates the design to the team of assistants, fitters and needleworkers who bring it to life. The abundance of hand work and attention to detail required in couture sewing means that a workroom team of four to eight people may require 70 to 90 hours to create a simple day dress and hundreds of hours to produce a richly embellished evening gown. Consequently, the cost of a couture design is very high, but in the haute couture industry, meeting high design and production standards takes precedence over controlling expenses.

Today, even though there are excellent couturiers in London and Rome, the center of haute couture remains in Paris, where there is an enormous support structure of skilled needleworkers and workshops specializing in hand embroidery, beading, feather work, braiding, fabric flowers and custom-made accessories. In France, the term *haute couture* is strictly controlled by the *Chambre syndicale de la couture parisienne* (Parisian High Fashion Syndicate), the governing body of French fashion houses. The use of this term is reserved exclusively for the group's 13 members, who meet the strict qualifying rules outlined below. The official 2000 list included the couture houses of Balmain, Chanel, Christian Dior, Christian Lacroix, Emanuel Ungaro, Givenchy, Hanae Mori, Jean Louis Scherrer, Jean-Paul Gaultier, Lecoanet Hemant, Lapidus, Torrente and Yves Saint Laurent. There are also four "membres invités": Adeline Andre, Dominique Sirop, Franck Sorbier, and Pascal Humbert, as well as two *"membres correspondants"*: Valentino and Gianni Versace.

To earn the right to call itself a couture house and use the term *haute couture* in its advertising or in any other way, a member of the *Chambre syndicale* must design fashions that are made to order for private clients and involve one or more fittings, have a workroom in Paris

Especially gifted at working with fabric, Spanish-born couturier Cristobal Balenciaga developed the graceful silhouette of this silk gazar gown in 1967 by cutting the front on the bias with flared seamlines and attaching the skirt with a buttressed seam (see p. 192). The toile, or muslin working pattern, shows the designer's penciled notations for cutting and executing the design. (Photo by Brian Gulick, courtesy of Threads *magazine, Balenciaga Archives and The Fashion Institute of Technology.)*

with at least 20 full-time workers, present a collection of at least 50 designs, day and evening garments, to the press in Paris in January and July during the Spring/Summer and Autumn/Winter seasons and show the Collection to potential clients in the respective couture houses in a determined place.

The *Chambre syndicale's* definition of a couture house is so limiting that it excludes such notables as the Italian couture houses of Mila Schön, Renato Balestra, Antonio Capucci and Lancetti, who both work and show their designs in Paris but maintain workrooms in Italy, as well as the houses of Renato Balestra, Antonio Capucci and Lancetti, who both work and show their collections in Italy. Also excluded are the English couture houses of Hardy Amies and Lachasse, who maintain workrooms and present their collections in London (the well-known English houses of Hartnell and Victor Edelstein had unfortunately closed their doors as this book went to press). Similarly excluded was the house of American designer Arnold Scaasi. Even the old, established French couture house of Jean Patou doesn't qualify because, although its workrooms are in Paris, it does not present a collection. For these designers, being unable to officially use the term *haute couture* in reference to their work means that their ability to sell their licenses in other countries for all manner of other products is greatly reduced (see p. 19).

WHAT MAKES COUTURE "HAUTE"?

What's so special about haute couture designs that simple day dresses range in price from $8,000 to $15,000, suits from $10,000 to $30,000, and evening gowns from $15,000 to as much as $150,000? There are many factors, notably the fabulous, exclusive fabrics used; the flawless design, cut and fit of each garment; and the exquisite craftsmanship.

Haute couture begins with strong, innovative design—the couturier's ability to interpret the mood of the time for the mode of the world. Whether classically styled or exaggerated, couture designs rely on such basic design principles as proportion, balance, color and texture, and they conform to the image of the couture house.

Maintaining the integrity of a design while making adjustments to suit a client's figure and personal preferences is a delicate balancing act. Most couture houses

Created by American designer Charles James in several versions from 1949 to 1972, these two classically styled ballgowns maintain their shape with the help of backings, underskirts and built-in foundations. On both the 'Four-Leaf Clover' design in the foreground and its companion in the background, the skirt is backed with Pellon interfacing and buckram, and is supported by several underskirts. (Metropolitan Museum of Art. Right, gift of Elizabeth Fairall, 1953; left, gift of E.J. Taylor, 1975.)

will go to great lengths to do both. Several years ago, for example, when I visited the workrooms of English designer Hardy Amies, the staff had just fitted a client's dress, which she felt was about 1 in. too short. The black velvet, asymmetrical design featured a 4-in. pleated taffeta ruffle inserted in a seamline that began at the left shoulder, curved gently downward and ended at the right side seam about 4 in.—a ruffle's width—above the hemline. Since the garment had a wide hem allowance, it could have been lengthened by simply lowering the hem, but then the proportion of the ruffle's width and distance to the hemline would have been spoiled. Rather than demean the design, the house decided to lower the seamline, even though it meant cutting a new right front that positioned the ruffle precisely 4 in. above the hem.

Couture designs are enhanced by the extraordinary fabrics from which they're sewn. Only the finest luxury fabrics are used in couture, and they frequently cost hundreds of dollars a yard—some cost more than a thousand dollars a yard. Although most fabrics are made of natural fibers, a few couturiers use metallic, plastic and man-made fibers for special effects.

Many printed fabrics are made with exclusive patterns or colorways (that is, the same design presented in different colors) designed by either the couturier or a fabric designer. A few couturiers work closely with a fabric house to develop new fabrics. Some fabrics, such as the silk gazar designed in 1958 for Balenciaga by the noted fabric-design firm of Abraham (see the photo on p. 69) and the printed silk muslin designed in 1947 for Dior by the firm of Bianchini-Ferier (see the photo on p. 192) are still widely used. Many other original fabrics are, of course, no longer available.

The long-standing liaison between the House of Chanel and the fabric firm of Linton Tweeds began with Chanel's first collection in 1919 and continues today. Used for Chanel's famous suits, Linton fabrics are usually a combination of wool and mohair, but some incorporate acrylic, metallic material and even cellophane. The House of Chanel chooses from 15 to 40 exclusive patterns for the firm of Linton to weave in lengths of 6 meters to 8 meters. Linton also weaves fancy selvages and supplies Chanel with matching yarns and narrow trims to accompany the fabric.

In the *atelier*, or workroom, of a couture house, printed fabric patterns are sometimes cut apart, rearranged and sewn back together to create special effects for a particular design. This procedure is most often used to rearrange the color bars on striped fabrics or to appliqué motifs where there is a void on the garment, but I've seen fabrics that were literally created in the atelier. Some are relatively simple creations—such as the red-and-blue striped Chanel blouse I saw that was made by

Yves Saint Laurent designed this two-piece evening suit for his Autumn/Winter 1985-1986 Collection so that the motifs would match exactly at the front opening and the print would seem to continue, uninterrupted, from the tunic to the pants. (Photo by Claude Ohm, courtesy of Yves Saint Laurent.)

cutting red and blue fabrics into narrow strips and seaming them together. Others, such as the fabric customized in Valentino's atelier for a wedding gown, are extremely labor intensive. That particular fabric had pink and white ruffled diamond patterns completely covering the gown's tulle skirt, which took four workers four weeks to make.

Buttons are often custom-made as well. They range from Chanel's signature metal buttons with the double-C logo or lion's head to Schiaparelli's more avant-garde, whimsical designs like the locust buttons made of molded plastic shown on p. 150 and her ceramic trapeze artists on p. 136.

A couture garment fits flawlessly as a result of multiple fittings on the client's dress form (customized to duplicate her figure), but more impressive than the fit are the subtle ways in which a couture garment is proportioned for the individual client. For an asymmetrical figure, for example, the collar, pockets and shoulder seam may be slightly narrower on one side. For a full figure, vertical seamlines are moved in or out as needed to create the most flattering line, while for a short figure, all horizontal seamlines are adjusted, not just the waistline and hem. On garments with embroidery or beading, the embellished design is scaled to the dimensions of the client's garment, so that it doesn't overwhelm a smaller figure or float against a sizable background on a larger one.

Impeccable craftsmanship is a hallmark of haute couture. In a couture atelier, every facet of a garment is treated with equal respect and attention, whether it's a perfectly rolled collar on a suit jacket or the seam allowances on a blouse finished with minute, evenly spaced, hand-stitched overcasting that no one but the client will see.

This attention to detail is the essence of haute couture, and it begins long before the fabric is cut. With the help of a muslin pattern, or *toile*, every design is planned so that motifs, stripes or plaids are not only matched, but also positioned most attractively for the client's figure. At garment openings, floral motifs match so perfectly you have to look twice to see the fasteners, and on suits and two-piece designs, the fabric pattern continues uninterrupted from neck to hem (see the photo of the Yves Saint Laurent pantsuit on p. 9).

During the construction process, most of the sewing is done by hand. Thousands of perfectly spaced basting stitches mark or hold the garment layers together temporarily so a design can be fitted on the client or dress form, stitched permanently or precisely pressed. Then these stitches are taken out so the construction can continue. Again and again, the fabric is painstakingly shaped and manipulated in the hands or on a form until the garment is completed. Even the seams may be permanently sewn by hand. The construction of the dress, gown or suit that emerges may look effortless, but it takes many hours to produce that effortless look.

In this inside view of an Yves Saint Laurent jacket (designed in 1978 and shown in full on p. 137), you can see a small portion of the considerable hand sewing that went into this design. (Photo by Susan Kahn. Author's collection.)

All of the hand sewing that goes into making a couture garment distinguishes it from a comparable design in luxury ready-to-wear, which is known in France as *prêt-à-porter*. Priced from $200 for a cotton shirt, for example, to $10,000 for an evening gown, luxury ready-to-wear is sewn from high-quality fabrics and sold in better stores and boutiques all over the world. Hundreds of copies of each design are sewn, primarily by machine operators, who are part of a piecework system—each one performs the same operation over and over. As a result, there's considerably less hand work on many luxury ready-to-wear garments by such designers as Geoffrey Beene, Bill Blass, James Galanos, Oscar de la Renta or Mary McFadden. The garments are nonetheless lovely, and most are clean-finished, or lined with rayon or silk that conceals pinked or unfinished seams.

LECOANET HEMANT
5, rue Lamennais - 75008 PARIS
S.A.R.L. au capital de 1.000.000 de F.
SIRET 320 518 370 00022 - APE 4704

When a client wants a one-of-a-kind design, the couturier will send her several sketches and fabric swatches to choose from. Shown above are a sketch and swatch for a short evening gown that were sent to a client of Lecoanet Hemant. (Original sketch courtesy of Lecoanet Hemant.)

CREATING A COUTURE COLLECTION

Twice a year, in January and July, each couture house spends a fortune—$750,000 to $3,000,000—to make and present its collections to important clients, celebrities and the press. Although the couture shows were once quiet, sedate affairs held in couture salons, they've become mad, theatrical extravaganzas produced in ballrooms and theaters with loud music and lights. Designed to lure almost 1,500 members of the media to Paris, the shows generate important publicity for the designers in the form of television and radio broadcasts and hundreds of articles on the fashion pages of newspapers and magazines throughout the industrialized world. With the help of the media, the couturiers make their fashion statements, heralding new silhouettes and hemlines, endorsing the fabrics and colors of the season, and occasionally delivering unexpected fashion jolts. The most successful designs that make headlines in January and July are eventually copied or translated into mass-produced clothing in all price ranges. As a laboratory for women's fashions, the couture industry has a major impact on what women wear.

A couture collection is frequently developed around a theme such as a major art exhibit, an exotic vacation spot or a period in fashion history. The collection will have some day dresses, some suits (and occasionally trouser suits), a few short evening designs and a number of long gowns. Some designs will be comfortable and may flatter older or less-than-perfect figures. Others may be memorable but less comfortable, including a few glitzy showstoppers to promote the house's image and excite the press. Some designs will be elegant, and a few will be unbelievably opulent.

DESIGNING THE COLLECTION

The first phase of assembling a collection begins in the couturier's design studio many months before the press show. Equipped with a thorough understanding of both human anatomy and the properties of fibers and fabrics, the couturier may begin with either the fabric or the silhouette. They must be compatible because the combined qualities of the fabric, that is, its weight, drape, texture and hand (a fabric's crispness or softness), will make it appropriate for some types of silhouettes and not for others. If the designer is contemplating an exaggerated, sculpted look, a crisp, tightly woven fabric will probably be chosen. If, on the other hand, the designer begins with a bolt of soft fabric, the design will probably fall more gently and follow the lines of the body. One designer known for his ability to use a fabric to its fullest potential was the Spaniard Cristobal Balenciaga. His gown shown on p. 6 was designed to show off the lovely architectural quality of silk gazar.

When the fabrics arrive, the couturier drapes unfolded lengths of each one over a dress form or a model to see how it hangs on the lengthwise grain, crossgrain and bias. Then, using this information as a guide, he makes hundreds of *croquis*, or design sketches, for his collection. Since it's impossible to develop toiles for every sketch, the editing process to select the best designs and fine-tune the focus of the collection begins at once. This is usually done by the couturier with the help of design assistants and the *premières*, the heads of the ateliers, whose technical expertise is highly regarded. The design sketches are then distributed to the workrooms.

Checking the effect in a mirror, Christian Dior drapes silk taffeta on a model to begin a design for his 1948 collection. (Photo by Bellini, courtesy of Christian Dior.)

THE WORK OF THE ATELIERS

Depending on the type of garment the couturier has designed, his sketch will go to the *atelier de tailleur* (tailoring workroom) or to the *atelier de flou* (dressmaking workroom). The jackets, dresses, skirts and other garments made in the tailoring workroom are more structured than those created in the dressmaking workroom, and the tailoring fabrics, usually woolens, tend to be heavier than dressmaker fabrics. In the tailoring workroom, the fabric is often shaped by stretching and shrinking it (see p. 59) and is supported by the garment's *entoilage*, or inner structure of interfacings and pad stitching. A few houses have two tailoring workrooms: one that concentrates on tailored, menswear-influenced designs made of fabrics similar in texture, weave and weight to those used for menswear; and a second that concentrates on softer dressmaker styles made of soft wools, mohairs, bouclés or chenilles.

In the dressmaking atelier, where many gowns, dresses, blouses and other garments are sewn, silk is the predominant fabric. Many of the garments made in this workroom are softly draped designs that have to be sewn on a dress form from the right side of the garment in order for the draped folds of the design to be accurately pinned and stitched in place. Some designs have no inner structure and rely completely on the body to give them shape (see the bias-cut dress designed by Madeleine Vionnet, shown on p. 118). Others, like the gown designed by Charles James, shown on p. 8, may be backed or rely on an elaborate inner structure. Designs sewn in the dressmaking workroom are rarely lined because the lining will not allow the garment to move easily with the body.

After discussing the design with the couturier, the première decides who will make the toiles and sew the prototypes, called *modèles*. The toiles and prototypes are usually sewn by the *premières mains,* (literally the "first hands"), the most experienced workers in the atelier, and a small group of workers, or *mains* ("hands"), with a variety of skills and training. Then a muslin fabric in the appropriate weight for the design is selected, and the toile is draped on a dress form to duplicate the couturier's design sketch and provide the basic pattern from which the garment will be sewn. Depending on the complexity of the design, this process usually takes four to eight hours.

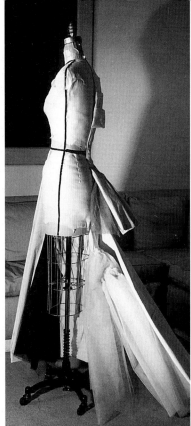

This muslin toile was made for a custom-designed wedding dress by Arnold Scaasi in 1991. The top skirt has a deep apron at the front with a short bustle at the back, while the lower skirt forms a short train. The bustle and train are supported by layers of tulle ruffles that are attached to the foundation and underskirt, as shown in the cut-away view above. (Photos courtesy of Threads *magazine.)*

Even though the toile is just a working pattern, it's made carefully with the necessary underpinnings and sometimes even with buttonholes. During its development, the toile is basted and rebasted for fittings on one of the house models and is examined and modified again and again until the couturier is satisfied.

Once the toile is approved by the couturier, he reviews the fabric selection for the prototype to make certain it's still appropriate for the design. The toile is then carefully ripped apart and pressed so that it can serve as a pattern for cutting the fashion fabric. After the fash-

ion fabric is cut and marked with thread tracing (see p. 39), the prototype is completely basted for a first fitting on a house model. Then it's modified and corrected as needed, which usually involves two or three fittings, until the couturier is satisfied with the results. To save time finishing the prototypes, the edges are sometimes serged or zigzagged, and it's not uncommon for tailored garments to be left unlined. Finally, jewelry, hats and shoes are selected by the couturier or his assistants for the press show and the design is entered in the *livre de fabrications,* or production book.

At the house of Christian Dior, every client has a personal dress form, padded and covered with a muslin body suit. (Photo by Ikes, courtesy of Christian Dior.)

ORDERING
A COUTURE DESIGN
AT THE HOUSE OF DIOR

Let me take you on an imaginary shopping spree at the famous House of Dior. The best times to visit are in February or September, when you can see the private fashion show, called the *défilé*, which is held several days each week immediately after the collection is shown to the press. If this isn't convenient, you can visit at another time and watch a videotape of the fashion show.

To make an appointment at Dior, you'll need to write the *directrice*, who manages the salon, or wait until you arrive in Paris and ask the concierge at your hotel to contact her for you. If you have a friend who shops at Dior, she may recommend that you ask for her *vendeuse* (salesperson); otherwise, one will be assigned to you. That assignment will be permanent unless you request a change. You'll get to know each other well, and she'll offer expert fashion advice on selecting the clothes that are appropriate for your lifestyle and figure and on accessorizing your wardrobe. In fact, a vendeuse is sometimes trusted so implicitly that the client allows her to select her garments and doesn't bother to come in until they're ready for the first fitting. Don't worry if you don't speak French; most of the salespeople speak fluent English.

If you arrive a little early on the day of the fashion show, you can browse in the beautiful pearl-grey and white ground-floor boutique, where you'll find the luxury ready-to-wear collection, lingerie, accessories, menswear and decorative items for the home. Furs, millinery and the couture salon are on the floor above. Present yourself at the reception desk so you can meet your vendeuse, who will show you to your seat. During the show, note the numbers of the designs you want to see. If you want to try some on, you can stay afterwards or make an appointment to come another day.

You'll probably want to "try the house" with a small order—a day dress or a suit. Although some clients will order an entire wardrobe from the same designer, most prefer nowadays to patronize several houses, unlike in the 1940s and 1950s when clients were dressed exclusively by a single couturier.

To look at the designs you've selected, you'll be escorted to a small room upholstered with silk moiré and mirrors. The designs will be brought from the *cabine*, or models' dressing room, where the prototypes are stored. Since they're custom-made for tall, extremely thin models, they may not fit, but don't worry.

Depending on your size, you can get an idea of what you'll look like in a given design by slipping into the prototype without zipping it, or by having it pinned to your slip. If you prefer, one of the house models will model it so that you can see it on the figure at close range. Since you probably aren't accustomed to shopping this way, you might be alarmed at the idea of ordering a costly garment that you haven't tried on in your size. But your vendeuse has had years of experience, and since the business of haute couture depends on loyal customers, she isn't going to let you purchase an unflattering design. She'll guide you to a better choice instead.

Once you've made your selection, discuss any changes you want with the vendeuse—for example, a different neckline or sleeve, another fabric, a longer or shorter skirt or possibly two skirts. How much you can change a design depends on the couturier. Most don't mind as long as they feel the integrity of the design remains intact.

Next, your measurements will be taken by the première of the tailoring or dressmaking ateliers. You'll be measured from head to toe—about 30 measurements altogether, which will be turned over to the première main, who will be responsible for your design. She'll pad a dress form with horsehair or lambswool to duplicate your figure, including any quirks or irregularities noted by the première, and cover the form with a muslin body suit, called a *toile de corps*, which zips up the back.

Using the design's original prototype or its muslin toile as a guide, the première main will make a toile of the design on your dress form. She'll drape, mold and pin pieces of muslin to the form until she's pleased with its design and fit.

If you were to lay your toile on top of the original toile for the prototype, you'd probably find that they're quite different in cut even though they look exactly the same on dress forms. This is one of the most fascinating aspects of the construction of a couture garment. Your toile will reflect the changes made to accommodate,

Designed by Gianfranco Ferre for Christian Dior's 1991 Spring/Summer Collection, this short, red damask evening dress features an asymmetrical bodice and a flared overskirt accented at the waist with an embroidered bow. Note how beautifully finished the toile to the model's left is. (Photo by Françoise Huguier, courtesy Christian Dior.)

flatter and fit your individual figure. It takes an atelier worker many years to learn which adjustments will be most flattering to the client and then execute them on a toile without visibly altering the design.

After the fabric for your garment has been cut, the garment sections will be marked with thread tracing. Then, almost every detail of the design, including the hem, zipper and sometimes even the lining, is hand basted for the first fitting.

About a week after you've ordered your garment, you'll have your first fitting. Although the garment may have thread tracings marking the garment centers and balance lines so that the fit can be easily evaluated, it may look finished to you because the basting stitches are so fine and regular. Fortunately, the fitting room is large enough to accommodate the your vendeuse and the directrice or couturier, who will evaluate the fit and design of your garment, and the première or première main, who will mark any necessary adjustments.

Back in the workroom, all the basted seams are ripped apart and the sections laid flat on the table. Called *mis à plat,* or "laying out flat," this procedure is one of the distinguishing techniques of couture construction. The corrections marked during the fitting are made on the garment sections and also on the toile for future reference, should you want another similar design. When necessary, a new garment section is cut to replace one that can't be corrected. If the garment has embroidery, beading or another type of embellishment, it's done at this point. Often the garment sections to be embellished are sent out to one of the small firms in Paris that specialize in ornamentation. Then the corrected and embellished garment sections are rebasted, pockets are added and the permanent stitching is completed on seams and details that don't require further fitting.

At your second fitting, the garment is checked to be sure it fits and hangs correctly, and any minor adjustments are indicated so the design can be completed. If the design is very complex or your figure is difficult to fit, there may be additional fittings.

Although heavily embellished designs may require several months to complete, most designs are finished in two to three weeks, but for the special client they're sometimes made in less time. Givenchy, for example, made a coat overnight for the Duchess of Windsor to wear to her husband's funeral.

When your own garment is completed, you'll have your final fitting, and assuming all is well, the *griffe* (label) will then be sewn in. It's considered bad luck to sew it in before the final fitting. At Dior, the date of the collection is woven on the label, and the fabrication number (the cumulative number of garments produced by the house) is stamped on it. Finally, the design is logged into the *livre de compte,* or sales book, carefully packed and delivered to your hotel or shipped to your home.

At Dior, as at most houses, your new outfit comes with an unspoken, unconditional guarantee of satisfaction. If the color is wrong, you may return it even though the error was yours. If you lose or gain weight, the garment will be altered, frequently at no extra charge.

A HISTORICAL GLANC

IN THE BEGINNING

France was already firmly established as the world's foremost fashion leader when Louis Napoleon Bonaparte established the Second Empire in 1852. About the same time, an Englishman named Charles Frederick Worth, a sales assistant at the famous Parisian fabric store, Gagelin-Opigez et Cie., persuaded his employers to allow him to open a new department with a few

Designed in 1898 by the House of Worth, this satin gown, with its woven velvet Art Nouveau pattern, exemplifies the luxury fabrics used then and now in couture designs. (Metropolitan Museum of Art. Gift of Miss Eva Drexel Dahlgren, 1976.)

dressmakers. By combining his extensive knowledge of fabrics and garment construction with a talent for promotion, Worth soon developed a flourishing department, establishing himself as the only male dressmaker in Paris. Worth executed each of his original designs in several Gagelin fabrics, distinguishing himself from conventional dressmakers, who were well-trained technicians who combined the customer's design and fabric. In so doing, he became the father of haute couture, a phrase coined in 1863 by one of his American clients, a Mrs. Moulton.

In 1858, Worth created his own couture house with his partner Gustof Bobergh. Within two years, he secured the patronage of the French Empress Eugénie, one of the most important fashion leaders of all time. He was the first to establish a house style and create a collection of seasonal designs shown on live models. In 1868 Worth established the *Chambre syndicale de la couture parisienne*, the governing body of French fashion (see p. 7).

Worth also pioneered revolutionary changes in garment construction. He was the first to understand the relationship of the fabric to the design. He began cutting garment sections with the grain and used one of the concepts of mass production—interchangeable, modular parts—to create a variety of different designs. But the fashion change he made that pleased him most was abolishing the "cage," or hoop skirt, in favor of a more relaxed silhouette.

When the Franco-Prussian War toppled the Second Empire in 1870, the fairy tale ended, and Worth lost his single most visible client when Empress Eugénie went into exile. Paris nonetheless continued as the international leader of high fashion—albeit more restrained fashion—and Worth continued to supply large and expensive wardrobes to women of wealth and note in Europe and America.

As La Belle Epoque dawned, the first important woman designer, Madame Pacquin, founded her couture house in 1891. Although she became known for glamorous evening gowns, exquisite workmanship and innovative mix of materials, Pacquin was also a practical designer. She introduced a dress style tailored enough for day wear but elegant enough for informal evening occasions. She was the first French designer to publicize her designs by sending several models to the races at Longchamps wearing the same outfit, and she was the first to open international branches of her couture house.

CHANGING TIMES

When the new century dawned, women were still confined in tightly laced corsets and elaborately ornamented clothing, but the fashion world was ready for a change. Credited with modernizing dress design, Paul Poiret introduced the straight silhouette in 1907, which has dominated fashion for most of the century. Worn with a less confining corset, the forerunner of the brassiere, his new design was a simple narrow tube with a high waist.

Unlike his predecessors, Poiret was inspired by the contemporary arts rather than by the fashions of the past. The first couturier to collaborate with artists such as Raoul Dufy, Poiret produced new fashions that were bold, brilliantly colored and exotic, and were distinguished more by their decoration than by their cut. Then in 1910, he introduced his infamous hobble skirt. Although so narrow that it had to be worn with "hobble garters" to limit the wearer's stride and keep her from splitting the fabric, it was popular among fashionable women, including suffragettes.

Madeleine Vionnet, another innovative designer, showed her radical new designs in 1907 while working for French couturier Jacques Doucet, one of the major competitors of the House of Worth at the turn of the century. Cut entirely on the bias and worn over corsetless figures, Vionnet's dresses appeared simple in design, but their construction was actually quite complex. More of an instant sensation initially than a success, Vionnet's designs didn't became popular until after World War I.

Mass production of various goods began during the war, and many women entered the work force. By the end of the war, the woman's role in society had changed. Women cut their hair, discarded their corsets for garter belts, and shortened their skirts first to the ankles (1917), then to the calves (1923), and finally to the knees (1927).

Even though clients from the Austrian, German, Balkan and Russian courts had vanished, the couture houses thrived after the war. They created simpler, less individualized designs intended for wealthy, fashionable women in France and abroad, but most sales were now made to retailers, who purchased hundreds of models to sell to their many wealthy American customers or to manufacturers who planned to copy them. As a result, many couture houses became small factories specializing in handmade designs.

During the 1920s, the "garçonne," or boyish look, became popular, introducing a new informality to the haute couture fashion scene, which was dominated by Coco Chanel and Jean Patou. Chanel put her rich clients, who had been wearing satin and lace day dresses, into casual, unstructured jersey dresses and woolen cardigan jackets accessorized with expensive costume jewelry. Patou's designs were more elegant, even though inspired by sporting clothing. The first to use his monogram as a design element, Patou invented the V-neck sweater and the short pleated skirt.

The 1929 Wall Street crash abruptly ended the prosperous Roaring Twenties. When the United States raised import taxes to as much as 90% on elaborately embellished couture designs, many houses began selling designs and toiles to retailers and manufacturers that could be imported to America duty free, along with a license to copy them.

In the 1930s, fashions changed dramatically. Influenced by Hollywood films, women returned to more feminine, elaborately designed clothing, proportioned to emphasize the bodice. Italian-born designer Elsa Schiaparelli created outlandish fashions in unique color combinations. Known for her hard-edge chic and fantasy, "la Schiap" created styles that often featured prints and embellishments designed by such artists as Dali and Cocteau. She is credited with inventing the long dinner suit and voluminous evening trousers, and she was the first designer to use zippers. Inspired by masculine uniforms, she introduced the broad-shouldered, boxy silhouette that dominated fashion from 1933 to the late 1940s.

After Germany invaded France in 1940, many couture houses closed, while others moved—Molyneux to London and Mainbocher to America—but most continued to present small collections. The Germans tried to relocate the French couture houses to Berlin and Vienna, but they were saved by designer Lucien Lelong, president of the *Chambre syndicale*, who persuaded the Germans that the French houses could not function without the thousands of small French-based businesses which supplied them with materials—a fact that remains true today, more than 50 years later.

During the war years, American designers like Gilbert Adrian, Charles James, Claire McCardell, Mainbocher, Norman Norell, Hattie Carnegie, and Sophie Gimbel developed an American style. Intended for a more active lifestyle, this style was straightforward and more youthful than the European tradition on which it was built.

THE NEW LOOK

Women's fashions remained virtually unchanged after the war until Christian Dior showed his first collection in 1947. Dubbed a "New Look" by Carmel Snow, editor of *Harper's Bazaar*, Dior's designs featured long, full skirts, wasp waists and narrow sloping shoulders. His timing was perfect. Greatly influenced by La Belle Epoque, Dior restored femininity to a world tired of uniforms and uniformity and made fashion exciting once more. The couture industry was revitalized, and Christian Dior ruled the fashion roost for the next decade.

Sewn from light wool crepe and silk shantung, 'Tailleur bar' is one Dior's most famous New Look designs. The close-fitting jacket with sloping shoulders and wasp waist sets off the full, pleated skirt, which required about 6 yd. of fabric. (Courtesy of Christian Dior.)

During the post-war boom and into the 1950s, haute couture flourished. Pierre Balmain created magnificent ball gowns, Jacques Fath introduced pastels to bridal wear and Hubert de Givenchy introduced separates to high fashion. In the early 1950s, an unfitted silhouette was ushered in with Cristobal Balenciaga's introduction of the sack dress in 1951 and the semi-fitted suit the next year. Although ridiculed at first, Balenciaga continued to create fashions with his revolutionary silhouette, and by the mid-1950s, many designers were showing designs that bypassed the waist. Notable was Yves Saint Laurent's trapeze dress, created for his first collection at Dior in 1958 (see p. 120). The new relaxed silhouette was off and running but, unfortunately, its success, later combined with fashion and fabric developments in the 1960s, would have a devastating effect on haute couture.

By the mid-1960s, couture fashions were less structured and even more casual, inspired by the loose-fitting fashions of the hippie movement. Many designs were so short and youthful that couture customers couldn't imagine wearing them. With the demise of the bra and fitted silhouettes, the fashions coming out of Paris were easily copied in all price ranges. For the first time in history, couture had lost its leading edge, and many couture houses launched *prêt-a-porter*, or luxury ready-to-wear, collections. Pierre Cardin, the first to do so in 1959, was promptly expelled from the *Chambre syndicale*. His expulsion was short-lived, however, and in the next ten years, many other couture houses followed his example. By 1975, luxury ready-to-wear was an important industry. Unfortunately, the success of the new luxury ready-to-wear clothing came at the expense of haute couture fashions. The easy availability of luxury ready-to-wear meant that retailers and manufacturers no longer had to purchase toiles and designs for copying.

THE "ME DECADE"

Dubbed the "Me Decade" by writer Tom Wolfe, the 1970s offered many choices. Fashions were romantic, individualistic and unstructured, with extravagant interpretations of Russian, Chinese, African, Indian and gypsy themes, as well as "retro" looks from the 1920s, '30s and '40s. The decade, however, was dominated by pants—from very short hot pants, stovepipes and bell-bottoms to Yves Saint Laurent's perfection of his masculine trouser suit for women.

With the 1980s came an English royal wedding, an infusion of Middle Eastern petrol dollars, the ostentatious Reagan Era and new clients from Japan. There was lots of new money, younger customers and a renewed interest in haute couture. Karl Lagerfeld was hired to modernize the Chanel style and resuscitate the couture house. The innovative Christian Lacroix revived the House of Patou and promptly left to establish his own label, putting us all in pouf dresses. Yves Saint Laurent perfected his classic styles for day and rich fantasies for evening, Pierre Cardin continued to perfect his geometric-inspired futurist shapes, and Givenchy and Valentino created the elegant luxuries their clients adore.

COUTURE TODAY

The finest jewel in fashion's crown, haute couture is an anachronism today. Having peaked in the 1940s and 1950s, when its sales were the major source of income for the great design houses, couture clothing has largely been replaced by luxury ready-to-wear. Couture sales have dropped to less than 10% of their all-time high, totaling approximately $48,700,000 in 1990. The couture customer base has dwindled to an estimated 2,500 with perhaps only 300 to 500 women purchasing regularly, and the number of couture houses has dropped from a high of 53 after World War II to 21 at the beginning of 1993.

Given the shrinking clientele and rising prices of haute couture, it's not surprising that its future is frequently a subject for speculation. A few houses have discontinued their haute couture collections altogether. Balmain did not show a Spring/Summer Collection in 1991, for example. Then, after receiving special permission from the *Chambre syndicale*, the house showed a collection of only 22 pieces the next season. In 1992, Balmain hired Oscar de la Renta as couturier for the Spring/Summer 1992 Collection with hopes of reviving its collection and clientele.

Today, couture is considered the engine that pulls the train as the most successful houses spin off lucrative licenses for ready-to-wear clothing, fragrances, cosmetics, fashion and home accessories, chocolates and even automobile interiors. The House of Cardin, for example, has 840 licenses in 94 countries, including one for car tires. Although supported by bigger and more profitable business operations, haute couture is still an art form practiced by a few creative men and women and a small group of skilled artisans. Whether classic in style or playfully outrageous, the designs that emerge from couture workrooms influence women's fashions throughout the industrialized world.

~

CHAPTER 2

THE ART OF
HAND SEWING

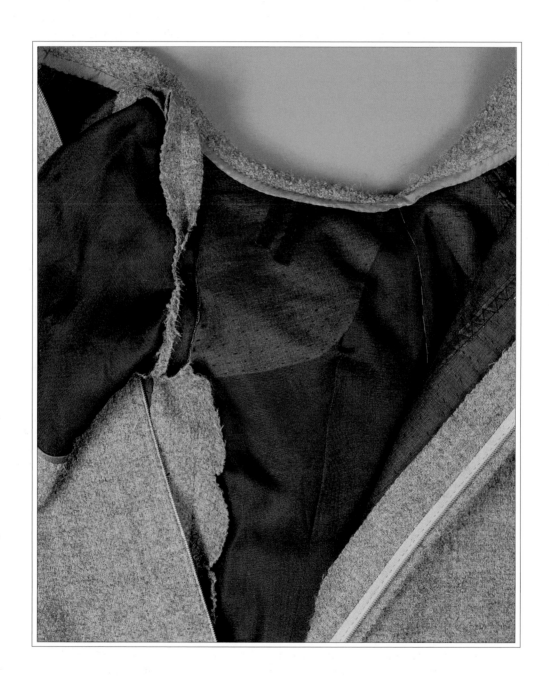

When I visited the house of Christian Dior in Paris, I asked Dior's archivist Marika Genty how the construction of haute couture garments differs from that of luxury ready-to-wear. Marika immediately responded, "They're made by hand." Her comment was repeated at every couture house I visited, and for good reason. There are thousands of temporary stitches sewn by hand into a couture garment during its construction, and hundreds of permanent hand stitches on the finished piece. And the first thing you notice when visiting a couture atelier is that the workers (referred to in French as *mains*, or "hands") are seated at tables, rather than at sewing machines, where they sew by hand. In fact, there are only a few sewing machines in the atelier. When machine stitching is required for added strength or absolute uniformity of stitches, the sewer takes her work to an available machine, completes the stitching and returns to work at the table.

Hand stitching has many virtues. You can control the construction of your garment more precisely, sew inconspicuously from the right side and work in corners of the garment that are too narrow to be sewn on a sewing machine. If the hand stitches must be removed, they're less likely to mar the fabric than machine stitches. And when permanently in place, hand stitches are softer than machine stitches because there is only one thread instead of the two linked by the machine.

THE BASICS OF HAND SEWING

In many European countries, children are taught the fundamentals of hand sewing when they're five or six years old. At the *Chambre syndicale's* school in Paris (see pp. 7-8), apprentices, who generally begin their apprenticeship after high school, perfect their hand sewing skills on samples before they undertake sewing a full garment. In this country, home sewers tend to be much more familiar with sewing on a machine than with sewing by hand, so it's worth reviewing some basics of hand sewing and choosing tools and supplies.

NEEDLES AND THREAD

Needles come in various types and sizes (see the needle chart on p. 22). The needle type is determined by its length, the size and shape of its eye and whether its point is sharp or blunt. Dressmaking needles are sized from 1 to 18, and tapestry needles and yarn darners are sized from 14 to 26. The higher the number, the finer and shorter the needle.

Use long needles for long stitches such as thread tracing, uneven basting and stab stitches; use shorter needles for general sewing, short basting stitches, hemming and other finishing techniques. Fine needles are appropriate for lightweight and medium-weight fabrics, and sturdier needles for heavier materials. Use needles with oval or long eyes for coarse threads and easy threading. To prevent rusting, store your extra needles in their original packages.

An emery bag, usually shaped like a strawberry, is used to sharpen and polish needles—simply push the needle back and forth through the bag several times. Don't leave needles in the bag for long periods, however, or they may rust.

Turned partly wrong side out, Yves Saint Laurent's famous trapeze dress, designed in 1958 for Christian Dior (and shown in full on p. 120), reveals the extraordinary amount of precise handwork in a couture garment. All seam allowances are finished with overcast stitches spaced exactly ⅛ in. apart, the interfacings are stitched to the backing with padstitches of equal length, and the zipper tape and bias neck facing are secured with tiny fell stitches. (Photo by Susan Kahn. Metropolitan Museum of Art. Gift of Imogene Schubert, 1958.)

A thimble is indispensable in couture sewing. It not only protects your finger, but it also helps you make neater stitches with greater speed. There are two types of thimbles: the more widely available and more often used closed-end dressmaker's thimble and the open-end tailor's thimble. Each type of thimble is used for similar tasks, but as their names suggest, they're worn by workers in different workrooms of a couture house.

Threads come in a variety of fibers and sizes. Most threads are sized by number from 16 to 150, but silk thread is sometimes sized by letter from A to F. When sized by number, the higher the number, the finer the thread. When sized by letter, the lower the letter (starting with A), the finer the thread. Thread size is generally described by the size and number of plies. For example, a 50/3 thread is composed of three size-50 plies.

Thread has twist. When you're hand sewing, your thread will knot and kink less if you work with the twist rather than against it. The twist usually runs in the direction from the loose end of the spooled thread toward the spool. So when sewing by hand, thread the needle with the end of the thread that first comes off the spool. Work with lengths of thread between 18 in. and 27 in., cutting the ends on a slant to make them easier to thread. If you've cut a length of thread and are unsure of the twist's direction, look at each end. Thread the end that's pointed like a flower bud and knot the end that flares open.

NEEDLES AND THEIR USES
(ARRANGED BY FREQUENCY OF USE)

TYPE	FEATURES	USES
Sharps	Medium long; round eye	General sewing
Crewels (embroidery)	Medium long; oval eye	General sewing, embroidery
Cotton darners	Long; oval eye	Long basting stitches, stab stitches
Milliner's	Long; round eye	Long basting stitches, stab stitches
Tapestry	Short; thick needle; blunt point; oval eye	Needlework, substitute for bodkin
Beading	Long; round eye; fine point	Long stitches, fine fabrics, beading
Chenille	Short; thick needle; blunt point; oval eye	Embroidery, handworked buttonholes
Glover's (leather needles)	Short; cutting point	Leather, fur, suede
Curved	Fine; round eye; fine point; half-circle shape	Sewing from right side

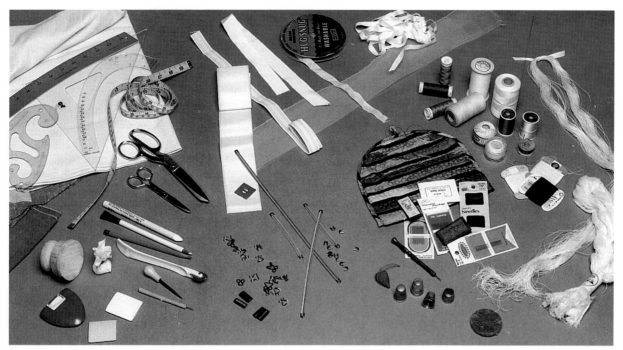

Most tools and supplies used in couture are familiar to home sewers. Among the various threads on the right, the only unfamiliar one may be the long skein of waxed silk (1) and the short skein of basting cotton (2). Each worker in a couture workroom has a silk bag (3), which she pins to her blouse to hold pins and needles. Below the needles is a tambour hook (4) for embroidery and beading, an emery bag (5), beeswax (6) and thimbles. At center top are tapes and bindings, horsehair braid (7) and petersham (8) topped with a drapery weight. At center bottom are spiral boning (9), hooks and eyes and more weights. Marking and cutting tools at left include assorted chalks and pencils, scissors and commercial and homemade pouncers (10,11). At top left are measuring and drafting equipment (12) on top of muslin, interfacing and backing materials, lambswool, collar linen and wadding. (Photo by Susan Kahn.)

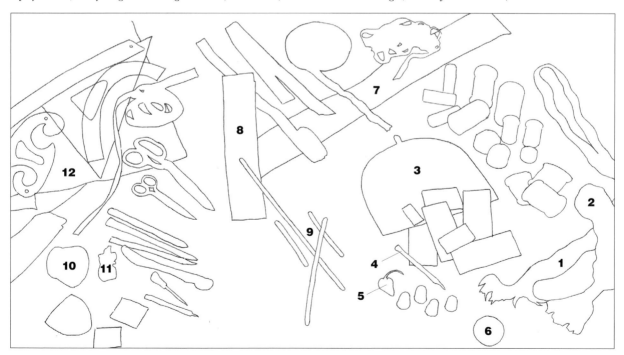

As is typical of couture construction, most of the sewing in the workroom of the London designer Hardy Amies is done by hand. Notice that the table supports both the sewer's arms and her work, and that she holds the edge of the garment on which she's working above the rest of it. (Photo courtesy of Museum of London.)

When used for sewing permanent stitches by hand (though not by machine), all varieties of thread should be pulled once or twice through a small cake of beeswax and then pressed to strengthen them. Pressing with a warm iron also prevents knotting and fraying and keeps the wax from rubbing off on the fabric. (Beeswax is not used on basting threads because it may leave a permanent stain on the fabric if pressed.)

In couture workrooms, a greater variety of threads is used than in home-sewing or ready-to-wear construction. The type of thread selected depends on whether it's to be used for hand or machine sewing, the kind of stitch it's intended for (temporary or permanent, decorative or utilitarian), the garment section to be sewn, the degree of strength required and the sewer's preference. On the facing page you'll find a chart of the various types of threads and their uses. Many other types of thread are used for embellishment (see the Bibliography on p. 214 for books that focus on embroidery.)

BEGINNINGS AND ENDINGS

Before sewing, be certain that your hands are clean. When sewing white and pastel fabrics, use talcum powder or drafting powder (available at art-supply stores) to keep your hands clean and dry. If you're sewing a fragile fabric and your hands are rough, rub your hands with a pumice stone or a mixture of equal parts of cooking oil and sugar, and then wash and rinse them well.

For most hand sewing, sit at your sewing table and let the bulk of the garment rest on the table. If you're right-handed, rest your left forearm on the table with the palm curled toward you and pick up the edge of the garment. Then rest your right forearm on the table and sew from right to left with the bulk of the garment below the needle—unless, of course, the stitch you're sewing requires reversing sewing direction or holding the garment vertically. (If you're left-handed, reverse these directions.)

THREADS AND THEIR USES

TYPE	FEATURES	USES
Skeined cotton or embroidery floss	Loose twist, soft finish; does not fall out of fabric; rarely leaves impression on fabric when pressed	Tailor's tacks, hand basting
Brook's basting cotton (on spools)	Breaks easily; may leave an impression when pressed	Basting, thread tracing
Glazed cotton (sizes 40, 50 or 60)	Strong, starched thread; easy to pull up; usually leaves an impression when pressed	Ease-basting, gathering, basting long seamlines
Mercerized cotton (size 50/3 or 3-cord cotton)	All-purpose thread for hand and machine, may fade or crock, or rub off	Basting, hemming, padstitching, zippers, button stems, buttonholes on cotton fabric, machine stitching
DMC cotton (size 50/2)	All-purpose thread for lightweight fabrics; has more sheen but less strength than mercerized cotton	Same as for mercerized cotton
Silk basting	Very fine; rarely leaves impression on fabric when pressed	Top basting, rolled hems, machine-stitching chiffon
Silk machine (size A and 50/3)	All-purpose thread for hand and machine sewing; has more sheen than mercerized cotton; stronger and more supple than all-cotton threads	Basting, zippers, hooks and eyes, buttonholes, button stems, machine stitching
Silk line stitch or silk embroidery (size 30/3)	Medium-weight silk thread; similar to silk machine thread but stronger	Buttonholes on light to medium-weight fabrics, machine topstitching, thread chains and loops, button stems
Silk buttonhole twist (size 8/3, D, E or F)	Heavy silk thread	Buttonholes on medium- to heavyweight fabrics, button stems
Extra-fine cotton-wrapped polyester	Strong, all-purpose thread	Same as for mercerized cotton and silk threads

KNOTS

SIMPLE KNOT

WASTE KNOT (BEFORE KNOT IS CUT OFF)

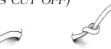

A waste knot temporarily anchors a thread until it can be secured with backstitches. It begins with a simple knot, is anchored with several back stitches, then is cut off.

TAILOR'S KNOT

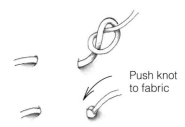

Push knot to fabric

Make a loose loop, hold it at exit point of last stitch, pull thread through and work knot down to fabric.

FIGURE-8 KNOT

Take a tiny backstitch and wrap thread under and around needle point before pulling needle through.

BACKSTITCH

As an alternative to a knot, take one or two backstitches after the last sewing stitch.

Once you're ready to begin stitching, fasten the thread with a simple knot or a waste knot at the beginning of your work and with a figure-8 knot or tailor's knot at the end (see the drawings above). Alternatively, backstitches can be substituted for any of these knots at the beginning or end of the work. It doesn't really matter which knot you choose, but be careful when working on lightweight fabrics to keep your knots small and inconspicuous to prevent an impression from the knot showing through on the right side of the fabric when it's pressed.

TEMPORARY STITCHES

Hand-sewn stitches fall into two basic categories according to their use: temporary and permanent. Temporary stitches, which are frequently referred to as basting stitches, are used for marking the garment, preparing it for fittings and keeping the various fabric layers in position during construction. Temporary stitches are sewn into a garment again and again throughout its construction, only to be removed a short time later after serving their purpose. By contrast, permanent stitches are sewn once and removed only if an error has been made or if the garment is altered.

In fact, most of the actual stitches used for basting—even, uneven, diagonal and slipstitch—are the same as those used for permanent functions. I've covered these four basic basting stitches below (listing them by order of frequency of their use), but have reserved the discussion of two other important temporary stitches used for marking a garment—thread tracing and tailor's tacks—for Chapter 3 (see p. 38-39). Also covered in Chapter 3 are gathering and ease-basting stitches, which are used as both temporary and permanent stitches (see p. 48).

Note that the directions for all the stitches in this chapter are given for right-handed sewers. Left-handed sewers should simply reverse these directions. Also note that the stitches are to be sewn from right to left unless otherwise indicated.

EVEN BASTING

Even basting is a slightly elongated form of the permanent running stitch (see "Running stitch" on p. 29), which is used to join two edges under some stress, for example, the seams of a closely fitted garment. It's  also used for easing one layer or a gathered section to another shorter layer or section. To make even-basting stitches, begin with right sides of the garment section together and sew running stitches so they're equal in length on both sides of the garment and no more than ¼ in. long.

There are several other uses of even basting, each of which is referred to by its own name. *Double basting* is used to hold two or more fabric layers securely and prevent shifting during construction. Not surprisingly, double basting involves two rows of even basting, one on top of the other, with the stitches of the second row placed to fill the "spaces" in the first row. (Alternatively, the first of these two rows could be slip basted, as explained on p. 28).

Top basting is used on the right side of the fabric to hold the garment layers in place when the garment is fitted or pressed. Top-basting stitches can be sewn with either even or uneven basting stitches. To top-baste seamlines for fittings, fold the seam allowances in one direction and even-baste through all layers ⅛ in. to ¼ in. from the seamline. To top-baste edges for pressing—or for fitting—even-baste through all layers, sewing about ¼ in. from the edge when possible to avoid distorting this edge.

Lap basting is used for basting bias seams that are stretched when stitched. To lap-baste, begin the seam with a simple knot and even-baste 6 in. to 8 in. Cut the thread, leaving a 2-in. tail. Then begin 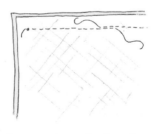 again, starting at a point that overlaps the last few stitches, using a 2-in. tail instead of a knot this time. Continue in this fashion to the end of the seamline and fasten with backstitches (see the facing page).

UNEVEN BASTING

As the name suggests, uneven-basting stitches are longer on one side of the fabric than the other. These basting stitches are used for marking a garment, basting hems and straight seams that don't  need to be particularly strong and for top basting. When basting long seams, pin one end of the work to a weight so you can hold the fabric taut while you sew.

Begin with the right sides of the garment together. After anchoring the thread, pick up a short stitch (⅛ in. to ¼ in.) on the underside of the fabric and insert the needle ¼ in. to 1 in. ahead of the first stitch. Continue, so that the stitches on one side of the garment are two to three times the length of the stitches on the other side.

DIAGONAL BASTING

Diagonal basting is used to hold two or more layers together (such as pleats, backings and interfacings) and keep them from shifting, as well as to baste pile fabrics together. This stitch can be worked verti-  cally or horizontally, depending on how you want to hold the fabric, and from top to bottom, or vice versa.

To begin diagonal basting, hold the fabric vertically and insert the needle horizontally from right to left. Then pull the thread through and make the next stitch ¼ in. to 2 in. directly below or above the first stitch, and continue in this fashion. On the other side of the fabric, the stitches will form a vertical column of short horizontal "dashes."

Cross stitching, a variation on diagonal basting, is made by working two rows of diagonal stitches in opposite directions, one on top of the other. The first row is worked top to bottom and the second row from bottom to top. As the name suggests, working the two rows produces stitches that cross one another. In couture, a large cross stitch is sometimes used to mark the front, right side or top of the garment sections and shoulder pads temporarily during construction. (See also "Cross stitch" on p. 32.)

SLIP BASTING

Slip basting is used to baste seams from the right side of the fabric when matching stripes and plaids, sewing intricately shaped seamlines and easing one edge to another. Generally 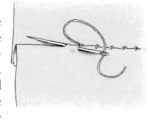 one slip-basted edge laps the other, but the two edges can abut, or the two garment sections and their edges can be sewn one on top of the other (as, for example, at the end of a belt or waistband).

Slip basting is sewn with the same slipstitch used for permanent seams joined from the right side (see "Slip-stitch" on the facing page). Since slip basting alone does not always keep layers from shifting slightly during construction, it's sometimes reinforced with an additional row of even basting. Fell stitching is often substituted for slip basting when you need to match patterns or edges precisely, since fell stitches shift less than slip-basted stitches. Fell stitching is also sometimes reinforced with a row of even basting (see "Fell stitch" on p. 30).

To slip-baste one edge lapped over the other, begin by folding under the seam allowance on the overlapping edge and pinning the two edges together so the seam-lines and any design match. Then anchor the thread in the top layer, and working right to left, pull the needle out through the folded edge $\frac{1}{16}$ in. to $\frac{1}{4}$ in. from the anchoring knot. Directly opposite this point, pick up a small stitch $\frac{1}{16}$ in. to $\frac{1}{4}$ in. long in the lower layer of fabric. Begin the next stitch in the folded edge directly opposite this small stitch. Make several stitches alternating between the two layers so that they form a perfect ladder. Then draw the thread tight.

PERMANENT STITCHES

Permanent stitches are used to manipulate the surface of the fabric (for example, to pleat, tuck or gather it), shape the garment and finish edges and details. These stitches can be simple and utilitarian, such as catch-stitches and running and hemming stitches, or they can be both functional and decorative, such as blanket stitches, buttonhole stitches and cross stitches. Although some permanent stitches can be used for a limited number of applications, others (such as backstitch) can be adapted for a variety of tasks. The stitches here are listed in order of frequency of their use.

Designed for Spring/Summer 1968 by Valentino, this two-piece ensemble displays some intricate handwork. The pintucks on the blouse, for example, are sewn by hand with small running stitches, and on the skirt, the silk double-cloth at the pocket edges is finished with tiny slipstitches (see also the detail photos of the blouse on p. 44). (Photo by Cathy Carver. Metropolitan Museum of Art. Gift of Mrs. Lyn Revson, 1975.)

RUNNING STITCH

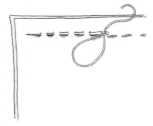

The running stitch is a small, even stitch used mainly for seams that require little strength, for example, on a lining or a pocket. By lengthening the stitch or sewing it unevenly, it can be adapted for other uses such as understitching, setting zippers, permanently joining two layers, or securing the folds of a draped design (see the Hanae Mori design on p. 53).

To sew a running stitch, anchor the thread and take several small, even stitches about ⅛ in. long on the needle. Pull the needle through the fabric and repeat the process to the end of the work.

When using a running stitch for a seam that needs more strength, add a backstitch after every third stitch. Combining running stitches and backstitches produces a *combination stitch*. This stitch is softer and weaker than the backstitch alone but can be sewn much more quickly.

Running stitches are also used for *staystitching* and *understitching*. Staystitching serves to prevent a curved or bias edge such as an armscye or neckline from stretching out of shape during the garment's construction. Understitching is used to keep the facing or lining from rolling out at the edge. These techniques, which are always done by machine in home sewing, are always sewn by hand in haute couture.

To staystitch an edge by hand, sew a row of short running stitches on the seamline, either before or after a backing has been applied to the garment section. Then tighten the thread as needed to prevent the edge from losing its shape.

To understitch an edge after it is finished with a facing or lining, position the garment wrong side up. Sew through the facing or lining and both seam allowances ¹⁄₁₆ in. to ¼ in. from the seamline using a running stitch or backstitch to anchor the facing on the underside. If you're understitching where there's no seam allowance (on an extended facing, for example), sew the understitches to the garment backing, interfacing or stay.

BACKSTITCH

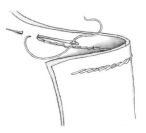

The backstitch is one of the strongest and most adaptable of permanent stitches. Its primary function is to join seams that need strength and elasticity, such as those used for setting sleeves. And at Gieves and Hawkes, a well-known men's bespoke tailor in London, the backstitch is the preferred stitch for stitching the crotch seam on trousers.

This stitch can be sewn two ways: as either a *full backstitch* or a *partial backstitch*. On the front side, the full backstitch looks like machine stitching, which makes it very useful for repairing seams. The partial backstitch looks like a simple running stitch on the front side. Sewn either way, these stitches can be varied in length and tension for a great deal of control over the work.

To sew a backstitch, anchor the thread, and working right to left, make a ⅛-in. stitch. Pull the thread completely through the material and then insert the needle ¹⁄₁₆ in. to ⅛ in. behind the thread. Complete the stitch by passing the needle under the fabric and out again ⅛ in. ahead of the thread. When you make the next stitch, insert the needle either at the end of the previous stitch for a full backstitch or with a short space separating the two stitches for a partial backstitch. (In this book, whenever the term *backstitch* appears, it refers to either the full or partial backstitch.)

SLIPSTITCH

A slipstitch is used to join permanently two layers from the right side of the fabric, for example, a waistline seam, intricately shaped seam or two folded edges on the end of a band or belt. It can also serve for hemming and for basting purposes. (For basic information on how to sew a slipstitch, see "Slip basting" on p. 28.) To prevent slipstitches from showing on the right side when hemming, be careful to pick up only a single thread on the garment.

A variation on the slip-stitch, the *drawing stitch*, is used in tailoring to join two layers (such as the collar and lapel). This stitch is worked from the right side of the garment and is made by alternately taking

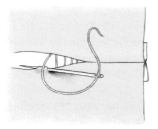

a short running stitch ¹⁄₁₆ in. to ⅛ in. long first in one folded edge then in the other, and drawing the thread taut so the two folded edges close together. It can be worked like a slipstitch or a fell stitch, but each stitch must be taken separately, and the stitches must be close together, evenly spaced and parallel to each other so the finished seam looks as if it's machine stitched.

FELL STITCH

A fell stitch is used to sew a raw or folded edge flat against the layer of fabric beneath it (to set an under collar, waistband or sleeve, for example), to sew seams permanently from the right side, to sew flat-felled

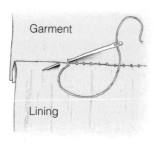

seams, and to finish narrow and rolled hems. When used for hemming, this stitch is called a *straight hemming stitch*.

The directions here are for fell stitching, or felling, a lining to a facing, but they apply equally to other uses of fell stitching, except for hemming and felling a French seam flat, which are described on pp. 46-47. Begin with the facing and lining right side up, and fold the raw edge of the lining under and match the seamlines. Work from right to left with the bulk of the garment below the needle. Anchor the thread and bring the needle out through the lining fold, and then insert it into the facing directly opposite the point it just exited. Take a deep stitch in the facing so the stitch will hold, then bring the needle out close to the lining fold ⅛ in. to ¼ in. away. Pull the thread taut and continue in this fashion. The finished stitches will be perpendicular to the edge of the lining and should be invisible on the right side. On the wrong side, there will be a row of diagonal stitches, unless the layers were so thick that your needle didn't pass entirely through them all.

When using the fell stitch for hemming (such as on a rolled hem) or when felling a French seam flat against the background fabric, take very small stitches, picking up only a single thread of the background fabric.

WHIPSTITCH

A whipstitch is similar to overcasting (see p. 32), but it's used for seaming and hemming rather than finishing raw edges. It can be sewn with either right or wrong sides of the garment together. It's used to make narrow seams when join-

ing selvages or lace; to join two folded edges when making bands, ties and belts; and to make a rolled hem.

When beginning a whipstitch, the best method for anchoring the thread is to leave a long tail and lay it over the seamline so that the first few stitches are worked over the tail. To whipstitch, insert the needle from the back of the fabric through all layers, bringing it out just below the edge and pointing toward you. Repeat, inserting the needle ¹⁄₁₆ in. to the left of the previous stitch. Pull the thread taut after each stitch. (If you're careful to insert the needle just a few threads below the edge, the finished seam will be smooth and flat without a ridge.)

When joining a new thread, cut the previous thread end to ½ in. and sew over it when you begin with the new thread. To finish a whipstitched seam or hem, sew six whipstitches in the opposite direction, and hide the thread end between the edges.

BASEBALL STITCH

The baseball stitch is used on interfacings to join two abutted edges without seam allowances. To make this stitch, butt the edges together with right sides up. Anchor

the thread and insert the needle between the edges, and then bring it out ⅛ in. to ¼ in. away from one edge. Then pass the needle point under the other edge and bring it out ⅛ in. to ¼ in. away from the last stitch. Pull the thread taut and pass the needle under the other edge, and bring it out at the same distance as the previous stitch. Repeat the procedure, alternating the stitches from one edge to the other.

STABSTITCH

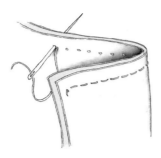

The stabstitch is used for sewing bound button-holes and pockets, setting shoulder pads and zippers, and joining especially thick fabric layers. With the garment right side up, anchor the thread and begin this stitch by stabbing the needle vertically into the fabric layers and pulling it through to the underside. Then reverse the procedure and stab the needle vertically into the fabric to bring the needle back to the surface, placing the stitches from $\frac{1}{8}$ in. to $\frac{1}{4}$ in. apart for a zipper to $\frac{3}{8}$ in. to $\frac{1}{2}$ in. apart for setting a shoulder pad. Keep the stitches loose to prevent dimples. All stitches should be inconspicuous on the right side of the garment and, when possible, located in the well of a seam.

DIAGONAL STITCH

Diagonal stitches are used to join two or more fabric layers together permanently and to shape collars and lapels. When used in tailoring, this stitch is referred to as padstitching. For information on how to sew diagonal stitches, or pad stitches, see "Diagonal basting" on p. 27.

CATCHSTITCH

Catchstitches look like a row of Xs on the right side of the fabric and two parallel rows of dashes on the wrong side. They're often used to hold one edge flat against another, as in hemming. A very elastic stitch, the catchstitch is also used to form casings for elastic and tapes and to tack pleats and attach labels.

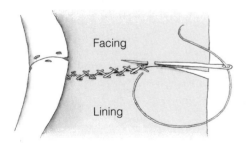

Facing

Lining

Working left to right with two layers or edges of fabric, anchor the thread in one layer, insert the needle horizontally so it points to the left and take a small stitch. Then move to the second layer, position the needle a little to the right and slightly below the first stitch, insert the needle horizontally and take a second stitch. Move back to the first layer to the right and slightly above the last stitch, position the needle as before and take the next stitch. Repeat this process, alternating between the two rows, always keeping the stitches in each row aligned with one another. Pull the thread taut after each stitch.

HEMMING STITCHES

The two hemming stitches used most often by both couturiers and home sewers are the blindstitch and the blind catchstitch. (See also the descriptions for the slipstitch and fell stitch on p. 29 and p. 30, respectively. These stitches can be used as hemming stitches, especially on edges that are visible from both sides, such as on a ruffle or a scarf.)

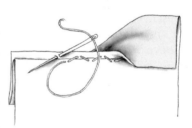

The *blindstitch* is the most frequently used hemming stitch and is worked inconspicuously between the hem and garment. To make this stitch (working from right to left), anchor the thread in the hem allowance and take a tiny stitch in the garment by picking up one fabric thread or just part of a thread. Pull the sewing thread through, then pick up a small stitch on the hem allowance $\frac{1}{4}$ in. to $\frac{1}{2}$ in. to the left of the previous stitch. Alternate the stitches between the garment and hem to create a series of small Vs, keeping the stitches loose and pulling the thread through on every stitch. Secure the thread on the hem allowance.

The *blind catchstitch* is stronger, more durable and more elastic than the blindstitch and is used for hemming heavy fabrics. This stitch is actually a catchstitch worked between two layers of fabric, like a blindstitch, but instead of working right to left as you would for a blindstitch, work left to right. Begin on the hem allowance and alternate the stitches between the garment and hem.

OVERCASTING STITCH

Used to prevent raveling, overcasting stitches are small, slanted stitches sewn over a single-layer raw edge. They can be worked in either direction and should be about 1/16 in. deep and evenly spaced 1/16 in. to 1/8 in. apart.

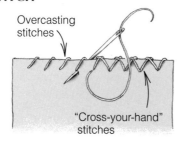

Overcasting stitches

"Cross-your-hand" stitches

To overcast, hold the raw edge horizontally so that it's parallel to your index finger. Anchor the thread on the underside with a simple knot and insert the point of the needle under the edge about 1/16 in. from it. Bring the needle out at about a 45° slant. Pull the thread through and the needle up, while holding the thread against the fabric with your left thumb. Insert the needle for the next stitch 1/8 in. from the first. Continue, making each stitch separately rather than trying to take several stitches on the needle at one time and then pulling the thread through.

For fabrics that ravel badly, overcast a row in one direction and then overcast a second row in the opposite direction. In haute couture, this maneuver is called "cross your hand," which produces finished stitches that look like machine zigzagging.

CROSS STITCH

A cross stitch looks like a catchstitch but is made by working a pair of diagonal basting stitches in opposite directions (see p. 27). In addition to their use as temporary marking stitches, cross stitches are also used on finished garments to indicate the center front on waistbands and dresses and the

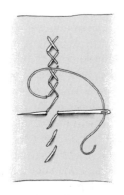

waistline on dresses, since the orienting label that is usually placed at the back neck in ready-to-wear is often positioned at a more obscure place in couture or may be absent altogether.

BLANKET STITCH

The blanket stitch is used, among other things, to cover hooks and eyes, thread bars and thread chains, and to serve as a decorative edging.

You can work blanket stitches from top to bottom, or vice versa, but in both cases hold the work right side up, with the raw edge positioned vertically in your hand. After anchoring the thread, insert the needle horizontally into the fabric about 1/4 in. from the edge. Loop the thread under the needle's point and pull the thread taut, but not tight. Once you get the knack of this stitch, you'll be able to position the thread loop at the edge before inserting the needle.

BUTTONHOLE STITCH

The buttonhole stitch is used to control fraying on hand-worked buttonholes as well as to make button shanks, decorative button loops and decorative edges. It's important to wax and press the thread

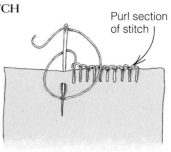

Purl section of stitch

used for buttonhole stitches, because waxing will strengthen it and keep it from twisting while you sew.

Buttonhole stitches can be worked in any direction and are begun by inserting the needle into the wrong side of the fabric and anchoring it with a waste knot. Then pass the needle point under the fabric edge and bring it out about 1/16 in. away. Loop the thread under the needle point in the direction in which you're working—right to left. Pull the needle through so that it's perpendicular to the fabric edge. Tighten the thread and use your thumbnails to position the purl part of the stitch on top of the fabric.

MAKING A THREAD BAR

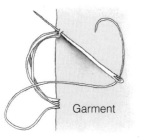

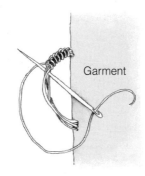

1. Anchor several strands at two points in fabric.

2. Cover strands with buttonhole or blanket stitch.

MAKING A THREAD CHAIN

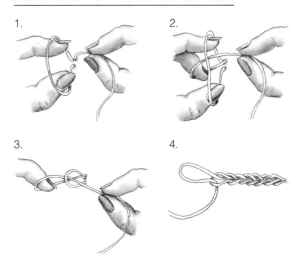

1.

2.

3.

4.

THREAD BAR

Made by sewing buttonhole or blanket stitches over several strands of thread anchored at two points in the fabric, thread bars serve various purposes and are referred to by different names, depending on their function and location on the garment. Used at the top of pleats and slits, at the bottom of zippers, at V-shaped openings and at any other point of stress on a garment, a thread bar becomes a reinforcing bar tack. Used at a garment edge instead of a fabric button loop or metal eye, the thread bar is called a thread loop (see the detail photo of the Norell blouse on p. 42).

Wherever positioned, a thread bar should be sewn with waxed and pressed thread for strength and to prevent tangling as you sew. To make a thread bar, anchor the thread and sew two to four stitches, one on top of the other. Make the stitches the length you need for the bar tack or loop. Then work blanket or buttonhole stitches over the length of the strands and at the end, push the needle to the wrong side of the fabric and fasten the thread securely. Work the buttonhole stitches tightly together on the thread bar, but don't crowd them.

THREAD CHAIN

A thread chain is made with a hand-crocheted chain stitch. When used to hold two or more layers or garment sections loosely together, the thread chain is called a French tack, or swing tack. A thread chain can also substitute for a thread eye to fasten a metal hook.

Thread chains are softer and less durable than thread bars and can range in length from ¼ in. to several inches. Scaasi uses long French tacks, among other things, to hold together the various layers of hems on his famous ballgowns. Chanel used short ones to attach ties to necklines.

To make a thread chain, anchor the thread in one garment section and sew a small backstitch to make a loop. With the loop held open over the thumb and index finger of one hand, hold the thread in the needle taut with the other thumb and index finger. Then, using the middle finger on the hand holding open the loop as a crochet hook, pull a new thread loop through the first one and allow the first loop to slip off the fingers. Open the new loop as you pull the last loop taut on the chain. Continue making loops in this fashion until the chain is the desired length, then finish by picking up a small stitch on the corresponding garment section before slipping the needle through the last loop of the chain. Fasten the thread securely.

CHAPTER 3

~

SHAPING THE GARMENT

SEAMS, DARTS AND PRESSING TECHNIQUES

Seams, darts and pressing techniques are crucial elements of garment construction. Combined with support fabrics, they shape a two-dimensional piece of fabric to fit the three-dimensional contours of a body. Although these techniques are essential to home sewing and ready-to-wear, they're practiced with the greatest skill in haute couture workrooms, where both the fit and construction of a garment are intended to appear flawless.

Seams and darts shape a garment visibly, while support fabrics and expert pressing shape it invisibly. For this reason, professionally sewn seams and darts are perhaps appreciated more than the selection of appropriate support fabrics and skillful pressing, but the latter are no less significant in a garment's construction. In fact, in the case of pressing, a couture pattern may appear to have little relationship to the final garment because many garment sections have been stretched and/or shrunk extensively during the pressing process.

One of the best examples I've seen of how effectively a garment can be shaped with heat and moisture was in the workroom of the London tailor Gieves and Hawkes. The presser was shaping the trouser legs on a uniform for one of the Queen's guards. He shrank and stretched the straight, narrow-legged pants again and again until they duplicated the shape of the guard's legs (for more information on pressing techniques, see pp. 57-59).

Only a few types of seams are used extensively in haute couture, and among them are the plain seam, lapped seam, abutted seam and French seam. Except for novelty seams, all other seams are variations of these four basic seams. (For information on sewing bias-cut seams, see p. 126.) The plain seam is by far the most frequently used and the most versatile. The lapped seam epitomizes the attention lavished on a couture garment (one of its variations, the appliqué seam, is painstakingly hand-stitched around the motifs of luxurious, costly lace and special-occasion fabrics). The French seam is very narrow and frequently used for sheer fabrics so that it will be inconspicuous on the finished design.

Novelty seams, such as piped, slot, tucked and welt seams, are not used as frequently in haute couture as in luxury ready-to-wear, and since basic directions for these seams are included in many sewing books, they have not been described in this chapter.

Unlike the seams on ready-to-wear and home-sewn garments, seams in couture are often sewn by hand, with machine sewing reserved for structural seams and darts. The shoulder and armscye seams on linings, for example, are always sewn by hand, as are those that join the lining to the garment. Seams joining a tailored collar to a neckline and lapels are always sewn by hand, and those attaching a skirt to a bodice are sometimes hand-worked.

Many of the seams discussed in this section can be stitched by hand or by machine depending on their location, whether they need to be sewn from the right or wrong side of the garment, and the strength and elasticity they need. One type of lapped seam, the appliqué seam for woven fabrics, is sewn by alternating between machine and hand stitches. (You'll find the basics of hand sewing reviewed in Chapter 2.) Before looking at seams, let's quickly review the fundamentals of machine stitching.

MACHINE-STITCHING BASICS

In haute couture, most machine stitching is done on a straight-stitch machine. If you're sewing on a zigzag machine, use a straight-stitch foot and needleplate.

Before machine stitching, clean the seams by removing all but the essential bastings. Also check the machine's stitch length, tension and needle size on a fabric sample. Since the seamlines are basted before machine stitching in couture, you'll have fewer stitching problems than you usually would and can disregard many of the rules you would otherwise observe, such as stitching with the grain of the fabric or with the sleeve on top.

A detail of American designer Gilbert Adrian's 1946 silk crepe ensemble, entitled 'Modern Art,' shows the technical wizardry of beautifully sewn curved seams on the right and wrong sides of the tunic (shown in full on p. 54). The seams are finished with hand overcasting. (Photo by Susan Kahn. Metropolitan Museum of Art. Gift of Miss Eleanor Lambert, 1958.)

Machine-stitched seamlines can be ended by fastening the machine threads with a tailor's knot (also called an overhand knot) or by threading them into a needle and sewing a few running stitches by hand on the seamline. Backstitching is never used because it adds stiffness and bulk to the seamline and it's almost impossible to remove without marring the fabric.

When making a tailor's knot on a machine-stitched seamline, pull the bottom thread through to the upper layer, so both ends are on the same side, and pull both threads sharply to be sure they're firmly locked. Then knot the ends as shown in the drawing on p. 26. To remove the bastings after you've machine-stitched the seamline, clip the basting threads every 3 in. to 4 in. and pull them out, using tweezers if necessary. (I try to avoid knots in the basting threads because they're particularly difficult to remove once they've been stitched over.)

The seams described in this chapter are permanent seams. In couture construction, however, before these seams are sewn, all the seamlines would be marked with thread tracing and matchpoints (see the sidebar "Marking the Garment" on pp. 38-39), and then top-basted for a fitting, as described below in the discussion of the plain seam. After the fitting, the top bastings would be removed and adjustments made as needed to correct the fit. Finally the seams would be sewn permanently (for more information on these steps, see the sidebar "Assembling the Garment" on the facing page).

PLAIN SEAMS

The plain seam is the flattest, least conspicuous and most versatile of all seams. It's suitable for almost any location on a garment and almost any fabric, and it serves as the foundation for many other seams. Although this seam is used on luxury ready-to-wear and home-sewn designs as well as on couture garments, there are important differences in how each sector constructs it. In ready-to-wear and home sewing, the cut edges of the seam allowances are used as guides for sewing the seamline. In haute couture, the seam allowances are frequently too wide or varied in width to be used as accurate guides. So, in couture, seamlines are marked with thread tracing, tailor's tacks and matchpoints. These markings become the guidelines for assembling and fitting the garment. In couture, most plain seams are basted together at least once before they're machine stitched, and many are basted, ripped and rebasted several times.

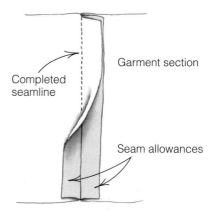

Completed seamline

Garment section

Seam allowances

Although the traditional plain seam is very inconspicuous when pressed open, it's not appropriate for all fabrics. For lightweight and transparent fabrics, the four variations on the plain seam described below—the narrow plain seam, the false French seam, the self-bound seam and the whipped seam—are more suitable. However, unlike the traditional plain seam, these seams cannot be altered.

To begin basting a plain seam, align the thread-traced seamlines and matchpoints and pin the seamlines together. Baste intricately shaped seams and those that join close-fitting sections of the garment with short, even basting stitches. For seams that will receive little stress, baste with long, uneven stitches. Check carefully as you sew to be sure that you're basting precisely on both seamlines.

When basting seams that cross darts or other seamlines, be careful to avoid catching the seam allowances or dart take-up. When basting seams and darts, begin basting at the intersecting seamline, rather than at the raw edge, to make it easier to fit the garment accurately. After you've basted a seam, lightly press it closed. Do not press the seam open unless you're certain it will not be changed after the fitting.

If you're matching fabric patterns or if you're assembling intricately shaped seams, it's more practical to baste the seams from the right side rather than the wrong side of the fabric. This is much easier to do in couture than in home sewing because the seamlines are thread-traced and can easily be aligned from the right side. To do this, turn under the seam allowance of one

ASSEMBLING THE GARMENT

The process of assembling a garment in haute couture is less straightforward than in home sewing and luxury ready-to-wear. The garment usually begins with draping several rectangles of muslin on the right side of a dress form that's padded to duplicate the customer's figure. Only half a pattern is usually needed for a symmetrical design since it can be used to duplicate the other half of the garment. The left side of the garment is draped in muslin only for bias-cut or extremely complex designs, fabrics with patterns that need to be matched, asymmetrical figures that are very difficult to fit, and embellished designs that need to be scaled to the garment's proportions.

The draper pins and shapes the muslin on a dress form to create a *toile*, or muslin pattern, for the customer's design. As the design takes shape, the excess muslin is trimmed away, and changes are made in proportion and scale to flatter and fit the client's figure. Once the draping is completed, the toile is carefully marked with matchpoints, unpinned and pressed for use as the garment pattern.

The toile's bodice and skirt sections are laid on the garment fabric with the lengthwise grains aligned and with ample space between the sections for at least 1-in. seam allowances. Then the backing is cut, but the sleeves, collar facings, pockets and lining are left uncut until needed.

All the cut garment sections are marked with thread tracings at stitching lines, hemlines, matchpoints, garment centers and horizontal balance lines. Since the garment fabric and muslin drape differently, the garment is hand-basted together and fitted on the dress form so corrections can be made. The bastings are then removed, the sections laid flat again and the fitting corrections made. For the client's first fitting, the garment is rebasted with a short basting stitch that makes the garment appear machine-stitched.

Instead of pressing and permanently creasing the seams, they're folded to one side and top-basted close to the seamline for the fitting. The edges are basted under at plackets, hems and seam allowances and clipped only as needed to turn under smoothly. Shoulder pads and stays are basted in place. Some premières even baste the zipper, pockets and lining in place, while others fit with few facings and may even fit a toile sleeve instead of a fabric sleeve.

After the fitting, corrections are carefully marked and matchpoints added as needed. Again the bastings are removed and the garment laid flat to make corrections. Any section requiring shaping is eased, shrunk or stretched to mold the fabric permanently, and the pockets and stays are set. At this point, the garment is rebasted and checked on the dress form.

If the garment has set-in sleeves, they're pinned into the armscye while the garment is still on the dress form.

The sleeves are basted in place with sleeve heads and shoulder pads so the garment appears finished for the second fitting. The fit is then examined to be sure earlier alterations are correct and to see if additional fine-tuning is needed.

After the fitting, the sleeves are carefully marked and removed so that underarm seams can be stitched and pressed, and cuffs, vents and any linings can be finished. Before permanently stitching the garment, each seamline is carefully checked to be sure that intersecting seams match precisely and that bastings are taut enough to keep the layers from shifting. Except for bastings that hold seams together, all other bastings, including thread tracings, are removed, and the seams are stitched precisely on the basted seamlines.

The sleeves are then basted and permanently stitched into the armscyes. Any remaining unfinished seams are basted, then stitched permanently and pressed. The garment is hemmed, lingerie guards added, the zipper set permanently and all raw edges finished.

After a final check to make sure all bastings have been removed, the garment is pressed lightly and is ready for the final fitting on the client. After the fit and drape are examined a last time and the client accepts the design, the label is sewn in place.

section using the thread tracing as a guide, and then pin the seam allowance in place with the pins perpendicular to the edge. Baste if necessary to control the seam allowance on a curved edge. With the right sides of the fabric up and the garment section with the folded seam allowance on top, match the seamlines, aligning matchpoints. Then pin the layers together, pulling each pin out of the upper layer just enough to reset it and catch the lower section. Baste the two sections together with slipbasting.

To prepare the garment for a fitting, fold the basted seam to one side and top-baste through all layers ⅛ in. to ¼ in. from the seamline. This top-basting is used instead of pressing to hold the seam flat, which lets you easily evaluate the garment's fit and visual effect. If there are no corrections to be made after the fitting, remove the top-basting, press the seam flat once more and machine-stitch on the basted lines. Remove the bastings. Then, to "marry" the seam and make the stitches sink into the fabric layers, press the seam flat. If the fabric is thick or heavy, turn the seam over and press the other side (see "Pressing techniques" on p. 57).

Next, spread the garment wrong side up and open the seam with your fingers. Then, using just the point of the iron, not the entire soleplate, press the stitched line firmly with a sharp up-and-down movement, without pressing the edges of the seam flat against the garment. This is easier to manage if you place the seam on a pressing cushion, point presser or seam roll. Press the entire section until it's almost dry (if you've used moisture), and let it cool before moving the work so the fabric will "remember" the pressed position. Finish the raw edges of the seams appropriately (see the sidebar "Seam finishes" on pp. 42-43), and press them flat.

An important element of couture sewing, marking a garment is essential for its assembly since, unlike in ready-to-wear construction and home sewing, raw edges are rarely used as a guide for seaming. In addition to indicating seamlines, hemlines, darts and matchpoints, markings are also used to note fabric grainlines and design details such as pocket positions and buttonholes.

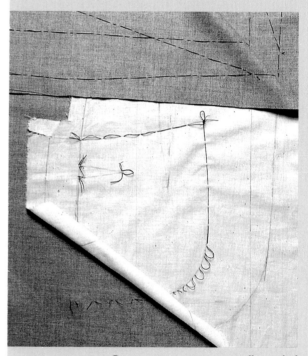

Couture garments are generally marked with thread because it's a durable marking visible on both sides of the fabric. At the top of the photo, thread tracings mark the edges, center fronts and roll lines of two garment sections. On the muslin jacket (at bottom), tailor tacks, most still unclipped, mark the position of a pocket. The clipped tack near the pocket center marks the position of a dart below the pocket. (Photo by Susan Kahn.)

A garment can be marked with thread, chalk or a tracing wheel. In couture, marking with thread is generally preferred because it's visible on both sides of the fabric and durable enough to stay in position as long as needed during construction without damaging the fabric. Since information on chalking and tracing-wheel markings is readily available in other sewing books (see the Bibliography on p. 214), I want to focus here on thread tracing.

If you've never marked with thread, the process may seem tedious at first, but you'll soon discover how invaluable it is for assembling and fitting garments. There are two basic marking stitches: thread tracings, most often used in dressmaking workrooms to mark dresses, blouses and gowns; and tailor's tacks, used in tailoring workrooms on suits, pants and tailored dresses. Both types of markings are made before the pattern is removed from the fabric and sometimes even before the fabric is cut.

THREAD TRACING

Thread tracings are usually made with basting cotton and a fine, long needle. But you may want to use silk basting thread to mark the garment centers and balance lines since silk will not leave an impression on the fabric when pressed. When thread-tracing seamlines and darts, you can first mark the stitching lines on the garment with chalk or dressmaker's carbon or transfer them directly from the toile.

To use a toile as a guide to mark a single layer of fabric, work with the fabric face side up and the toile on top of it. To transfer markings, fold the toile

back on the seamline, and mark the garment close to the folded edge. If the toile is spread on a double layer of fabric, thread-trace only the upper layer. (To avoid catching the lower layer, many sewers place scissor points between the two layers.) Then pin the layers together on the thread tracing, turn the sections over, and thread-trace between the pins.

To thread-trace, begin by anchoring the thread with a backstitch and mark the garment with alternating long and short basting stitches. At the end of the seamline, always insert the needle on the intersecting seamline or hemline so the intersection will be marked on both sides of the fabric. Continue basting at least ½ in. past the intersection without pivoting at the corner of the intersecting seamline. Then to turn the corner, take about a ¾-in. stitch on the diagonal that ends in line with the intersecting seam and begin thread-tracing that intersecting seamline (see the drawing below) in the seam allowance ½ in. from the intersection.

THREAD-TRACING INTERSECTING SEAMLINES

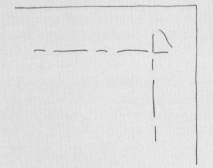

TAILOR'S TACKS

Tailor's tacks are generally used only to mark wool fabrics since they tend to fall out of slippery and open-weave materials and are cumbersome to use on a muslin toile. The tacks are made using a paper pattern without seam allowances—or with the seam allowances folded back—as a marking guide. They're usually sewn through two layers of fabric with a double strand of a soft, unglazed thread such as basting cotton or hand embroidery floss. The tacks themselves are a series of connected thread loops (see the photo on the facing page) that are cut apart, leaving thread markers in each layer of the fabric.

To mark fabric with tailor's tacks, cut out the garment sections first. Then, with the pattern still on the fabric, use tailor's tacks to mark all the seamlines, then garment centers, darts, placket openings, button and buttonhole locations.

To mark straight lines with tailor's tacks, take a short stitch, then take another short stitch about 1 in. away. To mark a curved line, make the stitches about ¼ in. apart and leave a loop as you pull up the thread. Then carefully clip the thread between the stitches, gently pull the two layers of fabric apart about ¼ in. and cut through the center of the loops, leaving tufts of thread on each layer.

NARROW PLAIN SEAM

This variation on a plain seam is trimmed and finished with the raw edges overcast together. Used frequently on the armholes of couture dresses, this seam is especially appropriate for curved seamlines that are not pressed open and for firmly woven, sheer fabrics.

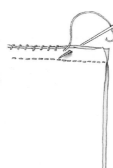

Begin this seam by sewing a plain seam with right sides together. Remove the basting and press the closed seam flat. Then baste the seam allowances together ⅛ in. from the seamline. If the fabric ravels badly, stitch next to the basting before overcasting the edges. Then trim the seam allowances so they're no wider than ¼ in. (although on armscye seams they can be as wide as ½ in.), overcast the edges together, remove the basting and press again. (The direction of the final pressing depends on where the seam is located on the garment. On an armscye, for example, it should be pressed flat and folded by hand—not pressed—toward the sleeve. On the shoulder, it should be pressed toward the garment front.)

FALSE FRENCH SEAM

Unlike the traditional French seam that it resembles (see pp. 46-47), the false French seam is stitched with right sides together and can be used on lightweight fabrics to finish shaped and closely fitted seams. Begin this

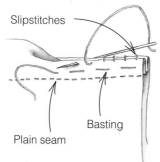

Slipstitches

Basting

Plain seam

seam by sewing a plain seam, then remove the basting and press the seam flat. Trim the seam allowances to between ¼ in. and ½ in. Fold one seam allowance in toward the other and pin along the fold. Then fold and pin the other seam allowance in the same way. Align the folded edges and baste them together. Then sew the edges together with slipstitches or whipstitches, and press the seam again.

SELF-BOUND SEAM

Called a standing fell seam in factory production, the self-bound seam is so named because one seam allowance wraps around and binds the other. The fin-

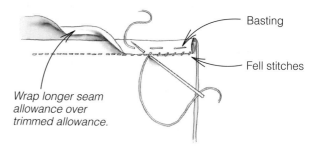

Basting

Fell stitches

Wrap longer seam allowance over trimmed allowance.

ished seam is generally less than ⅜ in. wide and is frequently used on the armholes of unlined blouses and dresses. This seam is only suitable for use on lightweight fabrics.

To make a self-bound seam, stitch a plain seam, remove the bastings, and press. Then trim one of the two seam allowances ¼ in. narrower than the other. When making a self-bound seam at an armhole, for example, the sleeve seam allowance should be trimmed to ⅛ in. to ¼ in. wide, and the bodice seam allowance to ⅜ in. to ½ in. wide. Wrap the wider seam allowance around the narrower one, and fold under the raw edge of the wider allowance. Baste this folded edge at the seamline, then sew it permanently with a fell stitch or slipstitch. Press the seam again.

WHIPPED SEAM

Another variation of the plain seam, the whipped seam is used on transparent fabrics like silk mousseline or organza. After a plain seam is stitched, the seam allowances are folded over together 1⁄16 in. from the stitched line. Then the fold is overcast and the seam allowances trimmed close to the overcasting. The finished whipped seam looks more like a heavy cord than a seam.

Overcast edge before seam allowances are trimmed

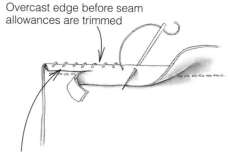

Trim seam allowance close to overcasting.

THE LAPPED SEAM

As its name suggests, a lapped seam is made by overlapping one garment section with another. The overlapping edge is folded under and permanently sewn to the underlap from the right side of the garment with a fell stitch or slipstitch.

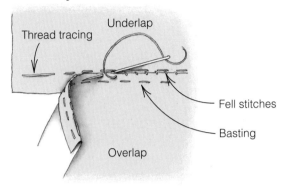

Compared with a plain seam, the lapped seam is more visually defined on the surface of the garment. Many couture houses use this seam to join a gathered skirt to the bodice. A few designers use it for setting sleeves, even though the stitches nearly always show, as you can see in the photo of Schiaparelli's circus jacket on p. 55. A lapped seam can also be used as an alternative to an abutted seam (see p. 46) to reduce bulk when joining seams and darts on interfacings and backings.

To sew a lapped seam, turn under the seam allowance of the overlapping edge using the thread tracing as a guide. Baste ⅛ in. from the edge. Then, with the wrong side up, press the folded edge lightly. Remove the thread tracing on the seamline and press the edge again. With the right sides up, align the seamlines and matchpoints on the two sections and top-baste them together on top of or alongside the earlier basting. Secure the seam permanently with slipstitches or fell stitches. Remove all bastings and press lightly.

If you're sewing a lapped seam on a curve, stretch or shrink the seam allowance if necessary to make it lie flat before turning it under. You may also find it necessary to clip or trim this seam allowance to flatten it. If the overlap is shaped with an outward corner, miter the seam allowances. If it has an inward corner, face the corner as needed (see p. 67 for instructions on both procedures).

When joining seams and darts on interfacings and backings, the overlap is left flat and has no seam allowance, but the underlap will need a small seam allowance. The layers are lapped and pinned, and then secured with a catchstitch or a running stitch.

APPLIQUÉ SEAMS
Among the most intricate seams sewn in couture workrooms are those used to seam lace and patterned fabrics. Variations of the lapped seam, appliqué seams are often used on couture bridal gowns and special-occasion designs. There are many ways to sew utilitarian appliqué seams, most of them labor intensive, difficult to alter and rarely used except in haute couture (see the discussion of purely decorative appliqué seams on pp. 202-203.)

Lace appliqué seams join intricately shaped lace designs without visible seamlines. Two different types of lace appliqué seams, one joining lace with lace and the other joining lace with woven fabric, can be seen on the Valentino blouse on p. 44.

In an appliqué seam joining patterned fabrics, the seamline is often adjusted to prevent disrupting the motifs of the fabric design. The resulting seam zigzags or meanders around motifs that cross the seamline and returns to a regular straight seam between motifs. The sections of the seam outlining a motif are sewn by hand; the straight sections between motifs are sewn by machine. This seam is inconspicuous but rarely invisible (see the photo on p. 46).

You need to plan for most appliqué seams before cutting out the garment fabric. For best results, begin with a fitted muslin toile, as is commonly done in couture workrooms. In order to see the motifs at the seamline when you place the toile on the fashion fabric, fold the seam allowances under.

Next spread the fabric right side up and lay the toile or pattern on top of it, positioning the motifs attractively on the garment sections. Wherever the major motifs cross the seamline, you'll need to appliqué that section of the seam. Leave plenty of room between garment sections for cutting around motifs to be appliquéd. Before cutting out the sections, thread-trace all seamlines and darts. Leave at least ¼-in. seam allowances around the motifs and 1 in. to 1½ in. along straight seamlines.

Seam Finishes

Seam finishes complete the edges of seams, facings and hems and prevent them from fraying when the garment is worn and cleaned (which is particularly important on unlined blouses and dresses). Overcasting seams by hand has always been the preferred finish in couture because it's the flattest, softest and least likely to show on the right side of the garment. Although it's the most popular finishing method, it's also the most time consuming and therefore the most expensive. Today, to reduce expense, a few couture workrooms use a narrow, machine-sewn zigzag finish. A bound edge, called a Hong Kong finish by home sewers, is also selectively used in couture since it creates a small ridge.

Hand overcasting

Hand overcasting is used to finish separately the individual allowances of a seam. It can also be used on the raw edge of a hem to reduce bulk, on a narrow plain seam that finishes two seam allowances together (see p. 40), and on narrow seams on transparent fabric. When two layers are overcast together, extra care must be taken to be sure there's no strain or pull that shows on the face of the garment.

To overcast by hand, use a short needle and fine cotton or silk thread. Sew the edge with overcasting stitches no more than ⅛ in. deep and ⅛ in. apart (see p. 32). For fabrics that ravel badly,

work a second row of stitches in the opposite direction. The seams on many of Balenciaga's designs were finished this way with astonishing precision.

Binding

A seam, hem or facing can also be completed with a bound finish that encases its raw edges. In the case of a seam, the allowances can be bound together or separately. Binding them together produces the bulkiest and stiffest edge, which may show as a ridge on the right side of a garment made of lightweight to medium-weight fabric. Binding the two edges separately is far more common in couture and suitable for fabrics that ravel

The raw edges of the facings and hem allowance on this silk crepe overblouse are finished with narrow silk organza bias bindings. Designed by Norman Norell for the suit shown on p. 134, the blouse has not only shoulder closures with fabric-covered buttons and thread loops overcast with tiny buttonhole stitches, but also an armhole design called a sleeveless flange (see pp.127-128). (Photo by Cathy Carver. Metropolitan Museum of Art. Gift of Mrs. Neal Sellin, 1969.)

Bias binding

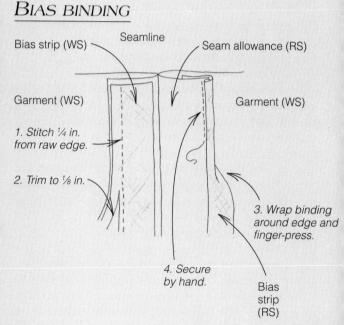

Bias strip (WS)   Seamline   Seam allowance (RS)

Garment (WS)   Garment (WS)

1. Stitch ¼ in. from raw edge.

2. Trim to ⅛ in.

3. Wrap binding around edge and finger-press.

4. Secure by hand.

Bias strip (RS)

or irritate the skin and for unlined or backed garments. This type of binding is also often used to finish a raw edge of a hem or facing on heavy or bulky fabrics. If you're working with lightweight and many medium-weight fabrics, however, this finish still may show through on the right side, in which case the edge should be overcast rather than bound.

To make a seam binding, choose a lightweight fabric like a plain-weave silk, organza or chiffon, no matter what weight the garment fabric is. The binding must be cut on the bias, and the bias strips should be 1 in. wide (see p. 76). As shown in the drawing on the facing page, trim the seam or hem allowances· so they're even in width and from ¾ in. to 1¼ in. wide. With right sides together, pin the strip to the seam allowance, matching the raw edges. Stitch a ¼-in. seam by hand or machine and trim to ⅛ in. or less. Wrap the binding over the raw edge and pin it in place. Secure the binding by hand with a short running stitch close to the first seamline. Press and trim the excess binding to ¼ in.

When finishing armholes or seams on transparent fabrics, apply the binding to the seam's two raw edges held together. When completing the binding, turn its raw edge under and fell it to the seamline joining the bias and seam allowances. At Valentino, the bias strip is cut from flesh-colored fabric to make narrow seams inconspicuous on transparent fabrics.

A *lace-on-lace appliqué seam* is the simplest kind of appliqué seam, which involves whipstitching a finished or cut lace edge to an underlying piece of lace. Only a small seam allowance is needed if you're working with a cut lace edge since this edge doesn't need to be turned under. Instead, to stop any raveling that may occur, the cut edge is whipstitched down to the underlaying lace and excess seam allowance trimmed away.

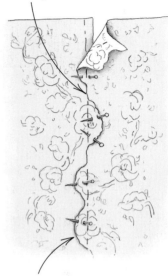

Match thread-traced seamlines, pin and baste. Motifs will seldom match exactly.

New seamline

Begin this seam with the right sides of each garment section up. Lap the sections, aligning the thread-traced seamlines and matchpoints. Consider lapping part of the seam in one direction and part in the other so that each garment section is at times the overlapping section and at times the underlapping section. To do this, clip to the seamline between the motifs each time you change the layering.

Pin all the seamlines together and examine your work, making sure the motifs are attractively positioned. (If you find a "bald spot" or two in the seam, you can cut out extra motifs and apply them where needed.) Baste, and then sew the new seamline with small whipstitches, and trim away the excess lace at the edges of the overlap (the underlaps are not usually trimmed). Remove the thread tracings and bastings, and press the garment wrong side up on a softly padded surface.

Frequently used in haute couture, a *lace-on-fabric appliqué seam* is suitable for fabrics that don't ravel badly and for curved seamlines. In the photo on p. 44, you'll see an example of this type of appliqué seam used on a blouse, this one by Valentino.

In the detail of the blouse at top, designed by Valentino and shown in full on p. 28, a lace-on-lace appliqué seam at the shoulder follows the design of the lace motifs and is very irregular. The sleeves and tucked bodice are hand-sewn to the lace yoke with lapped seams. The lace on the sleeve shown above is attached with a lace-on-fabric appliqué seam. (Photo by Cathy Carver. Metropolitan Museum of Art. Gift of Mrs. Lyn Revson, 1975.)

There are two ways to plan this seam: on the muslin toile or on the entire garment section. I prefer the latter because it allows more flexibility when positioning the lace and more control when sewing the seam.

The following directions for a sleeve trimmed with lace (see the photo at left) can be adapted for use on other parts of a garment. Once you've cut the sleeve, thread-trace all the seamlines except the appliqué seamline onto the fabric and indicate matchpoints. With the sleeve right side up, arrange and pin the lace on the cuff edge of the sleeve so the top edge of the lace will match at the underarm seam.

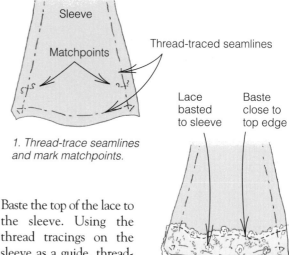

1. Thread-trace seamlines and mark matchpoints.

2. Thread-trace seamlines on lace and sew appliqué seam with whipstitches.

Baste the top of the lace to the sleeve. Using the thread tracings on the sleeve as a guide, thread-trace the underarm and cuff seamlines onto the lace. Do not trim away the sleeve under the lace until after the garment is fitted.

After the fitting, permanently sew the top of the lace to the sleeve with a small whipstitch and fine silk or cotton thread in a color that matches the lace. Remove the bastings. With the wrong side up, press the whipstitched seam on a softly padded surface. Trim away the sleeve fabric under the lace, leaving a ¹⁄₁₆-in. and ¹⁄₈-in. seam allowance. Complete the sleeve's underarm seam with a plain seam on the all-fabric sections and a lace-on-lace appliqué seam (see p. 43) on the lace section.

Suitable for fabrics with large, widely-spaced motifs, the *appliqué seam for patterned fabrics* has been used on wonderful designs by Schiaparelli, Lanvin, Dior, Balmain and other couturiers. This seam is usually

APPLIQUÉ SEAM FOR PATTERNED FABRIC

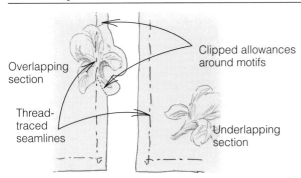

Overlapping section

Thread-traced seamlines

Clipped allowances around motifs

Underlapping section

1. Clip to seamline above and below motifs that will overlap.

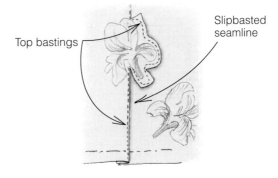

Top bastings

Slipbasted seamline

2. Fold back seam allowance between motifs on overlapping section and position sections. Top-baste seamlines between motifs and baste lapped motifs flat for fitting. Slipbaste between motifs and, right sides together, machine-stitch slipbasted seam.

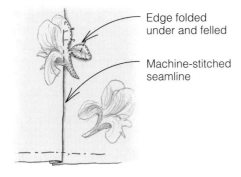

Edge folded under and felled

Machine-stitched seamline

3. Clip motifs as needed to fold raw edges under smoothly, and pin and baste around motifs. Sew to underlap with slipstitches or fell stitches.

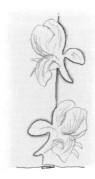

4. If overlapping motifs alternate side to side, completed seam will look like that above.

machine-stitched between the motifs and hand-sewn around them, and it must be planned for before the fabric is cut. The motifs on the two sections being joined don't have to match, but they should merge attractively. One section can consistently overlap the other, or they can alternate overlap directions.

To sew a simple appliqué seam with one section consistently overlapping the other, clip the seam allowance on the overlap section to the seamline above and below each motif to be lapped, as shown above. Using the thread tracing as a guide, fold the seam allowance between the motifs to the wrong side. With the wrong side up, press the folded edge lightly. With the right sides up, align the seamlines and matchpoints and top-baste the two sections together about ⅛ in. from the thread-traced seamline. Baste the edges of the motifs flat, and check and refine the garment's fit as needed.

Slipbaste or fell the part of the seam to be machine stitched. Remove the top basting and reposition the garment sections with right sides together. Machine-stitch the basted sections of the seam between the motifs. Then remove the remaining basting, secure the thread ends and press open the machine-stitched seam sections, clipping as needed to make it lie flat.

To sew the hand-stitched sections of the seam around each motif, first spread the garment right side up. Clip the motifs as needed at the curves and corners and trim the seam allowance around the motif to make it fold under smoothly. Use a fine needle to work the raw edges of the motifs under, and finger-press these edges. Pin and baste the motifs in place. Then use a tiny fell

In this detail of an appliquéd center-front seam, the motifs lap the seam left over right. (Photo by Susan Kahn.)

stitch or slipstitch to sew the edges permanently. Remove the bastings and trim away the excess fabric under the appliqué. Press lightly from the wrong side.

For an appliqué seam with overlapping motifs that alternate from side to side, establish one side as the primary overlapping side, clip above and below any motifs that are to overlap and handle the seam allowances and overlapping motifs as explained on p. 45.

ABUTTED SEAM

The abutted, or butted, seam has no seam allowances and is used for joining seams and darts on interfacings where you want to minimize bulk. Occasionally it is used for piecing fabrics. This seam can be sewn with or without an underlay, which adds strength. If you want an underlay, use plain-weave linen or cotton tape, rayon seam binding, lightweight selvage cut

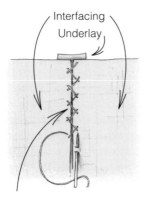

Butt edges together and catchstitch to underlay.

from silk organza or georgette, or muslin selvage. Cut away any seam allowances on the garment and the dart take-up, if used, at a dart. Center and baste one raw edge to the underlay and then butt and baste the second edge to the first. Secure the edges permanently by hand with a catchstitch or baseball stitch, or by machine with a straight stitch. Then press the seam.

Eliminating the underlay produces a softer, more flexible seam. To finish the seam without an underlay, sew the edges together with a catchstitch or baseball stitch and press.

FRENCH SEAM

Called an English seam in France and a French seam in the English-speaking world, the French seam looks like a tuck on the wrong side of the garment. Its neat appearance on both sides of the garment makes it appropriate for handmade silk lingerie and fine blouses and for some garments made of transparent fabric. Because of its strength, this seam is also suitable for fine infant's wear and other lightweight, washable garments. French seams, however, are unsuitable for intricately shaped seamlines and for garments that are closely fitted or might require alterations.

A French seam is actually two seams: the first seam is sewn in the seam allowance, and the second on the seamline. Either seam can be sewn by hand or machine, but if you sew them both by hand, they'll interfere less with the drape of the fabric.

To prepare the garment for a fitting before you sew a French seam, baste as you would for a plain seam, with the right sides together. After the fitting, and after any corrections are made, remove the seam bastings—but not the thread tracings—so you can lay the garment flat.

Reposition the garment sections with the wrong sides together. Match and pin the thread-traced seamlines together, and baste if necessary. On very lightweight fabrics like chiffon, georgette or organza, baste the first stitching line ⅛ in. from the thread-traced seamline. On heavier fabrics, baste a scant ¼ in. away. Then, with a short stitch length, machine-stitch over the basting, or if you're sewing by hand, use a short running stitch. Remove the seam bastings, but not the thread tracings.

FRENCH SEAM

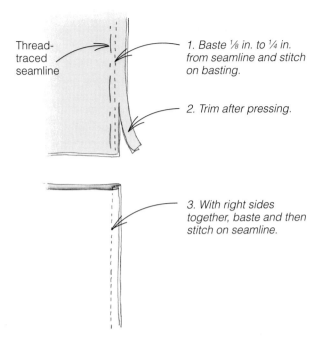

Thread-traced seamline

1. Baste ⅛ in. to ¼ in. from seamline and stitch on basting.

2. Trim after pressing.

3. With right sides together, baste and then stitch on seamline.

Press the seam flat, and then press it open. Refold the garment sections so that the right sides are together and the seam is at the fold. Press the fold with the point of the iron. Open the sections and trim the seam so it's slightly less than the finished width of the seam. Then, with the right sides together, baste on the thread-traced seamline and stitch. Next, remove the basting and press the seam flat, and then to one side. Press shoulder and side seams toward the front of the garment so they'll be inconspicuous when the garment is worn. For an even stronger seam, fell the free edge of the French seam to the wrong side of the garment.

SEAMS FOR SPECIAL SITUATIONS

Couture garments often feature intricate seamlines that require adapting a standard seam for a special use. The curved seamlines on Adrian's magnificent silk crepe ensemble on p. 34 and p. 54, for example, join reverse curves, which need to be handled differently from the standard plain seam. And on the colorful tunic overblouse by Yves Saint Laurent on p. 51, the seamline joining the cuff and sleeve has a reverse corner, which requires additional reinforcement since the inward corner is clipped to the seamline. More common than either seams with reverse corners or curves are in-

tersecting seams, which are unavoidable on virtually any garment you sew and which require special handling. When encountering some of these special situations, it's helpful to have some guidelines; they are presented here in order of the seam's frequency of use.

INTERSECTING SEAMS   Most designs have at least one or two seams that either meet or cross one another. In home sewing and ready-to-wear, the second seam is stitched across the seam allowances of the first seam. However, since this may interfere with the drape of the garment—that is, seam allowances caught in the seamline may cause it to pull when the body moves—many seams in haute couture are sewn without stitching across the seam allowances at the intersecting seamlines. Rather, the seam is stitched up to and ended at the intersecting seamline. Then it's begun again just on the other side of the seamline, with the seam allowances held out of the way (as shown in the drawing on p. 48). Shoulder seams are often stitched in this way when they intersect the armscye seam. When considering whether to cross one seam with another, base your decision on whether securing the seam allowances will create unwanted tension in the seam. If so, interrupt the seamline whenever it meets an intersecting seam.

To perfect your skill at matching seamlines and the first method of handling intersecting seams, make a patchwork sampler with 20 3-in. squares (just as the apprentices at the school of the *Chambre syndicale* do). First, make four long strips of five squares joined together with ½-in. seams and press all the seams open. Then, with right sides together, baste the strips together along their long edges with a ½-in. seam, sewing across the intersecting seam allowances. Double-baste at the intersections to keep the layers from slipping. Machine-stitch the basted seam. Check to be sure the intersections match exactly. Remove the bastings and press.

To practice the alternate method of handling intersecting seams, cut a new series of squares and repeat the exercise, this time basting the long edges of the strips together without stitching down the intersecting seamlines. When machine-stitching the seam, push the seam allowances away from the presser foot as you approach each intersection and sew precisely up to it. Cut your thread and rearrange the seam allowances to avoid stitching across them. Start the seam precisely on the other side of the seamline and stitch to the next intersecting seam. After stitching the seam, secure the thread ends with tailor's knots. Remove the bastings and press.

INTERSECTING SEAMS

WITH STITCHED-DOWN SEAM ALLOWANCES

WITH SEAM ALLOWANCES LEFT FREE

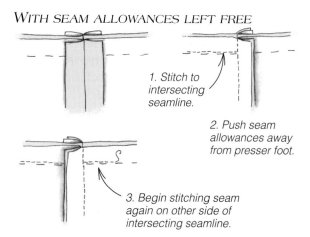

1. Stitch to intersecting seamline.

2. Push seam allowances away from presser foot.

3. Begin stitching seam again on other side of intersecting seamline.

SEAMS CROSSING A DART   When seaming over a dart, the garment will drape better if you don't stitch over the dart take-up. This situation is handled in the same way as the intersecting seam shown above whose seam allowances are left free.

To seam across a dart, first sew, cut and press the dart take-up open, and then baste the two garment sections together. Then, with the darted section on top, machine-stitch the seam to the dart, stop and cut the threads, leaving thread tails. Fold the dart take-up over the stitched section of the seam and begin the seam again just on the other side of the dart. When you've stitched to the end of the seamline, pull all the thread ends toward the undarted layer and fasten with tailor's knots before pressing.

ENCLOSED SEAMS   So named because it's enclosed between the garment section and its facing or lining, an enclosed seam can be located at any faced edge. Since these edges can be bulky, enclosed seams require some special handling to make them smooth, flat and inconspicuous.

Because all seams—especially enclosed ones—lie flatter if first pressed open, begin by pressing the seam open after it's machine-stitched. Then grade the seam in order to reduce its bulk, trimming the individual seam allowances to different widths. To ensure a smooth finish on the right side of the garment, trim the garment seam allowance to ¼ in. and the facing seam allowance slightly more.

At curved edges, clip or notch the seam allowances as needed after pressing them to make them lie flat and smooth. Make the clips on the bias, rather than on grain, in order to avoid weakening the seam. At corners, trim away only a small triangle.

After grading the seam, catchstitch one seam allowance to the interfacing or backing. Then sew the remaining seam allowances to the first. Turn the edge right side out so it's covered by the facing or lining and press it lightly from the wrong side.

EASED SEAMS   Used to shorten a longer section to fit a shorter one smoothly (such as a back shoulder joined to a front shoulder), eased seams are basted with tiny running stitches to hold in the excess fabric. Called ease basting, these stitches smoothly ease rather than gather or pleat the fabric.

To ease-baste a seam, begin with a simple knot on the wrong side of the fabric and baste a row of short, even stitches on the seamline, with approximately 20 to 30 stitches to the inch, leaving the thread slack with a long tail. Add two more rows of identical basting ⅛ in. above and below the first line of stitches. Pull up the threads and evenly distribute the fullness until the garment section is the desired length. Then fasten the threads by making a figure-eight with them around a pin. Shrink out the excess fullness with your iron until the eased area is smooth (see p. 59). Baste and complete the seam like a plain seam.

GATHERED SEAMS   A gathered seam uses a technique based upon the running stitch, which enables you to sew a large, full garment section to a smaller one. This technique is similar to ease basting, but the gathered fabric is much fuller, not shrunk with the iron and has a softly gathered decorative effect. This seam can be used to join gathered edges to waistbands, cuffs and yokes.

To sew a gathered seam, anchor the thread and begin the first row of gathering stitches on or just inside the seamline. Take five or six small stitches at once on the needle before pulling it out of the fabric, and continue in this manner until the entire section is gathered. Sew two more gathering rows ⅛ in. above and below the first.

Next, pin the beginning end of each row to a weight (such as a tailor's ham) and pull up all the gathering rows as tightly as possible. Fasten the threads by making a figure-eight around a pin. Then, with the top of the gathered section held in one hand, pull the bottom sharply with the other hand so the rucks (tops of the gathered folds) are parallel to one another. Remove the pin holding the gathering threads and loosen the threads, so that you can stroke the gathers with a tapestry needle to make them lie evenly side by side.

Adjust the gathered section to the length of the shorter section and fasten the threads in a figure eight around a pin.

To sew a gathered seam at a waistband, cuff or yoke, fold the seam allowance of the ungathered edge to the wrong side. With right sides up, align the seamlines and matchpoints on both edges for a lapped seam with the ungathered edge overlapping the gathered section and slipbaste the sections together for fitting. After fitting, machine-stitch or fell the seamline permanently. Trim the seam allowances to ½ in. and press first the band, then the gathered section, working carefully to press between the rucks to avoid setting creases. (See also the discussion of a variation of a gathered seam, the buttressed seam, on p. 192.)

STAYS

Stays made from strips of seam binding, plain-weave tape or selvage are used to stabilize seamlines or edges of a garment so they fit the body smoothly. A seam stabilized in this manner is called a stayed, or taped, seam. Stays are frequently used on eased or gathered seams to make the garment section easier to handle during construction and to prevent the finished edge from gaping away from the body. A stay will also keep fabric from stretching at foldlines on garment edges such as a zipper placket or a slashed pocket. When used for this purpose, the stay is called a grain stay.

Stays are usually sewn to a single garment section and don't cross seamlines. One notable exception is a waistline stay, which is usually sewn to the waistline seam after the skirt and bodice are joined.

To apply a stay, mark its position on the right side of the garment during the fitting, before sewing the seam permanently. If there's fullness to be removed from the edge, pin out a small dart—or series of small darts if there's a lot of fullness—indicating the excess to be eased. With the dart(s) pinned and the garment still on the body, measure the length for the finished stay. This length will vary, depending on how easily the fabric can be eased, the grain of the seam, the garment design and the amount of fabric pinched out in the dart. But the stay should always be a little longer than the section being stayed. The excess can be clipped away after permanently sewing the stay.

After the fitting, if a dart was pinned out, mark its width by thread-tracing a crossmark on the seamline at each "leg" of the dart. (Charles Kleibacker

leaves a connecting thread between the crossmarks to avoid confusion with nearby thread tracings.) Remove the pins from the dart. Press a ¼-in. to ½-in. wide strip of preshrunk silk organza or chiffon selvage, plain-weave tape or seam binding, and pencil-mark the finished length of the stay on the strip.

With the garment wrong side up, center the stay over the seamline, aligning and pinning the matchpoints on the stay and garment. With the garment right side up, find and pin the midpoint of the stay. Then distribute and pin any excess to be eased.

Sew the stay from the right side of the garment, with tiny running stitches just inside the seamline. As you sew, hold the edge of the garment with your index finger under the stay and your thumb on the outside of the garment. Use your thumb and the needle

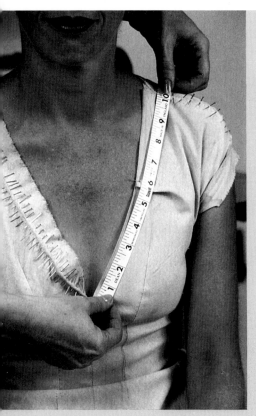

STAYING A SEAM

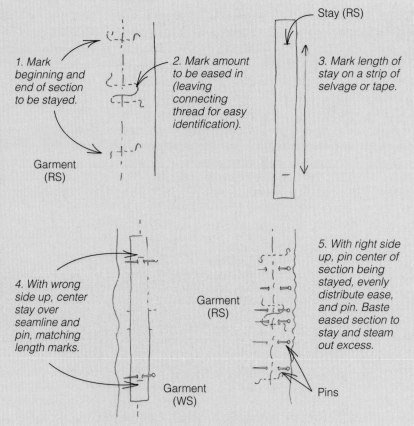

1. Mark beginning and end of section to be stayed.

2. Mark amount to be eased in (leaving connecting thread for easy identification).

Garment (RS)

Stay (RS)

3. Mark length of stay on a strip of selvage or tape.

4. With wrong side up, center stay over seamline and pin, matching length marks.

Garment (WS)

Garment (RS)

5. With right side up, pin center of section being stayed, evenly distribute ease, and pin. Baste eased section to stay and steam out excess.

Pins

Charles Kleibacker frequently uses stays to control V-necklines and keep them from sagging or gaping when the wearer moves. On this toile from Kleibacker's workroom, a dart has been pinned out on the left side of the neckline to make it fit snugly. On the right side, a stay has been pinned in place and the dart's fullness distributed evenly along the edge. (Photo courtesy of Threads *magazine.)*

to control the ease each time you remove a pin. When sewing the stay to a neckline or front opening, don't stop or release the edge until you finish. When you reach the end, check the stay's length before anchoring the thread securely.

To shrink the excess, work with just the point of the iron and a damp press cloth. Alternatively you could shrink some of the ease before pinning the stay on the garment and finish shrinking it after it's in place.

A grain stay does not hold in any ease, but rather simply preserves the lines of a design. When sewing a grain stay, work carefully from the wrong side, picking up only a single thread or back of a thread and not pulling the stitches too tight. If the garment has a backing, use short running stitches to sew the stay to the backing and reinforce the fabric. If the stay isn't covered by a lining, sew the stay's edges to the backing with a catchstitch.

To reinforce the seamline to withstand more stress, face the inward corner, as shown in the drawing on p. 52. To make this facing, cut a 3-in. square of silk organza and center it over the corner on the right side of the garment section. Match the grainlines and baste the square on the seamlines. Press what you've sewn flat.

Next, using a short machine stitch, sew just inside the seamline, beginning and ending 1 in. from the corner. When you approach the corner itself, shorten the stitch length a little more as additional reinforcement for the corner, and then lengthen the stitch again as you sew away from the corner. Clip the inward corner and reinforcing square precisely up to the machine-stitched corner, and turn the seam allowance and reinforcement to the wrong side. With the wrong side up, press the folded edge lightly. Trim away the excess reinforcing fabric, and with a tiny stitch, overcast together the clipped edges of the reinforcing square and garment section.

First turn the seam allowance on the inward corner to the wrong side and baste about ⅛ in. from the folded edge. With the right sides up and the folded edge of the inward corner lapped over the unfolded edged of the outward corner, align the seamlines and matchpoints and top-baste the sections together. Then slipbaste or fell the seam. Remove the bastings and reposition the sections with the right sides together and the faced corner uppermost. With the machine set for a short stitch, begin at the corner and stitch away from it for about 1 in. next to the facing seam. Then lengthen the stitch and finish that section of the seam. Finish the corner by repositioning your work so you can begin again at

SEAMS WITH REVERSE CORNERS

Designs with godets, gussets, square or pointed yokes and shawl collars have seams with reverse corners, that is, an inward corner on one edge and an outward corner on the adjoining edge (as shown in the drawing on p. 52). The sleeve on the Yves Saint Laurent tunic overblouse shown above, for example, has a seam with a reverse corner on its cuff. At the inward corner, the sleeve must be clipped to the seamline so the seam can be stitched and pressed open. Since the seam allowance tapers to nothing, the seam cannot withstand stress. When these seams are used on decorative godets or shawl collars, their weakness is not a problem. But on seams that will be stressed, for example, on gussets and yokes, the corner must be reinforced.

There is a variety of ways to reinforce an inward-corner seam. The simplest method is to back each garment section at the outset with a lightweight, firmly woven backing fabric, like silk organza or chiffon.

the corner, with the bulk of the garment to the right of the needle. Again stitch away from the corner, using a short stitch at first and then lengthening it. (By starting the seam at the corner and sewing away from it, you'll get a sharper corner and eliminate the shifting and mismatching of edges that might otherwise occur if you start away from the corner and sew toward it.)

When you finish sewing the seam, fasten the threads at the corners with tailor's knots, remove the bastings and press the seam toward the section with the inward corner. If the fabric is bulky, press the seam open so you can flatten the seam allowance on the outward corner. If you can't flatten it, trim away the overlapping layers at the corner and overcast the edges of the seam allowances.

MAKING A REVERSE CORNER

SLEEVE WITH REVERSE CORNER

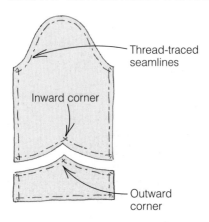

Thread-traced seamlines

Inward corner

Outward corner

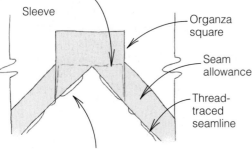

Clipped, overcast and folded-back seam allowance and reinforcing square

Sleeve

Organza square

Seam allowance

Thread-traced seamline

3. Fold back and press reinforced, clipped seam allowance.

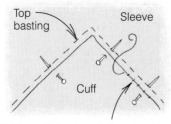

Top basting

Sleeve

Cuff

5. Then slipbaste or fell seam at corner.

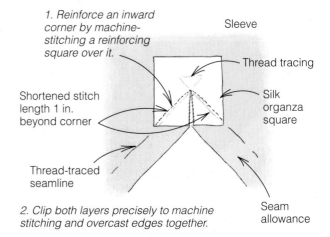

1. Reinforce an inward corner by machine-stitching a reinforcing square over it.

Sleeve

Thread tracing

Silk organza square

Shortened stitch length 1 in. beyond corner

Thread-traced seamline

Seam allowance

2. Clip both layers precisely to machine stitching and overcast edges together.

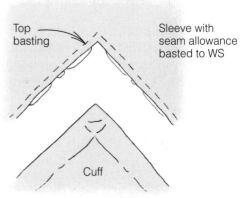

Top basting

Sleeve with seam allowance basted to WS

Cuff

4. To join sleeve and cuff, first align and pin thread-traced seamlines and baste.

INTERFACINGS AND BACKINGS

Used much more extensively in haute couture than in luxury ready-to-wear and home sewing, interfacings and backings are generally natural-fiber fabrics sewn to the interior of a garment to help shape and support the design. More malleable than synthetic and fusible materials, these natural-fiber fabrics can be applied to part or all of a garment section.

By contrast, linings, which are generally silk, serve for aesthetics rather than support. Although almost always used on tailored jackets and coats, linings are used much less frequently in couture than in luxury ready-to-wear for dresses and evening gowns since they add an unnecessary layer that may wrinkle or distort the garment's drape.

The distinction between an interfacing and a backing is somewhat blurred. They both help shape a garment, but a backing (sometimes called an underlining or mounting) usually lends body to the fabric itself, while an interfacing helps control or produce the shape of the garment. An interfacing is never used for modesty, but a backing is often applied to make a fabric opaque or change its color. And although a backing generally covers the entire garment section it backs, an interfacing can be cut either to duplicate and support an entire garment section or just an edge or another part of it.

Traditional couture interfacing and backing fabrics include hair canvas, silk organza, China silk, handkerchief linen, organdy, muslin, cotton flannel, net, tulle, crinoline and self-fabric. I've also seen more luxurious fabric used, like fine Egyptian cotton, faille and silk taffeta, charmeuse and chif-

fon. And I've found one stiffener, horsehair braid, used in several interesting ways—on the front edges of a Dior jacket, as the skirt backing for a Nina Ricci evening gown and as the support for one of Hardy Amies's off-the-shoulder wedding dresses.

Choose a backing or interfacing fabric by deciding how much support the interior architecture of the garment needs—the more support required, the stiffer the backing or interfacing (or both). To make a selection, try draping the garment fabric over the support material and examine the results: Does it hang stiffly or fall gently from your hand? Does it overwhelm the garment fabric? The support fabric can be crisper than the garment fabric, but it should not be heavier. (Note, too, that backing and interfacing fabrics hang less crisply when cut on the bias.) Experiment with various support fabrics to find the effect you want.

Many garments, particularly evening-wear, have extensive foundations, sometimes with several interfacings and backings in a given section. A few garments, like the Charles James's dresses on p. 8, are so structured that they can literally stand alone. More frequently designs are shaped with such subtleness that the shaping isn't noticeable—see, for example, the Dior dress on p. 125, which has a simple silk-charmeuse backing, and that on on p. 120, which is backed with two layers of silk organza and interfaced with hair canvas and nylon crinoline.

Backings and interfacings are used to create a variety of silhouettes. On this silk satin design from Hanae Mori's 1992 Spring/Summer Collection, the unbacked bodice is draped, while the fabric in the skirt is backed and stiffened with interfacing to produce its unusual shape. (Photo by Mamoru Sakamoto, courtesy of Hanae Mori.)

Adrian's 'Modern Art' ensemble, inspired by the fluid curves of Cubist painter Georges Braque, has striking examples of seams with reverse curves (see a detail of these seams on p. 34). The unusually shaped seamlines on this garment contrast with the classic lines of the tunic, long skirt and cape. (Photo by Susan Kahn. Metropolitan Museum of Art. Gift of Miss Eleanor Lambert, 1958.)

SEAM WITH REVERSE CURVE

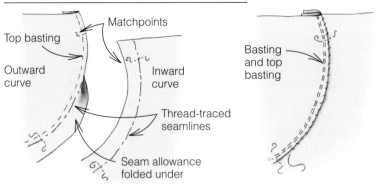

Matchpoints

Top basting

Outward curve

Inward curve

Thread-traced seamlines

Seam allowance folded under

Basting and top basting

With right sides up, match thread-traced seamlines and matchpoints, and top-baste overlapping curve in place. Slip-baste curves together, then remove thread tracing and top bastings on outward curve. With right sides together, machine-stitch seam and remove slipbasting.

SEAMS WITH REVERSE CURVES   A seam with a reverse curve joins an outward curve on one garment section with an inward curve on another section, as shown in the drawing above. The seam can either be decorative, as in the photo of the Adrian ensemble shown above, or it can be functional, as in the case of a princess fitting seam. Although the seamlines joining a pair of decorative inward and outward curves are the same length, the raw edges of their seam allowances are different: that on the inward curve is shorter than that on the outward curve. Successfully joining these two curved edges requires some manipulation—the more intricate the curve, the more the edges have to be manipulated. However, since seams in couture are

first thread-traced, matched and basted with right sides up, these seams are easier to sew than they would otherwise be.

To join an inward and outward curve for a decorative seamline, first turn the seam allowance on the outward curve to the wrong side and baste about ⅛ in. from the folded edge. With right sides up and the folded edge of the outward curve lapped over the unfolded edge of the inward curve, align the seamline and matchpoints, and top-baste the sections together on top of or alongside the basting on the folded edge (if you've indicated matchpoints at the beginning and end of each curve, you'll be able to match the curves more accurately). Slipbaste the two sections together. Remove the top-bastings so the sections can be positioned with right sides together for machine stitching. Then permanently stitch the seam. Remove the bastings, trim the seam allowances and press the seam open, clipping the inward seam as necessary to make it lie flat (the outward curve doesn't need to be clipped). Round any clipped corners, and when overcasting the edges, overcast the clips as well.

Unlike the decorative seams on the Adrian dress, fitting seams such as a princess seam or a sleeve-cap seam are frequently uneven in length. Once joined together, the excess fabric on the longer edge provides fitting ease. When seaming a fitting seam, ease-baste and shrink the longer edge to control the fullness before basting the two edges together. Then complete the seam like a plain seam.

BRACED SEAM A braced seam is a plain seam with a bias strip sewn atop it to hold the seam allowances open. Intended for fragile fabrics that are difficult to press crisply without marring the garment itself, the braced seam produces a smooth, flat seamline. To make this seam, first stitch a plain seam, then press it open and finish the raw edges. Choose a lightweight, crisp interfacing for the brace and cut a bias strip slightly narrower than the combined width of the two seam allowances. Center the brace over the seamline and pin it to the allowances. Then sew the edges to the seam allowances with running stitches.

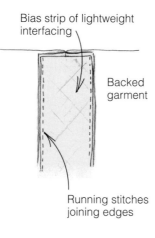

Bias strip of lightweight interfacing

Backed garment

Running stitches joining edges

DARTS

A dart is a stitched fold of fabric used to shape the fabric to the contours of the body. When positioned at the edge of a garment section, the dart tapers to a point at one end, as a skirt dart does. When positioned within a garment section, as for a dart below the bust on a jacket, the dart tapers to a point at both ends. Unlike the darts in ready-to-wear and home sewing, which are pressed to one side, darts in haute couture are often pressed open to make them lie flatter. Although darts are almost always stitched on the wrong side of the garment to hide their bulk, "stand-up" darts are stitched on the right side for decorative effect—a treatment Valentino frequently uses. To avoid disrupting a patterned fabric, darts can also be sewn as appliqué seams (see p. 41 and the photo on p. 136).

In haute couture, darts are used less often than in ready-to-wear and whenever possible are converted to ease (see pp. 56-57). Nonetheless, couture garments certainly use darts and occasionally put them in unusual places. For example, horizontal darts are sometimes used on the hem allowance to raise the hemline. On slips and underpinnings, which need to fit the bust closely, horizontal darts usually extend outward to the bust from a center-front seam (see the photo on p. 123).

Appliqué seaming techniques can be used to stitch a dart. In this detail of Schiaparelli's 1938 circus jacket (shown in full on p.136) the horse's tail is cut to lap over the dartline and secured with tiny fell stitches. The horse motifs also match perfectly on the sleeve cap, where the fullness is controlled with small tucks. (Photo by Cathy Carver. Metropolitan Museum of Art. Gift of Mrs. Pauline Potter, 1950.)

When stitched properly, a dart is barely visible on the right side of the garment. To sew a dart, begin by thread-tracing its stitching lines. If the dart is long or shaped, mark any matchpoints with tailor's tacks or crossmarks. Next, with the right sides together, baste the dart with short even-basting stitches, tapering the stitches to the point. To prepare the dart for a fitting, fold the basted dart into position and top-baste. If there are no corrections after the fitting, remove the top basting.

With the wrong side up, lightly press the dart flat and machine-stitch precisely on the basted lines. Secure the thread ends at the point, remove the bastings and press the stitched line. Carefully clip the dart open, stopping about ¼ in. from the point. If the dart is wide, trim it to 1 in. on each side of the stitched line. If the dart is too narrow to cut open, arrange the dart like a box pleat so that it's centered over the stitched line and baste the center so the dart will not shift when pressed.

Open the garment and spread the darted area over an appropriate pressing cushion so you can mold the dart to fit the body. Open the dart with your fingers and, with the point of the iron, press just the stitched line firmly with a sharp up-and-down movement. If necessary, insert a small metal knitting needle into the dart point to press it smoothly. Pressing over the needle keeps the fabric centered over the stitched line and prevents the dart from becoming crooked at the end. Press the entire section, molding it to fit the body and overcast the dart's raw edges.

When pressing double-pointed darts, stretch the folded edge of the dart at the widest point so it will fold back smoothly. If you're working with a cotton, linen or other fiber without much give, clip the dart before pressing it. If the dart is too narrow to be cut open, balance it with a strip of fabric (see below and the drawing at right).

To sew darts on a garment with a backing, apply the backing to the garment, then baste the dart centers together and work the two layers as one. After the darts are stitched, check to be sure the backing is not too tight. If it is, remove the bastings at the edges of the garment and rebaste.

If you're sewing darts on interfacing, you can eliminate extra bulk by adapting the instructions for lapped or abutted seams to make lapped or abutted darts. On the Yves Saint Laurent jacket on p. 10, the interfacing dart's take-up was cut away and the edges of the dart were catchstitched to the dart on the jacket.

BALANCED DARTS

A balanced dart is a dart to which a strip of fabric has been sewn and pressed in the opposite direction from the dart to balance its bulk. This technique is particularly useful for sewing small darts on bulky fabrics that ravel, although it is rarely used on lightweight fabrics.

To sew a balanced dart, baste the dart according to the directions above. Then, using self-fabric or an interfacing similar in weight to the fashion fabric, cut a strip on the lengthwise grain twice the width of the dart and about 1 in. longer. Center the strip over the basted dart so that when the dart is stitched, the strip will be sewn permanently with it. Baste the dart again to keep the strip from slipping, and stitch it permanently. Then remove the bastings and press the dart in one direction and both layers of the interfacing strip in the other.

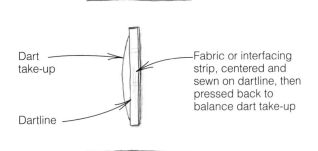

Dart take-up

Dartline

Fabric or interfacing strip, centered and sewn on dartline, then pressed back to balance dart take-up

CONVERTING DARTS TO EASE

In home sewing and luxury ready-to-wear, the practice of converting small darts to ease is often used at the elbow and back shoulder. In couture, darts are converted much more extensively to preserve the uninterrupted lines of a design. And sometimes they're converted in unconventional places in order to refine the garment's fit. Frequently used by Chanel on skirts to eliminate some or all darts, by Charles Kleibacker to prevent gaping décolleté necklines and by Yves Saint Laurent to tighten the back armscye on tailored jackets, this technique works best on fabrics that can be shrunk easily.

By converting darts to ease, you can avoid disrupting fabric patterns or the style lines of a garment. The waist dart in the right sample has been converted to ease in the left sample and the excess shrunk away with a steam iron. (Photo by Susan Kahn.)

The directions below include marking the dart during the fitting of a toile, but they can be adapted for commercial patterns. During the fitting of the toile or garment, pin a small dart anywhere it's needed or called for in the pattern. Note that to be a candidate for conversion, the dart must be relatively small and positioned at an edge or a seamline. Remove the garment and mark the location of the dart you just pinned on the uneased section. Remove the bastings and lay the garment flat.

On the wrong side of the darted section, mark the dart with chalk and measure its width at the seamline. Indicate matchpoints above and below the "legs" of the chalked dart equal to the dart's width, making the section to be eased three times the width of the dart. On the adjoining undarted section, indicate matchpoints equal to the dart's width above and below the stitching line of the dart location, making the uneased section twice the width of the dart. For example, if the pinned dart is ½ in. wide, the eased section would be 1½ in. wide and the undarted section would be 1 in. wide. Using the directions on p. 48 and p. 59 for eased seams and shrinking out fullness, ease and shrink the longer section to fit the adjoining section smoothly. Then complete the eased seams.

SETUP FOR CONVERTING DARTS TO EASE

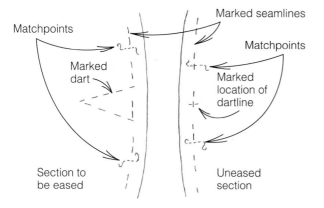

Matchpoints

Marked dart

Section to be eased

Marked seamlines

Matchpoints

Marked location of dartline

Uneased section

PRESSING TECHNIQUES

Pressing is such an important priority in couture sewing that many workrooms I visited had more irons than sewing machines. Pressing occurs throughout a design's construction—from shaping and molding garment sections before joining them, to pressing seams and edges during and after their shaping or sewing, to the final pressing of a completed garment.

The pressing tools I saw in couture workrooms are similar to many you may already have. An industrial steam iron with an outside water tank was generally used in tailoring workrooms, while a dry iron was used in dressmaking workrooms. Sometimes, however, a regular domestic iron was the only one used, and you certainly need not change irons if you have one you like and it works well. The issue is not the brand of iron you have, but how you use it. Other essential pressing tools include an ironing board or pressing table, point presser, sleeve board, large pressing pad or tailor's ham, lint brush and an assortment of pressing cloths in cotton, linen, wool and silk to press various types and weights of garment fabrics. (For useful but nonessential pressing tools, see the photo on p. 58.)

Pressing successfully is not difficult, but it requires some experimentation because there are no set formulas, and it's not uncommon for two people to press the same fabric differently. The key to getting professional results is understanding the essential elements of pressing—heat, moisture and pressure—and how they work together and affect the fabric. For general pressing techniques and more information on pressing specific fabrics, see *Claire Shaeffer's Fabric Sewing Guide* in the Bibliography on p. 214.

The amount of heat, moisture and pressure needed for successful pressing depends on the fiber content, weight, thickness and texture of the fabric. Cotton and linen fabrics need more heat than woolens, silks and synthetics. Thin fabrics are more easily damaged by excess heat than thick fabrics, even when both have the same fiber content. And, no matter what the fabric, pressing without a press cloth—or with a very thin one—requires a cooler iron than pressing with a regular press cloth.

Many fabrics become more malleable when pressed with both moisture and heat. You can apply moisture with a steam iron, damp pressing cloth, dauber or sponge. Steaming with an iron is both the easiest and

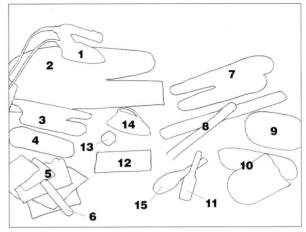

The essential pressing tools are a dependable steam iron (1), point presser (3), sleeve board (7), large pressing pad or ham (9), soap (13), lint brush (11) and an assortment of cotton, wool and silk press cloths (5). Other useful items include a pressing stand (2), clapper (4), assorted pressing pads (10), seam stick (8), dauber (6), needle board (12), teflon iron shoe (14) and spotter's brush (15). (Photo by Susan Kahn.)

most unpredictable method since it may leave water-spots. The damp press cloth and the dauber are much more dependable and versatile since you can use them directly on fabrics that don't waterspot. For fabrics that do waterspot, you can cover them with a dry press cloth and then apply the damp press cloth or dauber.

To dampen a press cloth, wet one end and wring it out. Then fold the cloth so the wet end wraps around the dry section and press it to distribute the moisture evenly. To dampen a dauber, dip one end in water and shake it so it's wet but not dripping. Then rub the wet end over the area to be pressed.

Most pressing requires some pressure, but the amount needed varies with the pressing task and fabric. For flattening seams and edges or reducing bulk on heavy fabrics, apply more pressure than for pressing light-weight or napped fabrics. You can apply pressure with several tools—an iron, clapper, bristles or handle of a spotter's brush, or your fingers. And you can vary the pressure by using different pressing surfaces. For press-ing pockets, buttonholes, hems, appliquéd seams and textured fabrics, place the garment section wrong side up on a softly padded surface or a needle board to avoid flattening it or causing pressing imprints. For a hard, crisp press at seamlines and edges, use an unpadded hardwood surface.

Always test-press on fabric scraps first. Make sample darts, seams and hems, then experiment with various amounts of heat, moisture and pressure, and with dif-ferent press cloths and pressing tools to determine which work best for your design and fabric.

Whenever possible, press from the wrong side. When pressing from the right side, use a press cloth to protect the surface. When pressing large sections or uncut yardage, check to be sure the grain is straight. To avoid stretching the fabric when pressing, slide the iron only with the lengthwise grain, and don't move the fabric or garment section until it's cool and dry.

Press at every stage of construction. Press flat areas on flat surfaces and shaped sections over a pressing cushion or curved board that duplicates the shape of the gar-ment. Press small garment sections before applying or joining them to other sections. Press darts well before joining the section to other sections. Press all seams and darts before crossing them with another line of stitching.

Before pressing seams and darts, check the fit and ex-amine the stitching. If it isn't perfect, correct it before pressing. Remove all bastings and thread tracings. Press the seam or dart flat in the direction it was sewn in or-der to "marry" the stitches. When pressing heavy or bulky fabrics, turn the seam over and press again. To avoid making unwanted impressions on the right side, place the seam wrong side up on a seam roll, point presser or seam stick so you can press just the stitched line. Then, using your fingers, a pin or the tip of the

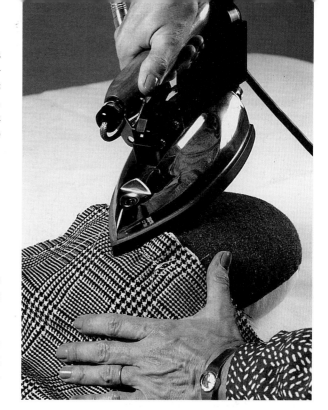

iron, open the seam without applying pressure. Press the seamline firmly with the point of the iron, using steam or a damp press cloth if needed.

For flatter, sharper edges, clip, notch and grade seams properly. Press enclosed seams open before trimming them and turning the section right side out. To flatten the edge after it's turned, place it on a firm surface, then fill the edge with steam, and cover it with a clapper. If the edge is bulky and doesn't flatten easily, spank it once or twice with the clapper to beat the steam out. Do not move the section until it's dry.

Avoid overpressing. You can always press again, but well-set creases, unwanted wrinkles, shines and scorches may be impossible to remove.

SHRINKING OR STRETCHING THE GARMENT

The ease with which you can shrink or stretch fabric when pressing it depends on the fabric's fiber content, its weave and the grain of the garment section or edge to be shaped. Wools, wool blends and loosely woven materials shrink and stretch more easily than silk, cotton, linen, synthetic or closely woven fabrics. Bias sections and edges are easy to shrink, while the lengthwise straight grain is more difficult to shape.

Although the technique for shrinking fabric is familiar to many home sewers, it's used much more extensively in couture and bespoke tailoring than in home sewing. Shrinking is used most commonly to reduce excess fullness when shaping sleeve caps, easing skirts to waistbands, controlling flared hems, tightening an armscye or converting darts to ease. It can also be used to restore a stretched edge, such as a neckline.

Shrinking within a garment section is slightly more difficult than shrinking at the edge, but the technique can be used to remove fullness at the waist or under the bust so the garment will conform to the contours of the body. To shrink an edge, begin by ease-basting as for an eased seam (see p. 48) and pull up the seam's stitched threads until the edge is the desired length. With the section wrong side up, press with a steam iron or with a dry iron and a damp pressing cloth. Moisten or steam the garment section and apply heat. As the fabric shrinks, apply pressure with your fingers or with the iron. When the surplus fabric has been removed, use a dry pressing cloth and a second, cooler iron to press the fabric dry.

Stretching a garment section to conform to the body will be a new technique for most home sewers. It is used to straighten and lengthen inward curves and to transform straight edges into outward curves. Frequently used in tandem with shrinking, stretching can also be used at the top or bottom of waistbands and the front edge of an upper sleeve.

To stretch an edge, begin with the section wrong side up. Dampen the edge with steam, a moistened press cloth or a dauber, depending on the fabric. Then, as you press, hold one edge of the fabric with one hand and use the iron as a weight to stretch the edge into the desired shape. Check your work often to be sure you don't overstretch it.

CHAPTER 4

EDGE FINISHES

HEMS, FACINGS AND BINDINGS

Unless finished in some way, the edges of a garment ravel and look incomplete. These edges—the neckline; the vertical front edges of jackets, coats and many blouses; and the bottom edge of sleeves, dresses, skirts, pants, blouses, jackets and coats—can be finished inconspicuously or they can become distinctive, decorative elements of the design. Three finishes are used extensively in couture: hems, facings and bindings.

The choice of edge finish depends on many things—the shape of the edge being finished; its position on the garment; the type, design and fabric of the garment; current fashion trends; and the preferences of the individual wearer and the designer. For example, if the bottom edge of a dress is straight, it might be completed with a hem, a facing or a binding. But if this edge is asymmetrical, curved, scalloped or otherwise unusually shaped, it will need to be finished with a facing. Even when the edge is visually the same on the neckline and hem, the two different edges are likely to require slightly different finishes to accommodate the curve at the neckline and the weight of the fabric at the hem. And although it's obvious that a tailored garment would require very different finishing from an evening gown, even similar designs worked in dissimilar fabrics would dictate finishes suitable for each fabric.

Although hems, facings and bindings are all edge finishes, each has a slightly different function. Hems are generally used on the lower edges of a garment or garment section (for example, a sleeve) and may help the garment hang attractively by adding weight to the edge. Facings, on the other hand, are applied to the upper and vertical edges of a garment. Bindings can be used on upper, lower or vertical edges, but they're used most often to replace facings rather than hems.

Generally cut as an extension of the garment section, hems can be wide or narrow, depending on the garment design, the hem location and the fabric weight or transparency. Hems can even be faced with a separate facing, but this treatment is generally reserved for unusually shaped hems.

Facings can be cut as separate sections and sewn to the garment to finish curved or shaped edges. Or, when used on edges that are straight or only slightly curved, they can be nothing more than a wide hem allowance, in which case they're called *extended facings*. Both hems and facings are visible on only one side—usually the underside—of the garment. Bindings, by contrast, are separate strips of fabric that encase the garment edge and finish both sides of the garment attractively.

Because in couture the cost of labor and materials takes a back seat to the desired results, edges are not always finished with the simplest method or the one most often used in ready-to-wear construction or home sewing. Whatever the finishing method, hems, facings and bindings can be sewn entirely by hand or machine, or by countless combinations of hand and machine work. The hand work visible on the finished product, however, is only a fraction of the hand work used to finish the edges of the traditional couture garment.

HEMS

Whether the hemline is to be long or short, the garment length and its relationship to the overall design are considered throughout the construction of the traditional couture garment. Before the first fitting of the garment on the customer (see pp. 15-16), the hemline is marked with thread tracing so the hem can be folded under and basted in place. This enables both the fitter and the customer to consider the overall effect of the design and its fit. After this fitting, the basting is removed so any necessary alterations can be made and the vertical seamlines stitched permanently. The garment length might be adjusted at this stage and a new thread tracing added for the altered hemline, since the entire process is repeated for the second fitting, when the final hemline is generally established.

On this bouclé wool jacket by Balenciaga for his Autumn 1959 Collection, the facing on the lapel was cut separately, while that below the waist fastener was cut as an extension of the jacket. To reduce the extra fullness at the curved bottom edge, the extended facing was eased and shrunk. (Photo by Cathy Carver. Metropolitan Museum of Art. Gift of Shirley Carmel, 1960.)

Hem

Facing

Binding

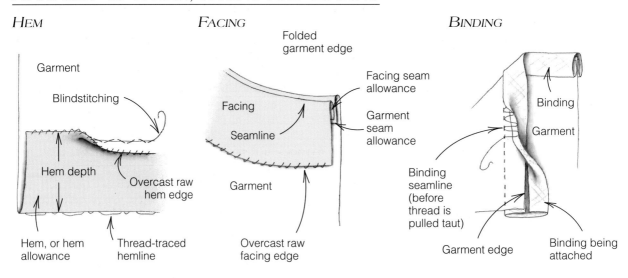

Hem
- Garment
- Blindstitching
- Hem depth
- Overcast raw hem edge
- Hem, or hem allowance
- Thread-traced hemline

Facing
- Folded garment edge
- Facing
- Seamline
- Garment
- Facing seam allowance
- Garment seam allowance
- Overcast raw facing edge

Binding
- Binding
- Garment
- Binding seamline (before thread is pulled taut)
- Garment edge
- Binding being attached

Christian Dior
30, AVENUE MONTAIGNE
PARIS

Christian Dior sketched this gown for his Autumn 1948 Zigzag Collection. The skirt's fullness was pulled to the back to create a dramatic hemline. (Courtesy of Christian Dior.)

Preparing to Sew a Plain Hem

Sometimes called a "couture hem" or "blind hem," the plain hem is the simplest hem possible and the foundation for many other hems. It's the most commonly used hem because it's the flattest and easiest to sew. It can be used on all types of garments and on all fabrics. Whether the bottom edge of the garment with a plain hem is wide or narrow, the vertical seamlines in the hem are on the lengthwise grain and the hem allowance has no excess fullness.

After the hemline is established and thread-traced, the plain hem is made by folding and basting the hem allowance to the wrong side of the garment; the raw edge is overcast, folded under or bound to prevent raveling and is secured inconspicuously by hand near this free edge of the hem. The hem finish at the raw edge should control raveling without forming a ridge. Properly finished, the hem is completely invisible on the right side of the garment.

HANGING A HEM   The process of establishing the finished garment's length is called "hanging a hem." Whether the skirt is straight or full, the goal is to create the illusion that the hemline is level and parallel to the floor. To create this impression, many designers actually finish the skirt ½ in. longer at the center back than at the center front, because when the hemline is an even distance from the floor all around, the contours of the body make the center back look shorter.

To begin the process of hanging a hem after the garment is cut, transfer the hemline on the pattern to each of the garment sections and thread-trace the hemline on each section. After basting the garment together, pin and baste the hem in place for the first fitting. Baste first about ¼ in. above the hemline and then baste again about ¼ in. below the hem's raw edge, and lightly press the hem. If the garment is for someone other than yourself, it's easy to hang the hem. If it's for you, you'll need a friend to help, or you can use the do-it-yourself pointers at the end of this discussion.

To start hanging the hem, try on the garment and match and pin the garment opening closed. Examine the hemline to see if it appears level and parallel to the floor. Use a yardstick to check the distance from the floor to the garment's hemline at center front and back and at the side seams.

To lengthen or shorten a level hemline, just mark the new hem length with one or two pins. Spread the garment on a table and then measure and mark the new hemline an even distance from the original one. Like workers in many couture houses, you may find it useful to use a second color of thread to mark a new hemline in order to distinguish it easily from the first hem.

If the original hemline is so uneven that it needs to be completely remarked, release the bastings, but do not remove the original thread tracing at the hemline. Measure the hem parallel to the floor and mark it with very fine pins or needles set horizontally to keep them from falling out. Pin up the hem so the folded edge at the center back is ½ in. below the pin at center back and ¼ in. below the pin on each side seam. The sections between these points should be pinned smooth. Examine the altered hemline to see if it looks level and, if necessary, continue to correct it until you're satisfied with the results.

When hanging a floor-length skirt, it's difficult to measure close to the floor. To make the task easier, you can use any line you mark below the fullest part of the hips that's parallel to the floor as a marking guide for the hemline. For example, you could pin a guideline around the skirt about 12 in. from the floor. Next you would mark the finished length at the center front. Then you would remove the garment and lay it on a table, measure the distance between the two pins at the center front and use this measurement to mark a new hemline.

DO-IT-YOURSELF TIPS FOR HANGING A HEM
When working alone, baste the hem in place and stand in front of a full-length mirror. You should be close enough to see the numbers on the yardstick easily. Measure the center front and mark this measurement on the yardstick with a piece of drafting tape. Then measure the sides and back, comparing the length of your garment with the mark on yardstick.

If a skirt has to be completely remarked, begin as you would for a floor-length skirt by marking a guideline. But this time, since you're working alone, use the top of your dining-room table as the guide.

THE HEMMING PROCESS
The hemming process begins with deciding on the hem depth. This depth can range from a narrow ¼ in. to as much as 12 in., depending on the type of garment being hemmed and the fabric. Hems are usually wider on dresses, skirts, pants and coats than on jackets, blouses and shorts.

The style of the garment and the weight of the fabric also influence the hem depth. For straight skirts sewn from medium-weight fabrics, the hem is usually 2½ in. to 3 in. deep. In general, heavy or stretchy fabrics and full skirts (including those with pleats, gathers or flares) require narrower hems, from 1 in. to 2 in. On garments sewn from transparent fabrics, the hem depth is visible and becomes an integral part of the design. It's usually very narrow on these garments, but if the skirt is straight and gathered, but unflared (like a dirndl), the hem depth can be as much as one-third of the skirt length.

Once the hem depth has been established, the actual hemming process can begin. Work with the garment wrong side up. If the fabric is heavy or bulky, reduce the seam allowances in the hem area as shown in the drawing at left on p. 64, but don't trim away any backing since it's lightweight and softens the look of the hemline. Fold the hem to the wrong side of the garment following the thread-traced hemline established when hanging the hem, and baste ¼ in. above the hemline.

Position the skirt on the pressing stand (or an ironing board set up next to a table) so that the table supports the skirt while you press the hemline. Firmly press only the folded edge of the hem. To avoid stretching the hemline and prevent rippling, don't slide the iron along the hemline, which is on the crossgrain. Instead, lower the iron onto the fabric, press, then lift the iron and reposition it. Continue pressing, working your way around the entire

REDUCING BULK OF SEAM ALLOWANCE IN HEM AREA

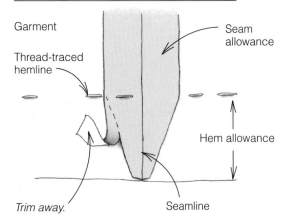

Garment

Seam allowance

Thread-traced hemline

Hem allowance

Trim away.

Seamline

PLAIN HEM FOLDED, PINNED AND BASTED FOR STITCHING

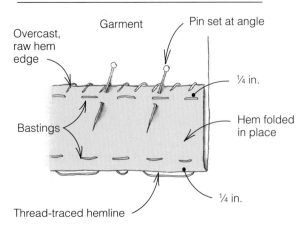

Garment

Pin set at angle

Overcast, raw hem edge

¼ in.

Bastings

Hem folded in place

¼ in.

Thread-traced hemline

hem. When pressing with steam or a damp press cloth, press a second time without moisture to dry this section of the hem before moving on to the next (see p. 57 for more information on pressing techniques).

Next mark the hem depth. Work with the garment on the table with the hem wrong side up and the hemline toward you. Measure the finished depth of the hem from the hemline. If the hem is to be finished with a folded edge, add ¼ in. to the desired finished depth and mark it with chalk. Trim away the excess above the chalked line and finish the raw edge appropriately (see the following pages for hem finishes).

Pin the hem flat against the garment, setting the pins on an angle with the heads away from you. If the garment is backed, pin the hem only to the backing. Then baste about ¼ in. below the pinned edge (see the drawing at right, above).

Almost all hems are stitched with a blindstitch or, if the garment is made of a heavy fabric, with a blind catchstitch. Arrange the garment for hemming by spreading it on top of the table, right side out, with the hem toward you. If the fabric does not wrinkle easily, pick up the hem of the top layer of the skirt, hold it perpendicular to the table and fold it back at the top of the hem allowance so the right sides of the folded garment are together (see the drawing at left, facing page). If the fabric creases easily, work on the bottom layer of the skirt, leaving the hem itself flat on the table and folding back just the top edge of the hem, rather than

the entire hem allowance. (For information on hemming a jacket or another garment whose lining is secured at the hem, see "Interfaced hem" on p. 68.)

Using a fine needle and matching thread, fasten the thread in the hem allowance. Hold the folded-back edge in place with one thumb while securing the edge with a fairly loose stitch. The stitches should hold the hem in place but not be tight enough to show. If the garment is backed, try to avoid sewing through the backing to the garment fabric.

Complete the hem and remove all basting threads. With the skirt wrong side up, press the hem carefully, stopping just shy of the top of the hem allowance to avoid creating an imprint on the garment. Then press the skirt itself, sliding the tip of the iron between the hem and the garment. Examine the right side of the garment. If there are any basting imprints, cover the hem with a self-fabric or woolen pressing cloth and steam-press to remove them.

VARIATIONS ON A PLAIN HEM

On flared designs such as gored, trumpet, A-line and circular skirts, the raw bottom edge is the widest part of the skirt. When it's turned under to create a hem, there's more material in the hem than in the skirt covering it. The excess fullness caused by the flare is concentrated near the seamlines. If this extra fabric isn't eliminated or controlled, the garment will not hang properly, the hem will not lie flat against the skirt, and the excess bulk may show through to the outside of the garment.

Two ways to hold garment for hemming

Hemming nonwrinkling fabrics

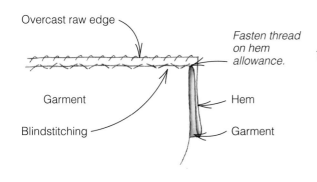

Overcast raw edge

Fasten thread on hem allowance.

Garment

Hem

Blindstitching

Garment

Hemming fabrics that wrinkle

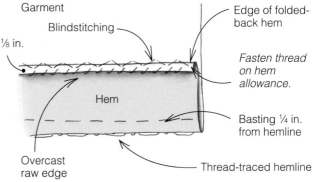

Garment

Blindstitching

Edge of folded-back hem

⅛ in.

Fasten thread on hem allowance.

Hem

Basting ¼ in. from hemline

Overcast raw edge

Thread-traced hemline

The simplest method of controlling fullness in a curved wool hem is to shrink out the excess fullness with heat and moisture. This tailoring technique is particularly well suited for wool, hair fiber, silk suitings and loosely woven fabrics that shrink easily. The curved corners on the bouclé wool Balenciaga jacket shown on p. 60 were finished in this manner (for directions on easing fabric by shrinking it, see p. 59).

Yves Saint Laurent designed this panné velvet circular skirt topped by a doubled, unstructured lace jacket for his Autumn 1984 Collection. The skirt could be ordered short or floor-length. Either way, the skirt draped gracefully without revealing the excess fullness skillfully controlled in the hem allowance (see the detail at left). (Photo by Cathy Carver. Metropolitan Museum of Art. Gift of Monika Dorsey, in memory of Hebe Dorsey, 1988.)

CONTROLLING FULLNESS IN HEM ALLOWANCE

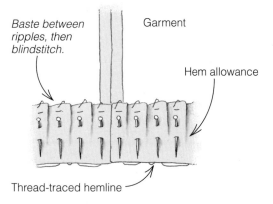

Baste between ripples, then blindstitch.

Garment

Hem allowance

Thread-traced hemline

Sewing small darts into a hem is an effective means of controlling the fullness when a medium-weight to heavyweight fabric cannot be shrunk with heat and moisture (shown above). Although the wrong side of the hem will not look as neat as a hem allowance shrunk with easing, the hem will hang attractively when the garment is worn. This method of controlling fullness is more likely to be used on a lined garment rather than on an unlined one.

Some cottons, linens, silks and other fabrics, like the panné velvet in the Yves Saint Laurent dress on p. 65 however, cannot be shrunk effectively, and the fullness in a curved hem of these fabrics would have to be handled with dressmaker techniques, that is, with either small darts in the hem or the hemming stitches themselves. Darting would be used on crisp fabrics, while eliminating fullness with hemming stitches would be preferable for lighter-weight fabrics. Both techniques can be used on either lined or unlined garments.

To control the fullness in a curved hem with the hemming stitches themselves, begin by folding the hem under and basting ⅛ in. from the folded edge. Then press just the folded edge without pressing the hem allowance. Measure and trim the hem allowance so it's even, reducing the depth as needed to reduce the bulk. Match and pin the seamlines. Then smooth and pin the hem allowance against the wrong side of the garment, working from the front and back center points to the seamlines. As the skirt begins to curve, the excess fabric will form ripples perpendicular to the hemline.

FINISHING CORNERS

When a facing and hem meet at the corner of jacket or coat openings, or at skirt or sleeve vents, the surplus fabric must be reduced or eliminated for a smooth finish. This can be accomplished by either hemming the lower edge, then cutting off the excess bulk at the corner and then hemming the vertical edge, or by mitering, a technique that creates a diagonal seam at the corner. On skirt vents, jackets and coat openings, the corners are generally hemmed, while sleeve vents can be hemmed or mitered. However these methods can be used interchangeably. Note that the instructions here are for a lined garment where the lining will cover the raw edge of the facing.

HEMMING A CORNER

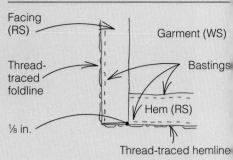

Facing (RS)

Garment (WS)

Thread-traced foldline

Bastings

Hem (RS)

⅛ in.

Thread-traced hemline

1. Fold back, baste and press hem allowance along thread-traced hemline. Fold back facing and fold under facing hem, tapering it from corner to be ⅛ in. shorter than garment hem. Baste and press lightly.

MITERING A CORNER

MAKING A RIGHT ANGLE

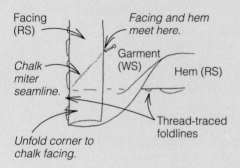

Facing (RS)

Chalk miter seamline.

Facing and hem meet here.

Garment (WS)

Hem (RS)

Unfold corner to chalk facing.

Thread-traced foldlines

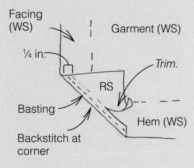

Facing (WS)

Garment (WS)

¼ in.

Trim.

RS

Basting

Hem (WS)

Backstitch at corner

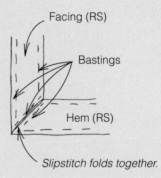

Facing (RS)

Bastings

Hem (RS)

Slipstitch folds together.

1. Fold and press facing and hem edges along thread-traced foldlines. Pin point where raw edges of facing and hem meet. Chalk diagonal line from pin to corner on hem. Unfold hem and chalk across facing from pin to corner.

2. Fold corner on chalked lines. Baste near folded edge, backstitching at corner. Press and trim to ¼ in.

3. Baste hem and facing in place, basting miter flat against garment. Hem garment and slipstitch miter.

MAKING AN ACUTE ANGLE

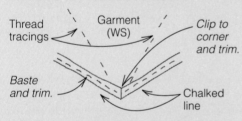

Thread tracings

Garment (WS)

Clip to corner and trim.

Baste and trim.

Chalked line

On an acute angle, chalked and basted lines will form very wide V from point at corner.

MAKING AN OBTUSE ANGLE

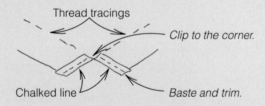

Thread tracings

Clip to the corner.

Chalked line

Baste and trim.

On an obtuse angle, chalked and basted lines will be shaped like an upside-down V.

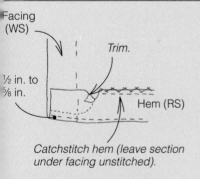

Facing (WS)

Trim.

½ in. to ⅝ in.

Hem (RS)

Catchstitch hem (leave section under facing unstitched).

2. If fabric is heavy or bulky, remove facing basting, trim as shown and catchstitch hem.

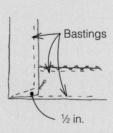

Bastings

½ in.

3. Baste edge of facing and press it and corner lightly. Pin facing edge ½ in. from hemline and baste to corner.

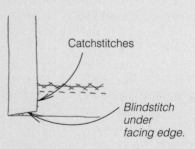

Catchstitches

Blindstitch under facing edge.

4. Hold back basted lower edge of facing and blindstitch to corner. Then catchstitch raw edge of facing to hem allowance.

Pin the hem allowance to the garment, setting the pins at right angles to the edge and from 1 in. to 5 in. apart—the tighter the curve, the closer together the pins will need to be—with the excess fabric falling in small ripples between the pins. To avoid distorting the hang of the garment, work carefully to keep the ripples perpendicular to the hemline. Baste near the top of the hem allowance without flattening any of the ripples and blindstitch carefully so the stitches on the hem allowance are between the ripples.

A word of caution: If you have the garment dry-cleaned, ask that the hem be pressed very carefully or not at all to prevent the pleats from showing through on the right side of the garment. Better still, remove the hemming stitches before sending the garment to the cleaners.

By contrast with flared skirts, the silhouette of a pegged skirt curves inward rather than outward at the bottom. Consequently the raw bottom edge of this skirt is shorter than the folded bottom edge that covers it. To create a smooth curved hem, before turning the allowance, trim it and stretch the edge with heat and moisture to make it conform to the curve.

DOUBLE-STITCHED HEM   If a garment is sewn from heavy fabric, the weight of the hem will pull on the hemming stitches, causing them to show on the right side. A simple solution is to hem the garment twice—first at the midpoint of the hem allowance, then, as usual, near the finished edge.

To do this, first mark the hem depth and place a row of basting stitches midway between the hem and the finished edge. Then, using a blindstitch or blind catchstitch, hem the garment at the basted line. Then move to the raw edge of the hem, fold it back and complete the hem.

INTERFACED HEM   Hems interfaced with bias strips add body and support to the lower part of the garment, reduce wrinkling and create smoother hemlines by camouflaging the edge of the hem allowance and preventing sharp breaks at the hemline. Depending on the interfacing material and how it's applied, the edge of an interfaced hem can be crisp or softly folded; and if it's a soft edge, it can be thin or thick and quilted.

INTERFACED HEMS

SOFT-EDGED HEMLINE

Lined garment

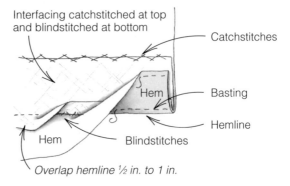

Interfacing catchstitched at top and blindstitched at bottom

Catchstitches

Hem

Basting

Hem

Hemline

Hem

Blindstitches

Overlap hemline ½ in. to 1 in.

CRISP HEMLINE

Unlined garment

On a flared hem, slash and lap.

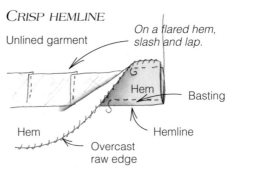

Hem

Basting

Hem

Hemline

Hem

Overcast raw edge

If you wish to add body to the garment, the best interfacing fabrics include traditional woven, nonfusible interfacing materials such as hair canvas, muslin, wigan, silk organza and silk shantung. For a soft, padded hemline, lambswool, wadding and cotton flannel are good choices. And for a quilted hemline, choose wadding, batting, polyester fleece or wool fleece. The best choice for a very crisp hemline is horsehair braid or crinoline.

To decide the width of the interfacing strip, first determine whether you want a soft or crisp edge and whether the garment is to be lined or unlined. For a soft edge, cut the interfacing to overlap the hemline by ½ in. to 1 in. For a sharper edge, cut the interfacing just wide enough to meet the hemline.

On unlined garments, the interfacing is generally hidden between the layers of the garment and the hem, with the upper edge of the interfacing ½ in. below the top of the hem allowance. On lined garments, the interfacing can be any width, though it's usually at least 3 in. wide so it will extend at least ½ in. above the hem

allowance to act as a buffer between the garment and hem, and keep the hem edge from showing on the right side of the garment. Generally, interfacings on the hems of special-occasion dresses, which are usually longer than regular daywear, are 10 in. to 12 in. wide, while those on daywear will be from 2 in. to 4 in. wide. However, there are always exceptions: the hem interfacing in Yves Saint Laurent's grey wool trapeze dress for Dior shown on p. 120 was about 20 in. wide and helps shape the skirt. The silhouette of the design, the weight of the fabric and the length of the skirt all determine how wide the hem, and consequently its interfacing, should be.

To interface a hem, begin by cutting enough bias strips to interface the hem's entire length, but don't join them. Cut off any selvages on the strips and turn the garment wrong side up. Piece the strips as you go by lapping the ends ½ in. and joining them with a short running stitch.

At the hemline, attach the interfacing lightly to the fabric with either a long running stitch or by folding the interfacing back at the hemline and securing it with widely spaced blindstitches. If the garment is backed, catch the backing but not the garment.

On an unlined garment, there's no need to secure the top of the interfacing strip since the hem will keep it in place. On lined garments, however, sew the top of the interfacing strip to the garment or its backing to keep it in place. To complete the hem, fold and baste it in place; then sew the hem to the interfacing with a running stitch or catchstitch.

If the skirt is flared, shape the interfacing when you lay it on the garment by stretching the bottom of the bias strip slightly and easing the top so the strip will lie smooth. If the strips are not flexible enough to shape easily, slash them where needed on the top edge and lap small darts, as shown in the lower drawing on the facing page. If you're using horsehair braid on a flared skirt, however, instead of slashing the edge, pull up the thread on the upper edge and ease.

NARROW HEMS   Although extremely versatile, the plain hem and its variations are simply not suitable for every garment design or fabric. One of the most common alternatives to the plain hem, especially for garments made of lightweight fabrics, is the narrow hem, which itself has several variations—the hand-rolled hem, felled hem and several types of blouse hems.

Of the many narrow hem styles appropriate for lightweight fabrics, the hand-rolled hem and felled hem are among the most useful. Narrow hems are a particularly attractive finish for designs where both sides of the hem are visible, as on ruffles, edges with sharp curves or corners, and any edge sewn from sheer fabric. On couture garments, narrow hems are usually sewn by hand, while on luxury ready-to-wear and home-sewn clothing, they are often machine-stitched. Generally, narrow hems hang more softly than wide hems or bindings, and hand-stitched narrow hems are softer and more elastic than machine-stitched ones. Regardless of which narrow-hem style you choose, carefully check the length of the garment before trimming away any excess fabric since you can't, of course, lengthen a hem that's too short.

Hand-rolled hems are used frequently on lightweight silks and wools, and on chiffons and organzas. They're not suitable for heavyweight fabrics or lightweight materials with weave variations, embroidery, metallic threads or beading because the edge will be difficult to roll smoothly.

The hand-rolled hem is most often sewn to the edge of the garment with a slipstitch or whipstitch. With the slipstitch, the sewing thread will be almost completely hidden within the roll. By contrast, the whipstitch thread passes over the roll and shows on the wrong side of the hem. Whatever the hemming stitch, the hand-rolled hem is softer than a machine-rolled hem.

For a smooth, bulk-free hem, begin by trimming any vertical seam allowances in the hem area to ⅛ in. and press them to the left (you're working from right to left and from the seamline to the raw edge of the seam). Then thread-trace the hemline, unless you're hemming a scarf, in which case, simply assume there will be a ½-in. hem allowance. Using a short stitch, machine stitch ⅛ in. below the hemline. In order to avoid excessive raveling, it's better to complete this hem in stages. Trim close to the stitched line only 6 in. to 9 in. at a time, rather than the entire length of the hem at once.

When rolling a hem, it's helpful to hold the section of the edge you're working on taut. When working at a table, pin the edge to a fabric-covered weight or brick.

With the wrong side of the fabric facing you, use your left thumb and forefinger to roll the edge, enclosing the stitched line. Stop at the thread-traced hemline. If you slightly moisten your index finger with the tip of your tongue before rolling the hem, the roll will be tighter. Hold the rolled edge over your index finger. Thread a fine needle with a single ply of unknotted silk thread about 15 in. long, or if silk thread isn't available, pull lengthwise threads from the fabric selvage to use. (You can also substitute mercerized cotton or fine polyester thread.) Anchor the thread in the hem roll.

When starting a rolled edge on the corner of a garment, hold the fabric wrong side up so the edge of the material is horizontal and parallel to your thumb. Lay the needle against the fabric and parallel to the top so the needle is positioned horizontally and roll the fabric and needle toward you until the stitched line is enclosed. You can secure the roll with either a slipstitch or a whipstitch.

HAND-ROLLED HEM

HEMMING WITH SLIPSTITCHES

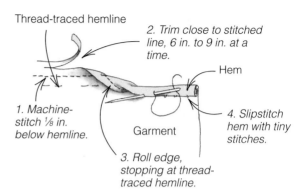

Thread-traced hemline

2. Trim close to stitched line, 6 in. to 9 in. at a time.

Hem

1. Machine-stitch ⅛ in. below hemline.

Garment

4. Slipstitch hem with tiny stitches.

3. Roll edge, stopping at thread-traced hemline.

HEMMING WITH WHIPSTITCHES

Thread-traced hemline

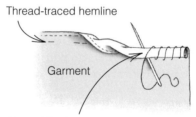

Garment

Slant whipstitches, sewing them parallel to one another.

To sew the hem with a slipstitch, pick up only a single thread on the garment, then pick up a small stitch on the garment at the edge of the roll and take several stitches before pulling the thread taut. To whip the edge, pick up a garment thread, slip the point of the needle under the roll and out the top. Bring it forward about ⅛ in. and take the next stitch on the garment. Sew several stitches, spacing them ⅛ in. apart before pulling the threads taut. The threads on the finished section should be slanted and parallel to one another.

Continue hemming until you've finished the trimmed section. Then trim and hem the next section and repeat until the entire hem is finished. Remove any bastings and press the garment, but try to avoid pressing the hem itself, which will flatten under the iron. If you feel it must be pressed, do so with the garment right side up on a softly padded surface.

A *felled hem* is a double-folded hem that can be used on lightweight fabrics unsuitable for a rolled hem. This hand-stitched hem is also suitable for medium-weight materials when machine stitching would be unattractive or when both sides will be visible. This hem can be as narrow as ⅛ in. wide, called a *pin hem*, or as wide as 2 in.

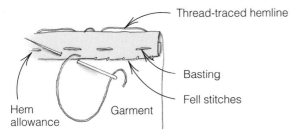

Thread-traced hemline

Basting

Fell stitches

Hem allowance   Garment

Begin by thread-tracing the hemline. Trim the hem allowance to the width of the finished hem plus ¼ in. (For a ¼-in. wide hem, for example, trim to ½ in.) With the garment wrong side up, fold a scant ¼ in. to the wrong side. Pleat the edge with your fingers every inch to crease the fold. Fold the hem under on the hemline and baste. Use a fell stitch to secure the hem inconspicuously. Remove the bastings and press lightly.

If the edge curves outward, as it would on a flared design or on circular ruffles, hand-stitch a row of ease-basting ¼ in.—the finished width of the hem—from the raw edge. Ease-basting is easier to pull up if the threads are only 15 in. to 20 in. long. Pull up the ease and fold the edge under. Baste the hem to the garment about ⅛ in. below the folded edge.

On tuck-in blouses, hems should be narrow and flat in order to avoid creating a ridge beneath the skirt. The hems used most often on such blouses are the overcast edge, edgestitched hem and pin hem (see "Felled hem" above for information on the pin hem).

The flattest hem of the three is the *overcast edge*, which is a simple variation on the overcast seam finish (see p. 42). To sew this hem, begin by thread-tracing the hemline. Then machine-stitch ⅛ in. above the thread-traced line, trim away the hem allowance and overcast the edge by hand. For a neater finish, overcast the edge in both directions.

To make an *edgestitched hem*, begin by thread-tracing the hemline and trimming the hem allowance to ⅜ in. Overcast the edge. Then fold the hem allowance to the wrong side on the thread-traced line and press. Machine-stitch ¹⁄₁₆ in. from the fold.

FACED HEM   Faced hems are especially appropriate for garments with sharply curved or unusually shaped hemlines. They're also well suited for reducing the bulk of a plain or eased hem, for covering interfaced hems on unlined garments and for lengthening a garment that does not have a generous hem allowance. The facing can be a traditional shaped facing that duplicates the garment edge, or a bias-cut strip that can easily be manipulated to fit the shape of the hemline. It can be applied by hand or machine using a variety of techniques. The directions here focus on the hand application used at the couture houses of Givenchy and Chanel. When sewing traditional, machine-stitched shaped facings, consult your favorite sewing manual.

For most designs, the finished bias facing should be between 1 in. and 2½ in. wide. Use the narrower width for sharp curves and the wider one for straight edges and gentle curves. Choose a firmly woven, lightweight lining material for the facing strips. Do not use ready-made bias because the material is inferior. Cut the bias strips ½ in. wider than the finished facing width and join as many bias strips as needed for the length of the facing. For instructions on cutting and joining bias strips, see p. 76. Press the seams open and trim away any selvages.

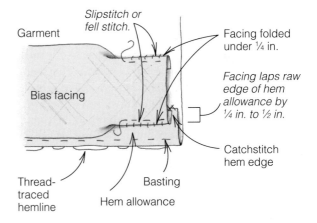

Garment

Slipstitch or fell stitch.

Bias facing

Facing folded under ¼ in.

Facing laps raw edge of hem allowance by ¼ in. to ½ in.

Catchstitch hem edge

Thread-traced hemline   Basting   Hem allowance

Thread-trace the hemline and interface it as needed. Fold the hem allowance to the wrong side and baste it in place. Trim the hem allowance to 1 in. if the skirt is straight or softly curved and the fabric isn't too heavy. If the hem is flared or shaped, trim it to ½ in. or ¼ in., or stretch and clip the raw edge to make it lie flat. Catchstitch the hem's raw edge to the wrong side of the garment or backing.

Spread the garment on the table, wrong side up, with the hem toward you. Place the bias strip on the hem and fold under the bottom of the bias strip ¼ in. so that the folded edge laps the raw edge of the hem allowance by ¼ in. to ½ in., as shown in the drawing at right on p. 71. Pin and baste it in place. Now fold under the top of the bias strip ¼ in. Pin and baste it in place for hemming. Secure both edges permanently with a fell stitch. Remove any bastings and press the hem.

FACINGS

Facings, like hems, are designed to finish the edge of the garment. Unlike hems, which hang free of the body and affect the garment's hang more than its overall shape, faced edges frequently fit the body's curves and subtly affect the garment's silhouette. Used on garment openings, curved edges and shaped edges like jacket lapels, facings contribute significantly to an overall impression of a well-constructed garment.

There are three types of facings: extended, shaped and bias. Two of these—shaped and bias facings—are cut separately from the garment and can be sewn from self-fabric or lightweight lining fabrics. The extended facing is cut as an extension of the garment section like a plain hem and is, of course, self-fabric.

The *extended facing* is nothing more than a ½-in. to 2-in. hem and is sewn exactly like a plain hem (see pp. 63-64). When the garment edge is on the lengthwise grain, the extended facing duplicates the shape and grain of the edge it faces. But when the edge is slanted on a bias or has a slight curve, the facing can't duplicate the grain and may have to be eased, stretched or clipped to fit the edge smoothly.

The extended facing is used extensively in couture because the folded edge of this facing is flatter and more supple than the seamed edges of shaped and bias facings and consequently drapes better. Edges with extended facings are generally interfaced and stabilized so that they maintain their original shape for the life of the garment.

As its name suggests, the *shaped facing* is cut to duplicate the shape of the edge it faces and usually duplicates the grain as well. This facing is often used on necklines and on edges intended to have a crisp, constructed look, and it's always used on intricately shaped edges like a scalloped hem.

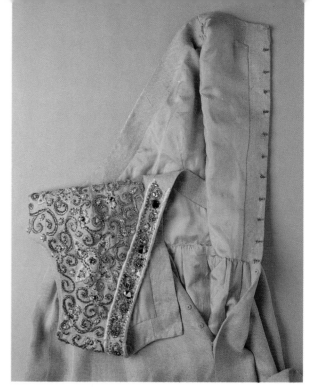

The back neckline of this evening gown is finished with a separate shaped facing, while the front surplice neckline is finished with an extended facing. Although the gown's designer cannot be identified because the label is missing, the hand-stitched waistline, hand-overcast seams, hand-finished facings and lining, and covered snaps leave little doubt that this is a couture garment. (Photo by Susan Kahn. Author's collection.)

The *bias facing* is a strip cut on the true bias. Because it doesn't duplicate the grain of the edge it faces, this facing must itself be shaped to fit the edge. Bias facings are made from lightweight fabrics and produce narrow, inconspicuous facings.

In couture, more than one type of facing is often used on a single garment or even on a single edge. The pink gazar dress shown above, for example, has extended facings on the front neckline and back opening with shaped facings on the back neckline. Similarly, the jacket on p. 60 has a shaped facing on the upper half of the front edge and an extended facing on the lower half of this edge.

Before applying any kind of facing, examine the garment's fit to determine whether the edge needs to be held in or stabilized with a stay tape (see pp. 49-50) or interfaced (see p. 68). Once you've handled the edge as required, then you can proceed to apply the facing you've chosen.

SHAPED FACINGS

Shaped facings can be applied by hand or by machine. Both types of applications are used in couture, while only machine applications are used in ready-to-wear. The machine application is, of course, faster, but it's sometimes more difficult to shape the facing so that it fits smoothly, and the seamline is sometimes visible at the garment edge. The instructions below are for applying the facing by hand. (For directions on applying shaped facings by machine, refer to your favorite sewing manual.)

These directions focus on neckline facings because they're most frequently used in couture workrooms. However, the directions can be applied to other edges such as waistbands, armholes, applied pockets, collars and cuffs, and they can be adapted for garment linings. The facing can be made any time after the neck edge is established, the seamline or foldline is thread-traced, and the edge is interfaced or stabilized appropriately for the design.

Facings can be cut from the original garment pattern if the edge wasn't changed during the fitting process, or the garment itself can serve as a pattern. When the garment is used as a pattern, the thread-traced neckline can be used to establish a corresponding stitching line on the facing. A finished neckline can also be used as a guide when you're applying the facing by hand.

Neck facings can be cut in several shapes. Two of the most popular are the traditional circular shape, which measures an even distance all around from the edge, and a rectangular shape, which extends into the armscye seams. When the larger shape is used, the facing edges can be anchored in the seamlines, holding them smooth and in place. The facing shadow may also be less obtrusive with the larger shape, depending on the design. The obvious disadvantage of this facing is the additional fabric introduced into the shoulder area, which may give the garment a bulky appearance.

One solution for reducing some of this bulk is to relocate the seamlines ½ in. to 1 in. from their original positions. In couture, the seams on facings are not always aligned with the corresponding garment seamlines, as they are in ready-to-wear and home sewing.

SHAPED FACINGS

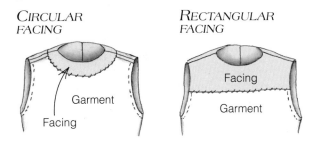

CIRCULAR FACING

RECTANGULAR FACING

Garment

Facing

Facing

Garment

The directions that follow are for cutting and applying the less familiar rectangular facing. They can easily be adapted for a circular facing. Start by selecting some scraps from your garment fabric for the front and back facings unless the fabric is bulky or heavy, in which case use a lighter, firmly woven material for the facings. Rectangular pieces of cloth are preferable because they make it easier to identify the grainlines. If you're cutting a rectangular facing for a garment with a high, round neckline with a closure in the back, begin with one large rectangle about 16 in. wide by 7 in. long for the front facing and two smaller ones about 8 in. wide by 6 in. long for the back facings.

When applying the facing by hand, it's easier to finish the garment edge before making the facing so that you can use the finished edge as a pattern. If the edge will be taped or interfaced, do so before starting the facing and clip the free edge of the interfacing as needed, to make it lie flat. Trim the seam allowance around the garment neck to ¾ in. and fold it to the wrong side. Baste a generous ⅛ in. from the edge. To minimize the seam allowance's tendency to curl around the neck, snip shallow cuts into the raw edge every inch or so as needed to make the neckline seam allowance lie flat (as shown on p. 74).

With the wrong side up, place the neckline over a pressing cushion and press just the neckline edge. With your fingers, gently try to flatten the raw edge. If necessary, trim the edge further to ⅜ in. for firmly woven fabrics and ½ in. for less stable fabrics. If the seam allowance still doesn't lie flat, clip the raw edge with short, closely spaced snips up to, but not through, the basting stitches around the neck edge. Use a loose catchstitch to sew the edge of the seam allowance to the underlining or interfacing. If the garment has neither, sew carefully so the stitches do not show on the right side of the garment.

Applying facing by hand

Making front facing

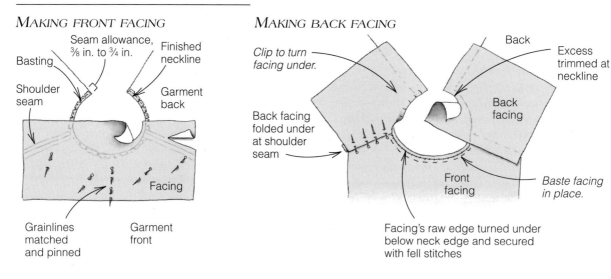

Seam allowance, ⅜ in. to ¾ in.

Basting

Finished neckline

Shoulder seam

Garment back

Grainlines matched and pinned

Facing

Garment front

Making back facing

Clip to turn facing under.

Back

Excess trimmed at neckline

Back facing

Back facing folded under at shoulder seam

Front facing

Baste facing in place.

Facing's raw edge turned under below neck edge and secured with fell stitches

Cut a rectangle for each section to be faced. Before proceeding, decide whether relocating the shoulder seams will redistribute the bulk. After relocating the seam, if you decide to do so, begin with wrong sides together, and match and pin the grainlines together at the center front of the garment and its facing. Then, holding the garment neckline curved, as it will be when worn, smooth the facing in place, pinning as you go. When you get to the shoulder seams, smooth the front facing over the seams so that the seam allowances are flat. Pin and then trim away the excess at the shoulder seams and at the neck edge, leaving ½-in. seam allowances on the facing, as shown above.

Pin the back facing(s) in place. At the shoulder seams, trim and then turn the raw edges under, then pin and slip-baste, as shown above. At this point, you can machine-stitch the shoulder seams. At the neckline, trim away the excess, leaving a ½-in. seam allowance. Turn under the raw edge so the facing is 1/16 in. to ¼ in. below the edge of the neckline and does not expose the clips on the garment's seam allowance. If necessary, clip the edge of the facing at intervals as needed to make it turn under smoothly and pin it in place. On edges with shallow curves, you can turn back the neck edge of the facing as much as 1 in. if the garment seam allowance is wide enough. With the facing toward you, baste the facing in place and press lightly. Using a fell stitch or slipstitch, sew the facing to the neck edge and join the shoulder seams if they weren't machine-stitched. Remove the bastings and press lightly.

Bias facings

A bias facing is a narrow strip of fabric cut on the true bias that's shaped, rather than cut, to duplicate the edge it faces. Well adapted to garments with soft edges, this facing is frequently used on blouses and dresses and on lightweight silk and cotton fabrics. In couture workrooms, most bias facings are applied by hand. Generally, self-fabric is used if the garment is sewn from lightweight fabric, but if the fabric is heavy, lining material can be used instead.

Bias facings are narrower and less conspicuous than shaped facings, and since they require less fabric, they're both more comfortable to wear next to the skin and more economical to sew. There are two disadvantages to these facings, however. When a bias facing is applied, the garment edge is rarely interfaced and may not be as smooth. And since the bias facing is usually slipstitched to the garment, it's sometimes difficult to prevent the stitches from showing on the outside of the garment.

Most bias facings are finished so they're about ½ in. wide, but they can be as narrow as ¼ in. on a jewel neckline and as wide as 2 in. at the waist of a skirt. Generally, the wider the bias facing, the more difficult it is to shape it to a curved edge.

Before applying a bias facing, finish the garment edge. Fold the seam allowance to the wrong side and baste ⅛ in. to ¼ in. from the edge. Clip as needed to make the edge lie flat. With the wrong side up, press the edge.

BIAS FACING

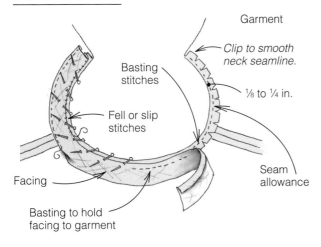

Garment

Basting stitches

Clip to smooth neck seamline.

⅛ to ¼ in.

Fell or slip stitches

Seam allowance

Facing

Basting to hold facing to garment

Measure the garment edge to be faced and cut a bias strip several inches longer, or join several strips for the length you need. For a ½-in. wide facing, the strip should be 1 in. wide for straight edges and 1½ in. wide for curved edges. Fold one of the long edges under ¼ in. This is best accomplished by folding 6 in. at one time and pleating the folded edge with your hands into 1-in. pleats so the edge will stay folded without pressing, which might stretch it.

Begin with the wrong side up and match the wrong side of the bias strip to the wrong side of the folded garment edge, aligning the bias edge with the basting, ⅛ in. to ¼ in. below the garment edge. Pin the bias, easing or stretching the strip until it fits the edge smoothly, and baste.

Place the edge over a pressing cushion with the right side up. Cover the edge with a press cloth and carefully press just the edge and the bias strip. The facing should lie smoothly against the wrong side of the garment. If it doesn't, release the basting and try again.

Using a slipstitch or fell stitch, sew the facing to the seam allowance. Trim the bias so it's an even ¾ in. wide. To finish the free edge, fold it under ¼ in., pin and baste. Using a very fine needle, sew the edge to the garment with a loose slipstitch or fell stitch. If the garment is backed, catch the backing but not the garment. Remove the bastings and press lightly.

When applying a bias facing to a neckline without an opening, begin at the left shoulder seam and work toward the front neckline (this is the most difficult part of the neckline to face and, in couture, is therefore tackled first). For a bias facing at the armscye, begin at the underarm. Finish by folding one end of the bias wrong sides together on the lengthwise grain. Lightly crease the fold with your thumbnail. Fold the other end under so the folded edges match. Then slipstitch the folds together.

BINDINGS

An elegant finish suitable for nearly every edge, a binding can be unobtrusive or, in a contrasting fabric or texture, add dash to your garment. Bindings are made by stitching a strip of fabric to the right side of an edge, wrapping it around the edge and securing it neatly on the underside. Often finished so they're attractive on both the right and wrong side of the garment, bindings are frequently used on transparent fabrics, two-faced fabrics and on reversible and unlined garments.

Black velvet bindings highlight the openings on both a coat dress and a tunic from Givenchy's Autumn 1983 Collection. (Photo by Jean-Pierre Ledos, courtesy of Givenchy and D-R.)

In order to shape and sew bindings to curved edges easily, most fabric bindings are cut on the true bias at a 45° angle to the lengthwise grain. But if the garment edges are straight or almost straight, bindings can be cut on either the crossgrain or lengthwise grain to enhance the design. The directions below focus on bias-cut bindings, but they can easily be adapted for nonbias strips and ribbon, although these other bindings do not take the shape of the edge as easily.

Selecting the fabric for bindings is particularly important. Lightweight materials like crepe, satin, chiffon and voile are suitable for bindings on almost any shell fabric. If you want a heavier bound edge, you could use fabrics like wool, rib-weaves, cottons and sturdy linens. But be aware that the heavier the binding fabric, the more difficult it is to work with and control its bulk, particularly at the ends.

Most bindings are finished about ¼ in. wide, but on very lightweight fabrics they can be as narrow as ⅛ in., and on bulky or heavy fabrics they can be as wide as 1 in. Bindings can be made with either a single-layered, open strip of fabric or with a double-layered, folded strip. Obviously, bindings sewn from a double layer are stiffer and thicker because they contain more fabric, an advantage when that binding fabric is lightweight or when you want a sharply defined edge. But if the binding fabric is heavy or bulky or if the garment edge is designed to hang softly, a single-layered binding is more suitable.

Generally, bindings are not applied until the garment is almost finished—that is, until appropriate interfacings and backings have already been set, the garment fitted and all corrections made. On lined couture garments, however, the binding is frequently applied first by hand or machine, and finished with the lining, which covers the raw edge of the binding.

CUTTING AND STITCHING THE BIAS STRIP

If you lived in Italy, you would visit your favorite *merceria*, or sewing-notions store, when you wanted to trim a design with bias bindings (I've looked in stores in France and England but have never seen fabric sold in this way). There you would find a large assortment of fabrics already cut with one edge on the bias. After you chose your fabric, a salesperson would cut a parallelogram for you, which would be ready to be cut into bias strips.

In America, however, the home sewer's first task in making a bias binding is to establish the true bias of the fabric. This is important because if the strips are not cut exactly at a 45° angle, the finished bindings will ripple, twist and pucker. The best way to establish the true bias is with an isosceles right triangle—a drafting tool that has two sides of equal length with a 90° angle between them.

Align one of the triangle's short sides with the lengthwise grain. The other side will be on the crossgrain, and the hypotenuse will mark the true bias. Mark parallel lines on the bias with chalk and cut as many strips as needed for the length of your edges (see the discussions on the following pages on single and double bindings to calculate the width of strip needed for a given finished binding width). For a short bound edge in a prominent place on the garment—for example, on a lapel—use one continuous bias strip. For longer edges, join as many strips as needed for your length. In general, it's better to join the strips on the lengthwise grain, but if the fabric has a prominent cross-rib or horizontal stripe, the seam will be less noticeable if the seam is parallel to the stripe or rib.

To join bias strips, first trim all ends of the bias strips so they're on the desired grain—usually the lengthwise grain. Begin with two strips, right side up. Fold one end under ¼ in., pin it to the other strip so the grainlines match and slip-baste at the fold. Repeat until all the strips are joined. Then, fold the basted strips together with right sides together and sew the seam with a very short machine stitch (20 stitches/in. or 1.25mm). Press the seams flat and then press them open. Trim away the ends of the seam allowance that extend beyond the width of the strip and trim the seams to ⅛ in.

Although bindings can be applied to almost any edge, the directions given here are for applying single and double bindings to a neckline, where they're most often sewn. To prepare the garment for either a single or double ¼-in. wide binding, thread-trace the finished neckline. Then thread-trace a guideline for the binding seamline ¼ in.—or the width of the finished binding—below the neckline. Do not trim away the seam allowance.

NECK EDGE PREPARED FOR A BINDING

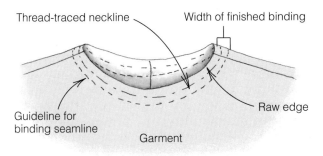

Thread-traced neckline

Width of finished binding

Guideline for binding seamline

Raw edge

Garment

SINGLE BINDING

The couture method of applying a single binding has several advantages over the regular home-sewing method. It's begun with the right sides up, allowing you to see the binding as you shape it to fit the edge. It can also be made entirely by hand rather than machine, which results in a softer finish. To determine the most suitable width for the finished binding, experiment with fabric scraps before cutting the strips until you arrive at a sample you like.

Thread-trace the garment edge, as explained on p. 76, and cut the bias strips so that the width of each strip is six times the desired finished width of the binding plus ½ in. (To make a finished ¼-in. wide binding, for example, cut a bias strip 2 in. wide.) Press the strip, stretching it slightly lengthwise. Fold under one long edge of the bias ¼ in., regardless of the desired finished width, and baste ⅛ in. from the fold.

Working with the right sides up, align and pin the folded edge to the garment so it barely laps the binding seamline. To apply the bias smoothly to a neckline, hold the folded edge of the strip taut when pinning it in place. Baste through all layers close to the folded edge and slip-baste the strip to the garment. Then remove the first row of basting that holds the binding flat, unfold the strip so the right sides are together and machine-stitch over the basted line. Trim the seam allowance at the neckline, remove any bastings and press lightly.

Fold the binding toward the neckline and finger-press the binding seam. Wrap the binding around the neckline's raw edge and finger-press again. Pin-baste the binding in place on the wrong side of the neckline, setting the pins just below the binding. Measure the binding width. If it's more than ¼ in., the finished neckline will probably be too tight. If this is the case, unpin the binding and trim the seam as needed to keep the finished binding width at ¼ in. Then fold the raw edge under so that the folded edge touches the seamline. If the folded edge overlaps the seamline, unfold the bias and trim it as needed to make a folded edge the width you need. Baste and then permanently fell or slipstitch the folded edge to the stitched line. Remove the bastings and press lightly.

Some binding fabrics are too bulky to produce a binding that looks the same on both sides. If the design has a lining that can be applied over the binding, bulk can be reduced by leaving the binding's raw edge flat on the wrong side of the garment instead of turning it under.

SINGLE BINDING

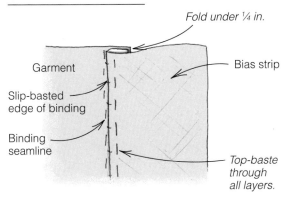

Fold under ¼ in.

Garment

Bias strip

Slip-basted edge of binding

Binding seamline

Top-baste through all layers.

1. Slip-baste folded edge of binding to seamline. Remove top basting, fold back strip and machine-stitch seam.

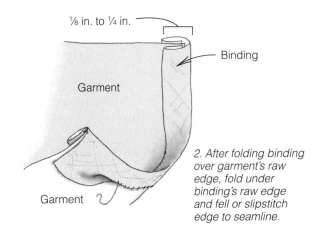

⅛ in. to ¼ in.

Binding

Garment

Garment

2. After folding binding over garment's raw edge, fold under binding's raw edge and fell or slipstitch edge to seamline.

DOUBLE BINDING

PREPARING BINDING STRIP

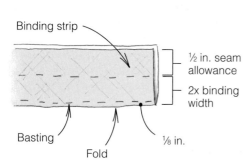

Binding strip

½ in. seam allowance

2x binding width

Basting

Fold

⅛ in.

SEWING GARMENT TO BIAS STRIP

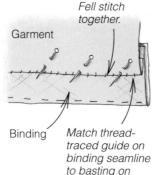

Garment

Fell stitch together.

Binding

Match thread-traced guide on binding seamline to basting on bias strip.

FINISHING BINDING

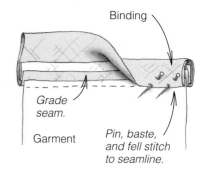

Binding

Grade seam.

Garment

Pin, baste, and fell stitch to seamline.

Sew the binding in place by hand with short running stitches. Then trim it ¼ in. below the seamline and apply the lining to cover the raw edge.

When binding outward curves, for example, on collars and pockets, trim away the garment seam allowance. Ease the folded edge to the binding seamline so the bias is smooth at the raw edge. Then proceed as above.

When binding corners on collars and lapels, a triangle of excess fabric will form at the corner. Use a needle to shape the triangle into a miter and baste it in place. Then proceed as above.

DOUBLE BINDING

American couturier Charles Kleibacker had an unusual method for applying a double binding, which he used to finish and trim the edges of his lace designs and to sew wide bias bands in the place of skirt hems. He laid the bias strip flat on the table and applied the garment to the bias strip, instead of the reverse. Working this way makes it easier to control the bias binding and produces fantastic results.

Because the finished binding for this application method will consist of at least seven layers, the weight and bulk of the binding fabric are particularly important and must be taken into account when deciding the width of the finished bias. Medium-weight fabrics such as four-ply silk and silk linen are suitable for bindings ranging from ¼ in. to several inches wide. For bindings as narrow as ⅛ in., lightweight crepes, chiffon and or-

ganza can be used. The instructions here are for a finished binding ¼ in. wide on a neckline. They can be modified to make a very narrow ⅛-in. wide binding or one that's much wider.

Begin with a bias strip four times the finished width plus two ½-in. wide seam allowances. (For a finished binding ¼ in. wide, for example, the strip will be 2 in. wide.) With the wrong sides together, fold the strip in half lengthwise and baste about ⅛ in. from the fold. Lay the strip flat on the table with the fold toward you. Using chalk or pins, mark a line along the length of the strip that is an even distance from the folded edge and equal to twice the finished binding width. (For a ¼-in. wide binding, mark ½ in. from the fold.) Put a second row of basting through both layers along this line to mark the binding seamline.

On the garment, thread-trace the neckline and seamline for the binding, as explained on p. 76. Spread the garment flat on the table with the edge to be bound toward you and right side up. Then, using the thread-traced binding seamline as a guide, fold the neck edge of the garment under ¼ in. To accomplish this neatly and without stretching the neckline, clip it as needed and fold under one small section at a time. Match and pin the folded edge of the neckline to the binding seamline on the bias strip (the one farther from the folded edge of the bias strip), as shown above. Baste the garment to the binding, using a small fell stitch or slip-basting. Reposition the layers with right sides together. Machine-stitch over the basted seamline. Remove the basting and press lightly.

Trim away the original thread-traced seam allowance on the neckline to reduce bulk. Wrap the binding around this raw edge. The binding's folded edge should just meet the stitched line on the wrong side of the neckline, and the finished binding should measure ¼ in. wide. If it doesn't, trim the neckline a little more. Grade the seam allowances as needed. Pin the binding in place, setting the pins at an angle with the heads toward the neckline and baste. Hold the edge in one hand with the wrong side toward you, and using a fell stitch, sew the folded edge to the stitched line.

FINISHING THE BINDING'S ENDS

Bindings often begin and end at garment openings such as neckline plackets and zipper closures. For a smooth, inconspicuous finish, fold the ends of the binding to the wrong side before wrapping the binding around the edge.

Complete the opening and trim away any excess bulk before beginning the binding. Pin the bias to the garment, allowing a 1-in. extension of the bias strip on each side of the opening. Then, after the strip is stitched to the right side of the garment, fold the end of the bias strip at the opening to the wrong side. Trim to about ½ in. and sew it with a catchstitch to the wrong sides of the bias strip and garment. Repeat for the other end. If the opening has a hook, eye or button loop, sew it in place now so the end will be hidden between the layers of the binding.

On couture and good-quality ready-to-wear garments, bindings applied to edges without openings (for example, circular necklines, armholes, sleeve edges and skirt hems) usually have the ends seamed on grain. Before beginning such bindings, decide where to locate the seam so it will be as inconspicuous as possible on the finished design. On necklines, the seam is usually deemed least conspicuous at the left shoulder; on armholes and the edges of sleeves, under the arm; and, on hems, at the left side seam.

Prepare a bias strip that's long enough to allow for a 4-in. tail on each end of the strip. Pin the bias strip to the garment. Fold back one tail on the lengthwise grain with wrong sides of the bias together and pin it in place. Repeat for the other end so the folded edges meet. Slip-baste the folds together. Unpin the bias about 1 in. on either side of the basted seamline so you can stitch the basted seam easily, or use a short backstitch to sew the seam by hand. Press the seam open and trim the seam allowances to ¼ in. Repin the bias to the edge and complete the binding, which encases the raw edges of the seam.

FINISHING BINDING'S ENDS

AT AN OPENING

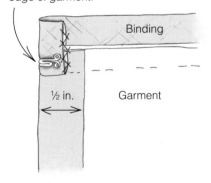

Sew hook so it's even with edge of garment.

Binding

½ in.   Garment

ON EDGE WITHOUT OPENING

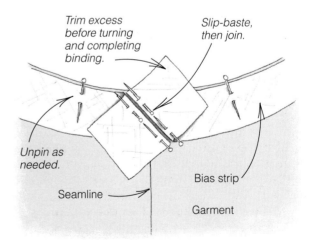

Trim excess before turning and completing binding.

Slip-baste, then join.

Unpin as needed.

Seamline

Bias strip

Garment

CHAPTER 5

CLOSURES

The word *closure* refers to both an opening, or placket, in a garment and to the fastener that joins a closure. Without closures, most fitted garments would be impossible to put on and take off.

Closures can be inconspicuous or ornamental. They can be located in seamlines or in slashes in the garment. They can be lapped or abutted, straight or shaped, visible or invisible, and even wiggling and winding in convoluted fashion within the garment's design.

Plackets can extend 2 in. or 3 in. from a garment edge or run the entire length of a garment. They can be located at the top or bottom edge of a garment section or within the body of the garment. They can be closed with any type of fastener, including zippers, hooks and eyes, snaps, or buttons with buttonholes or button loops.

In couture, the type of closure a garment will have, even when it's inconspicuous, is planned long before construction begins. The choice of closure depends on the garment's design and function, its fabric, the desired effect and the closure's location. A bound buttonhole, for example, would not be used on a sheer fabric, and buttons would generally be avoided under the arm.

Some designers are known for a particular kind or style of closure. Schiaparelli was the first couturier to use the utilitarian zipper as a decorative accent, which André Courrèges later took to new heights (see the photo on p. 95). Schiaparelli was also known for the unusual fasteners on her closures (see the buttons on her jackets on p. 86 and p. 136). And Chanel's gilded buttons, like those on the jacket on the facing page, were an important part of her signature suits.

PLACKETS

The term *placket* was first used in the 16th century to describe an underskirt, whose opening was, in turn, called the "placket hole." Today the term describes any finished slit or opening in a garment. Generally used at garment centers, side seams, necklines, sleeve edges and waistlines, well-made plackets are flat and neat. They don't gap when the garment is worn and are long enough to make dressing easy.

There are several types of plackets used in couture. Two of them, the faced placket and the continuous bound placket, are also often used in home sewing, and the directions for making these plackets are readily available in most sewing books. Four types of plackets (and a few of their variations) that home sewers may be less familiar with and may find useful additions to their sewing vocabulary are presented here: the hemmed slit, bound slit, hemmed seam placket and concealed placket.

HEMMED SLIT

A hemmed slit is the simplest of all plackets. It's made by hemming the edges of an opening at the top or bottom of a seam or a slit opening at an edge. Often used on blouses and dresses at sleeve openings and occasionally at necklines, the hemmed slit is not strong and may tear when stressed. To avoid tearing, make the slit longer and be sure when using it on a neckline that the opening is long enough to slip easily over the wearer's head.

To make a hemmed slit, start by thread-tracing the opening on the fabric grain. Beginning at the edge of the garment section, machine-stitch along one side of the opening 1/16 in. from the thread-traced line. About 1 in. before reaching the bottom of the opening, shorten the stitch length on your machine and then finish

On garments of woven fabric, such as this suit jacket designed in the mid-1960s, Coco Chanel often had the buttonholes hand-embroidered on the outside and finished as a bound buttonhole on the lining side (note that the welts for the bound side were cut to match the striped lining). Quilted horizontally, the lining can stretch comfortably with the wool shell. The jacket is trimmed at the collar, hem and seams with fabric selvage and weighted at the hemline with a gilt disc instead of the usual Chanel chain. (Photo by Irving Solero. The National Museum of Fashion at the Fashion Institute of Technology, New York. Gift of Mrs. Giorgio Uzielli.)

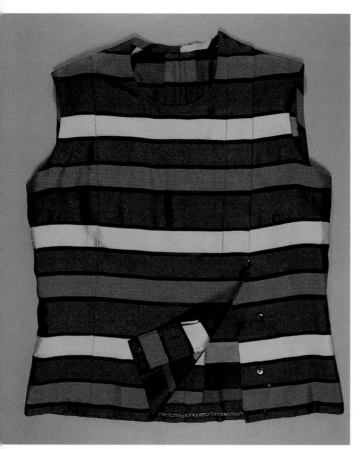

The concealed placket on this blouse, designed by Chanel to be worn under the jacket shown on p. 80, looks like a tuck when buttoned. Used on many Chanel blouses, this placket style has embroidered buttonholes on an underlay that's been hand sewn to the facing. Short swing tacks sewn between the buttonholes join and hold together the facing and underlay. (Photo by Irving Solero. The National Museum of Fashion at The Fashion Institute of Technology, New York. Gift of Mrs. Marti Stevens.)

sewing this side of the slit. Before turning to sew back up the other side of the thread-traced line, sew one or two stitches across the base of the opening. Then turn and sew about 1 in. up the other side before returning to your original stitch length and sewing back to the edge. Shortening the stitch length and sewing across the base of the opening makes the finished slit fold into a gentle U-shape rather than a V-shape and enables you to hem it more easily. Cut the thread-traced opening carefully. Then, using a fine needle and matching thread, hem the edges of the slit with a rolled hem (see p. 70) and remove all bastings.

HEMMED SLIT

HEMMED SLIT IN PROGRESS

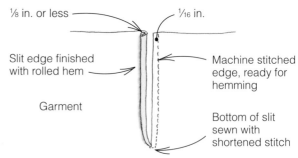

⅛ in. or less

1/16 in.

Slit edge finished with rolled hem

Garment

Machine stitched edge, ready for hemming

Bottom of slit sewn with shortened stitch

FINISHED HEM SLIT (RS)

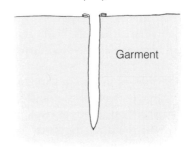

Garment

BOUND SLIT

Frequently used as a decorative opening at the neckline of blouses and dresses, a bound slit is made by cutting an opening at the edge of a garment section and binding each edge of the slit with a separate bias strip. When the garment is unlined or the edge is finished after the lining is applied, the binding is finished so that there are no raw edges on the inside (see pp. 78-79). When a lining is to be applied after the binding is sewn, the lining will cover the binding's raw edges.

The opening of a bound slit can be finished with a point at the end or squared off and finished like a bound buttonhole. The directions below are for a bound slit squared off at the end.

Begin by thread-tracing the opening on the grain and mark the end of the opening. Cut two bias strips about 1 in. longer than the slit and about five times the finished width of the binding. With right sides together, position one of the bias strips at one side of the thread-traced opening, centering it along the opening's length.

BOUND SLIT

STITCHING BINDING STRIPS

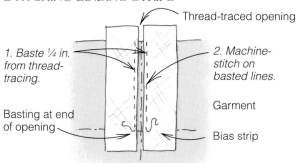

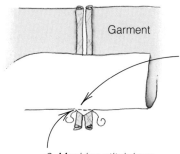

1. Baste ¼ in. from thread-tracing.

Thread-traced opening

2. Machine-stitch on basted lines.

Garment

Basting at end of opening

Bias strip

STITCHING ACROSS TRIANGLE

Garment

5. Fold back wrong side of garment to expose triangle at base of opening and stitch across end of opening, catching both binding strips.

6. Machine-stitch here.

CUTTING SLIT OPEN

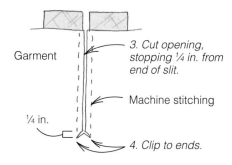

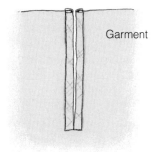

Garment

3. Cut opening, stopping ¼ in. from end of slit.

Machine stitching

¼ in.

4. Clip to ends.

FINISHED DESIGN

Garment

Baste the strip ¼ in. from the thread-traced line and stop at the end of the opening. Repeat the process for the other side of the opening.

Turn the work over and examine the basted lines. They should be evenly spaced, parallel to the opening and equal in length. Permanently stitch the binding, and tie the threads securely at the ends. Cut the slit open, stopping ¼ in. from the end of the slit. Make two diagonal clips at the end of the opening, one to the end of each stitched line, taking care not to cut the binding strip. Finish the binding using the steps described on pp. 78-79. Fold the bottom of the garment back to expose the triangle formed by the end of the opening and the bottom of the binding strips, and stitch across the bottom to catch all raw edges. Remove all bastings and press lightly.

HEMMED SEAM PLACKET

Easy to hide in the folds of a garment, a hemmed seam placket is most often used on full skirts. It can be used on both heavy and lightweight, transparent fabrics and is stronger than either the hemmed or bound slit. This placket is usually fastened with snaps or with snaps alternating with hooks and eyes, but it can also be closed with buttons and buttonholes. If buttons are used, the buttonholes can be made invisible on the outside of the garment by positioning them only in the seam allowance of the placket, or they can be sewn through all layers and show.

Plan for this opening before you cut the garment fabric. The seam allowances on the opening should be wide enough for the overlapping and underlapping edges of the placket. For a ½-in. overlap, cut the seam allowances on the opening at least 1½ in. wide and extend them about 1 in. below the opening, where you can return to your regular seam allowance. Mark the end of the opening on the seamline and complete the seam below the opening.

When working with medium-weight or heavyweight fabrics, interface both sides of the placket opening, then fold under the placket's overlap on the seamline and baste it in place. Mark the edge of the underlap ½ in. from the seamline, and fold this edge under on the marked line and baste it. Clip the seam allowance to the seamline about 1 in. below the opening so the allowance will lie flat, and press. After the garment is assembled, sew the fasteners in place. On the overlap, attach the fasteners so that the stitches do not show on the right side of the garment. Overcast the raw edges of the seams to finish them.

When working with lightweight fabrics, trim the seam allowance on the overlapping edge to 1 in. Fold the trimmed edge under ½ in. and crease the fold. Then fold the edge under again, this time on the seamline and baste it in place. Mark the edge of the underlapping edge ½ in. from the seamline. Then fold the edge under twice and baste it. Press the basted edges and set the fasteners.

CONCEALED PLACKETS

Designed to hide the fasteners that close the garment, a concealed placket has a separate underlay of fabric hidden beneath the finished edges of the garment opening. The garment edges are finished with extended facings, and the underlay of self-fabric or lining material is applied to the facing.

Concealed plackets are particularly useful when a more obvious closure would detract from the garment design. Usually fastened with buttons and buttonholes, snaps or zippers, these plackets can be lapped to produce a fly opening or abutted to make an inverted pleat.

FLY PLACKET   The fly placket was a favorite of Chanel, who frequently used it on the blouses and skirts of her famous suits with their numerous buttons. For the blouses, she preferred an asymmetrical design, inserting the placket so it opened off-center at the shoulder or base of the neckline, and extended to the hem. Some fly plackets were topstitched, while others were left plain. The underlays, however, were invariably made by hand and fastened with buttons and buttonholes or occasionally with snaps.

When planning the fly placket, decide first if the edge will be topstitched. If so, cut the extended facing ¼ in. to ½ in. wider than the width of the topstitching. Otherwise, cut the facing 1½ in. to 2 in. wide. Finish the facing and overcast the edge. Topstitch the garment section if planned.

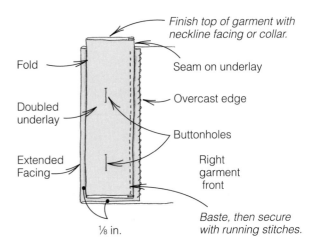

For the underlay at a blouse neckline, cut a rectangle on the lengthwise grain 3 in. longer than the opening and twice the width of the facing. Fold the underlay lengthwise, with right sides together. Baste, then machine-stitch the long edges together with a ¼-in. seam. Press the seam open and turn the underlay right side out. At the bottom, fold the raw edges in ¼ in. and slipstitch the edges.

Assemble the blouse and finish the hem, but do not finish the neckline. On the underlay, make the buttonhole locations and make hand-worked buttonholes. With the wrong side up, position the underlay on the facing of the overlap so the facing shows about ⅛ in. beyond the sides and bottom of the underlay. Baste the seamed edge of the underlay to the facing. Then sew it permanently using a short running stitch. Join the underlay to the facing with short thread tacks between buttonholes. Finish the neckline with a facing or collar. Remove all bastings.

INVERTED-PLEAT FLY PLACKET Used by Balenciaga on blouses and dresses made of silk gazar or linen, this fly placket looks like an inverted pleat. Generally used at the center front or back instead of a zipper, this placket begins at the neck and rarely extends to the hem. Balenciaga did not usually topstitch his plackets, but many designers do.

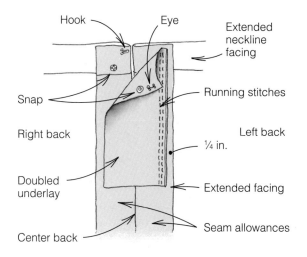

When planning for this placket, decide if it will be top-stitched. If so, cut the extended facings 2 in. wide. Otherwise, cut them 1½ in. wide. Finish the facing and overcast the edge. If desired, topstitch the fly placket. Next, cut the underlay 1 in. longer than the opening and three times the width of one facing. Fold the underlay lengthwise, with right sides together. Using a hand backstitch, make a ½-in. seam at the top and bottom of the underlay. Press the seam open, trim, and turn the underlay right side out. Baste the long edges together. Then, using a running stitch, sew the edges permanently and overcast them.

Assemble the garment and finish the neckline. With the wrong sides up, position the underlay on the left back if the opening is in the back of the garment, or on the right front if it's in front, so that the underlay is just below the neckline and the facing shows ¼ in. at the sides. Baste the underlay close to the long edge. Use a short running stitch to sew the edge permanently and sew again ¼ in. away. Sew a hook and eye at the top and use snaps with an occasional hook and eye on the rest of the placket to help the placket withstand stress.

MULTIPLE PLACKET A multiple placket is composed of two or more plackets located at the same or nearby positions on different layers of the garment. Double, triple and occasionally even quadruple plackets are a necessity for a design with a built-in foundation. The design of multiple plackets runs the gamut from a pair of simple center-back zippers on a dress and accompanying slip to far more convoluted combinations like the trio I saw on a Lanvin evening gown with a draped surplice bodice over an attached silk slip. The slip itself fastened under the arm with hooks and eyes. The left front bodice fastened to the slip with hooks and eyes at center front, and the right bodice similarly attached to the left bodice. Since the surplice edge was irregular, the hooks and eyes wiggled and wound from neckline to waist to create an invisible closure. (You can see examples of double plackets on the Dior gowns on p. 188 and p. 192, and on the bodice of the Worth gown on p. 16.)

BUTTONS AND BUTTONHOLES

Button closures are often an intrinsic part of a garment's design. They can serve as decorative accents as well as utilitarian fasteners and can be made from all kinds of materials.

Buttons can be used with a variety of buttonholes, four of which are commonly used in couture: bound, hand-worked, faced and in-seam buttonholes. The choice depends on the garment's style, function and fabric; the desired finished effect; the buttonhole's location; and the designer's preference. Sometimes the choice is straightforward, and sometimes not. Generally, bound buttonholes are used on soft feminine designs, afternoon and cocktail dresses, silk blouses and softly tailored suits and coats. Hand-worked buttonholes are most often used on fine lingerie, traditional menswear-tailored designs, skirts and sometimes on silk dresses and blouses. In-seam buttonholes are frequently used on structured garments and crisp fabrics. And faced buttonholes are reserved for furs and imitation-fur fabrics because they can be easily hidden.

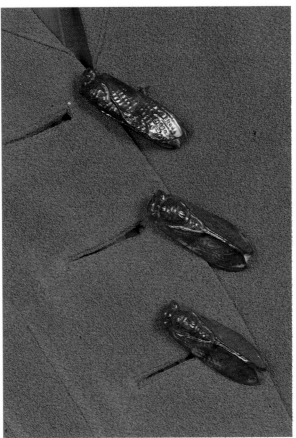

ning the selvage strip, measure the distance between the fold and pin. Add ⅛ in., since buttonholes always tend to shrink a little, and use this measurement to make a sample of the type of buttonhole you plan to sew.

Slip the button into the sample buttonhole. If the buttonhole is the least bit tight, it won't wear well. Once you've determined the buttonhole length, thread-trace horizontal placement lines to indicate each buttonhole location and vertical lines to mark the ends of the buttonholes (see the drawing on p. 87).

BOUND BUTTONHOLES

A bound buttonhole has two fabric welts that meet at the opening. This buttonhole is sewn in two separate steps: the first step finishes the buttonhole on the right side of the garment, and the second step finishes it on the inside or facing side. There are various methods for making bound buttonholes, but those described here are used most frequently in couture.

The welts for a bound buttonhole can be cut on the lengthwise grain, the crossgrain or the bias. They can be sewn from self-fabric, contrasting fabric, braid or piping.

In home sewing and ready-to-wear production, bound buttonholes are made on the garment section before the garment is assembled. In couture, the button locations and even the buttonhole size may not be finally decided until after the sections are sewn together and the garment's finished length is determined. If the garment is just basted together, the bastings are removed so the right front can be laid flat and the buttonholes sewn. If the garment is already machine-stitched, it's somewhat more cumbersome, but the buttonholes can nonetheless be completed without difficulty.

PREPARING TO SEW A BUTTONHOLE

Regardless of the style of buttonhole you choose, the garment should be carefully prepared before you actually sew the buttonhole. All buttonholes on a garment should be identical in length and width, spaced evenly and located an equal distance from the edge of the garment unless it's a novelty design. The garment should always be interfaced appropriately before the buttonholes are made. If it isn't, it will not maintain its shape, and the buttonholes will not wear well.

The thread-traced lines marking the garment centers are particularly important when fitting garments with button closures. They're always matched and pinned for each fitting so the closures are accurately positioned. Before beginning the buttonhole, measure the button's diameter and thickness. The easiest way to measure the diameter is to wrap a narrow strip of selvage, tape or a ribbon around the button and pin the ends together. Remove the button and, without unpin-

PATCH METHOD Well-suited for fabrics that ravel, the patch method for making bound buttonholes can be used on lightweight and medium-weight fabrics. It's generally not appropriate, however, for fabrics with patterns that need to be matched. Although welts sewn from a bias-cut patch are easier to shape, the patch can also be cut on the lengthwise grain or crossgrain.

For each buttonhole, cut a patch 2 in. wide and 1½ in. longer than the finished buttonhole length. Fold the patch in half lengthwise with the wrong sides together. Press the folded edge; if it's a bias patch, stretch the fold so the welts will maintain their shape on the finished buttonhole. With the right sides together, pin the patch to the garment so the folded edge is aligned with and centered on the thread-traced buttonhole place-

ment line. Using a short stitch, baste the patch to the garment along the foldline, which marks the placement line, beginning and ending ½ in. beyond where the ends of the buttonhole will be. Baste the stitching lines precisely above and below the placement line and at the ends.

Turn the garment section over. With the machine stitch length set to 15 stitches per inch (1.5mm)—or to a shorter stitch length if you're working on lightweight fabric—and the interfacing side up, stitch the basted rectangle around the buttonhole, beginning at its center. When you've stitched around the buttonhole and reach the first stitches again, overlap two to three of them. Turn the work over and check to be sure the stitched rectangle is perfect.

PATCH METHOD FOR BOUND BUTTONHOLES

SEWING PATCH TO PLACEMENT LINE

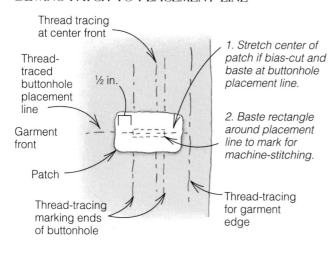

Thread tracing at center front

Thread-traced buttonhole placement line

½ in.

Garment front

Patch

Thread-tracing marking ends of buttonhole

Thread-tracing for garment edge

1. Stretch center of patch if bias-cut and baste at buttonhole placement line.

2. Baste rectangle around placement line to mark for machine-stitching.

CLIPPING TO CORNERS

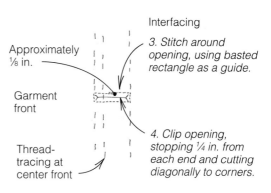

Interfacing

Approximately ⅛ in.

Garment front

Thread-tracing at center front

3. Stitch around opening, using basted rectangle as a guide.

4. Clip opening, stopping ¼ in. from each end and cutting diagonally to corners.

SECURING WELTS PERMANENTLY

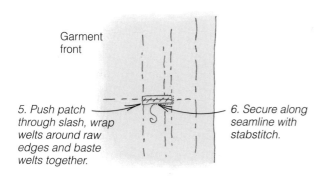

Garment front

5. Push patch through slash, wrap welts around raw edges and baste welts together.

6. Secure along seamline with stabstitch.

SECURING ENDS OF BUTTONHOLE

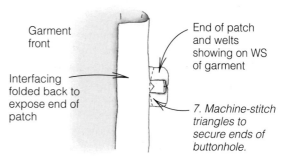

Garment front

Interfacing folded back to expose end of patch

End of patch and welts showing on WS of garment

7. Machine-stitch triangles to secure ends of buttonhole.

When making several buttonholes, stitch them all but don't cut the openings until you've measured them to be sure they're identical. With the interfacing side up, cut the buttonhole. Beginning at the center, clip toward the ends, stopping ¼ in. away, and carefully make diagonal clips to each of the corners. Press the stitched layers flat.

Push the patch through the slash and pull the ends of the patch back so you can see the seam at each end of the opening. Press each end carefully. With the right side up, wrap the welts around the long, raw edges of the opening and pin next to the seamlines. If the welts are too wide, unpin the buttonhole and trim the raw edges of the opening. Repeat the process until the welts just meet. Use a short diagonal stitch to baste the welts together, then press lightly. Using a fine needle and a stabstitch, secure the welts permanently along the long seamlines. Then, if the buttonhole is to be corded, thread the cord into a tapestry needle and run it through the welts.

For additional security, machine-stitch the ends of the triangles to the patch. Begin with the work right side up, fold the edge back to expose the triangle and welts. With a short machine-stitch length, stitch once across the base of the triangle. The line of stitches will be slightly bowed at each end in order to catch the corners. Round the corners of the patch with scissors and trim its edges. Then, with the buttonhole face down on a soft, spongy pad or towel, press it flat.

When the garment is almost complete, after the facing or lining is set, finish the back of the buttonhole. Baste around each buttonhole to hold the layers together, and from the right side, mark the ends with a pin. Turn the garment over and clip the facing or lining between the two pins. Clip another ¹⁄₁₆ in. at each end. Using a fine needle, turn under the edges of the opening a scant ⅛ in. and fell the folded edge to the welts of the buttonhole. At each end of the slit, use the needle point to shape the opening into a rectangle. Overcast the corners firmly to make them square. When sewing around the opening, I think it's easier to sew around twice instead of making the stitches close together.

For a design made of fragile or metallic fabric that can't tolerate the wear and tear of a functional buttonhole, or for buttons that are rough or jeweled, a blind buttonhole may be the best closure. To make a blind buttonhole, sew a regular bound buttonhole on the outside of the garment, but do not slash and finish the facing side. Instead, stitch the button to the facing in position in the buttonhole and sew covered snaps to the facing to fasten the garment. A blind buttonhole can also be made by sewing a hand-worked buttonhole on the outside of the garment and completing it as described below.

FINISHING BACK OF BUTTONHOLE

Garment

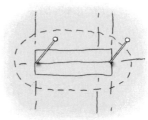

1. Baste around buttonhole and mark ends with pins.

Facing

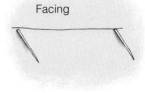

2. On facing, clip ¹⁄₁₆ in. beyond ends of opening.

Facing

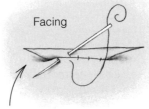

3. Turn under facing edge ⅛ in. and fell-stitch to welts.

Facing

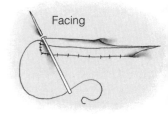

4. Shape corners of facing at buttonhole ends with needle—don't clip them.

STRIP METHOD The strip method for making bound buttonholes can be adapted for many uses. Not only can it be used on many different fabrics of various weights—including those that ravel—but it's also a good method when you're matching plaids and stripes, or when you're making triangular buttonholes, which are a striking addition to a plain design.

For each buttonhole, cut two strips on the lengthwise grain 2 in. wide and 1 in. longer than the finished buttonhole. When matching fabric patterns, cut the strips on the crossgrain so the fabric patterns match at the stitching line. Then prepare and sew the strips for the buttonhole opening as explained in the instructions for making a bound double-welt pocket on pp. 157-158. Then complete the back of the buttonhole as described above in the patch method.

HAND-WORKED BUTTONHOLES

Sometimes called thread or embroidered buttonholes, hand-worked buttonholes are used in couture on a variety of garments, from fine lingerie to tailored coats and suits. Unlike bound buttonholes, hand-worked buttonholes are cut before they're worked. They're frequently finished after the rest of the garment is completed, and in most workrooms, they're made by a buttonhole specialist.

All of the hand-worked buttonholes described below require the same careful preparation. Before beginning to sew buttonholes on the garment, perfect your buttonhole stitch and make some sample buttonholes on scraps of your garment fabric. On lightweight to medium-weight fabrics, use cotton thread or silk machine thread. On heavier fabrics, use silk buttonhole twist.

An easy formula for determining the thread length needed for a buttonhole is to cut the same fraction of a yard as the buttonhole length is of an inch. That is, if the buttonhole is to be two-thirds of an inch long, cut a length of thread about two-thirds of a yard. Prepare the thread for all the buttonholes before beginning by waxing and pressing it. Generally buttonholes are worked with a single strand of thread.

To reduce fraying and prevent the layers from slipping, while you're working, machine-stitch a rectangle around each buttonhole before cutting the opening. Set the stitch length for 20 stitches per inch (1.25mm) and sew 1/16 in. from the thread-traced opening. Overlap the beginning and ending stitches on one long edge by three or four stitches.

Cut the buttonhole opening precisely along a thread in the fabric, using a small pair of very sharp scissors or a mat knife. Overcast the edges of the opening, and if you're working with loosely woven medium-weight or heavyweight fabric, seal the edges with beeswax to retard fraying (see p. 90). Then work either a plain or a keyhole buttonhole by hand.

On tailored jackets and coats, stranding—that is, laying in a strand of thread before working the buttonhole stitches—is often used to create a raised texture that attractively defines the buttonhole. The buttonhole is stranded immediately after sealing and before overcasting and finishing the edge. Use matching thread to strand the buttonhole and anchor it securely at one end 1/16 in. below the opening. Then insert the needle at the other end of the buttonhole the same distance below the opening and take a short stitch between the layers so the needle exits 1/16 in. above the opening. Repeat this procedure above the opening, so that you end up where you began. Then add a second strand above and below the opening to produce a stronger, more attractive buttonhole, and fasten the thread securely.

PLAIN BUTTONHOLES A plain, hand-worked buttonhole is a simple slit in the fabric whose raw edges are finished with buttonhole stitches. Those edges can be finished with a bar at both ends, a fan at both ends, or a bar at one end and a fan at the other. Generally, double-bar buttonholes are used for vertical buttonholes on shirts, while those with fans are used on concealed plackets, blouses and fine lingerie. Buttonholes with a combination of fan and bar are used for horizontal buttonholes, bands and cuffs.

Complete the buttonhole by working a buttonhole stitch around it. Begin working the stitches at the end where the button will sit, making sure that the purls of the stitches sit on top of the fabric rather than inside the opening (see p. 32). You can work a fan at one end of the opening with five, seven or nine stitches, depending on the thread weight and closeness of the stitches. The fan stitches should be evenly spaced and

PLAIN BUTTONHOLE

STRANDING BUTTONHOLE

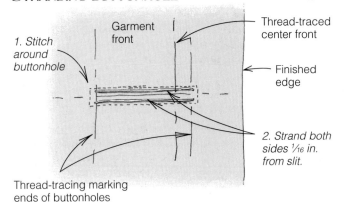

1. Stitch around buttonhole

Garment front

Thread-traced center front

Finished edge

2. Strand both sides ¹⁄₁₆ in. from slit.

Thread-tracing marking ends of buttonholes

MAKING A FAN AND BAR AT ENDS

1. Make fan with 5,7 or 9 buttonhole stitches.

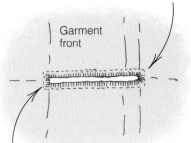

Garment front

2. Blanket stitch over bar.

the center stitch aligned with the opening. Complete the second side of the buttonhole and, after the last stitch, slide the needle into the knot of the first stitch to draw the opening together.

To make a bar at the end, take three short vertical stitches about ¹⁄₈ in. long across the end, pulling the threads taut. Then work blanket stitches over the bar, looping the thread toward the buttonhole. To finish, pass the needle to the facing side and secure the thread. Using a diagonal basting stitch, baste the buttonhole closed and press face down. Then remove all the bastings.

KEYHOLE BUTTONHOLE   Often used on tailored coats and suits, a keyhole, or tailored, buttonhole has one end slightly enlarged to allow the shank of a button to be seated in the buttonhole when the fabric layers are thick or bulky.

To make this buttonhole, insert an awl into the fabric at the end of the buttonhole where the button will sit to form the keyhole. Then stitch around the buttonhole about ¹⁄₁₆ in. from the opening.

Cut a straight line for the buttonhole opening and seal the edges with beeswax to prevent fraying. To apply the wax, fold the buttonhole slit lengthwise, with right sides together. Heat the blade of a small paring knife over an iron. Rub the blade over the wax, then rub the slit's raw edges with the waxed knife.

Work the buttonhole stitches from the straight end to the keyhole. Then work 11 stitches around the keyhole. Work the stitches on the second side and finish the end with a bar, as explained at left.

The keyhole buttonhole on this Yves Saint Laurent linen jacket from the late 1970s is as beautiful on both sides as decorative embroidery. (Photo by Susan Kahn. Author's collection.)

Like other meticulous designers, Norell changed thread colors when embroidering buttonholes on multi-colored fabrics. (Photo courtesy of Threads *magazine.)*

TWO-COLOR EMBROIDERED BUTTONHOLE American designer Norman Norell was extremely meticulous. When a buttonhole on one of his patterned fabrics crossed two colors, as it does in the photo above, Norell changed thread in mid-buttonhole to match the color of the pattern.

To embroider a buttonhole with two colors, begin the buttonhole as explained above. When you reach the point where you want to change colors, lay the first thread along the raw edges of the buttonhole so you can work the stitches of the second color over it. Do not cut the first thread. You'll need it to stitch the other side of the buttonhole.

Begin the second color with a waste knot and slip the needle into the purl of the last stitch. Hold the slit and the new thread firmly, and sew buttonhole stitches for the length of the new color. To change back to the original color, pick up the purl of the last stitch with the original thread and make two stitches over the second color. Secure the end of the second color, and then complete the buttonhole with the first color.

CHANEL BUTTONHOLE One feature that distinguishes a couture Chanel suit from a copy is the finish on the back of the buttonhole. A Chanel buttonhole is generally hand-worked on the shell fabric and finished with a bound buttonhole on the lining. This technique solves two problems: it makes the loosely woven suiting fabric that Chanel favored stable enough to support hand-worked buttonholes, and it hides their usually unattractive wrong side.

A Chanel buttonhole is worked on the shell fabric before the lining is sewn in place and is made with a large fan instead of a keyhole to accommodate the button shank. To finish the back of a Chanel buttonhole, cut two welts 1 in. wide and 1 in. longer than the buttonhole on the lengthwise grain of the lining fabric (if the lining has horizontal stripes that are to be matched, cut the welts on the crossgrain). Fold the welts lengthwise, with wrong sides together and press the folds. Pin the welts to the back of the buttonhole, aligning them with and centering over the hand-worked buttonhole, and secure them permanently with a short running stitch. Finish the lining as you would a facing for a regular bound buttonhole, as described on p. 88.

BUTTON LOOPS

Button loops are used on a variety of fabrics from sheers to satins (though rarely on heavier weight fabrics), and they're particularly attractive when used with ball buttons. Since they cannot withstand stress, however, they're often combined with a zipper or snaps.

Made of contrasting or matching fabric, decorative cords, narrow braids or thread, button loops can be set either individually or all together in a continuous strip, into a seamline or along a folded edge. They can be widely spaced or side by side, as they were for one Patou jacket made in the 1920s, which had 30 buttons and loops at the front opening and 10 on each of the fitted sleeves.

Fabric button loops should generally be narrow, round and firm, but if oversized, they can create an unusual effect. The actual width of the loop is determined by the fabric's weight and texture. Loops of lightweight, silky materials can be as fine as a single heavy thread.

BUTTON LOOPS

STITCHING TUBE

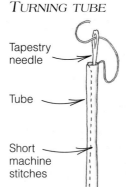

Tubing fabric

Funnel-shaped end

Machine stitching over basting

⅛ in.

1. Lap-baste, then machine-stitch on basted line, stretching as you stitch and widening width of tubing at end.

2. Trim close to seam.

TURNING TUBE

Tapestry needle

Tube

Short machine stitches

3. Thread tapestry needle with buttonhole twist and secure thread at wide end of tube. Push needle through tube to pull out to right side.

SETTING INDIVIDUAL LOOP IN A SEAM

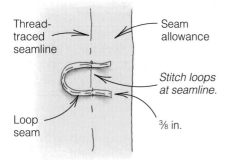

Thread-traced seamline

Seam allowance

Stitch loops at seamline.

Loop seam

⅜ in.

SETTING INDIVIDUAL LOOP IN A FOLD

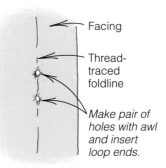

Facing

Thread-traced foldline

Make pair of holes with awl and insert loop ends.

SETTING MULTIPLE LOOPS

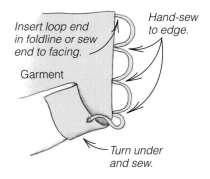

Insert loop end in foldline or sew end to facing.

Hand-sew to edge.

Garment

Turn under and sew.

Those of bulky or thick fabrics are necessarily much wider. The dimensions recommended here are only a guide; make samples from your garment fabric to be sure the loops are correctly sized.

To make loops in lightweight fabrics, begin with a 1-in. wide fabric strip cut on the true bias (see p. 76). If you're working with heavyweight fabric, make the strips 1½ in. to 2 in. wide. For individual loops, you can make several short strips. For loops set in a continuous strip, cut a strip long enough for all the loops and spaces in between, plus 3 in. To make the loops, fold the strip in half lengthwise, with the right sides together. Lap-baste a scant ⅛ in. from the folded edge, increasing slightly more than ⅛ in. at the end of the tube to make a funnel shape.

Shorten the machine's stitch length to 20 stitches per inch (1.25mm), and stitch on the basted line, stretching the strip as much as possible, which will narrow it. Then trim the seam allowances to slightly less than the tube's width. Remove the bastings.

Thread a tapestry needle with a short length of buttonhole twist and fasten the thread at the funnel end. Pass the needle inside the tube, pull it out the other end and turn the tube right side out. If the tube turns easily, it's probably too wide and you should try making a smaller strip of tubing.

After turning the tubing, wet it and squeeze it dry in a towel. Pin one end securely to the pressing board. Straighten the tubing so the seam is not twisted. Stretch it as much as possible, pin the other end securely and leave it to dry. (Don't worry about the water staining silk tubing since the entire strip is wet.)

Before setting the button loops, experiment with the shape you want. The loop can be held flat against the garment edge or it can extend out. Once you've selected a shape for the loops, thread-trace the top and bottom of each loop location on the garment. Mark the finished length of each loop on the tubing, leaving at least a ⅜-in. seam allowance at each end.

To set individual loops into a seam, begin with the garment section right side up. Pin and baste the loops in place so the marked finished length on the loops is aligned with the marked seamline and the seamlines on the loops are face up. Be sure the loops are identical in shape and length and are correctly spaced. With right sides together, baste and stitch the facing to the garment, securing the loops, as shown in the drawing on the facing page.

To set individual loops on a folded edge or extended facing, use an awl to make a hole for each end of the loop. Carefully work the garment threads apart without breaking them. From the right side of the garment, insert a loop end into each hole, adjust it to the desired length and baste it in place (as shown on the facing page). Repeat for the remaining loops and sew the ends securely to the interfacing or stay at the edge.

Several methods can be used to sew multiple loops side by side from a single length of tubing. One method is to sew them into a seamline along the garment edge (see how to set individual loops above). If the edge is folded rather than seamed, secure the two ends of the looped strip, using the directions above for setting loops into a fold, or fold under the tube's raw edges and sew them to the garment's facing (as shown on the facing page). To make the individual loops, sew the tubing to the finished edge, making sure to catch the interfacing so the garment will not tear when the loops are used. When the loops have space between them, make the first loop, then sew the tubing to the facing for the desired distance. Continue until all loops are sewn. Trim the excess tubing and sew the end under.

CHANEL-INSPIRED BUTTON

Chanel often used fabric-covered buttons on her signature suits, embellishing them with either a gilded motif, often a lion's head, at the center or encircling the fabric center with a decorative rim. After studying the buttons on a Chanel suit at the Victoria and Albert Museum in London, I decided to try to duplicate her gilded buttons with a fabric rim.

This Chanel-inspired button sets a metal button with a shank into the center of a fabric-covered plastic ring. Directions for making a Chanel button are in the drawing at left on p. 94. (Photo courtesy of Threads *magazine.)*

To make a Chanel-inspired button like that in the foreground of the photo above, you'll need a metal button with a shank and a plastic curtain ring that fits around the button easily. A ⅝-in. button fits nicely into a 1-inch ring. Measure the diameter of your ring and cut a fabric circle almost twice this diameter. Using buttonhole twist, sew around the raw edge of the circle with an overcast stitch, leaving a thread tail at both ends. Steam-press the circle and then place the ring on the wrong side of the fabric, pull up the thread ends tightly so the fabric fits the ring smoothly. Steam the drawn-up fabric again to shrink away some of the excess, and knot the ends. Sew back and forth across the back of the ring several times to flatten the fabric's raw edges.

Stabstitch around the inside of the ring on the right side of the button so the rim stands up at the edge. Use an awl to make a hole in the center of the ring for the button shank. Insert the shank and secure it to the fabric on the back of the ring. Continuing to work on the back, sew back and forth several times and fasten securely. To finish the back of the button, cut a circle of lining fabric slightly smaller than the ring, make a small hole with an awl for the button shank, and whipstitch the lining to the back of the button.

CHANEL-INSPIRED BUTTON

1. Cut fabric circle twice diameter of plastic ring, overcast edge and pull up overcasting thread gather fabric around ring.

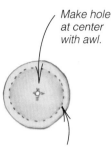

Make hole at center with awl.

2. Stabstitch around ring.

Button shank

Lining fabric

3. Slip button shank through hole and secure by stitching into gathered fabric. Back button with small, whipstitched circle of lining fabric.

SEWING ON BUTTONS

The garment should be finished and pressed before the buttons are sewn on. Use fine threads for lightweight to medium-weight fabrics and silk buttonhole twist or linen thread for medium-weight to heavyweight fabrics. Using a single thread, which you've waxed and pressed, make a waste knot, bring the needle out at the button location and take several tiny stitches in place to secure the thread and strengthen the base for the button. These stitches should not show on the facing.

If the button is only ornamental, it can be sewn flat against the fabric. If it's functional, it needs a thread stem (also called a neck) to allow the button to sit in the buttonhole without indenting the overlap. If the button has a shank, make the stem as long as the shank plus the thickness of the fabric overlap. If the button has no shank, make the stem the thickness of the fabric overlap plus ⅛ in.

On suits and coats, Yves Saint Laurent uses a braided, stand-up button stem, which is stronger than the regular shank and does not flop over when the button is unbuttoned. To make this stem, start with a shank of six

BRAIDED BUTTON STEM

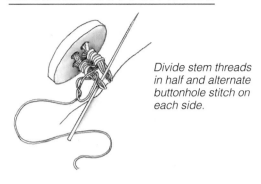

Divide stem threads in half and alternate buttonhole stitch on each side.

to eight threads. Hold the button slightly away from the surface of the fabric to make the stem. If the button has four eyes, take four stitches in each pair of holes to create the stem, adjusting the stitches to be the same length. If the button has a shank or two eyes, take six stitches.

Divide the threads in half, and beginning at the top of the shank near the button, sew a buttonhole stitch around one group of threads. Pass the needle under those threads and out through the center. Then sew a buttonhole stitch around the other group. Alternate back and forth until you reach the base of the stem and fasten the thread with several tiny stitches in the fabric.

ZIPPERS AND OTHER FASTENERS

Invented in 1893 as a fastener for boots, the zipper was first called a "clasp-locker" and later a "hookless fastener" or "slide fastener." In 1923, B.F. Goodrich coined the name "zipper." Even though early zippers were heavy and rusted if they weren't removed before garments were laundered, they were commonly found in inexpensive ready-to-wear clothing by the late 1920s.

Schiaparelli began showing zippers on couture designs in 1930. By 1935, her Fall/Winter Collection was filled with plastic zippers in contrasting colors and in unexpected places—at the shoulders of blouses and on evening gowns. Her enthusiasm for zippers was contagious, and by the mid-1930s, instructions for sewing zippers appeared in dressmaking books.

Less expensive and simpler to apply than other fasteners, the zipper continues to be a favorite of ready-to-wear and pattern-company designers, but it's less popular in haute couture. In addition to offering less design interest than other kinds of closures, a zipper adds bulk and can interfere with the drape of the design. It can also break when stressed.

Despite its drawbacks, however, the zipper can be a useful, unobtrusive closure. On couture skirts, zippers are frequently used in pairs to preserve a garment's symmetry. Used variously at garment centers, side seams and wrists of sleeves, a zipper can be centered under an opening with a narrow welt on each side (called a slot zipper), covered by one wide welt (a lapped zipper) or hidden under a fly placket (a fly zipper). I've focused below on the slot zipper because it's the most versatile and most frequently used zipper in couture. The directions for the slot zipper can easily be adapted for other types of zippers.

In couture workrooms, zippers are usually basted in place for fittings, even though they have to be removed after the fitting. And although they may appear to be machine-stitched, couture zippers are permanently sewn in place by hand because it's easier to control the fabric when sewing by hand.

Before permanently setting a zipper, complete as much of the garment as possible. To reduce bulk, trim the seam allowances of any horizontal seams that end at the zipper's opening.

To prepare any zipper placket, thread-trace the opening when you mark the seamlines. Then, using the thread tracings as a guide, baste a narrow stay at each side of the opening. Fold the raw edges of the opening under as indicated for the particular zipper type, and baste from the bottom to the top of each side of the opening ¼ in. from the folded edge. Measure the length of each side of the opening. When the opening is on grain, both sides should be the same length. If the opening is on the bias, the sides may differ in length.

Press the folded edges carefully. To avoid stretching the opening, don't clip or stretch the seam allowances to make them lie flat. If one edge is cut slightly longer than the other, shrink it to match the shorter edge (see p. 59) and reset the stay if needed. Then remeasure the opening to be sure both edges are now equal in length.

Press the zipper tape to remove any folds. If the zipper is too long, measure and mark the corrected length from the top and make a thread bar at the marked point (see p. 33). Since zipper lengths are frequently customized in couture, shortened zippers are not unusual.

APPLYING A SLOT ZIPPER

Sometimes called a centered or double-welt zipper, the slot zipper is centered under two narrow welts. Since this zipper is flatter than the lapped zipper and its balanced design is more aesthetically pleasing, it's used more frequently in couture than its lapped counterpart, even on side seams. It can be sewn in place before the facing is applied. Before applying this type of zipper, review the general instructions above.

The zipper opening should be from ⅛ in. to ½ in. longer than the zipper so the garment can be eased to the zipper tape, which helps prevent the zipper from rippling. When sewing a zipper to a bias or shaped opening, put the garment on a dress form or the human figure to pin the zipper into the opening rather than trying to work with the garment flat.

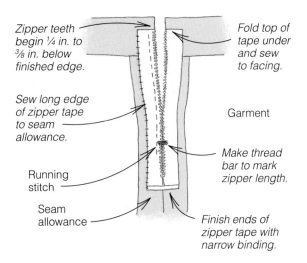

Zipper teeth begin ¼ in. to ⅜ in. below finished edge.

Sew long edge of zipper tape to seam allowance.

Running stitch

Seam allowance

Fold top of tape under and sew to facing.

Garment

Make thread bar to mark zipper length.

Finish ends of zipper tape with narrow binding.

Open the zipper and pin it in the opening from the top down, positioning the tab stop ¼ in. to ⅜ in. below the finished edge or seamline. Position the edge of the zipper teeth just inside the folded garment edge and set the pins vertically in the zipper tape parallel to the opening. Pin both sides of the zipper and zip it closed. Check to be sure the fabric doesn't pull or ripple along the zipper and that all horizontal seamlines and fabric patterns match.

Remove the garment from the model or dress form, and carefully reset the pins on the inside of the garment. With the garment wrong side up and the zipper open, baste one side of the zipper, starting at the bottom and using small stitches close to the zipper teeth. You should also baste the other side of the zipper from the bottom up, but, unless you're ambidextrous, you'll probably find it awkward to baste the second side. Some couture workrooms actually have two people basting and sewing each zipper, one of them left-handed and the other right-handed. I baste the awkward side, with the garment right side up. To prevent the layers from shifting when you're basting across seamlines, take a backstitch at the seamlines.

After you've basted both sizes, close the zipper. The two welts should form a small peak at the center where they meet. To check the zipper before sewing it permanently, put the garment on the form or figure again. The welts should flatten out without exposing the zipper teeth, and the peak should be gone.

To sew the zipper inconspicuously by hand, use a small-sized needle threaded with silk or mercerized cotton thread. Wax, press and knot several thread lengths before beginning. Open the zipper, and with the right side of the garment up, begin sewing along the basting at the bottom of the opening using a small running stitch. Unlike the traditional backstitch, the running stitch allows the fabric to move with the body so the stitches are less conspicuous. To conceal the tab for the last inch at the top, turn the work over and sew the zipper only to the facing or seam allowances without catching the garment. From the right side, sew small stitches on the garment without catching the facing or seam allowances to correspond with the rest of the opening. Since the basting is holding the layers in place, you can sew the second side of the zipper beginning at the top of the opening, which will be less awkward than sewing in the opposite direction.

To finish the zipper tape at the top, fold the ends under and trim and sew the folded edges flat. Then, for additional security, stitch by hand or machine the entire length of zipper tape to the seam allowances, close to the hand stitching—machine stitching offers more strength but is less supple. Sew the edges of the zipper tape to the seam allowances to keep them from curling.

To reinforce the bottom of the zipper, make a tiny bar tack on the right side of the garment. On the inside, trim the tails of the zipper tape and finish the end with a small bias binding. Remove all bastings and press lightly.

These instructions for applying a slot zipper can be adapted for sewing a longer, extended zipper, which is a classic detail on couture tuck-in blouses. This zipper is actually several inches longer than the blouse and hangs free below the hem. This added length allows the garment to open enough for dressing and undressing. Of course, the extended zipper could be replaced by a separating zipper, but separating zippers are heavier, available in limited colors and more difficult to close.

APPLYING A ZIPPER INTO A TOPSTITCHED PLACKET

Some designers machine-stitch the opening before sewing the zipper in place by hand. This method has several advantages: The opening can be topstitched more accurately because the topstitching is done before the zipper is actually sewn in; the topstitching can be sewn closer to the opening since the zipper teeth don't interfere with the zipper foot; and when you're working with thick fabrics, this method produces a much more secure zipper placket than if you stitch the zipper entirely by hand.

The directions here are for a fly opening, but they can easily be adapted for any zipper. Since the fly opening is rarely altered, the zipper can be set before the first fitting.

Before beginning, review the instructions on p. 95. Then fold under, baste and press the opening's seam allowances. Mark the stitching lines on the overlap with basting so the layers will not shift when you topstitch.

Select the thread and machine stitch length to correspond with other topstitching details on the garment. Stitch the opening as marked. Remove the bastings and press. Position the folded edge of the placket's underlap close to the zipper teeth, with any excess zipper at the waist and baste the zipper in place. Close the zipper and baste the garment together at the center front in order to position the zipper on the underneath side of the overlap. Turn the garment wrong side up and baste the zipper into the facing of the overlap. Sew the zipper permanently by hand with short running stitches strengthened by an occasional backstitch.

HOOKS AND EYES AND SNAPS

Hooks and eyes and snaps are frequently used instead of zippers in couture. Available in several sizes, hooks can be used with a straight or round metal eye or with a thread bar, which is less conspicuous but considerably weaker.

For skirt closures, the French prefer a fastener that's similar to the large coat hooks available in America. Since this hook is flat between the eyelets, it can be sewn to the wrong side of the waistband before the facing or lining is applied. The facing or lining can then be sewn in place by hand so that only the hook itself will be exposed on the finished garment. Select a mercerized cotton or machine silk thread that matches the garment and wax the thread for strength. Sew all hooks

in place first with a slipstitch, then sew the eyes to be sure they align correctly. When the eyelets on the hooks and eyes will not be covered by a facing or lining, use a blanket or buttonhole stitch to cover the eyelets. When making a thread eye, follow the directions for thread bars on p. 33.

For added security when sewing hooks at a placket on a waist stay or corselette, alternate the hooks and eyes so each side of the opening has both hooks and eyes. On delicate fabrics such as chiffon, lightweight metallics and lace, bend the hook before sewing to push the two eyelets on top of each other and make them less conspicuous.

Snaps are even less conspicuous than hooks and eyes because they're easy to cover with fabric, but they're not nearly as strong. Used on lapped edges in couture, they're usually combined with another fastener or used on loosely fitted designs and on overskirts. When used on coats and jackets, they're generally covered with a lightweight lining fabric in a matching color.

When sewing snaps, first sew the snap ball to the overlap, which will allow you to position the snap socket more accurately. Using a single strand of thread, secure the thread and make several stitches in the first hole without sewing through to the outside of the garment. After the last stitch in the first hole, run the needle between the fabric layers to the next hole. Repeat until all holes are sewn. To mark the location for the snap socket, rub the ball with chalk and arrange the garment in the snapped position. Firmly press the two edges together to mark the socket's position. Sew the socket in place the same way as the ball.

You can use a snap to fasten a heavy fabric at the top of a lapped zipper. To do this, sew the ball to the facing of the lap, then sew only one hole of the socket to the vertical edge of the underlap with a short thread chain.

To cover a snap on a coat, jacket or any garment that will be removed and may be seen on the inside, cut two circles of lining fabric twice the diameter of the snap. Knot the thread and overcast the edge of one circle. Place the ball face down on the circle and pull up the thread. Sew across the back of the snap several times to flatten the fabric. Fasten the thread securely and repeat for the snap socket. Snap the two sections together to make the hole at the center of the snap socket.

PART II

~

APPLYING COUTURE
TECHNIQUES

CHAPTER 6

~

SKIRTS AND PANTS

Whether long or short, straight or full, skirts have historically made fashion news. One of the most controversial styles was French couturier Paul Poiret's hobble skirt, which he introduced in 1910. Condemned by the Pope, it was so narrow—only 12 in. wide below the knees—that to avoid splitting the seams, women wore a hobble garter, or strap of fabric that held the ankles together and forced the wearer to take mincing steps or to hop. By contrast, Christian Dior's New Look skirts, designed about 40 years later, were so full that some required as much as 25 yd. of fabric (see the photos on p. 18 and p. 109).

A variety of silhouettes—pencil-thin tubes, pouffed pumpkin shapes, flares and circles—came and went in the decade after the New Look was introduced in 1947, but all skirts remained relatively long with traditional waistlines. In 1957, in his first collection at the House of Dior, Yves Saint Laurent raised eyebrows when he shortened skirts and raised the waistline, paving the way for the miniskirt, which dominated the 1960s. Despite the mini's reign, the 1960s saw a diversity of skirt styles, from long romantic skirts to traditional ethnic designs and maxicoats. By the end of the decade, women were wearing skirts of all lengths and silhouettes, which is still the case today, 30 years later.

Although the American feminist Amelia Bloomer urged women to wear loose trousers as early as 1850, they weren't included in haute couture collections until 1911, when Poiret showed Turkish trousers (with limited success). By the 1920s, pants in elaborate fabrics were popular for beach wear and lounging pajamas, but Poiret's corduroy pantsuit, designed in 1925, was largely ignored.

The pants revolution began in earnest in 1964, when André Courrèges showed pantsuits for day and evening wear in his couture collection. The Courrèges look featured long, narrow pants with hems that curved into slits in the front and dropped below the heel in back. They were an immediate success among those who bought couture garments, even though many fine restaurants initially refused to admit trouser-clad women. Three years later Yves Saint Laurent introduced two important trendsetters: the velvet smoking suit and the daytime trouser suit, a feminine version of the man's business suit. When Saint Laurent then introduced the culotte suit in 1968 and the safari suit in 1969, it became clear that pants had at last established a permanent niche in haute couture.

Compared to skirts, however, pants still play a secondary role in haute couture, where women continue to rely on dresses, suits and gowns for important occasions. Couturiers have taken their cues from their customers, focusing less on pants than on other garments, especially since women have proved resistant to the price of haute couture pants designs and often turn to luxury ready-to-wear pants instead.

When examined on the inside, couture skirts and pants are relatively easy to identify. Like all couture garments, the greater part of a skirt or pair of pants is often sewn by hand, including hems on the lining as well as on the garment itself, zippers, overcast seams, pleats, darts and waistline finishes. The bands, facings and bindings used to finish waistlines on skirts and pants are frequently abutted rather than overlapped and are fastened with large coat or fur hooks. Linings for couture skirts and pants are made of silk—lightweight plain weaves, charmeuse, crepe or organza. On some skirts, the skirt back has a backing of firmly woven cotton or linen to preserve the shape.

This undyed wool fleece skirt was created in 1961 by the American couturier Charles James for Lee Krasner Pollock, the wife of painter Jackson Pollock. Intended to be worn with James's famous tortoise shell-shaped coat, the skirt has a raised waist, shaped in front with two diagonal darts and finished with a wide, crisply interfaced facing to prevent wrinkling. (Photo by Susan Kahn. Metropolitan Museum of Art, gift of Lee Krasner Pollock, 1975.)

WAISTLINE FINISHES

Only three techniques are used extensively in couture for finishing the waists of separate skirts and pants: the the self-fabric band, the faced waistline, which doesn't have a band (like that on the skirt on p. 100), and the faced waistband. Of these, the faced waistband is used most frequently. Appropriate for lined or unlined separate skirts, the faced waistband is finished by hand on the inside of the skirt with a facing strip of lining fabric or grosgrain ribbon. This versatile method of finishing a waistband is suitable for a variety of waistband designs, fabrics and figures, and can be easily adapted for pants. Detailed instructions for sewing a faced waistband are provided on pp. 103-105.

SELF-FABRIC BAND

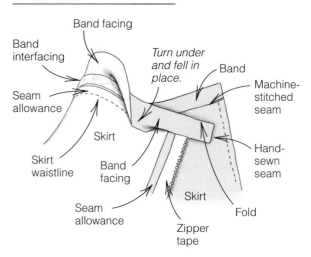

Band facing

Band interfacing

Turn under and fell in place.

Band

Machine-stitched seam

Seam allowance

Skirt

Skirt waistline

Band facing

Hand-sewn seam

Seam allowance

Skirt

Zipper tape

Fold

SELF-FABRIC BAND

Sometimes called a regular or one-piece waistband, the self-fabric band is used on lightweight and medium-weight fabrics. The band and facing are cut in one piece with a fold at the top. On most skirts, the facing is interfaced and then machine-stitched to the right side of the skirt before the raw edge is turned under and felled to the wrong side of the skirt. On Balenciaga skirts, however, the facing seam allowance was frequently trimmed away to reduce bulk and the raw edge was overcast by hand. To make this type of band, you can adapt the instructions for a blouse cuff, described on pp. 145-146.

FACED WAISTLINE

Usually finished with a grosgrain or lining-fabric facing, the faced waistline was favored by Chanel for many of her designs. Because it doesn't include a waistband, this finish is used on skirts that accompany overblouses and is flattering for short-waisted figures. The facing is applied by hand and can be designed so that either the bottom or top of the interfacing ribbon sits at the waistline.

Designed by Givenchy in 1964, this wool skirt was worn under a cropped jacket. The skirt is attached to a silk slip, which helps control the hang of the design, keeps the bias-cut midriff smooth and makes it more comfortable to wear. (Photo by Irving Solero. The National Museum of Fashion at the Fashion Institute of Technology, New York. Gift of Simplicity Pattern Company.)

FACED WAISTLINE

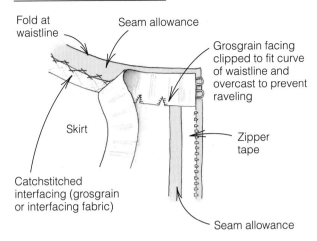

Fold at waistline

Seam allowance

Grosgrain facing clipped to fit curve of waistline and overcast to prevent raveling

Skirt

Zipper tape

Catchstitched interfacing (grosgrain or interfacing fabric)

Seam allowance

After interfacing top of skirt, shape grosgrain to body with steam iron, small darts or small snips (as shown), and overcast snips to prevent raveling. Then fell top of grosgrain to seam allowance.

To make a faced waistline using grosgrain ribbon, first fit the skirt with a stay tape at the waistline and interface the top of the skirt as needed. Then fold the raw edge of the seam allowance to the underside, enclosing the stay tape. Sew the seam allowance to the interfacing with catchstitches. Finally, shape the grosgrain to fit the curve of the waist with a steam iron, small darts or small snips (overcast to prevent raveling) at the bottom of the ribbon. Place the grosgrain on the inside of the skirt with the edge just below the top of the skirt and fell the top to the seam allowance.

Not all couture skirts have a separate waistline finish. Some, like the Givenchy design in the photo on the facing page, are joined to foundations—a full slip or camisole—that accommodate changes in waist measurement better than a separate skirt, but which would, in turn, greatly affect the hang of the garment. Admittedly, this design is not as versatile as a separate skirt. Yet in the couture atelier, controlling the hang of the skirt, supporting the fabric layers and providing comfort for the wearer are more important considerations than versatility.

Some skirts are actually sewn to the blouse with which they're intended to be worn, creating a dress that looks like coordinated separates. This technique was used extensively by Chanel and is discussed on p. 125.

FACED WAISTBAND

Usually sewn from the same fabric as the skirt, the faced waistband can be cut on the lengthwise grain or crossgrain if patterns are being matched because the interfacing will preserve its shape. In couture, the band is rarely cut on the bias (which is easier to shape and work with) except when it matches solid-color blouse fabric and a bias cut is unnoticeable.

Most finished bands are 1 in. to 1¼ in. wide. They can fasten with lapped or abutted ends. To determine the length of the finished band, measure the waist on the skirt and add 1 in. if the band ends are to abut and 2 in. if they're to lap. Then add 1 in. to the finished length and width for seam allowances, and cut the band.

To help it hold its shape, the band should be interfaced. For a band of medium-weight to heavyweight fabrics, choose a crisp interfacing material like hair canvas, tailor's linen, petersham, woven belting or grosgrain ribbon. For a lighter-weight fabric, select woven belting or grosgrain ribbon. Interfacing on wide or shaped bands should be crisper than that on straight, narrow bands. If one interfacing layer isn't crisp enough, use two. When using two layers of hair canvas or tailor's linen, quilt the layers together with rows of zigzag or straight stitching. To quilt, stack the two layers, then stitch the rows on the lengthwise grain, spacing the rows about ¼ in. apart. (When I quilt interfacing, I like to prepare enough for several bands at once.)

Cut the interfacings without seam allowances and trim all edges on the interfacing ⅛ in. to ¼ in. On the waistband, thread-trace all seamlines and guidelines at the garment centers and side seams. Baste the interfacing to the wrong side of the band, and wrap and pin the band's seam allowances around the interfacing and baste them in place. (Don't worry about the bulk at the corners at this point.) The thread tracing should be positioned at the edges of the folds. If the interfacing is too wide, the thread tracing will show on the right side; if it's too narrow, it will show on the underside.

FACED WAISTBAND

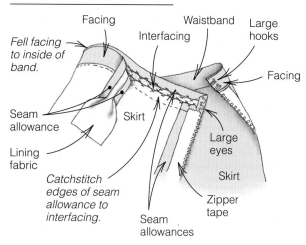

Facing

Fell facing to inside of band.

Interfacing

Waistband

Large hooks

Facing

Seam allowance

Skirt

Lining fabric

Large eyes

Skirt

Catchstitch edges of seam allowance to interfacing.

Seam allowances

Zipper tape

Next, using steam to build in some curve in the band for a smoother fit, stretch the upper edge so it's long enough to fit smoothly around the rib cage. To create a longer line for a short-waisted figure, stretch the bottom of the band so the top edge sits at the waistline.

FITTING AND SEWING THE BAND With the right sides up, match the bottom of the band to the thread-traced seamline on the skirt. Next, align all matchpoints and distribute the ease on the skirt smoothly. Using short, even basting stitches, baste through all layers about 1/16 in. from the edge of the band.

Try on the skirt with the band ends lapped and pinned as designed. If there's to be a zipper and it isn't basted in, pin the opening closed. The band should fit smoothly. If it rolls, the interfacing may not be crisp enough, the band may be too tight or not shaped enough, or the fabric may be bulky. Fabric that's bulky can cause the band to be to tight, and the band therefore needs to be longer. If there are horizontal wrinkles on the band above the side seams, the top of the band is probably too narrow for the rib cage, in which case you'll need to stretch the interfacing again or cut a shaped band.

Make any necessary corrections and fit the skirt toile as described in the sidebar on pp. 107-108. If you're happy with the fit, remove the skirt band and all bastings but not the thread tracings. Then, if you're lining the skirt, use the skirt sections to cut the front and back skirt linings, and also cut any pocket bags needed.

To attach the band, first remove the bastings holding the seam allowances in place at the band's ends and lower edge. Then remove just enough of the bastings at the top of the band to release the ends. Trim the interfacing at the ends as needed to keep it from extending into the seam allowances.

Next, prepare the skirt if you haven't already, shrinking away the ease at the top (see p. 59). Then baste, stitch and press all darts and seams. If there are pockets and belt loops, cut and sew them now (see the discussion on p. 116 on making belt and hanger loops). With the right sides together, baste one end of each belt loop to the skirt so it laps the seamline by 1/2 in.

Next, baste the lower edge of the band to the skirt with right sides together, aligning the seamlines and matchpoints. Then machine-stitch the skirt and band together, fastening the threads at each end with a tailor's knot. Press the seam flat and then open. If the fabric is bulky, clip the skirt seam allowance about 1 in. from the end of the band to eliminate bulk at the closure. If the fabric isn't bulky, press both seam allowances along the length of the band toward the band. Then trim the skirt seam allowance so the raw edge is about 1/8 in. below the raw edge of the band seam allowance.

On most lightweight and medium-weight fabrics, the corners of the band can be finished neatly without mitering. If the fabric is bulky, however, miter all the corners except the two bottom corners that are flush with the zipper placket (see p. 67 for information on mitering corners). To finish the ends of the band without mitering, baste the seam allowances at the top and bottom of the band to the wrong side. Baste the seamlines at the band's ends through the band and seam allowances without catching the interfacing. Next, taper the ends of the seam allowances at the top and bottom of the band as you fold them under to keep them from showing when the ends of the band are folded to the wrong side. Trim the excess bulk at the ends and the seam allowances as needed so they don't overlap at the center. Then press the band. Fold under the ends of the band, baste them in place and press again. Spank the

FINISHING ENDS OF BAND

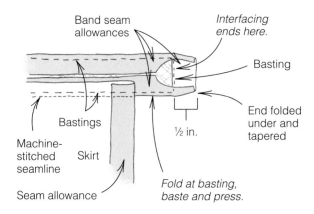

1. Baste seam allowances to wrong side and fold under and taper ends.

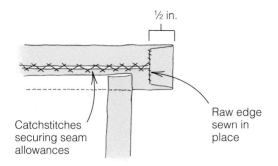

2. Sew ends securely and catchstitch seam allowances if fabric is wiry.

ends briskly with a clapper to flatten them. Trim away any stray threads and sew the ends securely with small whipstitches or catchstitches. If the fabric is wiry and prevents the long seam allowances from lying flat, catchstitch them against the interfacing.

Topstitch the band ¼ in. from the edges and waistline seam if you want. If the design has belt loops, fold the loops to the wrong side of the band so each has ⅛ in. to ⅜ in. of play, and sew each loop permanently by hand.

COMPLETING AND FACING THE BAND If the skirt will be lined, assemble the lining and place it inside the skirt with wrong sides together, match the seamlines at the waist and align the seams and darts. Pin and sew the skirt and lining together about ⅛ in. above the waistline seam with short running stitches.

SETTING FASTENERS AND HANGER LOOPS

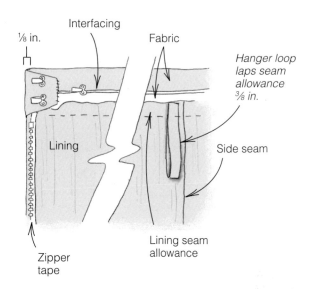

Use large regular hooks and eyes to fasten the skirt. To attach hooks and eyes, begin with the overlap wrong side up. Sew two hooks on the underside of the overlap with the top of the hooks ⅛ in. from the end of the band. Using blanket or buttonhole stitches, sew the corresponding straight eyes on the right side of the underlap, or if the band ends abut, sew two round eyes to the wrong side of the underlap so the ends meet. Continuing on the underlap, sew a round eye at the end. Sew the corresponding hook securely on the underside of the overlap so the band will fit snugly.

Before adding the facing to the band, attach hanger loops to the skirt so that they lap the seamline by ⅜ in. (see p. 116). Next cut the band facing out of lining fabric or use grosgrain ribbon. A fabric facing should be ¾ in. longer and wider than the finished band and cut on the lengthwise grain. Since the edges of grosgrain are already finished, it needs to be only ¾ in. longer.

With wrong sides together, center the facing over the band and mark the top point of the hook sewn farthest from the end of the band. Use an awl to make a hole in the facing for this hook, pushing the threads aside rather than cutting them. Then slip the hook through the facing and pin the facing and band together. When sewing a lining facing, turn under and pin the raw edges of the facing at the top and ends so the facing is

ADDING FACING TO WAISTBAND

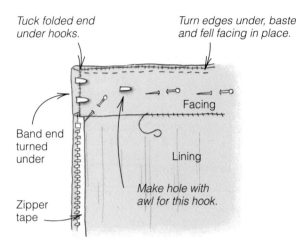

Tuck folded end under hooks.

Turn edges under, baste and fell facing in place.

Band end turned under

Facing

Lining

Make hole with awl for this hook.

Zipper tape

about ⅛ in. from the edges of the band. For a grosgrain facing, fold under the ends only. At the end of the overlap, tuck the folded edge under the hooks and pin it in place. At the waistline, turn the raw edge under if you're using lining fabric and pin the facing so that it barely covers the running stitches that anchor the skirt lining. Baste the edges of the facing in place and press lightly. Fell the facing to the band, remove the bastings and press.

JOINING A SKIRT TO A FOUNDATION

Couture skirts and underskirts are joined to foundations in several ways. Skirts can be sewn to a slip or camisole or to a waist cincher. These skirts are usually designed to be worn with a separate, but specific, overblouse or tunic, and thus actually become a two-piece dress. Alternatively, the skirt can be first joined to the foundation and then the bodice sewn to the foundation. When complete, the garment is a dress, but it begins with a skirt-foundation construction. This technique is one way to create a blouson bodice, but it's equally effective for a smooth, fitted bodice. (See the discussion of Chanel's skirt/blouse dresses on p. 125.)

Building a skirt or dress on a foundation is like making a birthday cake. You begin with the foundation, or cake, and then add the skirt, or frosting. First you need to decide which type of foundation—full slip, camisole extending several inches below the waist or form-

fitting waist cincher—is most appropriate for your garment design. A full slip or camisole is generally used for blouson and two-piece dresses, and a waist cincher for special-occasion dresses with a bouffant silhouette.

Once the foundation has been fitted and permanently stitched, thread-trace a seamline on the foundation to correspond to the seamline at the top of the skirt. This seamline can be parallel to the floor, more closely follow the contour of the waist (as on the Dior slip shown on p. 123) or be completely different (see the Givenchy skirt on p. 102). To reduce bulk at the waistline, the skirt can be set several inches below the body's natural waistline.

Next, put the foundation on the dress form if you have one and pin the skirt to it, aligning the thread tracings and any matchpoints. If you don't have a dress form, pin the skirt to the foundation, then try it on. You'll need an assistant to adjust and fit the skirt on the foundation. Depending on the desired effect, the seam allowance at the top of the skirt can be pressed flat with the raw edge pointing toward the shoulders to produce a flatter seam, or the seam allowance can be turned under with a buttressed seam (see p. 192) so the top of the skirt will stand away from the body, which is especially appropriate for bouffant petticoats and evening skirts. Check the hang of the skirt and correct it as needed.

Remove the foundation and skirt and baste them together. After checking that the skirt hangs properly, sew it in place permanently by hand. For a flat finish, trim the skirt seam allowance to ¼ in. to ⅜ in. wide. On most couture garments a simple catchstitch neatens the trimmed edge, but seam binding is sometimes used to cover it. For a buttressed seam, overcast the raw edge.

If you plan to attach a bodice to the foundation, put the foundation and skirt back on the dress form or fit them again on the figure. Then pin the bodice in place, aligning any matchpoints and adjusting the length as desired for a smoothly fitted torso or for a blouson effect. The waistline of the bodice can be finished by folding the raw edge under or by covering the raw edge with a band of matching or contrasting fabric. The attaching seam should be sewn by hand.

FITTING THE SKIRT TOILE

Perfect fit is one reason many clients purchase couture garments, which, according to one woman, feel like a second skin and are "more comfortable than sweats." This fit results from many fittings of the garment during the construction process, on both the client and a dress form duplicating the client's figure (see a description of the process on pp. 14-16). Since this book focuses on construction techniques rather than fitting, I can only include a few basic fitting principles with some suggestions for analyzing and correcting fitting problems. These basic principles will serve you well, but for more information on fitting, consult the Bibliography on p. 214.

I strongly recommend working with a dress form, even though you'll always need to fine-tune the fit of a garment on the actual figure. You can work with a new or used commercial dress form that's slightly smaller than your body measurements and pad it to duplicate your figure (see the article "Padding a Dress Form," *Threads* magazine, No. 44, pp. 35-37). You can use the readily available Uniquely You dress form, or you can make your own custom form. (See Sources of Supply on p. 215 for information on commercial dress forms, and the book by Judith King in the Bibliography for information on making your own custom form.)

Although it's physically much more difficult to fit yourself without a dress form, it isn't impossible to do. You'll need an assistant, however, for taking accurate measurements every time you fit a new design. But if you fit a toile, or muslin pattern, before cutting the garment fabric for a new design, you'll be able to do much of the fitting by yourself.

Before making a toile for a particular design, I suggest you begin by making a basic muslin pattern called a sloper (you can use a basic commercial pattern like Vogue 1000). Unlike a toile for a design, the sloper is a close-fitting, long-sleeve, jewel-neck pattern that serves as a basic fitting shell for fitting all other designs. Fitting a muslin sloper will help you analyze your body, posture and any figure irregularities you may have. It will also help you learn how grainlines—both lengthwise and crosswise grains—relate to the body and how they indicate the adjustments necessary to perfect fit. And even though most designs are more complex than the sloper, the basic principles for fitting remain the same. (For more information on fitting blouses and dresses, see p. 121; for fitting sleeves, see pp. 137-138.)

In couture houses, a toile is usually made for each design and fitted on the client's dress form before the garment fabric is cut (although simple garments like a straight skirt might proceed directly with fitting the actual garment on the client). Home sewers are often tempted to skip making and fitting a toile, but there are several important reasons not to do so. Working with a toile allows you to fine-tune many fitting adjustments and reduce the number of fittings after the garment fabric is cut. It also helps you evaluate the proportions of the design on the figure, practice any sewing techniques that are new or difficult before constructing the actual gar-

ment, and avoid handling the garment itself excessively. I strongly recommend working with a toile before cutting and sewing your garment.

The following instructions are for fitting a basic straight skirt with no flare below the hips. This is one of the easiest of all garments to fit, and your work is made even easier if you work with a muslin toile, using the skirt section of your basic sloper pattern. The toile can be marked with pencil and dressmaker's carbon rather than thread tracings, and seams can be added at the front and back garment centers, which makes it easy to adjust the skirt's width before the garment fabric is cut. If you prefer to fit the actual skirt rather than a toile, transfer all changes made during the fitting to the original pattern for future reference.

Before cutting the muslin, add seams at the garment centers. Then cut out the toile and add at least 1-in. wide seam allowances for the center seams. Next, mark all stitching lines on both sides of the muslin so that you can sew with right sides together and fit the garment with right sides out. Mark the crossgrain at the hipline about 7 in. below the waist at the center front.

Baste the skirt together, leaving an opening at the center front if you're fitting yourself. Do not baste the portions of seams or darts that extend into the waistline seam allowance. Press the toile lightly. Then make a grosgrain fitting band by cutting a piece of 1-in. wide grosgrain 4 in. longer than the waistline measurement. Mark the waistline length on the grosgrain, beginning 2 in. from the end so you'll have enough for an overlap closure and some inevitable raveling. Then mark the center front on the grosgrain. On most figures the front is 1 in. wider side to side than the back. With the toile right side up, pin the bottom of the grosgrain at the waistline with the garment centers and side seams aligned and baste the grosgrain to the skirt.

Try on the skirt, pinning the opening closed. First check and correct the width. The hang of the skirt is difficult to evaluate if it's too tight or loose. The skirt should have a minimum of 2 in. ease at the waist and hips, and should fit without distortion or tightness. Small additions in the width of up to 2 in. total can be made at the garment centers, but larger adjustments must be made at the side seams.

Next evaluate the hang of the skirt to see that the garment centers are straight, centered on the body and perpendicular to the floor. The side seams should not only appear straight and perpendicular to the floor, they should also divide the body into pleasing proportions. The hemline should be level and appear parallel to the floor. The crossgrain at the hipline should be parallel to the floor for several inches at the center front and back. As it approaches the side seams, this crossgrain will begin to drop on all skirts with any flare, but not on the basic straight design. On a correctly balanced skirt, the crossgrain will drop an equal amount on both sides.

Even though fitting problems on skirts (and other garments) are as varied as people's bodies, you can use the grain-

lines as a guide when correcting the fit. If one hip is higher than the other, the grainline at the center front will swing toward the higher hip, raising the crossgrain at hip level on that side. To hang properly, the skirt needs more length on the side with the higher hip. This can be corrected by either raising the skirt waistline on the low side or lowering the high side—or by doing both—until the crossgrain is level.

On a figure with a large abdomen, the skirt will swing toward the front, cupping under the hips, while the crossgrain at the hipline arcs upward at the center front. To hang properly, the skirt needs more length at the center front. This can be accomplished by raising the front waistline or by lowering the back waistline until the skirt hangs straight and perpendicular to the floor below the hips, or by doing both. If necessary, move the side seams toward the front to divide the figure more attractively. On most patterns, the skirt front is only 1 in. wider than the back, and a large abdomen may require more width.

Mark and pin any temporary adjustments you need to make while the skirt is on the figure. After the fitting, remove the bastings and mark the corrections with a colored pencil on the toile. Rebaste the toile and repeat until the fit is correct.

In the drawing at right you can see how the fitting principles are applied for a figure with a sway back. This technique can be adapted when fitting other figure problems.

FITTING A FIGURE WITH A SWAY BACK

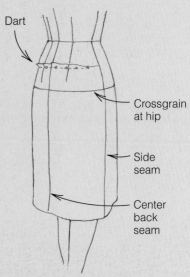

1. Pin out a horizontal dart so that the crossgrain at the hip is parallel to the floor and the vertical seamlines are perpendicular.

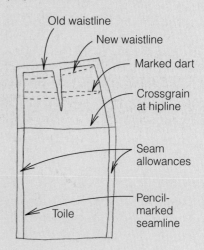

2. Measure the width of the pinned dart at the center back, dart and side seam. Draw a new waistline, transferring the measurements to the top of skirt so that the distance of the new waistline below the old waistline equals the width of the pinned dart.

SEWING PLEATED SKIRTS

A basic pleat is composed of a pair of folds of fabric that provide controlled fullness in a garment. A pleat can be functional, as in a kick pleat on a long, straight skirt that provides ease for walking, or it can serve simply as an attractive design element. There are many pleat variations, but most are developed from the simple knife pleat, which consists of a single fold on the right side of the garment and another fold in the opposite direction on the wrong side. Knife pleats are generally sewn in a series and all pressed in the same direction.

On skirts, pleats are usually held in position only at or near the top of the pleat, but on bodices and sleeves they can be secured at both ends. Used alone or in groups, pleats vary in width, sometimes narrowing at the top to conform to the slope from hip to waist, and they can be widely spaced or overlap. They can hang free or be partly stitched down, pressed crisply or hang in soft, unpressed folds. And they can be sewn on the lengthwise grain, crossgrain or on the bias.

Whatever their design, all pleats have an underlay, which is the bottommost layer of the pleat. The underlay can be the bottom fold of the pleat or, less frequently, a separately cut and attached underlay that substitutes for this bottom layer.

Pleats hold their shape best when made of fabrics that drape and press well, such as worsted, wool flannel, silk and linen. Avoid fabrics that are soft, wiry or textured and therefore difficult to press. Wide pleats maintain a crease longer than narrow ones, and pleats sewn on the lengthwise grain look crisper than those sewn on the crossgrain or bias. Kilts, however, which are traditionally made of fine worsted, twill-weave tartans, are pleated on the crossgrain because the design requires so many yards of uncut fabric—8 yd. of single-width (27-in.) fabric.

The most frequently sewn pleats are knife pleats, inverted pleats and box pleats. Unlike the knife pleat, which is a single pleat, inverted and box pleats are double pleats, which are frequently stitched down for several inches at the top. The inverted pleat is made with two knife pleats facing each other, while the box pleat consists of two knife pleats facing away from each other. On the underside, the underlays of box pleats can meet, overlap or have a space between them (see the pleats on the Chanel skirt in the photo on p. 112).

The tailored skirt of the often photographed 'Virevolte' suit from Christian Dior's 1955 Autumn/Winter Collection features two deep inverted pleats both in front and in back. To reduce the bulk at the waist of the wool twill skirt, the pleat underlays were first trimmed, then darted, and the tuck-in section of the accompanying blouse is made of silk. (Photo by Willy Maywald, courtesy of Christian Dior.)

TAMING KNIFE PLEATS WITH RUNNING STITCHES

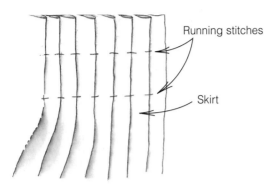

Running stitches

Skirt

These two skirts from Yves Saint Laurent's 1968 Haute Couture Spring/Summer Collection feature inverted pleats. The skirt design was planned so that the color bars on the fabric would match perfectly at each pleat. (Photo courtesy of Yves Saint Laurent.)

Skirts with many knife pleats will fall more gracefully if the pleats are tacked on the underside with several horizontal rows of running stitches. This technique was used on Dior's most famous New Look skirt, designed in 1947 (see the photo on p. 18), which has more than 60 small knife pleats and almost 6 yd. of fabric at the hemline. The ½-in. pleats on this skirt have very deep underlays and appear to hang free from a narrow yoke below the waist.

Another way to tame small pleats is to hand-fell each one vertically for 1 in. to 2 in. from the top edge. This technique is used on fine kilts and pants. On kilts, the pleats are all pressed in one direction and felled for about 7 in. For a more flattering fit on pants, the bulk of the pleats on the wrong side is pressed toward the side seams, and the pleats are felled for about 2 in.

MAKING A SKIRT WITH INVERTED PLEATS

These directions are for a skirt with inverted pleats without a separate underlay, like the pleats on the Dior skirt on p. 109. These pleats are stitched down for several inches below the waist, then hang in soft folds.

When marking the fabric for a skirt with inverted pleats, mark all the pleat lines as well as the stitching lines using a pattern as a guide. On a design like the Dior skirt, thread-trace the stitching lines above the pleat from the waistline to the top of the pleat. Mark the ends of these stitching lines precisely, and mark the pleat foldlines and placement lines. (The former is a continuation of the seamline, and the latter is a temporary line on the underlay that's aligned with the fold-

line to make the pleat). If the garment has a backing, baste the backing to the wrong side of the garment section. When planning a plaid skirt with pleats, position the pattern sections so the fabric design matches at the pleat foldlines. The easiest way to do this is to treat the pleat foldlines as if they're the stitching lines of a seam. On the Yves Saint Laurent skirts shown above, the placement line on the center of the underlay also matches the foldlines.

After the skirt is marked, stay the pleat foldlines to prevent stretching during construction and pressing. Cut the stay ½ in. wide and 1 in. longer than the pleat. With the skirt wrong side up, center the stay over the foldline and sew it in place with running stitches, keeping the stitches shallow so they don't show on the right side (see p. 49 for more information on stays).

Then, with right sides together, match and baste the seam between the waist and pleat, stopping at the top of the pleat. To baste the pleat, work with the skirt right side up and fold one side of the pleat on the foldline so that wrong sides of the fold are together. Baste through the two layers of the fold about ¼ in. from the

MAKING INVERTED PLEATS

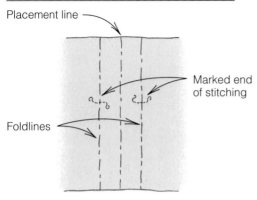

Placement line

Marked end
of stitching

Foldlines

1. Thread-trace all guidelines for making pleats.
Then baste pleat folds ¼ in. from folded edge.

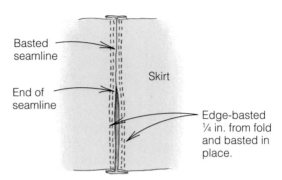

Basted
seamline

End of
seamline

Skirt

Edge-basted
¼ in. from fold
and basted in
place.

2. Bring foldlines to placement line and top-baste
length of pleat.

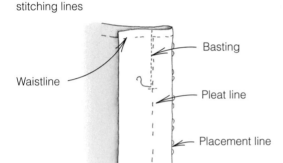

Matched
stitching lines

Waistline

Basting

Pleat line

Placement line

3. After fitting, remove top and edge basting, match
stitching lines and baste and stitch pleat from waist
to end of stitching line.

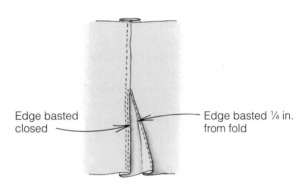

Edge basted
closed

Edge basted ¼ in.
from fold

4. Rebaste edges of pleat and then top-baste both
edges closed for pressing.

folded edge. Bring the basted edge to the placement
line at the center of the underlay and pin the edge in
place. Next, top-baste through all three layers of the
pleat along its entire length, using a single thread without a knot so that it will be easy to remove if necessary
at the fitting. When basting fabrics that mar easily, use
silk basting thread. Follow the above procedure to
complete the other half of the pleat. Turn the skirt
wrong side up and baste the top of the underlay to the
waistline seam allowance. Then repeat the process for
the remaining pleats on the skirt.

After basting all the pleats, baste the skirt together for
the fitting. Since pleats don't affect the fit of the design, they should lie smoothly—if they spring open, the
garment is too tight. If the garment is too small or too
large, you can reduce or increase the size of the pleats
or taper them. If you decide to change the pleat size, rebaste the skirt afterward and fit it again.

At the fitting, release the top bastings holding the
pleats in place to be sure the two pleats hang straight
and parallel to each other. If the hems lap, the stay
needs to be lengthened. If they gap at the hem, the stay
needs to be shortened.

After the fitting, remove the waistband or yoke and
any remaining top and edge bastings so you can reposition the pleats with right sides together. Baste and
stitch the seam from the waist to the top of the pleat,
and knot the thread ends.

From the right side, rebaste edges of pleat and top-
baste each pleat flat, as you did for the first fitting,
aligning the foldlines and placement lines. Examine
the pleats one last time before you press them because,
once pressed, they'll be difficult (if not impossible) to

change. It's a good idea to test the pressing method on fabric scraps, using a clapper and varying the amounts of heat and moisture (see pp. 57-59).

From the wrong side, press just the folds of the pleat underlay with the tip of your iron, without pressing the pleats flat against the garment, which might make an impression on the right side of the garment. Next, with the garment section right side up, pin both the top and bottom of each pleat to the pressing board to hold the pleats taut. Using a press cloth, press just the foldline of each pleat to avoid pressing an imprint of the underlay. Allow the section to dry completely before moving it. When you remove the bastings and thread tracings, clip the threads every 3 in. or 4 in. and pull them out gently. Press again to remove any thread imprints.

REDUCING BULK AND SUPPORTING PLEATS

If the pleats are deep or the fabric bulky, pleated skirts can be thick and unflattering. One method of reducing the bulk and weight of the skirt is to remove some of the excess fabric at the top of the underlay. To do this, first machine-stitch horizontally across the top of each pleat underlay. Then trim away the underlay section on each pleat that lies next to the skirt itself, trimming to ½ in. above the machine stitching, as shown at right. To further reduce the underlay while still supporting the pleat, stitch a vertical dart in the remaining underlay. Trim away the excess in the dart, press the dart open, and finish all raw edges with hand overcasting.

Another way to reduce bulk that's well suited for loosely woven, bulky fabrics is to trim the underlays in the stitched-down area of the pleats to ½-in. to 1-in. seam allowances. Use a lining stay to support the pleats and cover the trimmed edges like the Chanel skirt in the photo at right. If the skirt has a backing, trim the skirt fabric but not the backing.

TRIMMING AND DARTING PLEAT UNDERLAY TO REDUCE BULK

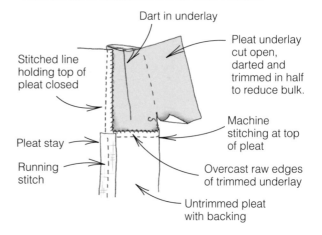

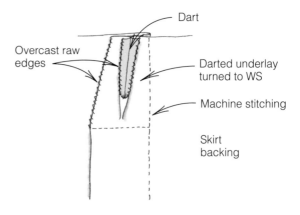

The skirt on this Chanel suit from the mid-1960s features double inverted pleats—two pleats, one on top of another. To reduce the bulk at the top of the skirt, the pleat underlays were trimmed and their seam allowances covered with a lining stay. As on many Chanel suits, this blouse and skirt are actually a dress, created by hand-sewing the blouse to the completed skirt. (Photo by Susan Kahn. Metropolitan Museum of Art. Gift of Kimberly Knitwear, 1974.)

HEMMING A PLEATED SKIRT

DRESSMAKING TECHNIQUE

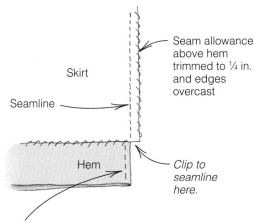

1. After sewing seam, trim seam allowance in hem area, baste hem in place and fold pleat at inside fold. Baste ¼ in. from edge, press and complete hem. Clip seam allowance just above hem.

2. Fold pleat into position and baste ¼ in. from edge to hold pleat for pressing. Sew permanently with running stitches and press.

TAILORING TECHNIQUE

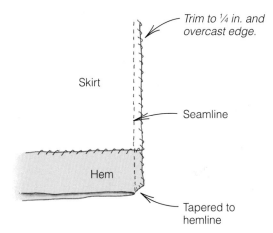

1. After hem is completed, trim allowance to ¼ in. and overcast edge.

2. Stitch side seams to 6 in. above hem. Separately hem front and back of skirt before finishing seams. Match hem at seams, complete seams, trim allowance and overcast edge.

HEMMING PLEATED SKIRTS

On a pleated skirt, seamlines are often located at the inside fold of a pleat, which can add considerable bulk to the hem area. In the dressmaking workrooms of most couture houses, the skirt is hemmed after the seams are stitched, which is appropriate for lightweight pleated skirts. In tailoring workrooms, however, the skirt is hemmed before the seams are stitched in the hem area, a technique that is suitable for a variety of fabrics.

The dressmaking hemming technique was used on the Dior dress shown on p. 125. To hem a pleated skirt after the seams are sewn and pressed, begin by trimming the seam allowance in the hem area to ¼ in., press the seam open, and baste the hem in place. Check to be sure the underlay doesn't show at the hemline when the skirt is on the figure, and if it does, shorten the underlay's hem. Fold the pleat with the seamline at the inside fold so the right sides are together. Clip the seam at the top of the hem allowance to release the seam above the hemline. Baste through all layers of the hem ¼ in. from the folded edge. Press and flatten the edge as much as possible, complete the hem and press it lightly.

To keep the pleat with the seamline from springing open at the hemline, use a short running stitch to sew the pleat together about ¼ in. from the edge and press again. Overcast the edges of the seam above the hem.

The tailoring technique for hemming pleated skirts is especially suited for wiry, heavy and bulky fabrics. It produces a crisper, sharper pleat than the dressmaking method and is particularly successful when used on a hem stiffened with horsehair braid, on a ballgown, for example. American couturier Scaasi frequently uses this technique on his gowns and binds the raw edges of the seam to keep the horsehair braid from scratching the wearer.

To make a hem with this method, begin by putting the garment on the dress form or figure and checking the hemline to be sure it's marked accurately and that the underlay does not show. Machine-stitch the skirt's vertical seams, stopping about 6 in. from the hemline. Remove the bastings of the vertical seams and press the seams flat. Hem the two separate sections of the skirt.

Then baste the side seams together again, carefully matching the hemline on either side of the seam. Stitch and press the seams. In the hem area, trim the seam to ¼ in., tapering to nothing at the hemline. Overcast the edges together and press lightly.

DIOR KICKPLEAT

The Dior kickpleat is a useful design. According to Madame Marguerite, whom Dior called his "première of premières," this pleat was created because the fabrics Dior used from the late 1940s to late 1950s were too heavy to make a traditional kickpleat. The separate underlay was sometimes applied to the lining or to the inside of the skirt if the skirt was unlined.

To make the Dior kickpleat, cut the center-back seam allowances on the skirt 3 in. wide. Cut the separate pleat underlay 6 in. wide and 10 in. long. First finish the hem and the pleat opening on the skirt, and set the skirt lining if it has one. Then finish the hem on the underlay, apply the lining and overcast the edges together. Next, with both the skirt and underlay lining side up, align the hems and pin the top of the underlay to the skirt lining or seam allowances. Using a catchstitch, sew across the top and down each side for 1½ in., taking care to sew into the seam allowances.

When using the Dior kickpleat on lightweight and medium-weight fabrics, place a pair of small weights in the skirt hem, one at each front fold of the kickpleat, to help the pleat hang more attractively. To use the round or square weights, first pound them flat with a hammer and cover them with silk organza. Then after hemming the skirt, but before finishing the pleat opening, sew the weights to the hem allowance so they'll be covered by the seam allowances.

SEWING PANTS

Ever since pants leapt onto the high-fashion runways in the mid-1960s, pants of all styles and lengths, from hot pants to menswear-inspired trousers, have become a routine part of our fashion vocabulary. No longer considered avant garde, pants are a staple of the modern woman's wardrobe, an alternative for unpopular hem lengths and an option for comfort and variety. Although many sewing techniques are applicable to both pants and skirts, the several below are unique to pants (see also the discussion of sewing a fly placket on p. 84).

DIOR KICKPLEAT

APPLYING UNDERLAY TO LINED SKIRT

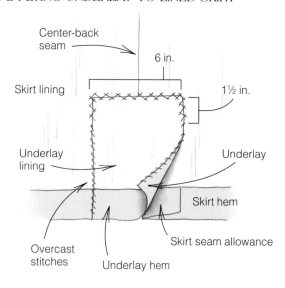

Center-back seam

6 in.

Skirt lining

1½ in.

Underlay lining

Underlay

Skirt hem

Overcast stitches

Skirt seam allowance

Underlay hem

WEIGHTING A HEM

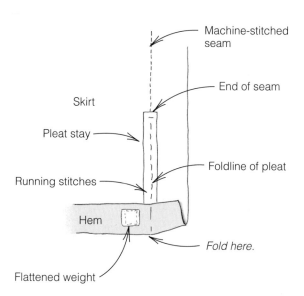

Machine-stitched seam

End of seam

Skirt

Pleat stay

Foldline of pleat

Running stitches

Hem

Fold here.

Flattened weight

At the fitting, check to see that marked crossgrains are parallel to the floor and the knee line is actually at mid-knee. Vertical seamlines and crease lines should be perpendicular, appear straight and divide the figure attractively.

Make any needed corrections, cut out the garment fabric and thread-trace all stitching lines, grainlines and crease lines. Shape the backs of the legs by stretching the back inseam and crotch. Then fold the front at the crease with the wrong sides together and baste ⅛ in. from the fold. Lay the folded front on the pressing table, curving it slightly so you can shrink the crease edge about ½ in. at the knee to avoid bagging. Press the crease lightly.

Baste the pants together with a grosgrain fitting band at the waist and hems at the bottom of the legs. Fit the pants and make any corrections necessary. Remove the waistband and crotch bastings so that you can machine-stitch and press the leg seams open.

FITTING AND SHAPING PANTS

To fit a toile for pants, mark the seamlines and then mark the crossgrain at the crotch and at the knee midway between the hemline and the crotch. Then, using the center of the knee line as a guide, mark crease lines on the fronts and backs of the legs from the hem to the waist. Before basting the sections together, use an iron and dauber to stretch and shape the toile back so it will fit the hips smoothly (see p. 59 for more information on shaping with the iron). First stretch the curved section of the back crotch seam ½ in. to 1 in. Then stretch the inseam ½ in. to ¾ in., beginning about 4 in. above the knee. The amount of stretch will depend on the roundness of the hips. Baste the toile together. If the pants have pleats, the crease line should form a continuous line with the closest pleat. If it doesn't, move the pleat so it does. If the front inseam is shorter than the back, lengthen the front inseam or shorten the back inseam.

To shape the crotch and set the creases permanently, lay the pant leg flat on a lightly padded pressing board with the inseam uppermost. Smooth the leg from the crease lines toward the crotch so the excess fullness is near the inseam. To shape the back crotch, fill the fabric with steam and, with your fingers, press the crotch seam allowance to the wrong side, stretching the raw edge as you work. Press the front crease from waist to hemline. When pressing hard-to-crease fabrics, firmly rub the wrong side of the crease with a bar of Ivory soap and press again (the soap will not hurt the iron). On tailored pants, press the back crease on the grain, stopping about 3 in. below the crotch. On dressy pants, do not press a back crease. Once you've pressed the pant leg, leave it on the pressing board until it dries completely.

The next step is to baste and sew the crotch seam. Since the crotch seam receives considerably more stress than most other seams on a garment, however, you may want to strengthen this seam as you sew it so it will not rip. In the bespoke workrooms at London tailor Gieves and Hawkes, the technique used on men's trousers relies on a hand-sewn backstitch to build stretch into the crotch seam so that it lasts for the life of the garment. I've never seen this technique used in women's couture garments, but I've seen many ripped seams on women's trousers!

To sew a crotch seam with this technique, begin with the right sides together, match all thread-traced seamlines and baste the pants together. Fit the pants and make any corrections. Then, using a double strand of

thread, sew the crotch seam permanently with a backstitch and press the seam (see the discussion on p. 115 on pressing pants).

Once you've sewn the crotch seam, press it open. Then trim the seam allowances of the curved section to ½ in. Next, using the iron, stretch the raw edges as much as possible. Arrange the crotch so the right sides of the pant legs are together (that is, with one leg stuffed into the other) and the seam allowances are folded back against the inside of the pants. Then press the crotch seam again.

BELT AND HANGER LOOPS

BELT LOOPS

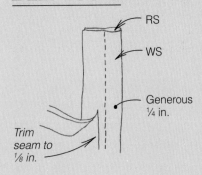

Belt loops are frequently used in couture on sport skirts and tailored trousers, but rarely on dressy skirts. For most lightweight to medium-weight fabrics, the finished belt loops are ¼ in. to ⅜ in. wide and ⅜ in. to ½ in. longer than the band width. To make a sample loop, cut a fabric strip 1½ in. wide and 3 in. long. Fold the strip lengthwise, with wrong sides together, and stitch the layers together a generous ¼ in. from the fold. Press the seam

open and trim it to ⅛ in. Using a tube turner or a tapestry needle and buttonhole twist thread, turn the loop right side out, center the seam on the underside and press. Topstitch the loop if you like.

If you're happy with your sample, make enough loops for the design. Generally skirts have a loop at the top of each vertical seamline and pants have loops at the center back, side seams and tops of the front and back creases.

To make loops in heavy or bulky fabrics, cut the fabric strip ⅝ in. wide and 3 in. long. Begin with the strip wrong side up and fold the long edges so they meet at the center. Baste and press, then sew the raw edges together permanently, using a catchstitch. Topstitch the loop if you want, and press it.

Hanger loops are used on better ready-to-wear, as well as haute couture garments—usually at the waistlines of dresses with heavy skirts and on strapless and one-shoulder designs, pinafores, and skirts and pants. Designed to reduce wrinkling and damage when the garment is hung for storage, the loops vary in location depending upon the style of the garment, but many are located at the side seams.

To make hanger loops for skirts or pants, follow the directions above for a belt loop, but use lightweight lining fabric and cut the loops 8 in. long. Instead of centering the loop's seamline on the underside, position it at one edge. To make hanger loops on special-occasion dresses, cut the fabric strip as long as needed so that the loops can be attached at the waist and support the hung garment without wrinkling the bodice.

HEMS AND CUFFS

Straight pants are usually considered more attractive when they are about ¾ in. shorter in front than in back. If the pant front is long enough to cover part of the instep at the side, the front crease will probably have a break. Although this is acceptable, you may prefer to avoid a break by adjusting the hem length so the pant front just skims the instep.

To produce a pant hemline that dips slightly in back, begin by thread-tracing the hemline so the front is straight and the back curves down over the heel. Measure and mark the hem allowance so that it is 1½ in. to 2 in. wide and trim away any excess. Because the hem allowance is shorter than the garment section it finishes, stretch the raw edge at the center front so that it can be turned under smoothly. If it will not stretch enough, clip the hem allowance and overcast the edges on heavy fabrics. On lightweight fabrics, sew in a small triangle of self-fabric. At the center back, shrink away the excess hem allowance or, if this isn't possible, make a small dart and sew it flat. Baste the hem in place, press and overcast the edge. Then blind-stitch the hem permanently.

A break at the back crease is far less acceptable than one at the front and should be eliminated. Pants made of lightweight fabrics frequently don't have enough weight, however, to hang smoothly in the back without a break. Unfortunately, this may not be apparent until the pants are finished and the excess hem allowance trimmed away. To correct this problem, a heel stay can be sewn to the hem allowance on the back of the pants. In addition to adding weight to the cuff, the heel stay protects the hem from wear.

To make a heel stay, cut a self-fabric stay 6 in. long and 2 in. wide. With the wrong side up, fold the long edges to the center and press. Overcast the raw edges at the ends. Then, center the stay on the back hem allowance just above the hemline. Fell the stay to the hem allowance without stitching into the pants.

Pant cuffs will also add needed weight to lightweight fabrics, and, for this reason, bespoke tailors always leave a 5-in. hem allowance just in case the client wants cuffs. When planning cuffs, make the hem allowance ¼ in. narrower than the width of the finished cuffs so that the hem can be finished with a catch-stitch and the edge will not need overcasting. Anchor the finished cuffs inconspicuously at each seamline with a ⅛-in. thread chain between the cuff and pants (see p. 33).

CROTCH LINER

The crotch liner on a pair of pants is designed to protect the crotch from moisture. It can be made from any lightweight silk, cotton or linen fabric and can be a single or double layer, though the latter is better for most individuals.

To sew a double-layer crotch liner, cut two 6-in. squares from lightweight silk. With the right sides together, stitch the edges of the two squares together with a ¼-in. seam, leaving one side opening about 2 in. for turning. Then turn the square right side out and slip-stitch the opening closed. Press the edges and fold the square in half diagonally. Press the fold, shrinking it as much as possible so the square will fit the crotch curve. Then open up the square, and, with the pants wrong side up, position the fold over the crotch seam so all four corners are aligned with seamlines. Pin and baste the corners to the seam allowances. Check to be sure the liner does not affect the drape of the pants, and sew the liner in place with short thread chains. (Crotch liners can also be made by adapting the instructions for a dress shield on p. 132.)

CHAPTER 7

BLOUSES AND DRESSES

Dresses, and before them, robes and gowns, have been worn by women since the mid-14th century. Blouses (or more accurately, shirts) became part of women's wardrobes in the 17th century, when women adapted men's fashions for riding. In the first half of this century, blouses were worn primarily for sports and leisure or as an integral part of an ensemble. Then in the late 1940s, Givenchy created a collection of mix-and-match separates for Schiaparelli's Paris boutique. As costume historian Robert Riley noted in his catalog for the 1982 exhibition "Givenchy—30 Years" at the Fashion Institute of Technology, the designer's notion that a lady could travel for extended periods without transporting a lot of clothing changed the wardrobes of women of all classes.

At first glance, couture dresses and blouses may be difficult to distinguish on the outside from luxury ready-to-wear garments. Yet on closer inspection, you'll find notable distinctions in couture designs—among them, hand-worked or bound buttonholes (never machine-stitched), hand-sewn zippers, and matched fabric patterns at seamlines, darts and pockets, sometimes even when the fabric is a single-color jacquard weave.

If you compared the inside of a couture garment and a luxury ready-to-wear garment, the distinctions would be more readily apparent. In contrast to the ready-to-wear garment, you would first notice that the couture garment is unlined—a common practice in couture since linings add bulk and may adversely affect the drape of the garment. You would also immediately see all the hand work on a couture garment, including hand-stitched seams, hems and facings, and raw edges beautifully finished, frequently with hand overcasting or with organza or chiffon bindings. You might also find that the couture garment was backed since backings are much more prevalent in couture than linings and are usually cut from silk. It's not uncommon to find an extra layer of backing on the garment back to balance the weight of buttons or bows on the front. And as you looked more closely at the couture garment, you would notice a variety of details used to control its drape on the body (for example, stays, lingerie straps and French tacks) and to give it shape (for instance, silk-covered shoulder pads, hip pads and bust enhancers).

DRESSMAKING BASICS

Today the vast majority of couture blouses and dresses are made in the dressmaking workroom of the couture houses, where the staff specializes in sewing silks and other soft fabrics. More tailored dresses, such as the Dior trapeze dress on p. 120, are made in the couture house's tailoring workroom.

Blouses and dresses are more difficult to fit and sew than most skirts, which we looked at in the last chapter, for several reasons. Their design is usually far more complex, and fitting the upper torso is much more demanding than fitting the lower torso (unless, of course, you're fitting pants!). Blouses and dresses are usually made from lighter-weight fabrics than skirts, and they require more skill to sew and rarely drape like the muslin toile. And, unlike wool often used for skirts, many dress and blouse fabrics cannot be shaped with heat and moisture because they're more firmly woven, less elastic and less able—or unable—to shrink or stretch.

Blouses and dresses frequently rely on backings and/or underpinnings to establish and preserve their silhouette. Backings add body and stability to lightweight and fragile fabrics, which consequently hold their shape better and are less stressed at seamlines. And, since backings also serve as a buffer between the shell fabric and edges of seams, hems and facings, they keep these edges from showing on the right side of the garment. Cut to duplicate each of the main sections of the garment, the backing sections are immediately basted to the wrong side of the garment sections. Then, when the garment is assembled, the two fabrics are handled as one.

Designed by Madeleine Vionnet in 1926, this silk crepe dress is cut on the bias, but the diagonal tucks are sewn by hand with the grain. At the neckline, the binding is finished like an appliqué on the right side of the garment and a facing on the wrong side. (Photo by Cathy Carver. Metropolitan Museum of Art, gift of Mrs. Aline Bernstein, 1945.)

Underpinnings like slips, petticoats, pantaloons, corselettes and waist cinchers provide support for the design and control the figure. The small sampling in this chapter of couture dressmaking techniques for underpinnings is intended to supplement, not replace, standard pattern guides. (For more information on underpinnings, see pp. 193-198.)

FITTING DRESSES AND BLOUSES

Among the first tasks in sewing a couture blouse or dress is fitting the toile because many changes are difficult, and sometimes impossible, to make after the garment fabric is cut. You can slash, lap, dart and otherwise adjust a toile as much as needed, however, knowing that the corrections can be made before you cut into the garment fabric.

When fitting a blouse or dress without a seam at the waist, fit the toile using the basic principles described in the sidebar on the facing page for fitting a bodice. If the design has shoulder pads, make and baste them into the blouse toile before you begin fitting. At the fitting, remember that blouses and dresses have more ease than the basic sloper bodice (see p. 107) and avoid overfitting the toile, which may destroy the lines of the design. When fitting a dress with a seam at the waist, fit the bodice and skirt separately, using the fitting principles for each found in the sidebars on the facing page and pp. 107-108.

BACKING THE GARMENT

Backing lends support to a blouse or dress. The backing fabric can be soft and its effect subtle, as in the silk Dior dress on p. 125, which is backed with a silk charmeuse lining that gently supports the garment design. Or the backing fabric can be crisp and add body, as it does in the trapeze dress designed by Yves Saint Laurent for Dior in 1958 (shown above right). In this dress, several layers of crisp backing are combined with an interfacing (see p. 20 for a look inside this dress).

When backing a blouse or a dress, select the backing fabric carefully. It should not be heavier than the shell fabric, but it can be crisper if your design calls for a more exaggerated silhouette. Its drape should be similar to that of the shell fabric so it doesn't restrict the hang of the design, and it should have enough body to keep its threads from pulling apart when the seams are stressed. And since the backing often lies next to the skin, it should be a fabric that both absorbs perspiration and feels luxurious.

The clean lines and complex construction of this trapeze dress epitomize couture at its finest. Designed by Yves Saint Laurent in 1958 for the House of Dior, the dress is completely backed with two layers of silk organza, and a third layer of crisp organdy backs the skirt. Hair canvas interfaces the collar and shoulder area (see p. 20 for a detail photo of the garment's inside). The dress was designed to worn over the multi-layered slip shown on p. 123. (Photo by Willy Maywald, courtesy of Christian Dior.)

Although the backing will not show, don't be tempted to choose an inexpensive material. Fine fabrics and couture construction deserve high-quality backings. Natural-fiber fabrics like silk muslin, chiffon, China silk, silk crepe, charmeuse, silk gauze, fine cotton batiste and voile are good choices when you want a soft, draped design. When you want to impart crispness to the silhouette without adding bulk, select organza, marquisette, shantung, taffeta, handkerchief linen, traditional interfacing or hair canvas. Self-fabric, if it's neither bulky nor heavy, can also be a good choice. Experiment by matching your garment fabric with various backings until you're happy with how it drapes.

FITTING A BASIC BODICE

If you've already perfected the fit of a skirt by using a toile, you understand basic fitting principles (for more information on working with a toile, see the sidebar on p. 107-108). Although the bodice is more complex in design than a straight skirt and the upper body is slightly more difficult to fit than the lower body, the basic principles still apply—garment centers are centered on the body and are perpendicular to the floor, designated crossgrains are parallel to the floor, and the side seams should divide the figure attractively. When all these fitting points are correct, the garment is said to be balanced. If you're sewing a dress, you must deal with balancing two areas of the garment: the skirt, whose balance is determined by the way it sets at the waistline; and the bodice, whose balance is established by the way it sets at the shoulders.

These directions for fitting a toile for a simple, close-fitting bodice can be modified for more complex designs (and once you've fitted the bodice, you'll want to fit the toile sleeve as described on pp. 138-139). Add 1-in. seam allowances at garment centers, then cut the toile bodice front and back and mark all matchpoints, seamlines and darts with a pencil or tracing wheel. Also mark the crossgrain at the cross-chest and cross-back lines and at the bustline. The cross-chest and cross-back lines fall at the narrowest part of the chest and at the midpoint of the armscye. The bustline falls at the base of the underarm and may not actually be at the bust point.

Baste the darts and assemble the bodice, but do not baste the sleeves into the armscyes. Baste a narrow piece of selvage at the waistline on the wrong side of the bodice, distributing the fullness as indicated by the design. Next, try on the bodice, matching the garment's center-front marks, and pin the opening closed. Adjust the garment so the garment centers are centered on the figure.

Begin making corrections by eliminating any excess looseness in the bodice or by letting out any seams or darts that are too restricting. Next correct the length if necessary. When fitting a basic close-fitting bodice for a master pattern, or sloper, there should be at least 2 in. of ease at the bustline and ½ in. at the waist.

Next analyze the relationship of the front to the back. Look at the marked crossgrains and the lengths of the front and back bodice. When the garment fits the shoulders properly, it will not shift when the body moves, even when the garment is worn unbuttoned.

Use the balance lines as a guide to correct the bodice. An easy place to begin is with the crossgrain at the cross-chest and cross-back, which can be used to determine the slope of the shoulders. If the crossgrain droops as it nears the armscyes, you have sloping shoulders. If it curves up instead, your shoulders are square. If only one end of the crossgrain line droops and the center-front seam swings toward the other side, you have one low shoulder. The shoulder slope can generally be corrected by taking up or letting out the shoulder seams until the crossgrain line is again horizontal.

Another common, more complex fitting problem is rounded shoulders, but the same principles apply. If the crossgrain at the bustline curves upward at the center back, your shoulders are rounded, and you need to add extra length at the center back. After adding length to the center back, you'll need to shape the fabric to fit the roundness of the shoulder. To do this, increase the fullness on the back shoulder by increasing the size of the shoulder dart or the ease or both until the crossgrain at the upper back is straight.

Once the bodice is balanced, check the armscye. It should fit the body smoothly without gaping or binding with the underarm about ½ in. below the armpit. Beginning at the cross-chest line, there should be a small fold of fabric extending downward from the armscye on the front, with a similar fold at the cross-back line.

MARKING TOILE BODICE

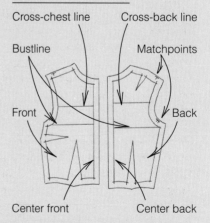

Mark all seamlines, darts and matchpoints as well as crossgrain at cross-chest and cross-back lines and at bustline.

Before cutting the backing and shell fabrics, press them on the wrong side with a steam iron to preshrink them. When using backing fabrics such as silk organza, China silk, handkerchief linen or cotton batiste, dip the fabric into a basin of lukewarm water and hang it to air dry to prevent shrinkage later. If the shell fabric is crisp, or if the shell and backing fabrics are similar in elasticity (for example, if the shell is silk jacquard and the backing is a silk charmeuse), the backing and shell are cut to exactly the same dimensions. If the shell fabric is elastic, like wool, the backing should be cut a little wider than the garment and "fulled," that is, have its excess fullness built into the backing so that the backing will not restrict the shell's movement (see the description below).

To cut the backing, use either the toile or garment sections as a pattern. Mark the garment centers, stitching lines, hemline and matchpoints on the backing with a tracing wheel and dressmaker's carbon. Next, place the garment section wrong side up on the table and position the backing on top of it. Match and pin the center fronts together.

If you plan to full the backing, adjust and pin it so that its vertical seamlines are about ⅛ in. inside the thread-traced vertical seamlines of the garment section (⅛ in. works with many fabrics and is the place to begin if you're unsure of how much to full the backing). The amount of fulling required depends not only on the weave and elasticity of the shell and backing fabrics but also on the width of the garment sections. Wide garment sections need more fulling than narrow sections. To be sure you haven't fulled your backing too much, firmly hold and stretch the sides of the garment section with the backing pinned in place. When you do this, the added fullness on the backing should disappear. If it doesn't, repin the backing with less fullness. If the backing is too tight, repin it to add some fullness. Once you've adjusted the fullness, use the thread-traced seamlines on the bodice as a guide to baste the layers together on the vertical seamlines.

If you don't plan to full the backing, match the seamlines precisely. If you're using a very crisp backing material, such as hair canvas, you'll need to "hold it short." To do this, cut the backing slightly narrower than the garment sections so it will not buckle under the shell fabric. With the centers basted together, hold the garment fabric and backing layers in the round with the backing on the inside to duplicate the way the

layers will fit the body. Holding the layers this way, baste their vertical edges together with diagonal basting, then baste the vertical thread-traced seamlines.

Next, pin and baste together the horizontal seamlines of the backing and garment sections, matching them exactly. Repeat the steps outlined above for all sections. Then baste the garment together and put it on the dress form or figure. Evaluate the way the shell and backing drape together, making certain there's no tightness or buckling in either layer. Then assemble the garment, treating the two layers as one. When finishing hems and facings, sew the stitches into the backing but not into the shell fabric.

PREPARING THE BACKING

FULLING A BACKING

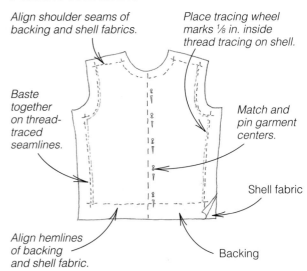

Align shoulder seams of backing and shell fabrics.

Place tracing wheel marks ⅛ in. inside thread tracing on shell.

Baste together on thread-traced seamlines.

Match and pin garment centers.

Shell fabric

Align hemlines of backing and shell fabric.

Backing

HOLDING SHORT A VERY CRISP BACKING

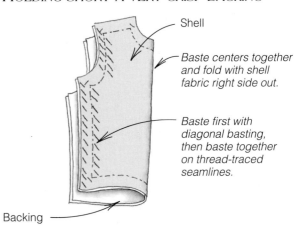

Shell

Baste centers together and fold with shell fabric right side out.

Baste first with diagonal basting, then baste together on thread-traced seamlines.

Backing

UNDERPINNINGS

A distinguishing characteristic of many couture dresses is an underpinning especially designed to maintain the garment's silhouette. The slip shown at right was designed to be worn with the Dior trapeze dress shown on p. 120 and has many elements that can be adapted for other designs. Made of China silk, the base slip is a fitted princess-line garment with three additional skirts of crinoline, net and organza. There's a small vertical dart at the center front of the slip, extending up from the waist, with two horizontal darts at the top of it. Combined with traditional bust darts beginning at the side front seams, the darts between the breasts create a snug fit and are common on couture slips and eveningwear.

Each of the slip's extra skirts is hand-sewn to the base slip with a running stitch, and the raw edges of the seam allowance are flattened with catchstitches. The stiff, black nylon crinoline top skirt is applied 1½ in. below the waist (though it looks at waist level on the dress form since the form is taller than the original wearer). Pleats and long, 3-in. wide darts at center front and back control the fullness at the top of the skirt and create an A-line effect. The machine-stitched, 4-in. wide hem measures 75 in. around and encases horsehair braid.

The first underskirt is made of net, gathered at the top and sewn to the slip 1 in. below the crinoline skirt. The second underskirt is made of silk organza and sewn 2⅛ in. below the top of the net underskirt. The fullness in the top of this skirt is controlled by 12 2-in. wide darts, with the balance gathered. Its hem measures 131 in. in length.

Sleeveless dresses and blouses tend to expose undergarments or the braless body underneath, especially when the armholes are deep. To solve this problem, some designers accompany these fashions with a camisole or slip that has side panels made from the dress or blouse fabric. One such design by Norell is shown on p. 124.

While these underpinnings offer some useful ideas for home sewers, they probably don't provide just the solutions you need for the project you're working on. In fact, it's likely that most of the time you'll have to create your own designs for underpinnings since the instructions for them in commercial patterns are often omitted altogether or, if included, are extremely simplified. Commercial patterns can nonetheless be helpful in devising and constructing underpinnings, but before deciding on the specifics of construction, you need to determine the kind of underpinning that's needed. To do that, look to the design itself. What parts of the design need support? The bodice—all or just part of it? The skirt? The waist? Does the body itself need control to wear the design? Whatever the answers, there's proba-

Created for the trapeze dress shown on p. 20 and p. 120, this full slip has three overskirts attached by hand with running stitches. The neckline and armscyes are finished with narrow bias facings. (Photo by Cathy Carver. Metropolitan Museum of Art, Gift of Imogene Schubert, 1958.)

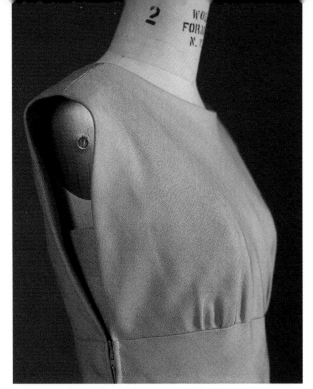

This linen dress designed by Norman Norell in 1964 was worn over a special camisole to preserve the integrity of the design and conceal the undergarments at the underarm. On the dress's lining-fabric camisole, self-fabric was used only at the sides, where it would be seen. (Photo by Irving Solero. The National Museum of Fashion at the Fashion Institute of Technology, New York. Gift of Mrs. John A. Dunbar.)

bly no single solution but rather several ways to create that support. To decide upon the best solution, you'll need to do some experimentation.

For simple underpinnings like the slip mentioned above, try beginning with existing commercial patterns for slips, camisoles or even simple dresses. For more complex, body-hugging support, look to bra, bathing-suit and evening-dress patterns as well as to your own wardrobe for ideas or solutions. For complex underpinnings, you'll probably need to use your imagination. It's always a good idea to start with a muslin to develop the silhouette you want before proceeding to the real thing. As you work with various support fabrics and underpinning designs, you'll soon learn which combinations are most effective.

DRESSES WITH WAISTLINES

Dresses with waistlines range from understated, tailored garments to exuberant creations for summer afternoon parties. Whatever their design, they're all sewn by separately assembling the bodice and skirt, and then joining the two at the waistline.

To join a bodice and skirt at the waistline, start by centering a ½-in. wide organza stay on the wrong side of the bodice over the thread tracing at the waist. Baste the bodice to the stay so the ease is appropriately distributed. Then baste a grosgrain fitting band to the skirt's thread-traced waistline (see the sidebar on pp. 107-108 for more information on fitting bands).

Before joining the sections, fit and mark them separately (preferably on a dress form), make any necessary corrections and remove the grosgrain fitting band from the skirt. Baste the bodice and skirt together with the garment centers and underarm seams aligned. Baste the grosgrain fitting band in once more and fit the basted dress on the figure.

After the fitting, mark the stay and fitting band with the finished length, seams, beginning and end of any fullness on the bodice or skirt, and perhaps even the dart locations so that the fullness will not have to be adjusted again. Remove the stay and fitting band so you can complete all vertical seams and darts on both the bodice and skirt. Then baste the organza stay into the bodice again and baste the skirt to the bodice. Stitch the waistline seam and press it lightly.

For a flat, inconspicuous waistline seam, turn the seam toward the bodice. To accentuate a full skirt with a buttressed seam (see p. 192), instead press the waistline seam toward the hem so the skirt will stand away from the bodice at the waist. Finish both types of waistline seams by separately overcasting the raw edges of the bodice and skirt, but trim the raw edges of an inconspicuous waistline seam to 1 in. before overcasting them.

Designed by Marc Bohan for the Dior 1985 Spring/Summer Collection, this elegant silk jacquard dress is completely backed with silk charmeuse. The edges of the surplice neckline and the bodice waistline are stayed with silk organza selvage. (Photo by Susan Kahn. Author's collection.)

CHANEL'S ATTACHED BLOUSE/SKIRT DRESS

For her suits, Chanel favored attached blouse-and-skirt ensembles that were actually dresses, though they didn't look it. She assembled these dresses using several methods, but the most practical and easiest to duplicate is to complete the blouse and skirt separately, then sew them together by hand.

Begin by putting the blouse on a dress form or the figure. Place a narrow linen fitting tape around the waist, and pin the ends of the tape together. Arrange the blouse's fullness as desired, and pin the tape to the blouse so the pins are parallel to the tape. Remove the blouse from the dress form, and mark the garment centers and seamlines on the tape. Turn the blouse wrong side out, and using the pins as a guide, thread-trace the waistline and unpin the tape.

Next, pin and baste the skirt to the blouse, aligning the waistlines, garment centers and side seams. If the skirt has a band, baste the layers together at the bottom of the band. If it has a facing, baste the skirt to the blouse $\frac{1}{4}$ in. to $\frac{1}{2}$ in. below the top of the facing. Check the fit and make any necessary corrections. Then sew the waistline permanently with a running stitch, reinforcing it frequently with a backstitch. Keep the stitches loose in order to avoid dimples on the right side.

BIAS-CUT DRESSES

Only a few designers have been truly successful with bias creations, among them the legendary French couturier Madeleine Vionnet, who introduced the bias-cut garment at the turn of the century (see one of her designs on p. 118). Her first designs, shown in 1907 over uncorseted figures with sandals or bare feet, shocked and infuriated many clients. A few appreciated the new freedom of these styles, which did not restrict movement even though they clung to the figure. It was not until after World War I, however, that Vionnet's innovative bias cut became high fashion.

In more recent years, American couturier Charles Kleibacker became known for his classic bias dresses for day and evening, many of which were made of 4-ply silk and designed to be worn without undergarments other than stockings. Because bias-cut garments are constructed with the bias hanging vertically, these fashions are more challenging to sew than traditional designs cut on the straight grain because the bias cut stretches more and is easily distorted. From Kleibacker, I've learned some useful tips for working with the bias.

When making a muslin toile for a bias-cut garment, be sure the muslin for each garment section has a selvage edge. That edge will make it easy to align the grainlines when you lay out the toile on the garment fabric for cutting.

Instead of folding the fabric lengthwise as you normally would to cut out two layers on the lengthwise grain, cut the unfolded fabric in two lengths long enough to accommodate your pattern. Mark the face side of each length with a thread stitched in the same position on each side. Stack the two lengths with right sides together and thread markers at one end. Smooth the stacked layers of fabric, and to prevent shifting, pin the layers together on all sides, setting the pins perpendicular to the edges. "Corner" the fabric so that one end and long edge are aligned with one corner and long edge of the table, which ensures that the grainlines are at right angles.

Slip large sheets of dressmaker's carbon under the fabric layers, and check to be sure the fabric is still cornered. Spread the muslin pattern on top of the fabric and pin the selvages on the muslin to the selvages on the garment fabric, allowing several inches between pattern pieces for seam allowances. Using weights or pins in the seam allowances, anchor the pattern. Then transfer all stitching lines and matchpoints to the wrong side of the lower layer with a serrated tracing wheel. As you wheel with one hand, hold the fabric layers flat with the just the fingertips of the other hand (as if you're playing the piano). Roll the wheel in only one direction, and move your fingers frequently so you're holding the fabric at the same place where you're "wheeling," as it's called in couture.

After you've wheeled the entire pattern, remove the muslin pattern, turn the two layers of fabric over so you can smooth and mark the second layer as you did the first. Lap-baste the garment centers and any other seamlines that are positioned with right sides together, ready for stitching. Thread-trace the remaining stitching lines and matchpoints. To avoid catching the underlayer, slip a ruler in between the layers to separate them. Cut out the garment sections, leaving at least 1-in. wide seam allowances.

Machine-stitch the dress only after it has been fitted, stretching the bias seams as much as possible as you sew so the garment will drape properly. Try to locate any zippers on the lengthwise grain rather than on the bias so they will hang correctly and will not buckle. If this isn't possible, make a slashed opening for the zipper and bind the edges of the opening with bias bindings (see pp. 82-83).

BLOUSE DESIGNS

Blouses are usually designed either to tuck into or hang over the waistband of a skirt or pants. Many tuck-in couture blouses, like the one shown on the facing page, have a seam at the waist and a separately cut section below the waist called a yoke, which reduces bulk, controls the fullness at the waist and hem of the blouse and ensures a better fit. The yoke is generally made of fabric that's both lighter in weight and less expensive than the blouse fabric, for example, organza, China silk or lightweight silk shantung. Most yokes are simple rectangles, darted to fit the waist and the upper part of the hip. They're usually 4 in. to 7 in. wide and are sometimes cut on the crossgrain so the selvage can be used at the bottom instead of a hem, further reducing bulk.

To make a yoke for a blouse, begin with a pattern for a close-fitting skirt. If you want to use the yoke fabric's selvage for a hem, place the top of the skirt's front and back pattern sections on the fabric the same distance from the selvage. Using a tracing wheel and dressmaker's carbon, transfer the stitching lines at the top of the front and back pattern sections to the fabric. Remove the pattern and baste the yoke together. Then baste it to the blouse for a fitting, make any necessary corrections, and permanently stitch and press the yoke and blouse. If you haven't used the selvage as the hem, finish the lower edge by machine stitching ¼ in. from the edge, trimming it to ⅛ in. and overcasting.

If a tuck-in blouse has a zipper, it usually extends 10 in. to 12 in. below the waist and several inches below the blouse hem so the wearer can step into the garment easily. Sometimes the zippers are sewn in upside-down in place of a separating zipper since the latter are heavy and available in only limited lengths and colors (see pp. 94-97 for information on sewing in a zipper).

Frequently used with her classic suits, Coco Chanel's overblouses and tunics are always comfortable, even when they aren't high fashion. The blouse should hang smoothly without shifting on the body toward the back or front, and the hemline should appear parallel to the floor, except, of course, when the design's hemline is intentionally uneven.

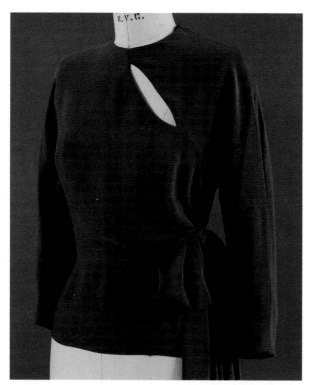

Designed by Madame Grès in 1977, this tuck-in blouse has an asymmetrical drape that ties on the left. To prevent wrinkling under the top of the skirt, the blouse is finished with a form-fitting yoke. And to make dressing easier, there are zippers at the shoulder and wrists and an extra-long zipper under the arm that extends several inches below the yoke. (Photo by Irving Solero. The National Museum of Fashion at the Fashion Institute of Technology, New York. Gift of Mrs. Marc Haas.)

In couture, the hang of the overblouse is controlled with weights. Chanel used a variety of weights, including brass chains and circle weights. Other couturiers have weighted the blouse with wide hem allowances, bands, bindings, embroidery, ribbon or braid trims, and even pockets and buttons. Noted in the 1920s for his Grecian-inspired, long, pleated silk, column-like dresses, Italian designer Mario Fortuny always used small glass beads as weights along the hemline of the blouse on his two-piece designs. More recently, Norell preferred silk-covered drapery weights, even though they had to be removed when the blouse was dry-cleaned. Many designs, including the tunic by Yves Saint Laurent shown on p. 51, have a bias binding at the hem to weight it.

SLEEVELESS BLOUSES AND DRESSES

Sleeveless designs were traditionally associated with casual dress and sportswear until American designer Mainbocher introduced haute couture to the bare-armed suit blouse in the 1930s. Although Chanel liked this innovation for the comfort it offered, she wanted her suits to look as if they had long sleeves. She achieved this effect by creating separate blouse cuffs that were sewn or snapped into the insides of the jacket sleeves.

On both sleeveless blouses and dresses, Norell and Balenciaga favored an unusual front armhole shape, called a sleeveless flange (seen in the photo on p. 42). The shallow front armhole hugs the body and covers the hollow between the armhole and bust, while a fold of fabric extending from the shoulder at the armscye covers the "crease" next to the base of the arm, one of the body's less attractive parts. On some Norell and Balenciaga designs with cap or extended-cap sleeves, the sleeveless flange was used on both the front and back armholes.

If you want to reshape an armhole to create the sleeveless flange, extend the shoulder seamline on your pattern front by 1¼ in. Connect the end of the shoulder seam with the armhole matchpoint, which creates a shallow sleeve cap, and add seam allowances to all edges as needed. Repeat on the pattern back if you want a rounder, softer edge on the back armhole as well. Finish the armhole with a facing or lining, then fold the extension under 1¼ in. and catchstitch it at the shoulder seam.

RESHAPING ARMHOLE INTO SLEEVELESS FLANGE

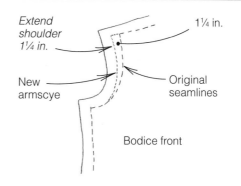

Extend shoulder 1¼ in.

1¼ in.

New armscye

Original seamlines

Bodice front

Any sleeveless design will be enhanced by interfacing the armscye with a bias-cut strip to soften the edge without causing any "breaks" in it and to make the edge drape better. Using the same technique as for interfacing hems (see p. 68), you can create a softly rolled edge that's usually more attractive than a sharp, hard-pressed finish. Depending on the amount of roll you want, choose an interfacing fabric like muslin, traditional interfacing fabrics, hair canvas, cotton flannel, lambswool or armo wool (listed here in order of the amount of roll they produce, from the least to the greatest) and cut a strip of interfacing 1½ in. wide. After the facings are stitched and the seam is pressed and clipped, hand sew the strip along the entire armscye seamline, positioning it so it laps the facing by ½ in. and the body by 1 in. Clip the strip as necessary so the outer edge will lie flat.

INVISIBLE DETAILS

The construction details on the inside of a couture garment are among its most important secrets. These details represent the finishing touches that imperceptibly keep necklines from shifting or gaping, help pleats hang as designed, make waistlines fit smoothly and generally hold the garment in place on the body.

PERFECT NECKLINES

A well-made neckline that lies precisely as the designer intended is a hallmark of couture construction. There are many ways to achieve this end, from small weights to elaborate elastic harnesses, and the design of the neckline determines the approach needed to tame it.

A draped cowl neckline, for example, can be held in place with small weights covered with plain-weave silk or organza and sewn with a small French tack to the inside fold of the drape. A deep, V-shaped neckline, like that in the photo on p. 125, will lie smoothly if anchored at the deepest point of the V with a boning stay.

To anchor a V-neck, first stay the neckline early in its construction to eliminate any gaping (see pp. 49-50 for information on neckline stays). After the neckline is finished, make the anchor by sewing a narrow silk tube and inserting a 3-in. piece of polyester boning or a

This detail of a two-piece silk matelassé dress designed by Balenciaga in 1961 shows the elastic harness used to hold the front of the blouson-style bodice firmly in place, while allowing the wrapping back sections to drape gracefully. (Photo by Irving Solero. The National Museum of Fashion at the Fashion Institute of Technology, New York. Gift of Mr. David Biberman.)

man's shirt stay into the tube. With the garment wrong side out, sew one end of the tube to the facing about ¼ in. below the neckline. When the garment is worn, the bottom of the anchor slips into the bra and the neckline clings to the body.

Designs with deep décolletés, or low-cut necklines, are more difficult to control, particularly when they're not close-fitting. To solve the problem, low-cut couture blouses and dresses have elastic harnesses that attach to elastic waistbands. The specific design of the harness varies with each neckline, but they usually have an elastic band that snugly fits the waist or under the bust. The shoulder straps extending from the elastic waistband are either sewn to the garment shoulder seams or held in place with lingerie straps to keep the shoulder straps of the garment from shifting when it's worn. The harness on the Balenciaga two-piece dress shown above is a good example of such an underpinning.

CONTROLLING A
SQUARE NECKLINE

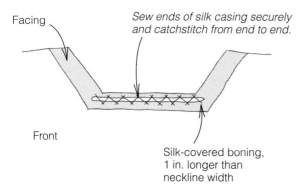

Facing

*Sew ends of silk casing securely
and catchstitch from end to end.*

Front

Silk-covered boning,
1 in. longer than
neckline width

CONTROLLING AN
OFF-THE-SHOULDER NECKLINE

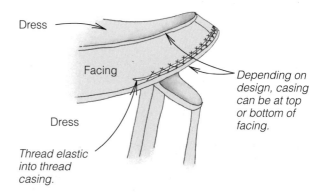

Dress

Facing

Dress

*Depending on
design, casing
can be at top
or bottom of
facing.*

*Thread elastic
into thread
casing.*

An elastic stay is used to control a square neckline and keep it from gaping. To make such a stay, cut the elastic long enough to extend from one front corner of the neckline around the back to the other front corner. Secure one end of the elastic to the one front corner of the neckline facing and sew a snap to the free end of the elastic. Then sew a matching snap socket on the other corner of the neckline facing. If the neckline sags a little despite the elastic, use a piece of polyester boning to keep it smooth. Cut the boning 1 in. longer than the neckline width, insert it into a narrow silk tube and catchstitch it to the neckline facing ¼ in. to ½ in. below the edge.

Another form of elastic stay is used to hold an off-the-shoulder neckline in position. This stay is a piece of elastic held in a thread casing of catchstitches sewn over the elastic. To make this stay, begin by pinning a piece of braided elastic (the kind that narrows when stretched) around the neckline facing without stretching it. Then sew catchstitches over the elastic. Baste one end of the elastic to the facing so it will not pull out. Then pull up the other end of the elastic so the elastic is about 1 in. shorter than the length of the garment's neckline. Baste the end of the elastic to the neckline facing and cut the elastic, leaving an extra 2 in. Adjust the fullness of the neckline along the elastic. At the next fitting, evaluate the neckline to decide if the elastic needs to be shortened or lengthened or if the fullness needs to be redistributed. After the fitting, trim the elastic ends and sew them securely to the facing. If the elastic needs to be replaced at a later date, remove the old elastic and sew a short length of buttonhole twist thread to the end of the new elastic and thread it through the casing.

Valentino uses elastic stays attached to the shoulder pads in a garment to control necklines. The elastic is inserted into a narrow silk tube, and the ends are sewn to the front and back of the shoulder pad to form a loop that fits snugly but not tightly under the arm. The exact placement of the elastic depends on the design, but it's usually in line with the armscye. Surprisingly, these stays are neither uncomfortable nor unattractive, and I've used them on several loose-fitting designs with excellent results.

WAISTLINE, UNDERBUST, PLEAT AND CROTCH STAYS

A waistline stay generally ensures a better-fitting and more comfortable dress. A stay can also ease the strain at the zipper on close-fitting garments, support the weight of a dress's full or heavy skirt, control the fullness on a blouson bodice and control the hang of dresses without waistline seams, thereby creating a smoother line on the figure. For most daytime dresses, a 1-in. wide grosgrain stay is suitable. Begin by cutting the grosgrain about 7 in. longer than the waistline measurement of the garment. With the garment wrong side up, align the bottom of the grosgrain with the seamline and pin it to the seam allowances. Then, beginning and ending 1½ in. from the garment opening, baste the center of the grosgrain to the seam. After the fitting, sew the grosgrain permanently with short running stitches. If the dress does not have a waistline seam, sew the stay to the vertical seams using short French tacks. Finish the stay ends neatly, as described on p. 130.

UNDERBUST STAY

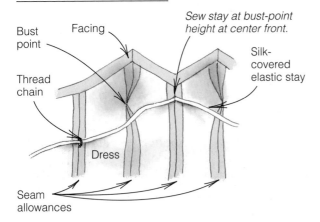

Bust point

Facing

Sew stay at bust-point height at center front.

Silk-covered elastic stay

Thread chain

Dress

Seam allowances

An underbust stay is made of elastic, rather than grosgrain ribbon, so that it will move with the body while holding the bodice securely in place. Sometimes encased in a silk tube, the stay is held in place by a series of thread chains placed on the inside of the bodice at the center front, side seams and back darts.

To sew an underbust stay, begin with narrow elastic 1/4 in. to 3/8 in. wide. Cut the ends the same length as the underbust measurement of the wearer, and finish the elastic ends with a hook and eye. On the inside of the bodice, make the thread chains for the stay at the side seams (see p. 33) just long enough to hold the elastic. For a closer fit at the bustline, sew the elastic to the garment midway between the bust points and locate the thread guides as needed to guide the elastic under the bust.

To finish a waistline or underbust stay on a garment with a side closure, place the hooks on the left front of the stay. For a garment with a center closure, place them on the right back. Before sewing on the hooks, mark the ends of the stay, leaving 2 in. free on the hook end and 4½ in. on the eye end. To finish the hook end, fold the stay under at the marked point (see the drawing at right). On a 1-in. wide stay, sew two hooks in place so that they don't extend beyond the folded end. Then fold the raw edge of the stay back to the wrong side to cover everything but the hooks themselves. Turn under the tip end of the raw edge and fell it in place. Finally, whipstitch the folded edges together.

To finish the eye end, fold the stay under at the 4½-in. marked point and sew the edges together for ½ in. Align the eyes with the hooks and sew them to the stay so they extend 1/8 in. beyond the folded edge. Fold the end back on itself for 1 in. with right sides together to make a 1-in. underlap beyond the marked foldline. At the end of the underlap, fold the stay with wrong sides together. To finish, fold the raw edge under ½ in., fell it in place and whipstitch the folded edges together.

FINISHING STAY ENDS

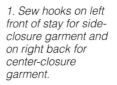

Ribbon folded back on itself covers most of hooks.

2-in. marked foldline

Ribbon

1 in.

Sew folded edges together.

1. Sew hooks on left front of stay for side-closure garment and on right back for center-closure garment.

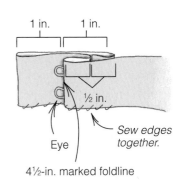

1 in.   1 in.

½ in.

Eye

Sew edges together.

4½-in. marked foldline

2. Sew eyes on other end of stay, folding stay as shown.

This black and white silk gazar gown (at left), designed in 1965 by Balenciaga, has a graceful pleat at each shoulder held in place on the inside of the garment by a pleat stay (shown below). This design relied on the cut, the fabric's characteristics and the wearer's movements for the intended effect: When the wearer walked, the raised front hem allowed the skirt to fill with air and billow out to form a cone. (Photo by Irving Solero. The National Museum of Fashion at the Fashion Institute of Technology, New York. Gift of Mrs. Ephraim London.)

A pleat stay makes a pleat hang softly in its intended position without being held by any stitching. Such a stay was used to secure the pleat at the armhole on the Balenciaga gown shown above, a treatment that would obviously work equally well for a daytime design. The inside view of the bodice shown at right shows the simplicity of this clever device, which could also be used on any other pleat stitched down at the top whose underlay has been trimmed.

To make a pleat stay, begin by sewing a ¼-in. tube for each pleat that is ½ in. longer than its finished length (for instructions on how to make a narrow tube, see p. 116). Fold the raw edge under on each end of the strap and pin it in place on the inside of the garment, anchoring one end to the shoulder seam at the neckline and the other end to the armhole facing. You may need to experiment a little with the placement of the end on the armhole facing to get the pleat to drape as you intend it. Once you've established the position of the stay's ends, sew them securely in place.

CROTCH STAY

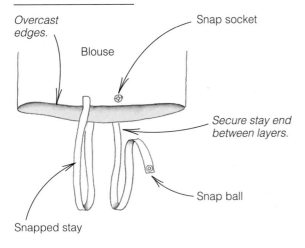

Overcast edges.

Blouse

Snap socket

Secure stay end between layers.

Snap ball

Snapped stay

A crotch stay is a simple, functional means of anchoring a tuck-in blouse to prevent it from riding up. The blouse in the Valentino ensemble on p. 28 has such a stay.

To sew a crotch stay, begin with the blouse on the figure and determine the needed length of the stay by measuring from the back hem of the blouse through the legs to the front hem. Then cut two strips of elastic this length. Insert the elastic strips into narrow silk tubes that are about 2 in. longer than the elastic. Stretch the elastic and sew the ends to the tube ends. Then sew one end of one strap to the inside back hem of the blouse, about 1 in. to the right of the center, and one end of the other strap to the back hem, about 1 in. to the left of center. Sew the ball half of a snap to the other end of each strap and the corresponding snap socket to the front inside hem of the blouse, positioning the sockets similarly to the right and left of center.

SHOULDER PADS

The shoulder pads used in dressmaking are generally softer and thinner than those used in tailoring. They're sometimes shaped irregularly to fit an unusual neckline, and they're always covered with fabric when not concealed by a lining. The pads themselves are made and shaped on a dress form in the same way as tailored shoulder pads (see the sidebar on pp. 180-181).

To cover the pads with backing or lining fabric, begin with a piece of fabric about 12 in. square and mark the true bias at the center. Before removing the pads from the dress form, align the bias with the armscye edge of the pad, and smooth and pin the backing fabric over the pad. Remove the pad from the dress form and wrap the fabric around the pad. Pin a dart in the center of the underside to remove the excess fullness, and then smooth and pin the fabric to the underside. At the edge of the padding, sew the layers together with a running stitch. Trim away the excess, fell the dart flat and overcast the edges of the silk by hand. Mark the front of the pad with a cross stitch, and baste the pad into the garment for fitting. To secure the pad permanently, use a blindstitch to sew it to the shoulder seam and the armscye for about 1 in. on each side of the shoulder point. Sew the corners to the armscye seam with a short French tack.

DRESS SHIELDS

Dress shields fit inside the garment at the underarm and protect the garment from perspiration. Made from the lining or backing fabric, they're about 5 in. wide and 5 in. long, with an inward curve at the top. For greater protection, they can be made double, with mirror-image sides and one of them extending into the sleeve, or they can be interfaced with cotton flannel for extra absorbency.

To make a dress shield, begin by drawing the shape of the shield you want and adding 1/4-in. seam allowances to all the edges. To make a pair of shields, cut four sections from the blouse or lining fabric. Begin with two sections with right sides together, and stitch around them, leaving a 1-in. opening on one side. Trim the seams to 1/8 in. and turn the shield right side out. Close the opening with a slipstitch and press the edges. On the inside of the bodice, snap or baste the shields in place.

In a couture atelier, dress shields are often sewn from silk lining or backing fabric, but on sleeveless designs they're often made from self-fabric so that they will be inconspicuous. On this black silk chiffon blouse by Chanel from the early 1980s, the shields are made from light-colored silk to make them similarly inconspicuous. (Photo by Susan Kahn. Author's collection.)

To make double shields, cut eight sections and join each of the two pairs at the armscye. Then line and finish the shields as above. For sleeveless designs, make the shields from self-fabric and position them so they show about ⅛ in. above the armscye. In this position, the shields will catch perspiration before the garment does.

CHAPTER 8

~

SLEEVES

Not long after "football shoulders" were introduced in the late 1970s, I went to Paris for the first time. One of the highlights of the trip was a fashion show presented by the House of Cardin. The shoulder widths Cardin featured that year on everything from soft silk dresses to wool suits and coats were enormous. I couldn't imagine wearing such an exaggerated look, but I did wear it, and perhaps so did you.

Although there is an endless variety of sleeve styles and silhouettes to choose from, there are only two basic categories of sleeves: set-in sleeves, which are made separately and sewn to the bodice; and cut-on sleeves, like raglan, dolman, batwing and kimono sleeves, which are cut as an integral part of the bodice.

While both sleeve types are used in haute couture, this chapter focuses on the separately cut, set-in sleeve because it's more difficult to fit and sew successfully. Designer methods for sewing cut-on sleeves are quite similar to traditional home-sewing techniques.

Set-in sleeve styles are known by a variety of names that describe their silhouette—bell, bishop, cap, lantern, leg-of-mutton, puff, shirt and tulip. A set-in sleeve can be long or short, close-fitting or full. The sleeve's cap, or top (see the discussion of the sleeve's anatomy at right and on pp. 136-137), can be set smoothly into the armscye (armhole) on the bodice, or it can be gathered, pleated, tucked or draped. The bottom of the sleeve can be finished with a self-hem, facing, binding, cuff or casing. And a separate, set-in sleeve type can be composed of one, two or even three pieces. But whatever the style and cut, the general method for hanging, or fitting, and sewing all set-in sleeves is fundamentally the same.

BASIC ONE-PIECE, FITTED SLEEVE

Frequently called a one-piece sleeve, the basic fitted sleeve is the simplest of all set-in sleeve designs. It follows the contours of the body and is the foundation for all other set-in sleeves. Once you've mastered this basic sleeve, the others will be relatively simple to sew.

Before exploring how to fit and sew a set-in sleeve, let's look at the anatomy of a fitted sleeve. When this sleeve is laid flat (see the drawing on p. 136), the *grainline* runs the length of the arm from the *shoulder point*, or highest point on the sleeve cap, to the back of the wrist. Above the elbow, the grainline is located at the *sleeve center*. Below the elbow, the grainline and sleeve center move apart.

The vertical grainline is used as a guide for marking the horizontal lines of the biceps, cap and elbow. The *biceps line* connects the top of the underarm seam and marks the crossgrain. It defines the base of the sleeve cap and the top of the sleeve body.

The *capline* is located on the crossgrain midway between the biceps line and the shoulder point. The cap is wider and higher in front than in back to accommodate the shoulder joint, which juts forward. The cap's front underarm curve is scooped out more than in back to allow the arm to move forward without binding at the front of the armscye. The cap's back underarm curve is just deep enough to allow the arm to swing forward without ripping the seam. The differences between the front and back of the sleeve cap are easy to see when you fold the sleeve in half.

The *cap height* is affected by the length of the shoulder seam and height of the shoulder pads—two details influenced by changing fashions. But whatever the fashion, the shorter the shoulder seam, the higher the

Designed in the 1960s by American ready-to-wear designer Norman Norell, this suit jacket exemplifies the attention to detail normally associated with haute couture. The plaid of the two-piece sleeves and bodice is meticulously matched, and the welt pockets and buttonholes blend invisibly with the jacket front. (Photo by Cathy Carver. Metropolitan Museum of Art. Gift of Mrs. Neal Sellin, 1969.)

ANATOMY OF BASIC ONE-PIECE SLEEVE

BASIC PARTS

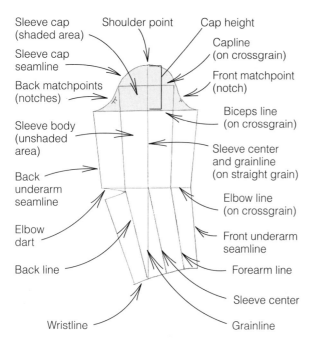

Sleeve cap (shaded area)
Sleeve cap seamline
Back matchpoints (notches)
Sleeve body (unshaded area)
Back underarm seamline
Elbow dart
Back line
Wristline

Shoulder point
Cap height
Capline (on crossgrain)
Front matchpoint (notch)
Biceps line (on crossgrain)
Sleeve center and grainline (on straight grain)
Elbow line (on crossgrain)
Front underarm seamline
Forearm line
Sleeve center
Grainline

Note: on a fitted sleeve, sleeve center and grainline are the same above elbow line but not below it.

PROFILE OF CAP AND ARMSCYE

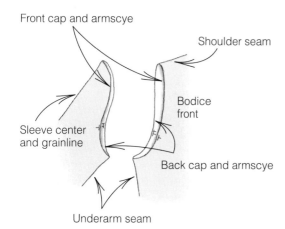

Front cap and armscye
Shoulder seam
Bodice front
Sleeve center and grainline
Back cap and armscye
Underarm seam

Schiaparelli's famous circus jacket, designed in 1938, features closely fitted, one-piece sleeves darted at the cap. Note the careful matching of the horses on the sleeves and bodice. This popular design varied slightly in construction from one jacket to the next, as you can see by comparing the dart placement on this jacket with that in the detail of the jacket on p. 55. (Photograph by Cecil Beaton, courtesy of Sotheby's, London.)

sleeve cap; and the longer the seam, the lower the cap. To accommodate a shoulder pad, the sleeve cap has to have some extra height, and the thicker the pads, the higher the cap needs to be.

The *sleeve cap seamline* outlines the top of the cap. Designed to fit the outward curve of the shoulder, the length of this seamline is 1 in. to 2 in. longer than the armscye of the bodice and must be eased in when the bodice and sleeve are joined. Generally located on the sleeve cap seamline about ¾ in. below the capline, the matchpoints (or notches on commercial patterns), are used to indicate the beginning and end of the ease on the upper part of the sleeve cap. Since they're only guides, however, the matchpoints are frequently changed when the sleeve is fitted.

Marked on the crossgrain, the *elbow line* indicates the level of the elbow. The *elbow dart* shapes the fitted sleeve to follow the curve of the arm and provides fullness to allow for bending the elbow. Sometimes this dart is converted to ease (see pp. 56-57).

In addition to the sleeve center and grainline, the other important vertical lines on the sleeve are the front and back underarm seamlines, the forearm line and the back line. The *forearm line* marks the center of the sleeve front and runs from the front end of the capline to the wrist. The *back line* marks the center of the sleeve back and extends from the other end of the capline through the point of the elbow dart to the wrist. The back line is frequently used to locate sleeve vents, cuff openings, darts and extra length for full sleeves.

CRITERIA FOR A WELL-FITTED SLEEVE

There are some basic elements of a well-fitted sleeve to keep in mind before you hang, or fit, a sleeve. The sleeve should fit the arm and shoulder smoothly and allow the arm to move easily without binding. When the sleeve is correctly balanced, the lengthwise grain will hang straight from the shoulder point and be perpendicular to the floor, and the crossgrain will be parallel to the floor.

When viewed from above the shoulder, the armscye seam at the top of the cap should appear to be a straight line. When viewed from the front or back, it should be appear to be a straight vertical line parallel to the garment center. The vertical line of the armscye seam should, in turn, be visually continued by the vertical lines of the sleeve's silhouette. On both the front and back, the curve of the underarm seam is concealed by a small fold of fabric extending down from the upper bodice.

The ease on the front of the sleeve cap should be concentrated near the top to fit the protruding shoulder joint, and the ease on the back armscye should be distributed evenly. The sleeve should have some ease provided for the elbow because even when the arm is relaxed, the elbow is slightly bent. Finally, the underarm of both the sleeve and garment should hang smoothly when the arm is down, and when silhouetted, the outside edges of the sleeves should be vertical.

The two-piece sleeves on this man-tailored jacket from Yves Saint Laurent's Autumn/Winter 1978 Collection shows how a well-fitted sleeve should look. The armscye seam appears straight and visually extends the vertical line of the sleeve, camouflaging the curve of the underarm. The upper two-thirds of the cap is backed with hair canvas to maintain its shape, and the ease is filled with a sleeve head to keep the cap smooth. (Photo by Susan Kahn. Author's collection.)

PREPARING, HANGING AND FITTING THE SLEEVE

The directions below are for hanging a basic, full-length sleeve on a toile or garment. They can be adapted for all garment sleeves—short set-in sleeves and other one-piece and two-piece set-in sleeves. The advantage of hanging sleeves on the toile is that, unlike the garment fabric, the muslin can be marked quickly and easily with a pencil. If you're sewing with fabrics that must be matched, such as plaids, stripes or large prints, the toile is particularly useful because you can fit the sleeve before planning the placement of the fabric patterns so that they'll match.

To prepare the sleeve, cut it out with 1-in. seam allowances, except at the cap seamline, which should have a 1½-in. allowance. Thread-trace all seamlines, elbow darts and matchpoints. Also mark the grainline and sleeve center, beginning at the shoulder point and continuing the length of the sleeve. Mark the crossgrain at the capline, biceps line and elbow line.

Baste the elbow dart closed. (You may prefer to convert the elbow dart to ease on the garment, as explained on pp. 56-57, but keep the dart intact while you hang the toile sleeve.) Baste the underarm seam. Then fold the hem under and baste it in place.

In a couture house, sleeves—both in muslin and garment fabric—are generally first fitted on the customer's dress form with a padded fabric arm, not on the customer herself. In home sewing, sleeves are usually fitted on the person who will wear the garment. If you're fitting a sleeve for yourself, you'll find it much easier to have someone to help you unless you have a dress form.

To hang the sleeve, you'll need to have already fitted, corrected and rebasted or permanently machine-stitched the bodice and to have basted in the shoulder pads if the design has them. Then try on the garment and slip the sleeve over your arm. The first step is to anchor the sleeve's shoulder point temporarily to the bodice so the grain at the sleeve center hangs perpendicular to the floor. Do this by setting a pin at a right angle to the sleeve's seamline without folding under the sleeve's seam allowance. Don't be concerned at this point if the shoulder point isn't pinned exactly to the garment's shoulder seam.

PINNING SLEEVE TO BODICE

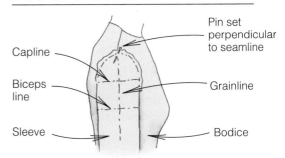

1. Without folding sleeve seam allowance under, pin shoulder points together, setting pin perpendicular to seamline.

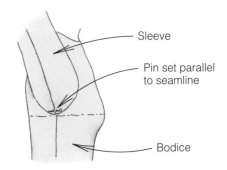

2. Fold under sleeve seam allowance at underarm. Pin sleeve and bodice together, setting pin parallel to seamline.

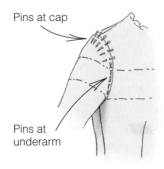

3. Fold under seam allowance on cap. Set pins on cap perpendicular to seamline and pins at underarm parallel to seamline.

With the arm held out, fold the sleeve seam allowance under at the underarm. Match the underarm seamlines of the sleeve and bodice and pin them together. Then, with the arm held down and relaxed, arrange the ends of the marked capline so the grainline is horizontal and the sleeve falls in a gentle vertical column. Pin each end of the capline to the bodice, but don't fold the seam allowance under yet. Since you're hanging the sleeve for a particular figure, don't worry if the matchpoints you transferred from the pattern to the sleeve and bodice don't match. But if the capline bows upward at the sleeve center, the cap is too short. In that case, release the pin at the shoulder point and repin it so that the capline is level and the sleeve is balanced.

Then, beginning at the underarm, fold the sleeve seam allowance under and pin the front of the sleeve to the armscye seamline, setting the pins parallel to it. Stop at the marked capline and repeat the process on the back of the sleeve.

Before pinning the top of the cap, check the grainlines again to be sure the sleeve is balanced. Then remove the pin at the shoulder point and fold under the sleeve seam allowance at the top of the cap. Ease and repin the top of the cap to the bodice, setting the pins perpendicular to the folded edge. The cap probably will not lie flat between the pins because you haven't yet ease-basted and shrunk the edge to control the excess fabric.

Now check the sleeve length. It should end just below the wrist bone when the arm is held down at the side. Bend the arm; the sleeve should be long enough so it doesn't pull away from the wrist. Check the location of the elbow dart; it should point toward the elbow.

Next check the underarm seam. It should end at the wrist at the center of the palm. Swing your arms forward and, bending them at the elbows, place each hand on the opposite shoulder. The bodice back and sleeve cap should be wide enough to allow mobility. Correct and repin any of the above sleeve points, as needed.

When hanging a fabric sleeve, examine the sleeve to determine whether the fabric has enough body to support the sleeve's shape. If the sleeve seems limp, it can be completely backed after you've fitted it, or backed just above the elbow or in part or all of the sleeve cap. The backings I've seen used on couture garments were variously made from silk organza, silk chiffon, polyester organza and traditional interfacing materials. You may need to experiment a little bit to decide on a backing fabric. You want to find one whose weight and hand, when combined with the garment fabric, produces the sleeve silhouette you're after.

If you're working with plaid, striped or patterned fabric that needs to be matched at the seamlines, now's the time to draw the fabric pattern at the bodice shoulder onto the sleeve cap so you can accurately match the patterns when cutting the garment fabric. At the House of Valentino, a fabric scrap with the appropriate pattern is basted onto the muslin toile so the patterns can be easily matched.

After you've checked the fit and considered whether you need a backing, remove the toile or garment and mark the bodice and sleeve carefully before unpinning the sleeve so the fabric sleeve can be basted into the armscye easily. Mark any changes made on the seamlines of the sleeve or bodice. Indicate new matchpoints as needed at the shoulder point and capline, and again midway between the two. If the sleeve's underarm seams don't match those on the bodice, decide which should be repositioned and mark the new location.

Unpin the sleeve, remove all bastings, and smooth and press it, if needed. Using a ruler and French curve, correct any irregular lines to "true" them.

CUTTING AND SHAPING THE SLEEVE

Using the corrected toile sleeve as a guide, cut out and mark the fabric sleeve. Once the sleeve has been fitted and corrected, cut out any backings you're planning to use and baste them to the wrong side of the sleeve. (If you know before you start that the fabric will need a backing, apply the backing to the sleeve before fitting it.) Baste first with diagonal stitches at the center on the lengthwise grain. Then fold the sleeve vertically and pin the thread-traced seamlines to the backing. Baste the layers together on the seamlines.

Baste and stitch the elbow dart. Remove the bastings, slash the dart open and press it. (If the dart was converted to ease, shrink and shape the elbow area, as explained on p. 59.) Then baste and stitch the underarm seam and press it. Finish the lower edge of the sleeve appropriately for the design.

To shape the sleeve cap, place a row of ease basting on the seamline between the matchpoints. Add a row $\frac{1}{8}$ in. above the seamline and another $\frac{1}{8}$ in. below it. Measure the armscye and pull up the ease basting on the cap so that the sleeve seamline equals the corresponding length of the armscye. Arrange the cap, right side up, on a tailor's ham. Cover the section with a

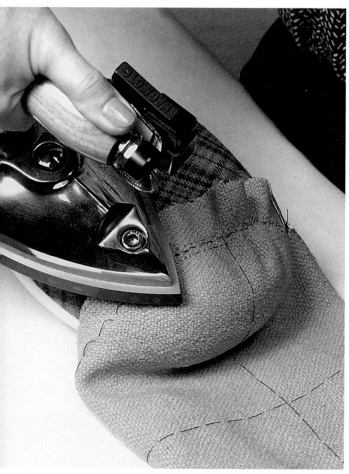

Press the sleeve cap on a tailor's ham to shrink the excess fullness, using a damp pressing cloth (absent in the photo since it would cover the sleeve) and moving the tip of the iron no more than 1 in. past the seam allowance. (Photo by Susan Kahn.)

damp press cloth and shrink out the excess fullness. When shrinking, work from the seam allowance inward, moving the iron no more than 1 in. over the seamline to keep from shrinking out too much fullness and distorting the hang of the sleeve. After shrinking, cover the work with a dry press cloth and press until the cap is dry. To preserve the shape and support the caps, pin the sleeves to a pair of shoulder pads that have been sewn to the ends of a coat hanger or stuff the caps with tissue paper. Set the sleeve aside until you're ready to finish it.

SETTING THE SLEEVE INTO THE ARMSCYE

If you haven't already, complete the bodice and tighten the armscye (see p. 177 and p. 179). Pin the sleeve into the armscye with the right sides together, using the matchpoints established earlier. If you're right-handed, begin with the left sleeve, which will be easier for you to baste; if you're left-handed, begin with the right sleeve.

Many home-sewing instructions advise against putting ease at the top of the sleeve because it's difficult to ease smoothly on the crossgrain. In haute couture, ease is added at the top of the sleeve so the cap will not fit too tightly over the seam allowances. However, since the top of the cap is cut on the crossgrain, not the bias, there will be only a small amount of ease.

Starting at the front matchpoint, baste along the seamline with a short, even basting stitch across the top of the cap to the back matchpoints under the arm, and back to the starting point. Distribute the ease with your thumb between the matchpoints as you baste.

If you're matching plaids, stripes or other fabric patterns, begin with the garment on a dress form so that you can baste with a fell stitch or slipstitch from the right side and be sure to keep the fabric patterns aligned. Then take the garment off the dress form and, working from the wrong side, even-baste the armscye seam a second time to make sure the layers are securely positioned.

To examine the sleeve to be sure it hangs correctly and to evaluate the ease and smoothness of the cap, the garment can be refitted on the figure, put on a dress form or simply held over your arm by putting your fist into the sleeve cap with the jacket shoulder over your forearm. Hold your arm forward so the jacket hangs naturally. The sleeve should hang straight without wrinkling.

Finally, baste the other sleeve into the garment so that the bodice can be fitted on the figure, and baste any shoulder pads in place. Check the fit of the sleeves and make any refinements necessary.

Next examine the sleeve cap. It shouldn't have pleats or gathers at the seamline, and the cap should look smooth and free of dimples. If the basted sleeve does have dimples, try to determine the reason. Dimples frequently occur simply because the sleeve head (see the sidebar on pp. 142-143) hasn't yet been set, which will be done when the sleeve is stitched permanently. If the fabric is tightly woven, however, and the cap was difficult to shrink, you may need to consider alternatives: using a thicker sleeve head, redistributing the ease so there's a small amount of ease—between ¼ in. and ⅜ in.—in the underarm area, or making the entire sleeve narrower by sewing a deeper underarm seam. To do either of the last two, remove the sleeve and rebaste. None of these solutions will significantly affect the hang of the sleeve.

When all else fails, you can increase the seam allowance at the top of the sleeve cap to make the cap fit smoothly. This lowers the sleeve cap and is a particularly effective way to reduce unwanted fullness in a short sleeve, which requires less ease. Although the shortened cap will cause the sleeve to hang at an angle from the shoulder instead of falling vertically, and the crossgrain will not be parallel to the floor, these imperfections will not be very noticeable in a short sleeve. If your sleeve is long, however, these problems will be more obvious and the hang of the sleeve will not be as attractive.

Today most sleeves are set in by machine because the method is less expensive than hand sewing. However, at Huntsman, the most expensive bespoke tailor on London's Saville Row, the tailors prefer setting the sleeve by hand since hand sewing is always easier to control than machine stitching. They use a hand-sewn full backstitch, which is much more elastic than the machine lockstitch. I've also seen fell stitches on designs by Yves Saint Laurent and Schiaparelli, but this stitch is generally considered old-fashioned and, in any case, is not a good choice for the home sewer because it's difficult to sew invisibly. If you want to set the sleeve by hand, choose a full backstitch.

When setting the sleeve by machine, double-baste across the hand-basted capline to prevent the ease from shifting when you stitch. Since the sleeve is securely basted in, you can stitch with either the sleeve or the garment uppermost. Then remove the bastings and press the armscye seam flat, allowing the tip of the iron to lap the seamline only ⅛ in.

At the bottom of the armscye, never press the seam open. It should stand straight up to prevent unwelcome underarm bulk and to allow the sleeves to hang in an

LOWERING A SLEEVE CAP

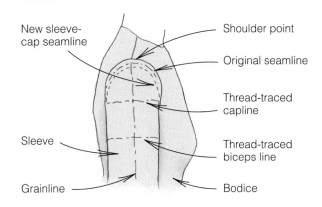

Establish a new sleeve-cap seamline ⅛ in. below shoulder point, tapering to nothing on original seamline.

attractive vertical line. At the top of the cap, you can turn the armscye seam toward the sleeve, creating a small ridge at the end of the shoulder, or, for a smoother line, you can press it open or toward the bodice. When pressing the seam open, clip the bodice seam allowance to the seamline on both the front and back at the capline, which frees the underarm seam to stand up. Then press the seam carefully to avoid introducing unwanted pleats into the garment or sleeve cap.

If you're working with a bulky fabric or want a smoother line at the shoulder, you can balance the bulk on both sides of the seam. You'll find directions for balancing a dart on p. 56, which you can adapt for balancing a seam.

Finally, to avoid a ridge on the sleeve cap, grade the armscye seam so the sleeve seam allowance is about ⅛ in. wider than the bodice seam allowance. (If you're turning the seam allowance toward the bodice, you don't need to grade the allowance.) If the garment is unlined, finish the raw edges with overcasting or a narrow binding (see p. 42). If you need to tighten the armscye more at the back or under the arm, backstitch as described on p. 177 and p. 179. Sew the sleeve heads and shoulder pads into the garment.

Notice the height of the sleeve cap on this detail of an Yves Saint Laurent jacket, shown in full on p. 137. A sleeve head is used to support such a cap so it will remain smooth and firm. (Photo by Susan Kahn. Author's collection.)

Most sleeves need some sort of support to maintain their shape, and couturiers often use sleeve heads and sleeve boosters for this purpose. While both devices generally serve the same function, a sleeve head is used to support a classic, eased sleeve cap, while a sleeve booster supports a full or exaggerated cap. Compared to a sleeve head, a booster is usually wider and fuller and extends farther into the sleeve cap. Both are used with or without shoulder pads but are sewn into the sleeve cap rather than the shoulder area of the garment.

Sleeve heads and boosters are made from a variety of fabrics, from silk organza to hair canvas, depending on how light or stiff a support is needed. They can be made with a single or double roll of fabric and be wide or narrow. A single roll usually just fills out any "dimples" in a sleeve cap, while a double roll produces the effect of a full, well-defined cap. To decide which fabric to use and whether to make a single-layer or double-layer roll, first determine the effect you want to achieve. Then, using the directions below as a guide, experiment with various fabrics and thicknesses until you're happy with the way your sleeve cap looks.

MAKING A SLEEVE HEAD

To make a sleeve head to preserve the shape of a flat, smooth cap, choose a lightweight material like silk organza, blouse-weight silk or muslin, and sew a sleeve head with a single roll. (For a subtle increase in the size of the sleeve head, use muslin, soft wool or hair canvas or wrap the sleeve head fabric around a piece of wadding.) Begin by cutting a bias strip about 8½ in. long and 1½ in. wide. Fold the strip lengthwise so one long edge is ⅛ in. wider than the other and, using a loose diagonal stitch, sew the layers together. Round the corners at the ends, cutting them so they don't curl or show on the right side.

Place the folded edge of the sleeve head on the armscye seamline so the wider side of the sleeve head lies against the sleeve. Adjust the sleeve head so it extends 5 in. into the back of the sleeve. With a blindstitch, sew the folded edge to the seamline stitches.

To support a high sleeve cap that you want to be well defined, choose materials like wadding, cotton batting, hair canvas, soft wool or lambswool. Cut the bias strip 2½ in. wide and 8½ in. long. Make the sleeve head using the directions above. When using wadding or cotton batting, fold it with the fuzzy side out. Tear the cut edges with your fingers to feather them so they will not make a ridge.

Place the sleeve head at the top of the cap, but lap the folded edge ⅛ in. to ¼ in. over the seamline instead of aligning the folded edge with the seamline. Sew through all layers at the seamline with a running stitch, just catching the seamline. Once you turn the armscye seam allowance toward the sleeve, the sleeve head will have a double roll.

MAKING A SLEEVE BOOSTER

For each booster, cut a strip of lightweight silk on the crossgrain, 3 in. wide by 14 in. long, and then cut a bias strip of interfacing 1¼ in. wide by 14 in. long. Baste the interfacing to the wrong side of the silk and fold the silk strip in half lengthwise, with the wrong side out. Stitch a narrow ¼-in. seam at the ends, rounding the corners as you stitch and trim away the excess at the ends. Turn the booster right side out, and gather the unfinished edge ¼ in. from the edge so it's 7½ in. long. Bind the raw gathered edges with chiffon or organza. Attach the bound edge to the armscye seam by hand with a running stitch or blindstitch.

This booster will support the cap on most sleeves. For the cap on a more extended shoulder, make the booster wider and shape it like a football.

MAKING A SLEEVE HEAD

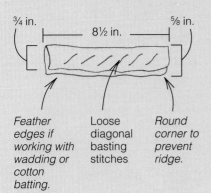

¾ in. 8½ in. ⅝ in.

Feather edges if working with wadding or cotton batting.

Loose diagonal basting stitches

Round corner to prevent ridge.

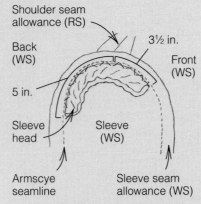

Shoulder seam allowance (RS)

Back (WS)

3½ in.

Front (WS)

5 in.

Sleeve head

Sleeve (WS)

Armscye seamline

Sleeve seam allowance (WS)

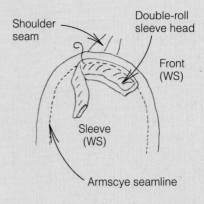

Shoulder seam

Double-roll sleeve head

Front (WS)

Sleeve (WS)

Armscye seamline

1. Cut a rectangle of fabric and fold in two, leaving ⅛ in. of one layer exposed. Baste two layers together.

2. To make a single-roll sleeve head, sew folded edge of head to armscye seamline with blindstitch, positioning sleeve head so it extends 5 in. into back of sleeve.

3. To make a double-roll sleeve head, sew head to armscye seamline about ⅛ in. from folded edge, using a running stitch.

MAKING A SLEEVE BOOSTER

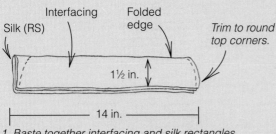

Silk (RS)

Interfacing

Folded edge

Trim to round top corners.

1½ in.

14 in.

1. Baste together interfacing and silk rectangles and fold in half. Trim top corners round and turn inside out.

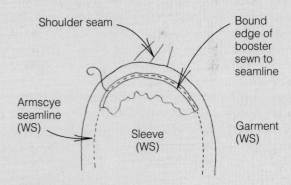

Shoulder seam

Bound edge of booster sewn to seamline

Armscye seamline (WS)

Sleeve (WS)

Garment (WS)

2. Gather edge of booster, reducing it to 7½ in. long. Bind edge and sew edge to wrong side of sleeve seamline with running or blind stitch.

MAKING A
BLOUSE SLEEVE

The basic principles for hanging and setting a one-piece sleeve can be applied to the classic, one-piece blouse or shirt sleeve with a cuff. Unlike the basic one-piece sleeve, the classic sleeve with a cuff does not have an elbow dart. Instead, the lower edge of the sleeve is cut longer at the back to provide enough length for the elbow to bend easily. The length on the sleeve front remains shorter than in back so the sleeve doesn't droop over the hand. At the wrist, the sleeve is pleated, gathered or tapered to fit into the cuff, and a small placket is added to enable the wearer to pull the cuff over the hand.

SHAPING THE SLEEVE PATTERN

On most commercial blouse patterns, the wrist edge of the sleeve has a shallow S-curve, which generally needs to be exaggerated a little to create a sleeve that hangs more attractively. To do this, first pin the underarm seam together and fold the sleeve pattern so the sleeve center and underarm seam are aligned. Then square a line (that is, draw a right-angle line) from the forearm line to the back line, and extend the back line and underarm seamline about 2 in. below the original wrist seamline. Establish the new base of the back line 2 in. below the squared line and connect it with a gentle S-curve to the unchanged base of the forearm line. Use the modified pattern to cut out the sleeves, thread-tracing the seamlines and placket location.

MAKING A TAILORED PLACKET

The tailored placket is particularly attractive on shirts and tailored suit blouses made from lightweight fabrics. The opening is finished with a wide band on the overlap (called a gauntlet by custom shirtmakers) and a narrow binding on the underlap. The band on the overlap duplicates the grain of the sleeve and is generally finished about 1 in. wide and 3½ in. to 4½ in. long. The binding on the underlap is a bias-cut strip, usually finished ¼ in. wide by 1 in. shorter than the band on the overlap. The end of the placket can be finished with a point or squared off, and usually extends about 1 in. beyond the end of the opening. Unlike similar plackets on luxury ready-to-wear, the couture tailored placket is finished by hand without topstitching.

This Yves Saint Laurent blouse from the early 1980s has a tailored placket, turned-back French cuffs and button cufflinks. The cuff covers the blouse/cuff seamline so it can't be seen when worn. Note the way the sleeve echoes the curve of the arm. (Photo by Susan Kahn. Author's collection.)

RESHAPING WRIST EDGE OF BLOUSE SLEEVE

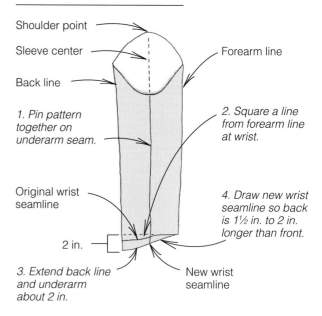

Shoulder point
Sleeve center
Back line
1. Pin pattern together on underarm seam.
Original wrist seamline
2 in.
3. Extend back line and underarm about 2 in.
Forearm line
2. Square a line from forearm line at wrist.
4. Draw new wrist seamline so back is 1½ in. to 2 in. longer than front.
New wrist seamline

To make a 1-in. wide by 4-in. long tailored placket with a point, begin by thread-tracing the opening. Mark the opening's end 3¼ in. from the wrist seamline. Then, using the blouse fabric, cut a band for the overlap on the lengthwise grain, 2¾ in. wide by 6 in. long. For the underlap, cut a bias strip from the blouse fabric 1¼ in. wide by 5 in. long. With right sides together, align the edge of the bias strip with the thread-traced opening on the side of the underlap (the side nearer the underarm seam). Baste the bias strip ¼ in. from the thread-traced opening on the seam allowance, starting about ½ in. below the wrist seamline and stopping at the other end of the opening. Then, with right sides together, match the raw edge of the band to the other side of the thread-traced opening and baste it ¼ in. from the opening, starting and stopping at the same points as for the bias strip.

Machine-stitch the basted lines and tie the threads securely at the ends. Cut the slit open and clip straight or diagonally to the ends of the stitched lines. Press both the strip and band toward the opening and then wrap the bias strip around the edge of the opening to the wrong side. Finish the bias strip on the underlap so that it's no more than ¼ in. wide, using the directions for binding an edge on pp. 75-79.

To finish the band on the overlap, baste a guide on the band 1 in. from the seamline. Fold the band with wrong sides together on the basted line so the band wraps around the raw edge of the opening and press it lightly. Turn the sleeve wrong side up, then turn under the long raw edge and pin it to the seamline. Fell the edge in place and press it.

To finish the point, begin with the sleeve right side up. Mark the point 4 in. from the wrist seamline, then thread-trace the sides of the point so they intersect at a right angle. Fold and baste the end of the band to make the point, trimming as needed so the raw edges will not show. Check to be sure the end of the underlap binding is on top of the sleeve so it will be enclosed between the band and sleeve, trim the end to ¼ in. and cover it with the band. Baste the point to the sleeve and fell around the point and about ¼ in. down the sides.

To prepare the sleeve for setting a cuff, stitch the underarm seam with right sides together and press it. Then set the sleeve aside until you're ready to set the cuff.

MAKING AND SETTING THE CUFF

Cuff styles range from very narrow straight bands to wide shaped cuffs, but simple barrel and French cuffs (with and without turn-backs) are the usual choice for a classic shirt or blouse. Hand-worked and bound buttonholes, as well as button loops, are used to fasten barrel cuffs, while hand-worked buttonholes are generally preferred for French cuffs. The pattern for the barrel cuff included with most commercial patterns can be easily adapted to make a French cuff without a turn-back by replacing the button with a second buttonhole.

MAKING A CUFF

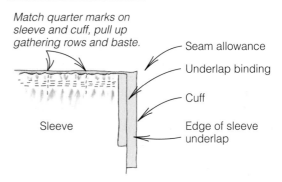

Match quarter marks on sleeve and cuff, pull up gathering rows and baste.

Seam allowance
Underlap binding
Cuff
Edge of sleeve underlap
Sleeve

1. Baste cuff to sleeve, with right sides together.

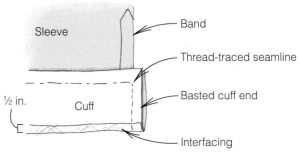

Sleeve
Band
Thread-traced seamline
Basted cuff end
½ in.
Cuff
Interfacing

2. Baste both ends of cuff.

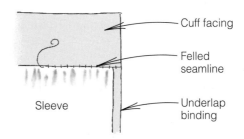

Cuff facing
Felled seamline
Sleeve
Underlap binding

3. Fell cuff facing to cuff/sleeve seamline.

Cut out the cuffs, thread-trace the seamlines and fold-line and mark the button and buttonhole locations. Choose a lightweight interfacing such as silk organza, fine cotton batiste or silk-weight interfacing. Cut the interfacing so it extends into the seam allowances and lap the folded cuff edge at the wrist by ½ in. With the wrong side of the cuff up, baste or fuse the interfacing to the upper-cuff section, which will join the sleeve.

To set a barrel cuff, divide the wrist edge of the cuff (excluding the seam allowances) into quarters so that you can distribute the fullness evenly on the blouse sleeve when sewing on the cuff. Mark the sleeve center, then align it with the underarm seam so you can mark the wrist seamline at the front and back folds. Then put in two or three rows of gathers along the wrist seamline. With the right sides together, pin the cuff to the sleeve with the matchpoints aligned. Pull up and adjust the gathers on the cuff, and baste the cuff and sleeve together. Machine-stitch the seam and trim the seam allowances to ½ in. Remove the bastings and press the seam toward the cuff. (If you want to redistribute the fullness so there is more on the back of the sleeve, do so before basting the cuff and sleeve together.)

On a French cuff, the fastened cuff will be more attractive when worn if you hide the bound edge of the underlap by folding it under ¾ in. before dividing the wrist edge into quarters and gathering. Then join the sleeve to the cuff as you would a barrel cuff.

To sew the ends of the cuff, fold the cuff on the foldline with right sides together, and baste the ends without catching the blouse sleeve. Baste the ends on the other cuff, and then turn both cuffs right-side out to be sure their shapes and ends are identical. When you're satisfied the cuffs are the same, turn them wrong side out again and machine-stitch their ends. Remove the bastings, press the seams open, and trim them to ¼ in. Sew the corners of the seam allowance to the interfacing with a catchstitch, and turn the cuffs right side out again and press them lightly.

To finish the cuffs, fold under the remaining raw edge on the inner wrist and pin it to the seamline. Fell or slip-stitch it permanently. Remove the bastings and press.

MAKING A TAILORED SLEEVE

The basic principles for hanging and setting the basic one-piece sleeve can also be applied to the tailored sleeve. Generally used for coats, suits and tailored dresses, the tailored sleeve differs in several ways from a one-piece sleeve. First, it's cut with two or three pieces rather than one. It may also have a higher cap and has fullness for the elbow built into the seam. It may have a vent at the wrist, and it's usually lined. The sleeves on both the Yves Saint Laurent jacket shown in detail below and in full on p. 137, and the Norell jacket on p. 134 are excellent examples of tailored sleeves.

A tailored sleeve has at least two sections—an upper sleeve (the one here with buttons) and a narrower under sleeve. (Sometimes a tailored sleeve might have a third section inserted between the other two for additional shaping.) The sleeves on this Yves Saint Laurent jacket, shown in full on p. 137, also have short vents finished with blind buttonholes. (Photo by Susan Kahn. Author's collection.)

TWO-PIECE SLEEVE (SHOWN THREAD-TRACED)

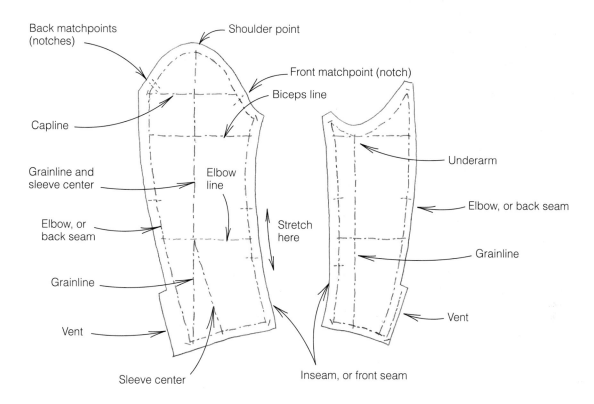

Back matchpoints (notches)

Shoulder point

Front matchpoint (notch)

Biceps line

Capline

Grainline and sleeve center

Elbow line

Underarm

Elbow, or back seam

Elbow, or back seam

Stretch here

Grainline

Grainline

Vent

Vent

Sleeve center

Inseam, or front seam

The tailored sleeve is most often composed of two sections—an upper sleeve and a narrower under sleeve. The elbow, or back, seam is located on the back of the sleeve, approximately midway between the sleeve center and underarm; and the inseam, or front, seam is located on the underside of the sleeve front about ¾ in. from the center of the front.

The tailored sleeve is basted and hung in the same way as the one-piece sleeve. If you make a toile, use the muslin as a pattern for cutting out the fabric and the lining. The sleeve lining should have a 1-in. seam allowance at the cap and a 1¼-in. hem allowance at the bottom.

SHAPING AND LINING THE SLEEVE

Before assembling the sleeve, you must shape the upper sleeve so the front of the sleeve will curve to the shape of the arm instead of wrinkling unattractively. To do this, the shorter edge of the upper sleeve is stretched to fit the longer edge of the under sleeve.

To shape the sleeve, begin with the upper sleeve section of both sleeves, laying them one on top of the other with right sides together. You'll be stretching both sleeve sections at the same time to be sure they're shaped identically. Lay them on the pressing table with the front edge away from you. Using a moistened dauber when working on wool and a moistened press cloth for silks or other fabrics, dampen the curved edge of the sections at the elbow. Place the iron at the wrist end of the seam, pressing from the edge as you stretch it with one hand. Turn the sections over together and repeat the process with the other section on top. To determine when you've stretched the edge enough, make a vertical fold ¾ in. from the seamline. The folded edge should curve nicely from top to bottom without wrinkling at the center (see the photo on p. 148).

Baste the sleeves together, then baste them to the garment for the fitting. After the fitting, take out the bastings, lay the sleeve flat and make any corrections necessary. Then permanently stitch the front seam. Press the seam flat, stretching the seam allowances as you

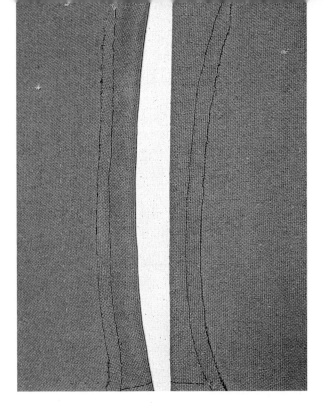

press them open. Fold the sleeve in half vertically and mark the foldline with basting, which will serve as a guide for the next pressing.

With the sleeve wrong side up, smooth it flat on one side of the basted line, then press, stopping at the basting. Repeat the process for the other half of the sleeve. Machine-stitch and press the elbow seam, interface the sleeve hem, hem the sleeve and finish the vent, if the garment has one. Then remove the bastings. If the sleeve has a vent, baste it closed.

In tailoring, the sleeves are generally lined before they're sewn to the garment. This is because tailored sleeve vents are complex to sew and should be hemmed and lined before the sleeve is set. In dressmaking, by contrast, if the garment has a lining, it's often not sewn into the body or sleeve until the garment is almost complete.

To sew the sleeve lining, stitch the vertical seams on the lining so that the seam allowances are slightly narrower than on the sleeve seams. This will make the lining a little larger than the sleeve, which is important since the lining material, often a firmly woven silk, has less give than the shell fabric, which is usually wool on a tailored jacket. Press the seam open.

To sew the lining into the sleeve, begin with both the sleeve and lining wrong side out. Lay the sleeve on the table with the under sleeve down. Place the lining on top of the sleeve (under sleeve up) so the elbow seams are aligned. Depending on how wide the sleeve-cap seam allowances are on the lining and garment sleeve, the two may not align, but the important alignments are the matchpoints on the elbow and inseam seamlines. Pin the seam allowances together. With a running stitch, sew the lining and sleeve seams of the under sleeves together, sewing close to the seamline and beginning and ending about 4 in. from each end of the seam, as shown in the drawing on the facing page. Keep the stitches loose so the lining will not distort the sleeve when the garment is worn. Join the front lining and sleeve seams with two or three stitches about 6 in. above the hem. Turn the sleeve and lining right side out, and arrange the lining inside the sleeve.

To anchor the lining temporarily to the sleeve, baste around the sleeve using large diagonal basting stitches about 5 in. from the wrist and just below the cap. At the wrist, trim the lining hem so it's ½ in. longer than the finished length of the sleeve. Turn the sleeve wrong side out. Fold the lining under so that ½ in. to ¾ in. of the sleeve hem shows. Baste ⅜ in. from the folded edge. Then, holding the fold of the lining out of the way with your thumb, use a blindstitch to sew a single layer of the lining to the hem. Now fold the top of the lining out of the way so you can set the sleeve (see pp. 140-141).

After setting the sleeve, adding the shoulder pads and sleeve heads (see the sidebar on pp. 142-143) and lining the body of the garment, hold the garment right side out and baste around the armscye of the garment close to the seamline. (This holds the lining in place and marks the seamline on the lining.) Bring the cap of the sleeve lining up into the sleeve cap, and smooth and pin the two together about 4 in. from the top. Align and pin the seams of the sleeve and lining. At the underarm, smooth the lining over the armscye seam with-

ATTACHING LINING TO SLEEVE

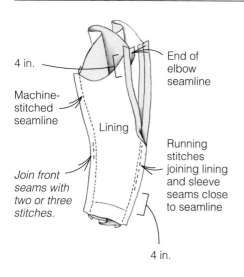

4 in.

End of elbow seamline

Machine-stitched seamline

Lining

Join front seams with two or three stitches.

Running stitches joining lining and sleeve seams close to seamline

4 in.

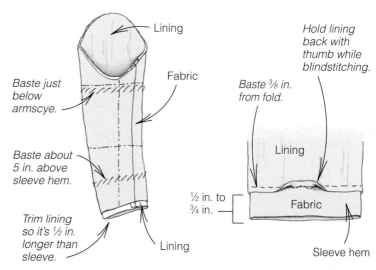

Lining

Baste just below armscye.

Fabric

Baste about 5 in. above sleeve hem.

Trim lining so it's ½ in. longer than sleeve.

Lining

Hold lining back with thumb while blindstitching.

Baste ⅜ in. from fold.

Lining

½ in. to ¾ in.

Fabric

Sleeve hem

1. Lay lining on top of sleeve with wrong sides out, and align sleeve and lining elbow seams with lining extending ¼ in. below sleeve hem. Sew lining and sleeve seam together on elbow seam, beginning 4 in. above wrist and ending 4 in. below armscye.

2. Turn sleeve right side out and baste it to lining from right side, using large diagonal stitches.

3. Hem lining to sleeve, using a blindstitch.

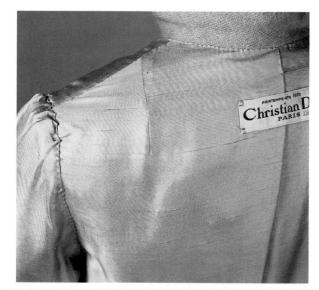

In haute couture, the sleeve lining is always sewn in by hand, as on this Christian Dior coat from 1970. Hand-stitched linings often have excess fullness that cannot be eased in as smoothly as with machine stitching. (Photo by Susan Kahn. Author's collection.)

out flattening the seam allowances. Fold the raw edge of the lining under and pin the folded edge to the seamline. Trim the lining as needed to remove any excess at the underarm.

At the top of the cap, smooth the lining in place. Trim away any excess lining, adjust the fullness and pin the lining to the armscye seam. Baste around the armscye about ⅛ in. from the folded edge of the lining and fell the lining permanently. The fold at the seamline should be neat, but it will not be as smooth as a machine-stitched lining on ready-made designs. Remove the bastings.

CHAPTER 9

~

POCKETS

Pockets can be decorative as well as functional, and they adorn a variety of couture garments from Yves Saint Laurent's handsomely tailored jackets to Christian Lacroix's whimsical evening dresses. During the first half of this century, when she was one of the reigning influences on the couture industry, Coco Chanel applied pockets lavishly to all types of garments from sportswear to formal wear. According to legend, she designed pockets to be used, rather than just to decorate a garment (most of the pockets on menswear, by contrast, have always been designed for real use). Many photographs of *la grande Mademoiselle,* as Chanel was frequently called, show her with her hands hidden inside the pockets of her jacket, while other pictures show her in garments whose pockets sag badly from use.

In contrast to Chanel's simple pocket designs, those of her contemporary, Elsa Schiaparelli, featured unusual shapes, like the pocket on the 1938 jacket shown on the facing page, with fanciful embellishments of beads, embroidery and even metal springs. And designer Christian Dior sometimes used pockets to add roundness to the hips, which in turn make the waistline look smaller.

Whatever their shape or design, pockets fall into two basic categories: patch pockets and set-in pockets. The patch pocket is a "pocket bag" sewn to the outside of the garment, while the set-in pocket is a pocket bag sewn into a seam opening or slash, which rests unseen inside the garment. These two basic types of pockets have numerous variations.

Since the scope of this book permits only a selection of the many techniques used in couture sewing, I've chosen to look at the pockets most used by couturiers that are made with techniques different from those generally used in home sewing and in ready-to-wear construction. In many instances, these couture techniques can be applied to other pocket styles and even to other design elements. For example, the directions for patch pockets and flaps can also be applied to belts and tabs, and the instructions for the bound pocket can be adapted for zipper openings and bound plackets.

PATCH POCKETS

Patch pockets are generally used on tailored dresses, suits, sportswear and casual garments, but a few designers such as Chanel, Givenchy, Schiaparelli and Lacroix have even applied them to after-five dresses and dinner suits. In a recent collection, Karl Lagerfeld, the current couturier at Chanel, even placed beaded patch pockets on the organza bodice of a formal evening gown.

Unlike pockets on ready-to-wear garments, patch pockets on couture designs are always applied by hand. In fact, a hand-applied patch pocket is one of the identifying characteristics of a couture garment, even though many such pockets are first topstitched to look as if they've been applied by machine.

Patch pockets usually match the pattern and grain of the fabric section they cover, and they generally consist of three layers: the pocket itself, the interfacing and the lining, which usually matches the garment lining. When the pocket is made of transparent or open-weave fabrics, it may also be backed to hide the construction details or to match other sections of the garment, or it may be cut with a self-fabric lining and with an interfacing. Before the pocket is sewn, its location is marked on the garment with thread tracing.

Patch pockets can be made before or after the first fitting. If the pocket shape and size is established before the fitting, the pockets are usually finished and basted in place for the fitting. If the pocket's shape, size or location is in question and to be determined at the fitting, or if the pocket and garment are patterned and require matching, a temporary pocket shape is cut from a fabric scrap and basted onto the garment for the fitting.

Designed by Elsa Schiaparelli in 1938, this jacket features pockets whose shape suggests spilled liquid. Hand-sewn to the garment, the pockets are lined to the edge but not interfaced, and the jacket front's darts consequently show through. The molded-plastic locust buttons are typical Schiaparelli witticisms. (Photo by Susan Kahn. Metropolitan Museum of Art. Gift of Mrs. J.R. Keagy, 1974.)

MAKING A PATCH POCKET

The following directions are for an interfaced patch pocket with a separate lining. As you'll see, these directions can be adapted for a pocket with a backing or for a pocket with a flap.

Cut out a muslin pocket pattern the size and shape of the finished pocket, but do not add seam or hem allowances. If the fabric has a design that must be matched, cut a pattern for each pocket so that the design can be marked on the pattern.

To match the fabric pattern or grain of the garment, complete any seams on the garment body that may affect the pocket. Then, working on the right side of the garment, place the pocket pattern on the thread tracing that marks the pocket's location. Draw the continuation of the grain or the color bars of the fabric pattern onto the muslin pocket. To cut the actual pocket, match the muslin's drawn pattern or grain to that on a piece of the garment fabric and pin the pattern in place. Chalk around the pattern and cut the pocket, adding ½-in. seam allowances and a 1¼-in. hem allowance at the pocket opening. Since the finished edges of the pocket will be thread-traced, the seam and hem widths don't need to be exact. Thread-trace the foldline of the hem and all of the seamlines. If there are two matching pockets, repeat the procedure for the other pocket.

Interfacing the pocket will help it hold its shape. The interfacing material for a pocket is often crisper than interfacing used in other parts of the garment, and its weight should, of course, be appropriate for the weight and drape of the garment fabric. Muslin, linen, hair canvas and crisp lining fabrics are all suitable for interfacing, as are knit and weft fusibles when an especially crisp finish is preferred. The interfacing can be cut on the straight grain or on the bias.

The dimensions of the interfacing will be determined by the type of interfacing you use and the look you want. Cutting the interfacing the finished size of the pocket produces crisp edges, while cutting it to extend past the seamline yields softer, more rounded edges. However, a few woven interfacings, particularly hair canvas, should not extend into the seam allowance because the edges will be too bulky. These interfacings can extend into the pocket hem by ½ in. to 1 in. to help the opening hold its shape and give it a slightly rounded edge instead of a hard crease. Fusible interfac-

INTERFACING THE POCKET

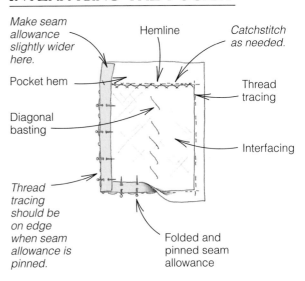

Make seam allowance slightly wider here.

Hemline

Catchstitch as needed.

Pocket hem

Thread tracing

Diagonal basting

Interfacing

Thread tracing should be on edge when seam allowance is pinned.

Folded and pinned seam allowance

ings can be cut to the finished size of the pocket or extend into the seam and/or hem allowance, with similar effects to those mentioned for woven interfacings.

The following directions are for a finished pocket with crisp edges and a tailored effect. Therefore, use hair canvas as the interfacing and cut it to the size of the finished pocket. Place the interfacing on the wrong side of the pocket with the top of the interfacing just below the pocket's hemline. Using a diagonal basting stitch, baste the centers of the pocket and interfacing together. To check the size of the interfacing, fold and pin the pocket's hem and seam allowances over the edges of the interfacing. The thread tracings on the pocket should be seen only on the very edges of the pocket and be invisible from the pocket's right side. If the thread tracings are visible from the right side, unpin the hem and seam allowances and trim the edges of the interfacing. If the pocket isn't going to be topstitched, catchstitch all edges of the interfacing to the wrong side of the pocket. If it will be topstitched, baste the guideline for the topstitching ¼ in. to ⅜ in. from the finished edge.

To finish the pocket edges, fold and pin the pocket seam allowances at the sides and bottom to the interfaced side. To prevent the hem allowance from showing at the sides of the pocket when it's folded back, the seam allowance should be slightly wider in the opening's hem area than elsewhere on the pocket.

FINISHING POCKET EDGES

ROUNDED-CORNER POCKET

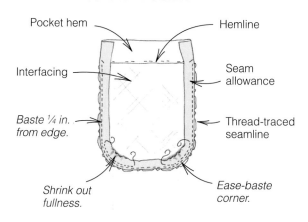

Pocket hem

Hemline

Interfacing

Seam allowance

Baste ¼ in. from edge.

Thread-traced seamline

Shrink out fullness.

Ease-baste corner.

SQUARE-CORNER POCKET

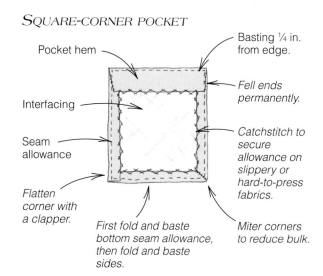

Pocket hem

Basting ¼ in. from edge.

Interfacing

Fell ends permanently.

Seam allowance

Catchstitch to secure allowance on slippery or hard-to-press fabrics.

Flatten corner with a clapper.

First fold and baste bottom seam allowance, then fold and baste sides.

Miter corners to reduce bulk.

If the pocket has rounded corners, ease-baste the seam allowance at the corners about ¼ in. from the edge of the pocket as shown in the drawing above. Hold the pocket in your hands with the interfacing side up so it's slightly cupped and use a short basting stitch to baste ¼ in. from the edge. Pull up the thread so the seam allowance fits smoothly against the pocket, and shrink out the excess fullness with an iron (see p. 59). To avoid shrinking the pocket itself, place a piece of brown paper between the seam allowance and the interfacing.

If the pocket has square corners, fold the bottom seam allowance in place first. Baste ¼ in. from the seamline and press. Then fold and baste the side seam allowances. Trim the excess bulk at the corners and press the edges. When working with bulky fabrics, spank the pocket corners with a clapper to flatten them. On the Dior coat pocket shown on p. 154, the corners were finished very neatly with a raw-edge miter. To do this, trim away the excess bulk, butt the raw edges together, flatten them with a clapper, and baste. Then secure the edges with a small diagonal stitch.

Complete the pocket by folding the hem to the wrong side and trimming the seam allowances at the corners as needed to reduce the bulk. Fell the ends to secure them permanently. Baste ¼ in. below the pocket opening and press. If the fabric is slippery or doesn't press well, sew the raw edges of the pocket to the interfacing with a catchstitch. If the design has topstitching, topstitch around the pocket on the basted line.

When making a pair of pockets, compare them before proceeding further to be sure they're identical. If the person for whom the garment is intended has an asymmetrical figure and one hip larger than the other, the pocket for the larger side can be made slightly larger (up to ¼ in.); but when worn, the difference between the two pockets should be imperceptible.

To line the pocket, cut a rectangle on the same grain as the pocket and at least ¼ in. larger on all sides. At the top of the lining, fold it under about 1 in. and press. Then, with the wrong sides together, place the lining on the pocket so the folded edge is about ¾ in. below the top of the pocket. Match the centers and baste them together with a diagonal basting stitch. Fold the remaining raw edges of the lining under so they're ⅛ in. to ¼ in. from the pocket edges. Trim the lining as needed to remove excess bulk. Pin and then baste the lining to the pocket. Press lightly and fell the lining in place. Remove all bastings and press more thoroughly, using a damp pressing cloth. This is the last opportunity to press the pocket before it is applied to the garment.

If you want to add a flap to your patch pocket, you can make one using the directions above for a patch pocket. But, instead of sewing the sides and bottom of the patch to the garment, sew the top of it to the garment. If you want to add a flap to a bound pocket, you can easily adapt these same directions.

Both the patch pockets and flaps on this Dior coat, designed by Marc Bohan in 1972, were topstitched before they were lined. (Photo by Susan Kahn. Author's collection.)

DIOR FLAP

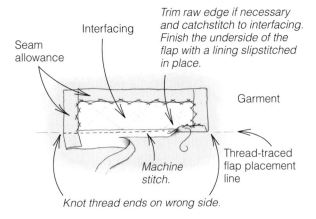

Seam allowance

Interfacing

Trim raw edge if necessary and catchstitch to interfacing. Finish the underside of the flap with a lining slipstitched in place.

Garment

Machine stitch.

Thread-traced flap placement line

Knot thread ends on wrong side.

APPLYING THE POCKET TO THE GARMENT

Before applying the pocket to the garment, decide whether the garment should be stayed, that is, stabilized with interfacing at the pocket location. If the pocket is simply decorative or if the entire front is backed with interfacing, a stay is unnecessary. But if the pocket is designed for occasional use and the front is not entirely interfaced, consider staying the opening.

To do this, cut a stay from interfacing on the straight grain about 2 in. wide and long enough so the ends of the stay can be sewn to the interfacing at the front opening and to a dart or seam at the side. (For more in-

formation on stays, see pp. 49-50.) With the garment section wrong side up, baste the stay over the thread-traced opening. When you sew the pocket, you'll machine-stitch through the stay to secure it.

The finished pocket is usually basted on the garment before the first fitting. After all the fitting corrections have been made, the pocket is permanently sewn in place.

Pockets should be applied to fit the garment smoothly, but not tightly. To apply the pocket, place the garment section on a pressing cushion that simulates the curve of the body where the pocket will sit—for example, on the long side curve of a tailor's ham if the pocket is a hip pocket. Pin the pocket in place on the garment section and baste it with a large "X" to hold it. Baste again an even ¼ in. from the edges. Examine the pocket to make sure it's not too tight. If it doesn't fit the garment smoothly, which may cause it to have ripples around the pocket—or if it just looks too tight—rebaste the pocket in place.

With the garment section wrong side up, and using short running stitches or stronger diagonal stitches if the pocket will get a lot of use, permanently stitch the pocket to the garment. Use the basting as a guide to stitch ⅛ in. from the pocket's edge, and be careful not to sew through the seam allowance to the face of the pocket. For extra strength, sew two rows around the pocket. At the top of the pocket opening, sew several cross stitches at each side for reinforcement. Remove the bastings and press lightly using a pressing cloth.

SET-IN POCKETS

There are two types of set-in pockets: the in-seam pocket sewn into a seam, and the slash pocket set into a slash. Unlike the single-layer pocket bag of a patch pocket, the pocket bag of a set-in pocket has two sections that are sewn together—an under pocket, which sets nearest the lining, and an upper pocket.

One particularly attractive—and unusual—in-seam pocket is found on the detail of an evening gown designed in 1987 by Christian Lacroix, shown on the facing page. The opening of each of the gown's two in-seam pockets is outlined with a wide ruffle, which echoes a similar ruffle at the neckline. By contrast, most in-seam pockets are inconspicuous and purely functional.

In 1987, Christian Lacroix designed an evening gown for his friend Hebe Dorsey, which featured this fanciful in-seam pocket with a 2⅛-in. ruffle around the opening. The pocket is understitched by hand, and the ruffle is anchored with six short French tacks. (Photo by Susan Kahn. Metropolitan Museum of Art. Gift of Monika Dorsey in memory of Hebe Dorsey, 1988.)

On both couture and ready-to-wear skirts, an in-seam pocket often hides the skirt opening. However, couture skirts usually have zippers inside the pocket, while even very expensive ready-to-wear garments often do not.

MAKING AN IN-SEAM POCKET WITH A ZIPPER

The directions that follow are for a lined skirt with an in-seam pocket in a side seam and a 7-in. zipper inside the pocket. Begin by measuring and marking the pocket opening 8 in. below the thread tracing at the waistline, as shown in Step 1 in the drawing on p. 156.

Cut out the skirt with a 1½-in. seam allowance on the side seams. Cut a rectangle 10 in. wide by 12 in. long from lining fabric for the pocket bag. Thread-trace the seamlines and baste the skirt together. On the left side, baste in a zipper temporarily for the fitting and fit the skirt. After fitting and making any necessary corrections, permanently stitch the seam below the 8-in. pocket opening and knot the thread ends. Then remove the basting. At the bottom of the opening on the skirt back, clip the seam allowance to the seamline so you can press the seam open below the clip. With the skirt right side up, chalk a line on the front seam allowance 1⅜ in. from the side seam. On the seam allowance of the skirt back, chalk and thread-trace the placement line for the zipper placket 1 in. from the seamline. Mark the bottom of the zipper opening on the zipper placement line 7¼ in. below the thread-traced waistline.

On the wrong side of the skirt front (Step 2), stabilize the pocket opening with a narrow strip of organza (see pp. 49-50 for directions). Fold the seam allowance at the pocket opening to the wrong side and baste ¼ in. from the edge. With right sides together, match and pin the raw edge of one side of the pocket bag to the chalk-marked line on the skirt front seam allowance. Baste the pocket (this is the upper pocket) and skirt front together with a ⅜-in. seam. Stitch the seam and knot the thread ends. Remove the basting and press the seam flat, then press it toward the pocket bag.

Fold under the raw edge on the opposite side of the pocket bag (this is the under pocket) ⅜ in. and baste it. Then turn the skirt wrong side up and fold the bag in half vertically, with the right sides together. Smooth the pocket bag toward the center front and pin and baste the top of the bag to the skirt. Mark the waistline on the pocket bag, using the thread tracing at the skirt waistline as a guide. Mark the bottom of the zipper opening on the folded edge of the under pocket 7¼ in. below the thread-traced waistline.

With the right sides up, align the seamlines of the skirt front and back at the pocket opening, and top-baste them together so you can position the pocket bag. Pin the pocket bag in place (Step 3) so that the right sides of the pocket bag are together and the thread tracings at the waistline and bottom of the zipper opening match on the pocket bag and skirt back. To complete the seam below the zipper opening, slipstitch the pocket to the skirt-back seam allowance from the mark for the bottom of the zipper to the point at which the seam allowance has been clipped (about ¾ in.). Remove the bastings and press the seam open. Knot the thread ends.

INSEAM POCKET WITH ZIPPER

1. POCKET SETUP

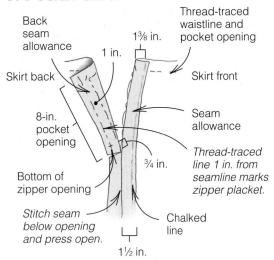

Back seam allowance

Skirt back

1 in.

1⅜ in.

Thread-traced waistline and pocket opening

Skirt front

Seam allowance

8-in. pocket opening

Thread-traced line 1 in. from seamline marks zipper placket.

¾ in.

Bottom of zipper opening

Stitch seam below opening and press open.

Chalked line

1½ in.

2. JOINING SKIRT FRONT AND POCKET BAG

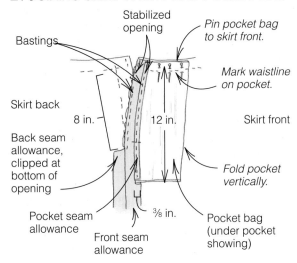

Bastings

Stabilized opening

Pin pocket bag to skirt front.

Mark waistline on pocket.

Skirt back

8 in.

12 in.

Skirt front

Back seam allowance, clipped at bottom of opening

Fold pocket vertically.

Pocket seam allowance

⅜ in.

Front seam allowance

Pocket bag (under pocket showing)

3. JOINING SKIRT BACK AND POCKET BAG

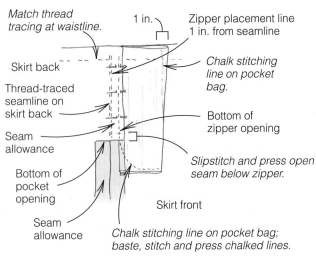

Match thread tracing at waistline.

1 in.

Zipper placement line 1 in. from seamline

Skirt back

Chalk stitching line on pocket bag.

Thread-traced seamline on skirt back

Seam allowance

Bottom of zipper opening

Bottom of pocket opening

Slipstitch and press open seam below zipper.

Skirt front

Seam allowance

Chalk stitching line on pocket bag; baste, stitch and press chalked lines.

4. PREPARING ZIPPER OPENING

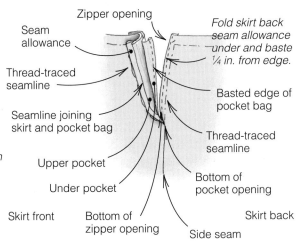

Zipper opening

Seam allowance

Fold skirt back seam allowance under and baste ¼ in. from edge.

Thread-traced seamline

Basted edge of pocket bag

Seamline joining skirt and pocket bag

Thread-traced seamline

Upper pocket

Under pocket

Bottom of pocket opening

Skirt front

Bottom of zipper opening

Side seam

Skirt back

5. ATTACHING SKIRT LINING

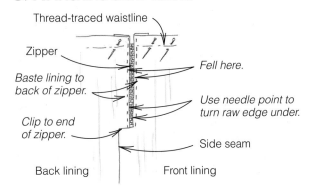

Thread-traced waistline

Zipper

Baste lining to back of zipper.

Fell here.

Use needle point to turn raw edge under.

Clip to end of zipper.

Side seam

Back lining

Front lining

COMPLETED POCKET AND ZIPPER

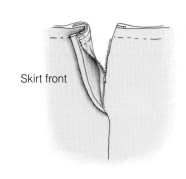

Skirt front

Lay the skirt wrong side up, with the pocket uppermost. Smooth the pocket toward the front and pin the bottom edges of the pocket bag together. To indicate the bottom of the pocket, chalk a line from the bottom of the opening on the skirt to the front edge of the pocket. Also, chalk a line along the front edge of the pocket, beginning at the top about 1 in. from the fold and ending on the fold about 5 in. from the bottom. Begin basting at the bottom of the pocket opening and hold back the skirt seam allowances to avoid sewing through them. Stitch on the basted lines. Knot the thread ends, remove the bastings and press flat. Trim the pocket seams to ¼ in. Overcast the raw edges of the pocket together.

On the skirt back, stabilize the zipper opening, with a narrow strip of organza. Fold the seam allowances to the wrong side and baste ¼ in. from the edge (Step 4). Press the opening. Baste and sew the zipper into the opening by hand (see pp. 94-97).

If you plan to line the skirt, cut the seam allowances on the lining 1½ in. wide—at least on the left side, where the zipper is to be placed—since the placket is 1 in. from the side seam. Pin the lining seam with right sides together, then measure and mark the bottom of the opening 7¼ in. below the waistline. Stitch and press the seam below the zipper, but do not press the seam allowances in the placket area.

Pin the skirt and lining with the wrong sides together so the seamlines at the waist and sides are aligned. Place the skirt, lining side up, on a large pressing stand. Adjust the back lining first. Let out the seam allowance as needed in the placket area so the lining will cover the skirt back and zipper tape. Baste the lining in place.

Mark the end of the zipper on the lining front and clip to the marked point (Step 5). Using the point of your needle, tuck the seam allowance under at the bottom of the zipper and pin it. Repeat this process at the side and then baste. Press the lining lightly and fell it in place.

Remove the skirt from the pressing stand so you can trim the seam allowances of the lining as needed in the zipper area. Trim the seam allowances below the zipper to 1 in. (if you haven't already), remove all bastings and overcast the edges.

Always a smart touch for a tailored jacket, a double-welt pocket can be made with or without a flap. On this linen Yves Saint Laurent design from the 1970s, the pocket flap has been tucked inside the pocket to show the opening. (Photo by Susan Kahn. Author's collection.)

BOUND SLASH POCKET

There are many styles of slashed pockets found in couture garments. I've included directions for two, a bound pocket and an applied-welt pocket, because these styles are the most popular as well as the most difficult to sew.

The bound pocket is a type of double-welt pocket, which has two narrow welts visible on the right side of the garment and a pocket bag hidden between the lining and garment. A bound pocket can be plain, like that on the Balenciaga jacket on p. 60, it can have a flap covering one or both of the welts, or it can have an applied welt covering both welts.

There are many couture methods for making bound pockets, but I particularly like one that uses two fabric strips to bind the edges of the pocket opening. Even though this method is similar to home-sewing methods, the differences are so important that they determine the success or failure of your results. This method can be adapted for making a bound buttonhole (see pp. 86-89) and is suitable for many fabrics, including those with an obvious grain or pattern to be matched. The finished pocket is flat, and the two welts are exactly the same depth. Each welt is interfaced with its own seam allowance and can be cut on the bias and shaped as needed for a curved opening.

Before beginning to sew this pocket, you'll need to thread-trace the pocket opening and the stitching lines on the garment for the first fitting so you can check the pocket placement and size of the opening. After the fitting, remove the bastings and lay the garment flat.

Unless the entire garment section is interfaced, the opening should be stayed on the wrong side to support the weight of the pocket. If the garment is already interfaced in the pocket area and the interfacing is heavy or very crisp, you can cut a rectangle out of the interfacing at the pocket opening and use a lighter-weight material for the stay under the pocket. Cut the stay 2 in. wide and several inches longer than the pocket opening. Baste it in place and thread-trace the pocket opening precisely.

Each pocket requires two welts and an under pocket cut from garment fabric, and an upper pocket cut from lining fabric to complete the pocket bag. Generally, the welts are cut with the lengthwise grain parallel to the opening, but they can also be cut on the crossgrain to match an obvious pattern or on the bias. If the welts are cut on the crossgrain or bias, or if sewn from stretchy or soft materials, they should be interfaced with a very lightweight interfacing. The under pocket, visible under the opening, should duplicate the grain of the garment and the pattern of the fabric.

Cut the welts 1½ in. wide and at least 1 in. longer than the pocket, and the under pocket 1 in. wider than the pocket opening. The under pocket's length varies according to the garment style and pocket's location and size. The pocket bag should not extend below the jacket's finished edge or overlap the hem allowance.

With the right sides together, align and pin the edge of one welt to the thread-traced pocket opening. Repeat for the other welt, butting the edges together. Baste the welts in place on the stitching lines (when matching a fabric pattern, match the pattern at the stitching line, not the pocket opening). If this is one of a pair, baste the welts on the second pocket as well.

Machine-stitch on the basted lines. Then examine the wrong side of your work to be sure the distance between the stitched lines is even, the lines are straight and the proper length, and that paired pockets match. When satisfied with the stitching, pull the thread ends sharply and knot them securely. Then remove the bastings.

Slash the pocket opening, beginning and ending ½ in. from the ends and taking care not to cut the welt strips. Then clip diagonally to the ends of the stitched lines. From the wrong side, press the welt seams open, ironing the interfacing and garment seam allowances away from the opening. If the fabric is very lightweight, press the allowances flat instead.

BOUND POCKET

BOUND POCKET SETUP

1. Sew stay over marked opening on wrong side of garment, and a welt above and below marked opening on right side.

2. Slash opening, beginning and end ½ in. from ends.

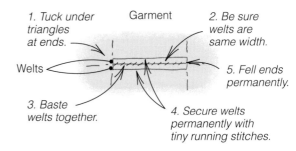

3. Clip ends diagonally to corners of opening.

4. Press welt seams open, then push welts through slash.

6 in.

Stay

Garment

Welt

Welt seamlines

Seam allowance

FINISHING WELTS

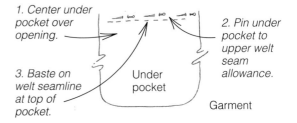

1. Tuck under triangles at ends.

Garment

2. Be sure welts are same width.

Welts

5. Fell ends permanently.

3. Baste welts together.

4. Secure welts permanently with tiny running stitches.

JOINING UNDER POCKET TO UPPER WELT

1. Center under pocket over opening.

2. Pin under pocket to upper welt seam allowance.

3. Baste on welt seamline at top of pocket.

Under pocket

Garment

Turn the garment right side up, push the welt strips through the slash and wrap them around the welt seam allowances. Tuck under the fabric triangles at each end of the opening so they lie between the garment and welts. The welts should lie flat and barely touch. If necessary, trim the edges of the welt seams to make the welts lie flat. Pin each welt from the right side in the well of the seam. Check to be sure the widths between the seamlines and folded edges are even and that both welts are identical. Baste the welts together at the opening with diagonal basting stitches, which makes them easier to sew, and secure the welts in the well of the seam with tiny running stitches.

With the right side up, fold the garment back to expose the triangles. Give them a sharp tug to keep them from showing at the corners. Then, from the right side, fell the ends of the welt strips permanently. Now place the garment section face down on a softly padded surface and press the opening lightly. Remove the bastings and press again.

With the garment section wrong side up, center the under pocket over the opening. If the fabric has a prominent pattern, align the under pocket with the fabric design on the garment section. Pin the under pocket to the upper welt seam allowance, and baste on the original seamline. To stitch the under pocket permanently, first turn the garment right side up and fold back the garment section to expose the basted seam.

Next cut a rectangle of lining fabric for the upper pocket 1 in. wider than the opening and about 1 in. shorter than the under pocket. With right sides together, baste the upper pocket to the lower welt with ¼-in. seams and stitch them permanently. Remove the bastings and press the seam toward the pocket bag.

Pin the two sides of the pocket bag together, keeping the bag flat. Hold the under pocket taut to prevent the pocket from curling toward the outer shell, and baste the bag together. Then machine-stitch it, rounding the corners to prevent them from catching lint. Remove all bastings and press.

Before lining the garment, fasten the stay's front end to the garment interfacing at the front edge. Fasten the other end to a dart or seam allowance, and trim away the excess fabric on the stay. If the bottom of the pocket overlaps the interfacing at the hem, sew them together with a running stitch.

APPLIED-WELT POCKETS

The applied-welt, or stand, pocket is a slash pocket with a single welt attached to the bottom edge of the pocket opening. The welt is usually interfaced and sewn from self-fabric, and it's always lined. The lining can be made from regular lining fabric and cut separately, or it can be made from self-fabric and cut in one piece with the welt itself.

The applied-welt pocket can be set either straight or at an angle. Breast pockets in traditionally tailored jackets are set at a slight angle, even though they appear at first glance to be straight. Hip pockets on dresses and coats are often set at a flattering 45° angle.

This traditional man-tailored jacket from Yves Saint Laurent's 1978 collection has an applied-welt breast pocket and two patch pockets at the hips (see the full view of the jacket on p. 137). The topstitching on the welt is decorative, and the ends are sewn securely with catchstitches. Both the pocket and jacket are lined with silk charmeuse. (Photo by Susan Kahn. Author's collection.)

The following directions are for a single-piece breast welt set at a slight angle, with a folded edge at the top and self-fabric lining. When making a two-piece welt with a separate lining, you can adapt the directions for a patch pocket on p. 152.

If you're using a commercial pattern for the welt, begin by trimming away the seam allowances from the paper pattern so you can mark the seamlines accurately. To make your own pattern for the welt, fold a rectangle of brown paper horizontally and outline the finished shape of the welt on the paper, with the top of the welt positioned on the fold. (Note that for a welt set at an angle, your pattern will need to have an angle between the adjoining welt and welt lining, as it does in the drawing on p. 160. If you make a welt set perfectly straight, the overall pattern will be a simple rectangle.) You don't need to add seam allowances to the welt pattern. You can add them when you cut the welt out of garment fabric.

On the garment section where the pocket is to be placed, thread-trace the stitching lines on the pattern. In order for the pocket opening to be completely hidden behind the welt, you may need to make the top stitching line about ⅜ in. shorter on each end than the bottom stitching line. To decide if you need to shorten the upper stitching line, pin the paper welt pattern on the garment to see if the top stitching line extends beyond the pattern.

APPLIED-WELT POCKET

1. CUTTING OUT ANGLED WELT

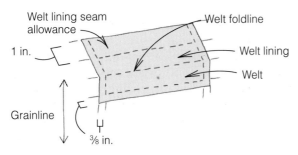

Welt lining seam allowance

1 in.

Welt foldline

Welt lining

Welt

Grainline

⅜ in.

Chalk-mark 1-in. seam allowance above welt lining and ⅜-in. seam allowances on all other sides. Cut out welt on chalked lines.

2. JOINING WELT TO POCKET OPENING

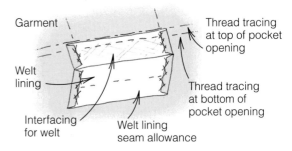

Garment

Welt lining

Interfacing for welt

Thread tracing at top of pocket opening

Thread tracing at bottom of pocket opening

Welt lining seam allowance

Interface welt, then baste and stitch it to lower edge of pocket opening.

3. JOINING UNDER POCKET TO POCKET OPENING

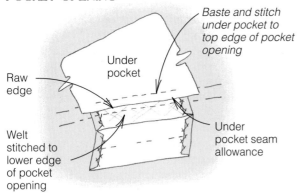

Under pocket

Baste and stitch under pocket to top edge of pocket opening

Raw edge

Welt stitched to lower edge of pocket opening

Under pocket seam allowance

4. FOLDING WELT INTO PLACE

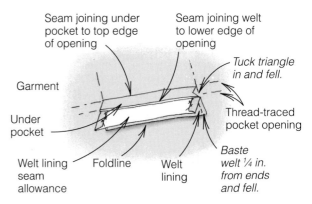

Seam joining under pocket to top edge of opening

Seam joining welt to lower edge of opening

Garment

Under pocket

Welt lining seam allowance

Foldline

Welt lining

Tuck triangle in and fell.

Thread-traced pocket opening

Baste welt ¼ in. from ends and fell.

Slash opening, push under pocket through to wrong side and complete ends of welt.

5. FINISHING WELT

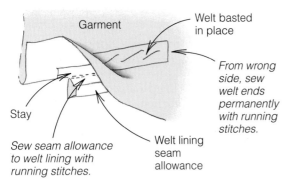

Garment

Welt basted in place

Stay

Welt lining seam allowance

From wrong side, sew welt ends permanently with running stitches.

Sew seam allowance to welt lining with running stitches.

6. SEWING UPPER POCKET TO LOWER EDGE OF OPENING

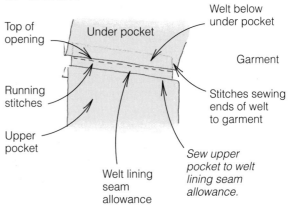

Top of opening

Under pocket

Welt below under pocket

Garment

Running stitches

Upper pocket

Stitches sewing ends of welt to garment

Welt lining seam allowance

Sew upper pocket to welt lining seam allowance.

When you're satisfied with the size of the welt, thread-trace its shape on a piece of garment fabric, matching the fabric grain and any pattern on the garment fabric as needed. Chalk-mark a ⅜-in. seam allowance at the bottom of the welt and at each end, and a 1-in. seam allowance at the top of the welt lining, the edge that will join the pocket bag (Step 1 in the drawing on the facing page). Cut the welt and under pocket from the garment fabric, making the under pocket 1 in. wider than the welt opening and matching the grain and pattern of the garment section.

Thread-trace the fold and seamlines onto the welt and interface the welt (Step 2), using the directions for interfacing a patch pocket on pp. 152-153. Fold and press the seam allowances at each end of the welt to the wrong side. Clip as needed so the seam allowances will lie flat, and catchstitch the seam allowances to the interfacing.

Check the size of the welt against the pattern and re-work the welt if it needs to be larger or smaller. Then fold the welt on the thread-traced foldline, check the size of the welt lining (which should be slightly narrower than the welt itself) and press the folded welt. If you plan to topstitch the finished welt, topstitch only the welt, not the welt lining.

The pocket opening is usually just a slash in the fabric, with the welt stitched to the lower edge of the opening and the under pocket sewn to the upper edge. To make the pocket opening and attach the welt, begin by staying both edges of the opening with a strip of organza (see p. 158). Then, with the garment right side up and with the right sides together, align the welt seamline with the lower stitching line on the garment. Pin the welt in place, with its ends positioned precisely at the ends of the stitching line. Baste on the lower stitching line, catching the welt, but not the welt lining.

With the right sides together, place the under pocket on the garment (Step 3), aligning the under pocket's raw edge with the stitching line at the lower edge of the opening. Pin the under pocket in place and baste on the stitching line.

With the garment right side up, fold the welt lining in place along the foldline (Step 4). Then fold the welt into its finished position, making sure that if the fabric has a pattern, the welt matches the garment and that the ends of the top stitching line are under the welt.

Matching patterns and carefully positioning the ends of the stitching lines are particularly important when the pocket is on a slant.

Open out the welt again and machine-stitch the basted lines above and below the pocket opening to secure the welt and under pocket, knotting the thread ends securely. For added control when stitching the welt, begin and end your machine-stitching one stitch short and then hand-sew the final stitches (be sure to leave ample thread tails at the beginning and ending of the machine stitching).

From the wrong side, press the marked opening flat and then slash the opening to the ends of the stitched lines without cutting into either the welt or under pocket. Push the under pocket to the wrong side and press open the seams of the opening.

Fold the welt horizontally along the foldline with the wrong sides together. Baste the welt ends together ¼ in. from the edge, then fell them permanently. Push the welt lining and the triangles at the ends to the wrong side. From the right side, use a pressing cloth and lightly press the seamline at the bottom of the welt. At each end of the opening, fell the triangles to the under pocket.

With the garment right side up, baste the welt in its finished position with a diagonal stitch (Step 5). Fold back the garment below the pocket to expose the seam allowances at the bottom of the opening. Use a running stitch to sew the welt lining to the seam allowances.

From the wrong side, sew the ends of the welt permanently to the garment with two rows of running stitches at each end, one near the edge and the other about ¼ in. away so that the felled ends of the triangles will be caught in between, strengthening the ends of the pocket opening.

To finish the pocket bag, cut the upper pocket from lining fabric, making it 1 in. wider than the pocket opening. Fold under and pin the end of the upper pocket to the welt lining so it covers the raw edge about ¼ in. (Step 6). If the pocket has a slant, adjust the fold at the top of the pocket section so the pocket will hang perpendicular to the floor, not perpendicular to the opening. Fell the upper pocket to the welt lining. Smooth, pin and baste the edges of the pocket sections together. Then machine-stitch around the pocket bag, remove all bastings and press.

CHAPTER 10

~

JACKETS AND COATS

The modern tailored jacket for women is the product of a long history of tailoring, which began during the Middle Ages. Initially, tailored clothing was made just for gentlemen. It was not until sometime in the 17th century that women began wearing tailored coats to ride or join the hunt.

By the middle of the 19th century, several tailors in London and Paris had ladies' departments. English tailor John Redfern is generally credited with creating the "tailor-made"—a lady's suit made by a tailor and composed of a tailored jacket and skirt.

Located in Cowes, a seaport on the Isle of Wight, Redfern's shop specialized in mourning suits. When Cowes became the center of yachting in the early 1870s, the enterprising Redfern adapted his designs for yachting outfits. The success of his flourishing business was assured when actress Lillie Langtry wore one of his trainless tailor-mades to the Cowes Regatta in 1879. The tailor-made quickly became a staple in the wardrobes of leisure-class women.

The success of tailor-mades continued for several decades. Dressmakers modified their techniques to compete with tailors, and a few tailors made only ladies' garments. Although today only a few tailors on London's famous Saville Row serve women clients, English tailoring has had a permanent impact on women's wardrobes in the Western world, and many couturiers in London, Paris and Rome create beautiful tailored designs each season.

At most couture houses, jackets are made in the tailoring workroom, but some houses have a second tailoring workroom that specializes in softer, more feminine designs (see pp. 12-13 for a discussion of how a couture house's workrooms are set up). Haute couture suits begin in price at $2,000 in London and at three times that amount in Paris. However, a suit from a well-known house costs at least $15,000. Although these figures may sound astronomical, they're understandable when you consider the time invested in an average suit: from 100 to 130 hours to complete the jacket and an additional 25 to 40 hours for the skirt.

TAILORING BASICS

The jacket is by far the most common garment produced in couture tailoring workrooms. Coats, on the other hand, account for only a very small percentage of the orders at any given house. Many of the techniques described here for tailoring jackets can also be applied to coats and tailored dresses. This small sampling of couture tailoring techniques is intended to supplement, not replace, standard pattern guides.

When buying your garment fabric, purchase an additional ½ yd. to allow for the wide seam allowances needed in couture construction and check to be sure the fabric is "needle-ready," or preshrunk. If not, you can shrink it at home using the London shrinking method described in many sewing books or you can ask your dry cleaner to shrink it for you.

Many couture jackets are interfaced and completely backed so they'll be smooth and wrinkle-free. Interfacings and backings are, in fact, the skeletal framework of the jacket that controls its shape so inconspicuously that only the tailor knows they're there (see p. 53, p. 120 and p. 122 for basic information on selecting and working with interfacings and backings).

When choosing an interfacing, consider the garment fabric's weight, fiber content, color and hand (that is, whether it's soft or crisp) in relation to the garment's design and the effect you're after—for example, an exaggerated silhouette or one that softly skims the body. Fabrics like hair canvas, hymo, collar linen, Utica linen, French canvas, handkerchief and dress linen, organdy, muslin and fine cotton are all good choices for interfacing and backing a tailored jacket. By contrast, fusible materials are rarely used because they're not as

---

This classic ensemble from Yves Saint Laurent's 1982-83 Fall/Winter Collection features a plaid jacket in the Prince of Wales pattern and a houndstooth-check skirt. On the lapels, the check is positioned so the grain is parallel to the edge of the surplice-cut jacket, even though the edge of the jacket is cut on the bias. (Photo by Susan Kahn. Author's collection.)

supple as woven backings and interfacings, and when used, they're frequently applied to another support material rather than to the garment fabric itself.

For the collar on a wool jacket to be crisp and have a sharp roll, choose collar linen as an interfacing. For a collar with a soft roll, choose hair canvas. For a linen or silk collar, Utica and handkerchief linens, cotton and even self-fabric are good choices. And for interfacing the body of the garment, hair canvas or hymo with a high wool and goat's hair content is always the tailor's first choice when sewing wool because it's more malleable than other interfacings. When sewing linen or cotton, consider either self-fabric or a plain-weave linen interfacing for the body.

Tailors often use a variety of interfacings cut on different grains within the same garment because each element of a garment—collar, pocket, lapel and hem—has different requirements. The interfacing for a collar, for example, is generally cut on the bias to produce a nice roll, while the interfacing for a patch pocket is cut on the same grain as the pocket itself (generally the straight grain) to produce a firm pocket that holds its shape.

Backings and interfacings are applied to the wrong side of each garment section before the garment is assembled. Then the two layers are handled as one when most of the seamlines are stitched. All support fabrics should be preshrunk. Soak the fabric in cold water for two hours, hang to air-dry and press it with a steam iron.

As you've seen in previous chapters, constructing a couture garment involves a number of fittings. In the case of a tailored jacket, you'll need one fitting for the muslin toile (in couture this fitting is usually done on the dress form rather than on the figure) and three additional fittings for the garment itself. If you're an experienced tailor, you may be able to compress these last three fittings into two. As we get to each point where a fitting is required, I'll explain what to look for.

MAKING A TOILE AND BASTING THE JACKET

Before a couture jacket body is cut and sewn, a muslin toile is prepared. As we saw in preceding chapters (see p. 37, p. 107 and p. 121), the toile is easy to mark, and it can be ripped and rebasted again and again until it fits well. The time spent perfecting the toile is saved later, and the garment itself maintains its pristine appearance because it doesn't need to be ripped apart or have major alterations made.

Begin the muslin toile by cutting all the pattern sections of your commercial jacket pattern except the top collar, front facings and pockets, and providing 1-in. seam allowances. With a tracing wheel and carbon, mark the toile with all stitching lines, garment centers, waistline, grainlines and cross-chest and cross-back lines (see the sidebar on p. 121 for more information on marking the balance lines). Draw the pockets and buttons on the muslin and baste the toile together. Baste the sleeve seams, but do not baste the sleeves into the armscyes until the body of the jacket is fitted. At the edges of the sleeves and body, turn under and baste all hems and seam allowances and press them lightly. Next baste the undercollar in place, and then make the shoulder pads (see the sidebar on pp. 180-181) and baste them in place.

Now you're ready to try on the toile and evaluate its fit. To do so, pin the center fronts together as they would be when buttoned, and begin by analyzing the relationship of the design to your figure. It should look the same on the right and left sides, even though your body may be asymmetrical. Check the line and proportions of the silhouette. If it isn't becoming, correct it (or start again with a new design).

When checking the fit of the toile, look for the following: The garment should fit smoothly without wrinkles—if you have horizontal wrinkles at the waist, the jacket is probably too narrow for your hips. Check the back shoulder width—if it's too narrow, the jacket will ride up, forming horizontal wrinkles just below the collar; if it's too wide, the back will wrinkle vertically. Examine the roll line of the lapel, and if it gaps, pin out one or more small darts to indicate how much it needs to be held in. Check the button and pocket locations to make sure neither are too low or too high. Check the hemline to be sure it's parallel to the floor and that

CHARACTERISTICS OF A COUTURE JACKET

Creating a couture jacket requires skill that comes with practice, but above all it requires attention to detail. All the jacket's edges should be interfaced to maintain their shape. When well interfaced, these edges are thin and curl slightly toward the body. Even seamlines on edges, like those on the lapel, roll slightly inward so they don't show on the right side of the garment. The garment centers are perpendicular to the floor even when the jacket is unbuttoned. Seams and edges are straight and well pressed, all hand sewing is even and inconspicuous, and any topstitching is straight and even.

Fullness at the back shoulder, back armscye, back neckline, sleeve cap and elbow has been shrunk out so the garment conforms to the body. The armscye seams are reinforced, and the sleeves, which are usually two-piece, hang in vertical cylinders without diagonal ripples. Sleeve heads are inserted into sleeve caps to keep them from "breaking" (collapsing) or dimpling.

Lapels and collars are interfaced and hand padded so the points don't curl up. Lapels lie gracefully against the chest, and the lapel roll lines hug the body. The collar fits the neck smoothly without standing away from it. The collar's outside edge covers the neckline seam and fits the shoulders smoothly without rippling. The gorge line is finished by hand.

Large darts are slashed and pressed open to distribute the bulk, while small darts are balanced with an extra layer of fabric. Buttons are attached with hand-sewn stems that don't show on the facing. Buttonholes are hand worked on tailored jackets with a keyhole opening, and hand bound on more feminine dressmaker jackets.

Linings, which are usually silk, don't interfere with the drape of the jacket. Sewn in by hand, they're loose but fit smoothly with a pleat at center back. The lining usually takes the place of a back-neck facing for a softer, more comfortable garment.

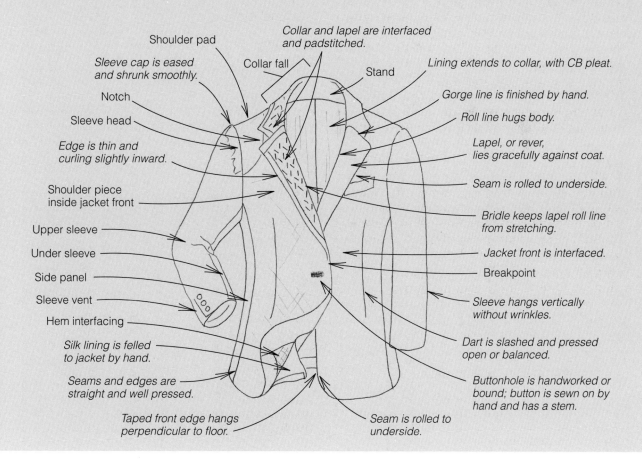

Shoulder pad

Collar and lapel are interfaced and padstitched.

Sleeve cap is eased and shrunk smoothly.

Collar fall

Stand

Lining extends to collar, with CB pleat.

Notch

Gorge line is finished by hand.

Sleeve head

Roll line hugs body.

Edge is thin and curling slightly inward.

Lapel, or rever, lies gracefully against coat.

Seam is rolled to underside.

Shoulder piece inside jacket front

Bridle keeps lapel roll line from stretching.

Upper sleeve

Jacket front is interfaced.

Under sleeve

Breakpoint

Side panel

Sleeve vent

Sleeve hangs vertically without wrinkles.

Hem interfacing

Dart is slashed and pressed open or balanced.

Silk lining is felled to jacket by hand.

Buttonhole is handworked or bound; button is sewn on by hand and has a stem.

Seams and edges are straight and well pressed.

Taped front edge hangs perpendicular to floor.

Seam is rolled to underside.

the length is attractive. When the toile fits perfectly, pin the sleeves in and make any necessary adjustments. (For information on how to fit a sleeve, see p. 138.)

After fitting the toile, mark all new seamlines and matchpoints carefully before removing the bastings and any pins. Press the sections with a dry iron and lay them flat to check the corrections. Remark the corrections if necessary, using a ruler or curve to true any uneven lines. You may need to fit the toile several times before you're satisfied.

ASSEMBLING AND FITTING THE JACKET BODY

Before cutting out the garment fabric for the jacket, convert any small darts on the toile to ease (see the discussion on pp. 56-57). Then, using the corrected toile as a pattern, cut the fronts, backs, any side sections, sleeves and undercollar from the garment fabric (if the fabric has a pattern to be matched, you may want to wait to cut the sleeves until after the first fitting). The undercollar and its interfacing should both be cut on the bias with a seam at the center back. Do not cut the lapel facings, top collar, pockets or linings at this time. Thread-trace all stitching lines, garment centers, matchpoints and grainlines as well as locations for buttons, buttonholes, roll lines, pockets and decorative details.

Next, cut and assemble the canvas. The tailoring term *canvas* refers to all the interfacings and backings after they've been cut, even though they may not actually be cut from hair canvas.

Today most jackets have both backings and interfacings because jacket fabrics are so lightweight that they will not drape well without wrinkling. And, even though the backing and interfacing can be combined in numerous ways, the method used by Valentino for dressmaker jackets and that used by Yves Saint Laurent for tailored blazers are good models for home sewers.

At Valentino, a silk organza or silk muslin backing is cut for the entire jacket, and hair canvas interfacings are cut to support the front edge, front and back shoulder areas, underarm, sleeve cap and hemline, leaving the waist area without interfacing so it's very supple. The backing is applied to the garment fabric at the outset, and the two layers are handled as one throughout the garment's construction.

PREPARING JACKET-BODY INTERFACING

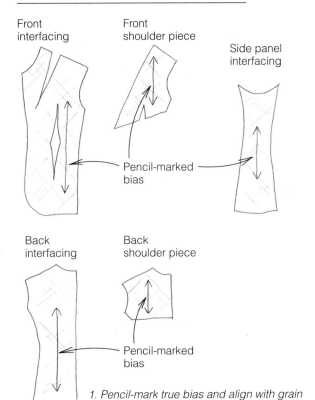

Front interfacing

Front shoulder piece

Side panel interfacing

Pencil-marked bias

Back interfacing

Back shoulder piece

Pencil-marked bias

1. Pencil-mark true bias and align with grain on pattern or toile before cutting two of each interfacing section.

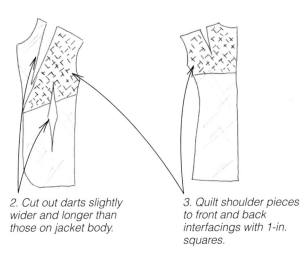

2. Cut out darts slightly wider and longer than those on jacket body.

3. Quilt shoulder pieces to front and back interfacings with 1-in. squares.

At Yves Saint Laurent, a hair-canvas backing, which also serves as the interfacing, is cut on the bias with seam and hem allowances for the fronts, backs (sometimes only partial backs), underarm panels and two-thirds of the sleeve cap. Then a second, smaller layer of hair canvas is cut on the bias for the front shoulder piece, which fills in the area above the bust but doesn't extend into the lapels. Occasionally a back shoulder piece is also cut to fill in the area in the upper back. Since the hair canvas is very crisp and resilient, darts have to be sewn into the separate layers of the garment fabric and backing before the canvas is applied to the shell fabric. Sometimes to reduce bulk, however, darts are not sewn in the interfacing but instead are cut out of it, as described below.

You can cut out the backings on the lengthwise grain, or, for a more supple look, like those on the Yves Saint Laurent jackets in the photos on p. 137 and p. 162, cut them on the bias, leaving ⅝-in. seam allowances and no hem allowance. If you cut them on the bias, mark the true bias at the center of each section so you can align it with the lengthwise grain on the wrong side of the garment section. Cut a second backing layer for the front shoulder piece (as well as one for the back shoulder piece if your design needs one).

Since many of the materials used for the canvas cannot be shrunk or stretched, the interfacing for the shoulder piece, which needs to accommodate the protruding shoulder joint, must be shaped instead by making several perpendicular cuts at the front shoulder seam that are spread open like wedges. To mark the location for each wedge on the front interfacing, draw a line from the shoulder seam 1½ in. long, which you will slash open shortly. Then mark the two angled stitching lines on each side of the slash line that will create a triangular wedge when the slash is spread open. Place the front interfacing on top of the canvas shoulder piece and pin them together just below the marked lines. Stitch the marked triangles and slash the centers in the interfacing layer only. Then quilt the interfacing and shoulder piece together by stitching 1-in. squares parallel to the grainlines, and press the canvas. As you press, stretch the shoulder seam slightly so the slashes open a generous ⅛ in., as shown in the photo above.

To shape the canvas and eliminate bulk, cut out the darts so they're slightly wider and longer than the darts on the jacket itself. Then join the legs of the dart with a baseball stitch (see p. 30). Alternatively, you can baste the darts for the fittings, then remove the bastings, slip the unstitched darts over the sewn darts in the shell fabric and loosely catchstitch the two together along the seamline of the darts (see an example of this in the photo on p. 10). Handled in this way, the inter-

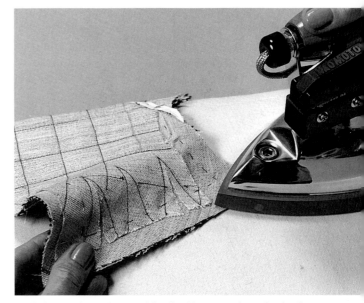

With the interfacing on top of the shoulder piece, shape the shoulder by first stitching several wedge shapes at the shoulder seam to join the two layers. Then slash the center of the triangles only in the interfacing and slightly stretch the shoulder seam as you press it. (The middle triangle would be slashed if more shaping was needed.) (Photo by Susan Kahn.)

facing serves as a buffer for darts in the garment fabric, reducing shadows and ridges produced by the darts on the right side of the garment.

Baste any darts on the garment-fabric fronts and backs, then baste the front canvas into the jacket, beginning with the left front wrong side up and canvas on top so the shoulder piece is uppermost. Arrange and pin the interfacing around the darts if you're using the interfacing as a buffer, as described above. Then turn the front over so the neckline is to your right. Smooth the fabric over the canvas, and check to be sure the darts are still aligned. Baste a vertical row of stitches beginning about 2 in. below the midpoint of the shoulder seam and ending at the hemline. Baste another row of stitches close to the roll line and down the front of the jacket about 1 in. from the edge. Then baste a third row around the armscye about 1 in. from the armscye seam and continuing to the hem.

To prevent the lapel roll line (sometimes called the creaseline) from stretching and to shape it to the contours of the body at the same time, tape it with a woven

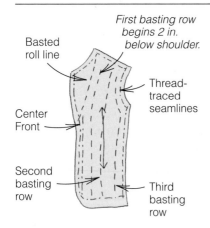

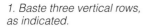

Basted roll line

First basting row begins 2 in. below shoulder.

Thread-traced seamlines

Center Front

Second basting row

Third basting row

1. Baste three vertical rows, as indicated.

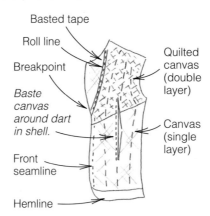

Basted tape

Roll line

Breakpoint

Baste canvas around dart in shell.

Front seamline

Hemline

Quilted canvas (double layer)

Canvas (single layer)

2. Align edge of tape with roll line and baste through center of tape.

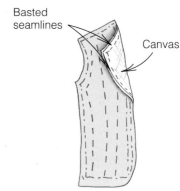

Basted seamlines

Canvas

3. Baste canvas and fabric together on lapel seamline.

tape or a piece of lightweight selvage. The best choice for this tape, which works like a stay tape and is called a bridle, is ¼-in. wide cotton or linen plain-weave tape. (Twill tape is too heavy and polyester tape does not shape well.) Begin by measuring the length of the roll line on the toile and chalk-mark this length on the bridle. Position the bridle with its outer edge on the roll line and the balance on the body of the garment rather than the lapel, and pin one end to the seamline at the neck. Pull the bridle taut and pin its end at the breakpoint, or beginning of the roll line on the front edge. On most figures, the bridle will be ¼ in. to ½ in. shorter than the roll line. For a softer roll at the breakpoint, end the bridle about 1 in. above the breakpoint.

Distribute and pin the ease evenly under the bridle, setting the pins at right angles to the tape. Using a short basting stitch, baste through the center of the bridle. Fold the lapel at the roll line; if the jacket front and canvas are cut exactly the same size, the jacket fabric should show at the edge of the lapel. Baste the layers together on the front seamline.

Next, apply the backing to the remaining garment sections. Baste the canvas and garment sections together at the center on the aligned grainlines. If your backing fabric is crisp like hair canvas, hold the garment fabric and backing layers in the round with the backing on the inside to duplicate the way the layers will fit the body. Holding the layers this way, baste the backing and fabric together at the vertical seamlines. If you're

using a soft backing fabric, full it in (see p. 122) and baste the vertical seams like any other seam. Later, after the seams are stitched, trim the backing to ⅛ in.

Next baste the center-back seam, stopping at the neckline seam, and then baste the side seams, stopping at the armscye seam. Fold under and baste the hems and seam allowances at the edges. And baste the shoulder seams, easing the back to the front. On most figures, the shoulder seam will fit better if it's slightly scooped, rather than straight. (Note that if you're backing with hair canvas, the canvas is *not* sewn into the shoulder seam. Instead it's lapped over the shoulder seam after the seam is stitched.) Although it's possible to try on the jacket at this point, you run the risk of stretching the neckline unless you first baste the interfaced undercollar to the jacket.

BASTING CURVED SHOULDER SEAM

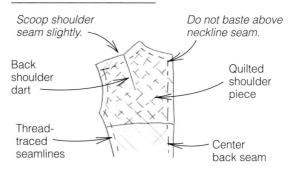

Scoop shoulder seam slightly.

Back shoulder dart

Thread-traced seamlines

Do not baste above neckline seam.

Quilted shoulder piece

Center back seam

PRESSING UNDERCOLLAR

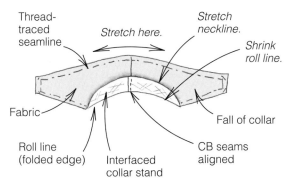

Thread-traced seamline

Stretch here.

Stretch neckline.

Shrink roll line.

Fabric

Roll line (folded edge)

Interfaced collar stand

Fall of collar

CB seams aligned

Press and shrink roll line, and move iron in arc outward to stretch outer edge.

SEWING THE UNDERCOLLAR

Begin assembling the undercollar fabric and interfacing by basting and stitching the center-back seam on the garment fabric. Trim the seam to ³⁄₈ in. and press it. To make the center-back seam on the interfacing, lap the raw edges, matching the seamlines and join them with a short running stitch.

Begin interfacing the undercollar with the wrong side of the collar up. Place the interfacing on top, matching the center-back seams, and baste them together on the roll line. Fold the undercollar on the roll line, with right sides together. Press the roll line in a curve to shrink it and then stretch the undercollar's outer edge at center back. The height of the curve is determined by the slope of the shoulders. If the wearer has square shoulders, the arc should be higher and requires more shrinking and stretching than if the wearer's shoulder slope. Whatever the height of the arc, the roll line should hug the neck and the outside edge should fit the shoulders smoothly. If you're unsure of how much to shrink and stretch the undercollar, check it frequently on a dress form or try it on to avoid stretching the edges too much.

Next, using the thread tracings on the undercollar as a guide, pin the interfacing and fabric together on the seamlines. Mark the seamlines on the interfacing with a sharp pencil and baste the seamlines together. For the first fitting, the seam allowances should be folded toward the interfacing and basted flat.

Before attaching the undercollar to the jacket body, measure the necklines on both—the undercollar should be about ½ in. larger. Pin the undercollar to the neckline at the center back and shoulder seams, and ease it slightly for 1 in. on each side of the shoulder seams. Beginning at the center back, baste the undercollar to the jacket for the fitting.

After attaching the undercollar, make and baste the shoulder pads in place for the first fitting. They extend about ½ in. beyond the armscye seam.

THE FIRST FITTING

Now you're ready for the first fitting of the jacket. Pay special attention to the undercollar. The ease on the lapel roll line should be distributed evenly and smoothly, and the collar roll line should hug the neck closely. The outer edge of the undercollar should cover the neckline seam and lie smoothly without rippling. If the neckline seam shows below the outer edge of the undercollar, the edge is too tight or the wearer's shoulders are very square, and you'll need to stretch the edge

FIRST FITTING OF JACKET (WITHOUT SLEEVES)

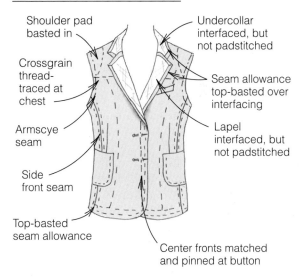

Shoulder pad basted in

Crossgrain thread-traced at chest

Armscye seam

Side front seam

Top-basted seam allowance

Undercollar interfaced, but not padstitched

Seam allowance top-basted over interfacing

Lapel interfaced, but not padstitched

Center fronts matched and pinned at button

Check:
- *Roll line on lapels (should hug body)*
- *Undercollar (should hug neck and cover CB neckline seam)*
- *Back armscye (should hug body)*
- *Button and pocket placement*
- *Hemline*

more so it will cover the neckline seam. After stretching the undercollar to fit the body, mark it with matchpoints at the shoulder seams.

Next check the front armscye. There should be enough room to insert your index finger between the fabric and body. If the armscye is just a little tight, it can be stretched by pressing. If it really binds, the shoulder seam needs to be let out. Next check the back armscye, which should hug the body without gaping. If it gapes, ease and shrink the excess before setting in the sleeve. Then check the shoulder pad size and placement, and pocket and button locations.

Pin in the sleeves and adjust their hang (see p. 138). Finally, correct the hemline for the jacket and sleeves as needed.

STITCHING THE JACKET

After the first fitting, remove the bastings, lay the sections flat and remove the backing and interfacing only when needed to make corrections. Indicate the corrections on the toile for future reference.

On the two jacket backs, complete the darts. Then mold the backs to fit the shoulder blades by shrinking away the excess at the shoulder seams and armscye and stretching the fabric in the shoulder blade area (see p. 59 for instructions on shrinking and stretching). Then stitch the center back seam permanently and trim the backing to ⅛ in. At the waistline, stretch the edges of the side and back seam allowances so they will lie flat against the jacket, and shrink away any excess on the body of the jacket.

On the jacket fronts, complete the darts. Balance small darts with a piece of self-fabric or interfacing (see p. 56), and for large darts, cut the dart take-up down the center and press them open. If the dart take-up was cut out of the interfacing, align the darts on the jacket and canvas and loosely catchstitch them together along the stitching lines of the darts. If the design has underarm panels, join the panels to the fronts. Then make the pockets.

FINISHING THE UNDERCOLLAR

Before you padstitch the undercollar, remove the bastings on the seamlines that join the interfacing and undercollar. Made by sewing small diagonal stitches (see p. 31), padstitching is used to shape and add firmness to the undercollar so it maintains its shape. Begin the padstitching with the collar stand. Hold the stand over one hand with the interfacing side up, and starting at the roll line, work the padded rows horizontally down to the penciled seamline at the neck. The stitches should be short and closely spaced, approximately ¼ in. long and ¼ in. apart. The result will be a crisp, sturdy stand.

PADSTITCHING UNDERCOLLAR

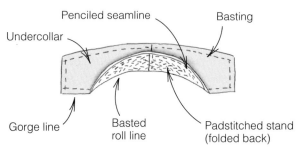

1. Padstitch stand parallel to roll line.

2. Padstitch fall of collar on crossgrain and mark collar points.

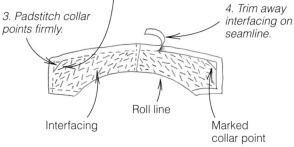

3. Padstitch collar points firmly.

4. Trim away interfacing on seamline.

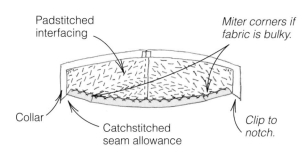

5. After the second fitting, finish neck edge and gorge line by catchstitching seam allowance to interfacing.

Next, on the undercollar interfacing, mark a small triangle at each collar point, penciling the base of the triangle 1 in. from the point. With the undercollar still in the rolled position and the interfacing side up, begin at the center back working out on each side and padstitch the fall of the collar on the crossgrain. Use slightly longer stitches than you used on the stand (from ⅜ in. to ½ in. long) and space them about ⅜ in. apart. Finally, using stitches about ⅛ in. to ¼ in. long and spacing them from ⅛ in. to ¼ in. apart, depending on the firmness you want, pad the collar points, beginning at the penciled base of the triangle and working toward the collar point. Pad to the penciled seamlines so the points will be firm and will not curl up on the finished jacket. Examine the collar carefully to be sure both sides look the same.

Remark the penciled seamlines on the interfacing so they're aligned with those on the undercollar and trim away the interfacing seam allowances. With the interfacing side up, press the undercollar, using a moderately hot, dry iron. Moisten the fall of the collar with a damp dauber and press the ends flat. Press up to the roll line but not over it. Continue pressing until the interfacing is dry and firm, and repeat this procedure for the collar stand.

Trim the undercollar seam allowances to ¼ in. and fold them over the edge of the interfacing. Baste them for the second fitting as you did for the first. Also baste the gorge line. After the fitting, catchstitch the seam allowances to the interfacing, mitering the corners as needed.

PADSTITCHING THE LAPELS

Prepare the lapels for padstitching by basting the bridle back on the roll line, as you did for the first fitting. Using cotton thread and a felling stitch, sew both long edges of the bridle to the interfacing, stopping ¼ in. from the seamline at each end. Repeat for the other front and check to be sure the roll lines are the same length.

With the front right side up, hold the lapel in one hand between the thumb and fingers and roll it back over the garment so that it's positioned as it will be when worn. Baste the edges of the fabric and interfacing together at the front seamline. On the interfacing, pencil a small triangle at the lapel point, marking the two legs of the triangle along the seamline and the triangle's base 1 in. from the point. Using a soft cotton or silk thread, begin the first row of padstitching on the lapel about ¼ in. from the bridle and parallel to it, barely catching the fabric so the threads don't show on the right side. This and all subsequent rows should be-

PADSTITCHING LAPELS

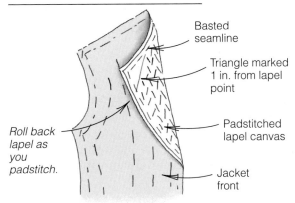

1. Make padstitches ½ in. long and space rows ½ in. apart, staggering stitches in rows to avoid ridges.

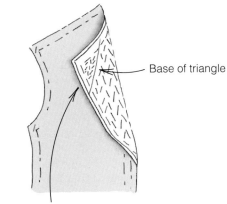

2. Padstitch lapel point with short, closely spaced stitches parallel to triangle's base.

gin and end about ¼ in. from the neckline and front seamlines. Make the padstitches about ½ in. long and space the rows ½ in. apart, staggering the stitches to avoid ridges between the rows of padstitching.

The degree of firmness the padstitching supplies is determined by the length of the stitches and distance between the rows. For softer lapels, make the stitches longer and the rows farther apart. Continue to work the rows toward the edge but do not padstitch the triangle at the point. If the canvas begins to pull the fabric, release the basting on the front seamline and rebaste.

For a firm lapel point, hold the lapel so you can padstitch rows parallel to the base of the triangle at the lapel point and work shorter, more tightly spaced stitches. Padstitch the other lapel, checking periodically to be sure the two lapels look the same.

TAPING FRONT EDGE OF JACKET

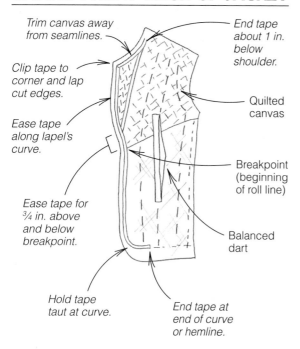

Trim canvas away from seamlines.

Clip tape to corner and lap cut edges.

Ease tape along lapel's curve.

Ease tape for ¾ in. above and below breakpoint.

End tape about 1 in. below shoulder.

Quilted canvas

Breakpoint (beginning of roll line)

Balanced dart

Hold tape taut at curve.

End tape at end of curve or hemline.

TAPING THE FRONT EDGES AND PRESSING THE JACKET BODY

To establish the hang of the jacket and preserve its shape, tape the front edge of the jacket to the hemline. For sharp, flat edges, trim the interfacing short of the seamline so that it will not be stitched and cover the raw edge with the tape. Before trimming the interfacing, check to be sure the edges are straight and redraw the seamlines as needed. Then trim away the seam allowance plus an additional ³⁄₁₆ in.

Using preshrunk ¼-in. cotton or linen plain-weave tape, begin pinning the tape to the interfaced side of the lapel at the breakpoint. Place the outside edge of the preshrunk tape on the seamline with the rest of the tape on the garment front rather than the seam allowance. Holding the tape loosely, ease and pin it for about ¾ in. above and below the breakpoint. Then pin the tape on the lapel so its curved outer edge is smooth but not taut. If there's a point at the corner of the lapel, cut the tape to the seamline and lap the cut edges. Continue pinning the tape to the neckline, easing the tape slightly at the top of the roll line and stopping about 1 in. below the shoulder.

Below the breakpoint, pin the tape to the jacket-front edge down to the bottom button so the tape is smooth but not taut. Below the bottom button, hold the tape taut as you pin it down to the hemline. When pinning around a curve at the hem, continue to hold the tape taut. Baste the tapes in place, remove the pins and press lightly. Compare the two front edges to be sure they've been taped identically and that they hang straight without curling at curves and corners.

Next, press the lapels carefully until they're very thin. Begin with the interfacing side up, positioning the lapel with the roll line on the edge of the pressing stand. Cover the lapel with a damp pressing cloth and press only to the roll line, but not over it. You're trying to build in some curve at the roll line, not press it flat. Next remove the damp cloth and press the lapel without moisture until it's firm and dry. Then press the other lapel.

With the interfacing side up, place the front on the pressing stand, with the roll line aligned with the stand's edge and the lapel hanging off the stand. Press the taped edge below the lapel from the hem to the breakpoint, first with a damp cloth, then without moisture until the edge is firm and dry. Then press the remainder of the interfacing between hem and waist.

With the canvas uppermost, use the iron to stretch the fabric slightly around the bust point, holding up the edge of the front section. Notice that the front dart is balanced and that the edges of the canvas have been catchstitched to the dart's stitching line. (Photo by Susan Kahn.)

With the interfacing still up, press the bust area, beginning at the roll line. At the bust point, shape the front to fit the bust. Do this by holding the top edge of the front off the pressing stand and using just the point of the iron at the bust point, as shown in the photo on the facing page. Finally, fold the lapel in place and steam the roll line, pressing firmly with your fingers as you steam. The fronts are now ready to be assembled for the second fitting, so baste the side and shoulder seams and the hem and baste in the sleeves and undercollar again.

THE SECOND FITTING

At the second fitting, check the hang and length of the sleeves. Also pay special attention to the taping. If the jacket's front edges swing toward the side seams, the tape should be tighter below the breakpoint. If the edges overlap, it's too tight. In either case, take the tape out, and sew and press it again.

After the fitting, remove the bastings at the shoulders and fell both sides of the tape to the front edge with small, even stitches. Begin at the hemline and stop at the notch of the lapel. Between the notch and shoulder seam, sew the tape only to the interfacing. Remember, since the interfacing will not be stitched into the shoulder seam, the fabric and interfacing shouldn't be sewn together in the neckline area. Finish the other lapel and compare the two to make sure they're equal.

SECOND FITTING OF JACKET

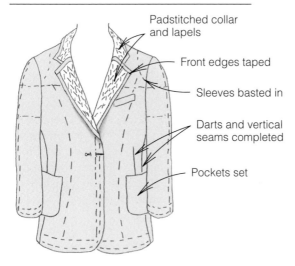

Padstitched collar and lapels

Front edges taped

Sleeves basted in

Darts and vertical seams completed

Pockets set

Check:
• *All previous fitting corrections*
• *Hang and length of sleeve*
• *Garment edges (should hang perpendicular to floor)*

After this fitting, also remove the collar and the bastings to release the seam allowances and press the undercollar again as needed. Before proceeding to the top collar, finish the neckline edge and gorge lines of the undercollar. If the fabric is bulky, miter the corners. Then baste the seam allowances of the neckline edge and gorge line to the wrong side and secure them with catchstitches. Clip the seam allowances at the notches and press with the interfacing side up, flattening the edges with the clapper.

FACING THE LAPELS

In luxury-ready-to wear and home sewing, jacket facings are cut so the lengthwise grain is parallel to the center front. The facings imitate—more or less—the jacket edges they face; and, when made from a plaid or horizontal stripe, the facing and jacket front match horizontally at the seamline joining them. In haute couture and bespoke tailoring, the lengthwise grain of the lapel facing is usually parallel to the lapel edge. This is particularly important when the fabric has a vertical stripe, even if the lapel section below the breakpoint is cut on the bias. However, when the fabric has a horizontal stripe or rib, the lapel is sometimes cut with the crossgrain parallel to the lapel edge so the rib or stripe is parallel to the edge.

In a couture workroom, a facing pattern is rarely used. Instead, a rectangle of fabric is usually pinned and shaped to fit the garment section, and then cut. Initially, shaping the facing may appear difficult and it does take more time, but it's actually a very practical approach that eliminates worry about whether the facing is cut with too much or too little ease and also makes it easier to position and match fabric patterns. This same procedure is often used for cutting couture linings and facings for other types of garments.

The finished size of the facing depends on the jacket, but most are about 5 in. wide at the bottom and 1 in. or less at the shoulder. To make a facing, begin with a rectangle of fabric that's large enough to make one facing, that is, at least 6 in. wide by the length of the jacket plus 2 in. If you're working with plaid or patterned fabric, decide which section of the pattern or which color bar of the plaid will be at the finished edge before cutting out the rectangle. A dominant color will generally be the most attractive. Pin and mark the lapel seamline temporarily. If the seamline is placed at the pins, part of the color bar will be lost at the edge, so position the seamline about ⅛ in. to ¼ in. away and thread-trace this line.

Next, with right sides together and beginning at the breakpoint and working up, pin the facing to the lapel, setting the pins parallel to and on the seamline so you can turn it right side out after you finish pinning to check the edge and how the patterns match. Ease the facing to the front as you pin it, leaving a little additional ease just above the breakpoint and at the lapel corner. This is called fulling in the facing.

If you full the facing too much, it will bubble at the edge. If you don't full it enough, the seamline will show on the right side and the lapel point may curl up. Let the fabric talk to your fingers. If it's thick and heavy, it will need more fullness than if it's lightweight or medium-weight. Once you're satisfied with the edge, trim away the excess at the edge, leaving ½-in. seam allowances so that you can make adjustments later on.

With a short even-basting stitch, baste the layers together—the basting should be at the outer edge of the tape beginning at the notch and ending at the breakpoint. Carefully turn the lapel right side out, but do not trim it. The facing should lie smoothly, with the basted seamline sitting just to the underside of the lapel so it's not visible on the right side of the jacket.

Turn the lapel wrong side out once again, and pin and baste the facing to the jacket front, beginning at the breakpoint and ending at the hem. Ease the facing for ½ in. just below the breakpoint. If the design has bound buttonholes, ease the right facing slightly in the button-hole area so there will be enough fabric to finish the facing side of the buttonholes smoothly. Below the button-holes, pull the facing taut to the hemline. Turn the facing right side out again to check that the edges don't curl.

After you've tailored a few jackets, you may prefer to baste the entire edge before turning it right side out to check it. I prefer to begin basting at the breakpoint so that if part of the facing needs to be repositioned, there's less stitching to be ripped out. When you're satisfied the lapel is perfect, repeat for the other lapel, then check to be sure they look the same.

If the lapel point comes to an acute angle, redraw the seamline with a slight curve at the point so you can stitch both exactly the same. If the point comes to a

FACING A JACKET WITH STRAIGHT LAPELS

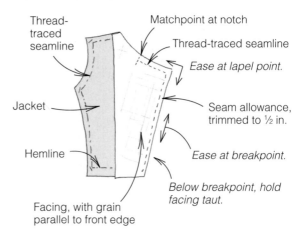

1. With RS together, pin facing to front's thread-traced seamline. Ease facing at breakpoint and at lapel. Baste, easing at breakpoint, then keeping facing taut to hemline.

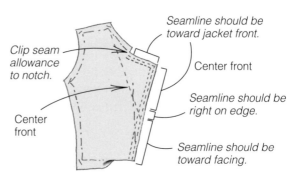

2. After permanently sewing facing seam, turn facing right side out and top-baste faced edges ¼ in. from edge and again ¾ in. from edge.

right angle, take one or two short stitches across the point so the corner will turn neatly and look square. To prevent the ease from shifting when you stitch, double baste and then steam-press the basted seamline. Since the facings are basted securely, you can stitch both fronts from the notch to the hem. Tie the threads using a tailor's knot at the beginning and end.

Turn the sections right side out and check the stitching before clipping and grading the seams. Remove the bastings and clip the seam allowances to the notch, where the seamline ends, and press the seam flat. Then with a point presser, press it open. Grade the seams so the seam allowance nearer the outside of the garment is ¼ in. On the lapels above the breakpoint, this seam allowance will be on the facing, while below the break-point it will be on the garment body. Trim the remaining seam allowance to ⅛ in. and trim away any excess bulk at the corners and curves. For added control and a flatter edge, sew the seam allowance on the garment to the tape. Then sew the facing seam allowance to the garment seam allowance and press.

Turn the fronts right side out. If the lapels have a corner, use a small needle and unknotted thread to work the corner out without distorting it. Take a short stitch in the seamline and, holding the needle and the unknotted end, tug gently to pull the seamline to the edge. Repeat until the corner has been turned out.

To prepare the garment for pressing, hold it right side up and top-baste through the garment and facing layers ¼ in. from the edge, shaping the edge as you baste so that the seamline rolls to the underside when the jacket is worn and is therefore invisible. At the lapels, the seamline should roll toward the jacket front while below the breakpoint, it should roll toward the facing so it doesn't show on the right side of the garment. For about ½ in. both above and below the breakpoint, the seamline should be right on the edge. Baste another row of stitches about ¾ in. from the edge. Next, fold the lapel into its finished position and smooth the facing over the lapel line. Baste on the roll line with a long diagonal stitch. Then baste through all layers from the shoulder point to the hem, and chalk a line on the facing about 1 in. away. Trim on the chalked line, baste around the buttonhole markings, and press.

FACING SHAPED LAPELS

Unlike the almost-straight lapels on Yves Saint Laurent's plaid jacket on p. 162, the lapels on his herringbone jacket on p. 137 have a more pronounced curve at the edge. Fitting the rectangular facing to this curved edge requires additional easing and shrinking. Although you can shape the facing using the directions above, it's easier to begin by shaping a pair of simple rectangles to the toile so both facings will be shaped the same. Then you can determine how much to ease and shrink the facing rectangle at the breakpoint to make it fit the shape of the jacket edge.

To determine the size of the facing rectangles, first mark the finished shape of the lapel on the jacket front toile by drawing the facing's unnotched edge 1 in. wide at the shoulder and 5 in. wide at the hem (see the drawing above right). Then measure the facing's width at the widest point of the lapel and add 2 in. for seam

MARKING TOILE TO ESTABLISH DIMENSIONS FOR FACING RECTANGLE

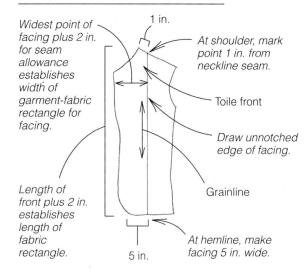

Widest point of facing plus 2 in. for seam allowance establishes width of garment-fabric rectangle for facing.

1 in.

At shoulder, mark point 1 in. from neckline seam.

Toile front

Draw unnotched edge of facing.

Grainline

Length of front plus 2 in. establishes length of fabric rectangle.

5 in.

At hemline, make facing 5 in. wide.

allowances. Finally measure the length of the facing from the highest point of the shoulder seam to the hem and add 2 in.

If you're using patterned fabric, before cutting the facing rectangles, decide which color bars or part of the pattern will be most attractive at the lapel's edge. Cut the rectangles accordingly using the measurements you arrived at above.

Thread-trace seamlines on one long edge of the rectangles for the front edge of the facings. With the facings right sides together, pin a small dart at what will be the breakpoint, then pin the facings to the toile front, matching the seamlines at the front edge. Repin a larger dart at the breakpoint for more shaping so that the thread-traced seamlines on the facings fit the edge of the toile smoothly. Then convert the dart to ease, and baste the facings and toile together on the front seamlines. The unnotched edge of each facing will ripple since you're basting the facing's straight edge to the curved edge of the toile.

Lay the facings on the pressing board with the neckline to your right and the unnotched edge toward you. Use a steam iron to fill the fabric with steam, and begin pressing at the basted seamline. Move the iron in a counterclockwise arc while you gently pull the facings

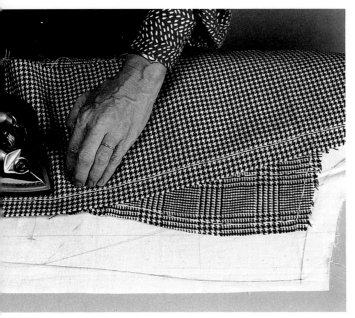

As the author shrinks the fullness out of a houndstooth lapel facing that's been basted to the plaid jacket front below the breakpoint, you can see the relationship of the grainlines on the lapel and facing. The jacket front and penciled toile laid below it have a slightly curved lapel edge, while the thread-traced seamline on the facing is on the straight grain. Notice that the facing's thread-traced seamline is at the edge of a white color bar, but when sewn and pressed, as it is in the photo at right, it appears to be at the edge of a black color bar. (Photo by Susan Kahn.)

After the facing is basted to the front, carefully turn it right side out to examine the results. (Photo by Susan Kahn.)

toward you. As you shape the lapel into an outward curve, ripples will form at the unnotched edge. Shrink them away carefully to avoid unwanted creases.

When working with some worsteds, linens and cottons, the fabric will not always shrink enough to fit the shape of the edge. To resolve this, some designers shape the lapel and ignore the direction of the grain below the breakpoint, while others cut the facing into two sections and place the seam between the first and second buttons. If you make a seamline, position the top of the lower section on the crossgrain. On a jacket with bound buttonholes, locate the seam behind the top buttonhole, leaving an opening in the seam to finish the back of the buttonhole.

After the facings have been shaped, trim the seam allowances to ½ in., and remove the bastings and muslin. Pin the facings to the lapel edge and finish them using the directions in the section on p. 175.

MAKING THE LINING

The lining finishes the inside of jackets and coats attractively, covers the inner construction, and makes it easier to slip the jacket on and off. Even though it lies inside of the jacket, it should be slightly larger in length and width than the garment because the lining material is generally more firmly woven and less elastic than the shell fabric.

Unlike linings in ready-to-wear and home sewing, couture linings are not completely assembled before they're sewn into the garment. As discussed in Chapter 8, the sleeves are lined before they're set, and the lining for the jacket body is usually put in before the shoulder seams are sewn.

The lining can be cut using the toile or jacket sections as patterns. This works well when the lining sections more or less duplicate the garment sections. If there are extensive alterations or design changes, however, the lining can be cut or torn into rectangles that are fitted to the inside of the garment. Making a lining this way isn't nearly as difficult as it seems, especially if the lining is fitted before the shoulder seams are machine-stitched so the garment can be spread flat.

When cutting the lining, make sure the seam and hem allowances are at least 1 in. wide (see Step 1 in the drawing on p. 178). Cut the front lining so the front edge is on the selvage and laps the front facing by about 1½ in. Cut the back lining, allowing for a 1-in. center-back pleat. Do not cut out the neckline on either the back or front lining. Mark the vertical seamlines and matchpoints with chalk or tracing carbon, but don't mark the hem or any darts or seamlines on the front edges, back neckline, shoulders or armscyes.

Before stitching the vertical seamlines, pin them as marked and baste them a scant ⅛ in. away from the seamline, toward the raw edge, so the lining will be slightly larger than the jacket. Stitch the seamlines, remove the bastings and press the seams open, clipping them as needed.

To prepare the jacket for the lining, join the backs to the side panels, as shown in Step 2 in the drawing on p. 178, and then interface the hem (for directions on interfacing a hem, see p. 68). If you want to control the hang of the garment at the opening, side vents, seamlines and back, you can do so by placing weights inside the jacket hem. Lead drapery weights are suitable and readily available in most notions departments. If the weight is too heavy or too large, use an old pair of scissors to cut it into smaller pieces and pound them flat with a hammer so that they won't show when the garment is worn. To eliminate sharp edges, cover each weight with a 3-in. square of organza. Place the weight in the center of the square and wrap first the sides and then the top and bottom around the weight. Secure the covered weights with a few stitches and sew them to the interfacing on the hem. Then hem the jacket.

Next spread the jacket on the table wrong side up. On the front facing, mark the facing/lining seamline with chalk so that it begins 1 in. or less away from the neckpoint. If the facings haven't been sewn to the interfacing, secure them with a loose catchstitch or blindstitch.

With wrong sides together, place the lining on the jacket so that the center backs and vertical seamlines are aligned and pin them together. The lining should be fulled so it's a little larger than the jacket itself and fits inside it with some ease. If the lining is too tight, the jacket will be uncomfortable and the lining will pull at the seams. If it's too loose, the lining will wrinkle and it may show when the jacket is worn.

Beginning at the side back seam, smooth and pin the lining toward the center back and pin the pleat in place so the underlay is toward the left (Step 3). Then smooth and pin the back around the armscyes. If there are any darts, pin in small pleats to control the fullness. Next, fold the side panel linings out of the way so you can sew together the side back seams of the lining and jacket. Using a loose running stitch, begin and end about 3 in. from the beginning and end of the seamline. Repeat to join the side front seams of the lining and jacket.

Smooth and pin the front lining around the armscye, then toward the facing. At the front edge, fold the lining under on the lengthwise grain and align the folded edge with the chalked seamline on the facing (Step 4). As you pin toward the shoulder, you will have excess lining, and you can fold more of the lining under or put a pleat in at the shoulder, or do both. If there is still some excess fabric, repin with a small pleat at the armscye. Trim only as needed.

Baste the lining to the jacket about 3 in. below the shoulder seams and armholes. To tame the fullness at the waist, make vertical pleats on the front and back linings. To sew pleats permanently, make a small thread bar (see p. 33) across the folded edge. Next, pin the lining and jacket together about 5 in. above the jacket hem. Trim the lining so it's even with the jacket and turn under the lining hem so that ¾ in. of the jacket hem shows. Baste about ½ in. above the folded edge of the lining. Hold the folded edge back with your thumb. Then, using a blindstitch, hem a single layer of lining to the jacket hem and press lightly (Step 5). When you remove the basting, the lining will have a soft fold at the bottom to provide ease in the length.

Before finishing the lining, you must stitch the shoulder seams on the jacket, and complete and set the sleeves (see pp. 140-141 for information on completing a sleeve). To sew the shoulder seams, first pin the front interfacing out of the way and then stitch and press the seams. Smooth the interfacing back over the shoulder seam and baste it to the seam allowance (Step 6).

Before permanently setting the sleeves, tighten the back armscye between ¼ in. and ½ in. by shrinking out the excess. Beginning with a doubled thread, place a

LINING THE JACKET

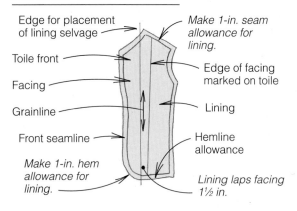

- Edge for placement of lining selvage
- Make 1-in. seam allowance for lining.
- Toile front
- Facing
- Grainline
- Front seamline
- *Make 1-in. hem allowance for lining.*
- Edge of facing marked on toile
- Lining
- Hemline allowance
- *Lining laps facing 1½ in.*

1. Cut the lining using either jacket front or toile.

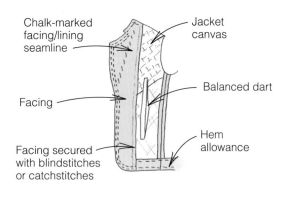

- Chalk-marked facing/lining seamline
- Jacket canvas
- Facing
- Balanced dart
- Facing secured with blindstitches or catchstitches
- Hem allowance

2. Prepare jacket for lining by chalk-marking facing/lining seamline and securing facing.

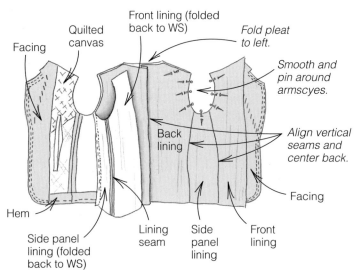

- Facing
- Quilted canvas
- Front lining (folded back to WS)
- *Fold pleat to left.*
- *Smooth and pin around armscyes.*
- Back lining
- *Align vertical seams and center back.*
- Facing
- Hem
- Side panel lining (folded back to WS)
- Lining seam
- Side panel lining
- Front lining

3. Sew lining seams together, beginning and ending about 3 in. from ends of seamline. Pin lining to sides and back of jacket.

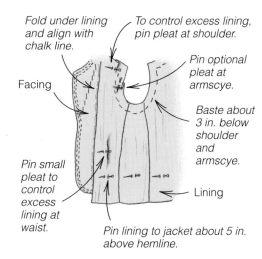

- *Fold under lining and align with chalk line.*
- *To control excess lining, pin pleat at shoulder.*
- Facing
- *Pin optional pleat at armscye.*
- *Baste about 3 in. below shoulder and armscye.*
- *Pin small pleat to control excess lining at waist.*
- Lining
- *Pin lining to jacket about 5 in. above hemline.*

4. Pin lining to jacket fronts.

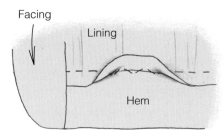

- Facing
- Lining
- Hem

5. Hem lining with a blindstitch, catching only one layer of lining.

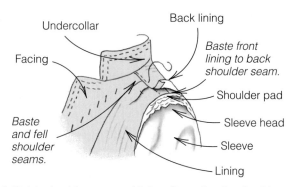

- Undercollar
- Back lining
- Facing
- *Baste front lining to back shoulder seam.*
- Shoulder pad
- *Baste and fell shoulder seams.*
- Sleeve head
- Sleeve
- Lining

6. Finish shoulder seams of lining. (In reality, the shoulder pad would curve upward, not, for clarity's sake, as it's shown above.)

row of backstitches on the back armscye just inside the seamline, starting about 1½ in. below the shoulder seam and ending about 2 in. from the underarm. Pull the stitches taut to hold in the excess fabric. Place the garment, wrong side up, on a flat pressing surface and use the point of the iron to shrink out the ease on the back itself near the armscye for 1 in. to 1½ in.

If the fabric is tightly woven or you've pulled the stitches too tight and can't shrink away all of the ripples, remove the stitches and try again. Otherwise, the ripples will be permanent and will look unattractive on the finished design. Finally, fold the linings out of the way and set the sleeves, which have already been lined. Sew in the sleeve heads and shoulder pads (see p. 180).

To finish the lining, smooth the front lining over the shoulder seam, baste to the back seam allowance and trim away the excess lining. Smooth the back lining to the neckline, clipping as needed so you can turn under and pin the edge. Continue pinning the back lining over the shoulders, easing it slightly at the shoulder seam. Trim the shoulder seam allowance to 1 in., turn it under, and baste it to the front lining. At the top of the armscye, trim the lining so that it's even with the garment seam allowances and baste the lining around the armscye.

Next pin the sleeve lining in place at the armscye, making sure that there will be extra length at the underarm to cover the bulk of the seam without flattening it. Trim as needed, turn the raw edge under and baste the sleeve lining around the armscye (see pp. 148-149).

Now you're ready for the third and final fitting. At this fitting, check to be sure your jacket exhibits all the points listed in the sidebar "Characteristics of a couture jacket" on p. 165. Also at the fitting, check the lining to make sure it isn't too tight. If not, then neatly fell the lining's shoulder seams, edges and armscyes.

LINING STAYS

On double-breasted jackets, asymmetrical designs, wraps without buttons, and jackets worn without a blouse, extra precautions must be taken to keep the underlapping front section from sagging below the hemline of the overlapping section. The most common solution for this problem in ready-to-wear and home sewing is to locate a buttonhole on the underlap and a button on the facing or lining of the corresponding section. Although this closure solves the problem of a sag-

ging underlapping layer, it sometimes pulls unattractively on the outer layers of the garment. On couture garments, ties or stays are used to control the underlap while permitting it to shift slightly when the body moves.

The technique described below for sewing lining stays was used on a Dior jacket made in the 1950s. The lining stay consists of a narrow strap sewn to the right front lining which hooks to an eye at the edge of the underlap. Less bulky than traditional ties, it can be used on jackets, coats and coat dresses, and can be added to a finished garment. The length of the stay and its placement will depend on the garment design, but on many jackets it's located the same distance from the hemline of the garment as the top button.

Begin the stay by sewing a strap that is ¼ in. wide and 8 in. to 10 in. long from the lining fabric (see the discussion on belt and hanger loops, p. 116). Place the jacket on a dress form or try it on, and pin the center fronts together. On the right front, mark the edge of the underlap with a pin (you can feel it through the overlapping layer) so that the pin is even with the top button. Then remove the jacket. Next, measure the distance on the right front between the pin marking the underlap and the side seam. Mark that length plus ¼ in. on the stay. Beginning at the side seam, baste the stay to the lining, leaving an extra ½ in. at the side seam for finishing and stopping 2 in. to 3 in. from the pin mark. Try on the jacket and pin the stay to the underlap. Then check the stay position when moving and sitting and correct as needed.

MAKING A LINING STAY

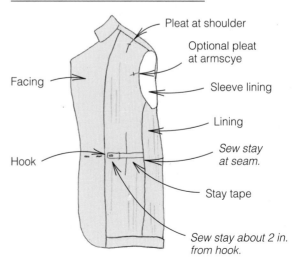

- Pleat at shoulder
- Optional pleat at armscye
- Sleeve lining
- Lining
- *Sew stay at seam.*
- Stay tape
- *Sew stay about 2 in. from hook.*

Facing

Hook

MAKING AND SETTING SHOULDER PADS

Shoulder pads create an attractive shoulder line and help the jacket hang smoothly. To do this, they must fill the hollow between the shoulder and bust in the front, and between the shoulder blades and armscye in the back. They can be unobtrusively thin or very thick, depending on current fashion and the wearer's build. They should always be flexible enough to be shaped to fit the body and be unnoticeable when the jacket is worn. If the wearer has one low shoulder, a pad can be used to "raise" it as much as ½ in.

In both tailoring and dressmaking workrooms, pads are built to the desired thickness by layering wadding or cotton batting. Tailored pads are usually built on a hair-canvas base, while dressmaker pads are often constructed on muslin. Unlike dressmaker pads, tailored pads are not covered with fabric since they'll be hidden by the jacket lining. At the armscye edge of both types of pads, all wadding layers end evenly about ½ in. beyond the seam-

line. At the neckline edge, the edges are feathered in graduated layers to prevent creating a ridge.

To make a pad, first pin the shoulder seams of the front and back toile together and mark a point on the shoulder seam 1 in. in from the neckline seam. Then, on the toile front, mark a point on the armscye seamline 5 in. below the shoulder point. On the toile back, mark a point on the armscye 6 in. below the shoulder point. Then trace the armscye seamline between the two armscye points.

Draw the shoulder pad shape, beginning at the marked point on the shoulder seam. Draw a deep curve on the front to the armscye, trace the armscye seamlines and, on the back, draw a shallow curve. Using a stiletto tracing wheel, transfer the pattern to brown paper, marking the shoulder seam and adding a 1-in. seam allowance at the armscye. Mark the true bias at the

shoulder seam, and cut two sections for each pad from hair canvas.

Align two of the hair-canvas layers, fold them at the shoulder seam and pin the ends together so the top layer is ¼ in. shorter than the bottom layer. This will make the top layer buckle and build in the curve for the shoulder. Repeat for the other pad, and then check to be sure you have a pair instead of two pads for one side. With the shorter layer on top, quilt the two layers by hand with large diagonal stitches. Then pin the quilted sections to the dress form with the shorter layer on top and steam-press them.

Use the pattern to cut six or more layers of wadding or cotton batting for each pad. Separate the wadding or batting into thin layers. Make a base layer of wadding by tearing one of the pieces half the size of the pattern and feathering the edge closest to the neckline. Press it in place on the canvas base with your fingers. Add several

MAKING SHOULDER PADS

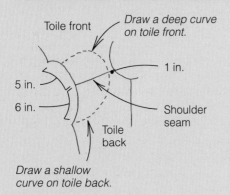

Draw a shallow curve on toile back.

1. Draw shoulder pad shape on toile.

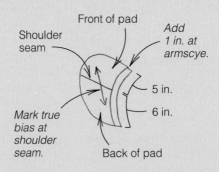

2. Create a paper pattern for pad.

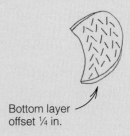

3. Align hair-canvas layers, pinning top layer ¼ in. shorter than bottom layer to build in shape and baste layers together with large diagonal stitches.

more layers of wadding, making each slightly larger than the last. Remove the pad from the dress form and use a few large diagonal stitches to sew the layers together. Put it back on the form and press it with the steam iron to pack the layers down. Repeat until the pad is the desired thickness, then trim it as needed at the armscye and press it again.

To make very thick pads, begin with several base layers of wadding half the size of the pattern to add thickness at the armscye. Then continue building the pad as described above.

Setting the shoulder pads is tricky because they've been shaped to fit the shoulders, and when you turn the jacket wrong side out to set the pads, the shoulder curve will be reversed. Fold back the lining to insert the pads and adjust them as needed to fit the shoulders. Pin and sew them permanently at the armscye and shoulder seams, keeping the stitches loose to prevent pulling at the shoulder.

Feather edges of wadding as you layer it.

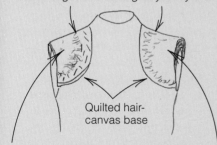

Quilted hair-canvas base

Begin with small piece of wadding over hair-canvas base (for very thick pad, begin with several small wadding layers).

Then add progressively larger pieces of wadding until pad is desired thickness.

4. Build pads on dress form.

Remove the stay to finish the ends. Fold one end under ¼ in. and catchstitch neatly. Place the hook over the raw edges of that end and sew it in place permanently. Trim the other end of the stay, leaving ¼ in. for finishing it. Fold this end up instead of under and catchstitch it. Then fell it to the lining side seam, enclosing the raw edge. With several backstitches, fasten the stay to the lining 2 to 3 in. from the hook end. Finally, make a permanent thread eye in a corresponding position on the edge of the underlap.

FINISHING THE BODY AND MAKING THE TOP COLLAR

To make the top collar, cut a rectangular piece of garment fabric that is 2 in. longer and wider than the undercollar. Since the grain of the top collar should match the grain of the jacket at the center back both vertically and horizontally, the top collar rarely matches the lapels at the grainline. When sewing stripes or plaids, plan carefully before beginning the garment so both ends of the collar are the same or look attractive as a pair.

Using a steam iron, begin pressing the top collar with the wrong side up. Press the two long sides separately, using a circular motion to stretch the edges and shrink the center so the top collar will fit the undercollar smoothly and the crossgrain will follow the collar's edge. If you can't follow the grain at the edge easily, thread-trace the seamline. To see if you've shaped the top collar enough, check it occasionally as you're working by laying it on top of the undercollar.

To join the top collar and undercollar, begin with right sides together. Match and pin the roll lines. Then pin the seamlines together at the outer edge, beginning at center back, stopping at the notch and easing the top collar to the undercollar along the outer edges. To check the collar, set the pins parallel to the seamline, unpin the roll line, and turn the collar right sides out. The top collar should have enough ease so the seamline will roll under, but not so much ease that it ripples. The ends should appear identical. Adjust as needed, reset the pins, and baste the collar securely with short stitches. Then check the collar once again, and double-baste.

Press and stitch the edges permanently, stopping at the notch at each end of the collar without stitching into the seam allowance. Remove the bastings, press the

JOINING TOP COLLAR AND UNDERCOLLAR

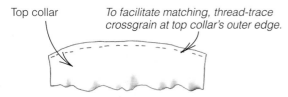

Top collar

To facilitate matching, thread-trace crossgrain at top collar's outer edge.

1. Stretch top and bottom edges of top collar.

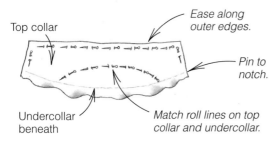

Top collar

Ease along outer edges.

Pin to notch.

Undercollar beneath

Match roll lines on top collar and undercollar.

2. Pin top collar and undercollar together.

3. Sew top collar to jacket seam allowance with a running stitch.

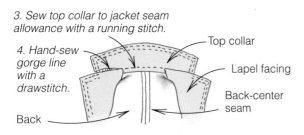

4. Hand-sew gorge line with a drawstitch.

Top collar

Lapel facing

Back-center seam

Back

seam open and grade the seams. Then catchstitch the edges of the seam allowances, as you did at the front edges of the jacket, and repeat for the top collar seam allowances.

Next, turn the collar right side out to baste the edges and the roll line. With the undercollar toward you, baste about ¼ in. from the edge. Hold the collar in the finished position and smooth out the top collar. Then baste the roll line. At the gorge line, trim the seam allowances to ¼ in., turn them under and top baste.

Before attaching the collar to the jacket, trim the neckline seam on the jacket to ⅜ in. Then fell the undercollar to the neckline and finish the gorge line with a drawing stitch (see p. 30). With the jacket wrong side up, smooth the neck edge of the top collar over the

jacket seam allowance and secure it neatly with a running stitch. (The raw edge of the top collar will be covered by the lining.)

To finish the gorge line, use a drawing stitch to join the top collar and the lapel facing. Make the stitches short and parallel to one another, like a ladder, so that they will disappear into the seamline and look machine-stitched. If they slant, they will show and the gorge will be unattractive.

"CHANELISMS"

The details and construction techniques on Chanel's legendary suits were so distinctive that the editors at *Vogue* magazine in the 1960s dubbed them "Chanelisms." Most of these techniques are labor-intensive and are still used today by the House of Chanel. They control the garment's hang and prolong its pristine appearance—and increase its price.

The classic Chanel suit appears to be a loosely fitted cardigan and skirt with a well-coordinated blouse. Casual in appearance, the ensemble is actually assembled with meticulous attention to details. Nothing is left to chance, either in the way the suit is to be worn or in its construction and fit. Linings for jackets and skirts are often cut from the same fragile fabric as the blouse, which means it's almost impossible to wear the suit with a different blouse. In fact, as noted earlier, many of the skirt and blouse ensembles designed by Chanel are actually dresses that look like separates.

Lightweight and comfortable to wear, the suits are assembled without traditional interfacings, backings, facings or heavy linings. Instead, there are only two fabric layers—the shell fabric and the lining. Many of the shell fabrics are textured Scottish wools or Linton tweeds (see p. 9) that most designers would consider too loosely woven and too fragile for skirts and jackets. Others are made from guipure lace, chenille, brocade and cotton or sequin embroideries. Most of the linings are delicate materials that feel wonderful next to the skin but aren't suitable for heavy wear, for example, silk gauze, China silk and charmeuse. They often contrast with the shell fabric in color, design or texture.

On many suits, the shell fabric and lining are machine-quilted together so the loosely structured shell fabric will not sag and the garment maintains its shape. On traditional suits, this support is provided by backings

The signature Chanel suit, worn here by Coco Chanel herself, is made of a loosely woven tweed and assembled without traditional interfacings, backings and facings. The lining is quilted to the jacket, and decorative trim (braid mounted on grosgrain ribbon) edges the cuffs, pockets and perimeter of the jacket. (Photo by Cecil Beaton, courtesy of Sotheby's, London.)

The lining of this Chanel jacket is quilted in rectangles to the plaid shell fabric, which is less conspicuous than would have been the traditional vertical lines of quilting used by the designer for fabrics without prominent patterns. Note, too, the Chanel buttonholes— bound on the facing and hand-worked on the face of the jacket— the jacket's trim and the chain weight at the hem to make the jacket hang smoothly. (Photo by Irving Solero. The National Museum of Fashion at the Fashion Institute of Technology, New York. Gift of Mrs. Samuel M.V. Hamilton.)

and interfacings. The quilting on Chanel's suits is almost invisible, since the stitching thread usually matches one of the colors in the shell fabric. If the thread does show, it becomes almost a status symbol, since most of the innumerable copies made are not quilted.

Other finishing touches on Chanel suits include signature buttons and buttonholes (see p. 91 and p. 93), functional sleeve vents and brass chains on the inside of the jacket hems, which act as weights. Many of the jackets are also trimmed imaginatively at the edges, pockets and sleeve vents with braids, ribbons, yarns, bias bindings, decorative selvages or pipings.

QUILTING THE LINING

On most Chanel jackets, the sections are quilted to the lining before the side, shoulder or sleeve seams are stitched. Since quilting tends to reduce the size of the garment section, the pieces are quilted together before they're cut into garment sections. Large, rectangular pieces of fabric and lining are pinned together and then basted and quilted. Next the garment sections are thread-traced onto the quilted rectangles before they're cut. The jacket is then basted together, fitted and stitched at the side seams and shoulders. Finally, the lining seams are sewn together.

The quilted pattern can be vertical, horizontal or rectangular, depending on the shell fabric and garment design. The quilting rows should be inconspicuous and parallel to grainlines and stripes. Generally, tweeds and

fabrics without prominent fabric patterns are quilted vertically. If the design has princess seams, horizontally quilted rows, perpendicular to the seamline, may be less conspicuous than vertical quilting. On plaid fabrics, quilted rectangles are sometimes the most unobtrusive choice, and when quilting lace or large prints, hand quilting is sometimes best.

Begin making a quilted lining by cutting rectangles for each jacket section from the shell fabric and the lining fabric about 4 in. wider and longer than the finished garment section. Outline the section shapes on the right side of the rectangles with chalk or thread tracing. This is a temporary guide, and it doesn't have to be exact. Next, spread the lining fabric wrong side up. With the right side up and the grainlines aligned, place the fabric rectangle on the lining. Plan the quilting pattern and pin the sections together on the proposed quilting lines. Do not pull the lining taut. Then, with a diagonal basting stitch, baste between the pinned rows so the lining will not shift, and remove the pins between the bastings.

Silk machine thread, fine cotton machine-embroidery thread and mercerized cotton are all suitable for quilting with a machine. Begin with the shell fabric on top and machine-quilt each section, stopping and starting about 2 in. from the sides and hemline so you can complete the seams and hem without ripping the quilting. Leave long thread ends and pull them so they are caught between the shell and lining. Knot and trim the ends, remove the bastings, and press lightly.

The garment sections are cut next. Place the toile sections on the quilted rectangles, with the shell fabric uppermost, and mark all stitching lines with pins. Remove the toile and thread-trace the shell fabric without catching the lining. Then trim away some of the excess fabric at the edges, leaving 1 in. seam allowances and a 2-in. hem. Sewing through both the shell and lining, baste all the seams and any darts, then top-baste the seams. Baste the dart centers and then baste the darts together with the lining like a backing. Then fold and baste the hems in place for the first fitting.

After the jacket has been fitted, the bastings removed and the necessary changes made, fold and pin the lining fabric out of the way and baste and stitch the vertical seams of the jacket. Press the seams open and trim the seam allowances evenly to ¾ in. or less. Then trim the lining seam allowances so they're slightly narrower than those on the jacket. Fold one raw lining edge under, aligning the folded edge with the seamline, and baste about ⅛ in. from the folded edge. Repeat for the lining edge on the adjoining garment section. Slipstitch the lining together. Remove the bastings and press lightly.

On some Chanel suits, particularly on the skirts, the lining and shell fabric are seamed together like a backing. If you prefer this method of attaching the linings, after the seams are pressed and trimmed, cover the seam allowances with a strip of lining fabric. Turn under the long edges of the lining strip and baste, then fell them to the lining.

ADDING A CHAIN WEIGHT

The House of Chanel uses a brass chain at the hemline on the inside of the jackets to make them hang smoothly and remain level without "catching" on the top of the skirt. On most jackets, the chain is sewn around the entire hem, starting and ending from 3 in. to 4 in. from the edge of the front openings. On the occasional jacket with many heavy buttons, which provide enough weight for the front, the chain is only used on the back.

MAKING A QUILTED LINING

QUILTING SHELL FABRIC TO LINING

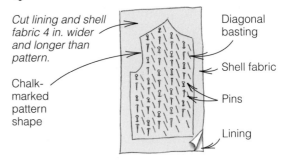

Pin shell fabric to lining along proposed quilting lines, and diagonal-baste between rows of pins. Then remove pins and machine-stitch between basted rows stopping 2 in. from edges.

SEAMING JACKET AND LINING

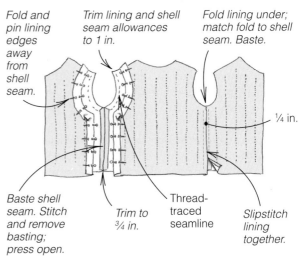

FINISHING SEAMS WHEN JACKET IS BACKED

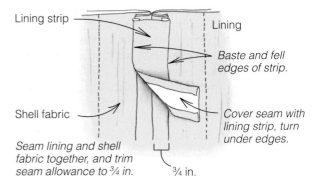

When the jacket is lined to the edge, the chain is usually located just above the hemline. When lined to the top of the hem allowance, the chain is located just below the lining. On one Chanel jacket I examined, the chain was positioned at the top of the hem allowance between the jacket and silk chiffon lining.

When sewing a chain weight onto a jacket, make certain that the jacket has had its final pressing. Then hand-sew both sides of the chain links to the inside of the jacket. To prevent unsightly press marks when the suit is dry-cleaned, remove the chain for cleaning.

CHANEL TRIMS

Chanel fashioned striking, imaginative trims from unusual materials, and this custom continues today at the House of Chanel. Many trims incorporate yarns that are braided, crocheted or embroidered onto the fabric. Some trims are made from decorative selvages enhanced with matching yarn or transformed into pipings. Others feature grosgrain ribbons, bias strips or ordinary topstitching. Most trims are applied after the jacket is quilted but before the lining is sewn to the jacket edge and the buttonholes are made. While some trims are sewn on the right side of the jacket, others are joined to the edge itself.

Grosgrain ribbon is used frequently on tweeds as a base for custom-made or purchased braid. On some Chanel suits there's a single piece of grosgrain under the braid, while others use two narrow pieces on either side of the trim because they're easier to shape at corners and curves. When making this trim yourself, try to use imported grosgrain with tiny scallops at the edge. It's more attractive and easier to shape around curves than the straight-edged American grosgrain. The braid can be ready-made, or you can make it yourself from yarn.

Begin this trim by shaping the grosgrain with a steam iron so that it will fit around any curved edges. Small hand-sewn darts work well on sharp curves. Starting at a side seam, sew the grosgrain to the garment by hand with small running stitches placed in the center of the ribbon. Miter the ribbon with a fold at the corners when needed.

To make a plaited braid, cut six to twelve strands of yarn at least three times the finished length of the trim. Knot the strands together at one end and pin this end to your pressing stand. Hold the strands taut while you

Always interesting and unique, most Chanel trims are easy to make. From left, yarn embroidery enhances selvage piping; ½-in. wide tubing made from the suit's blouse fabric laces the jacket's cuff; narrow, self-fabric bias strips are felled to the cuff; and a contrasting bias cuff provides a dramatic edging. (Photo by Irving Solero. The National Museum of Fashion at the Fashion Institute of Technology, New York. Gifts of Mrs. Samuel M.V. Hamilton, Mrs. Lawrence Cowen, Mrs. C.L. Cartwright and Mrs. Donald Elliman, from left, respectively.)

plait them. To finish the ends, secure the yarns with machine stitching. Then center the plaited braid on the ribbon and sew it in place by hand.

Many Chanel jackets are also trimmed with selvages, which are themselves embellished with embroidery or another trim. Sometimes when the edges of the jacket coincide with the edge of the shell fabric, they are true selvages, but in most instances the selvages are first cut from the fabric, then joined to the edge or are used as pipings.

To trim a jacket with selvages, cut the selvages at least ½ in. wider than the desired finished width and mark the finished width on the selvage with thread tracing. With right sides together, align the thread tracing with the seamline on the garment and baste them together.

Another simple but elegant Chanel trim features parallel rows of topstitching on the collar, pocket flaps, sleeve vents and the front edges of the jacket front. To sew this trim, use a regular stitch length (1.75mm, or 15 stitches to the inch) to edgestitch ¹⁄₁₆ in. from the edge of the garment. Stitch eight to twelve parallel rows, spacing them ¹⁄₁₆ in. apart. Don't worry if the topstitching isn't perfectly regular—neither is Chanel's.

CHAPTER 11

EVENINGWEAR

Eveningwear designs run the gamut from unadorned, body-clinging dresses of bias-cut silk charmeuse to richly ornamented ballgowns with multiple skirts and extravagantly shaped garments that are almost impossible to sit down in (see the Hanae Mori design on p. 53). Any type of garment—even shorts—can be eveningwear. The difference between an evening design and a comparable daytime garment may be as subtle as the choice of fabric, but eveningwear is usually more luxurious in both fabric and embellishment and more complex and exaggerated in design.

When planning a garment for eveningwear, there are numerous details to consider and questions to ask. Perhaps the most crucial questions in terms of the garment's construction are: What kind of shape, or silhouette, will the garment have? What special support is needed inside the garment to maintain this shape? What kind of support will the body itself need to look attractive in the garment and minimize stress on the fabric and construction? And if the garment is to be embellished, how and when during the garment's construction is that embellishment applied?

Some answers to these complex questions are found in the techniques described in this chapter. Although sometimes used on daytime clothing, most of these techniques are characteristic of eveningwear, and many are also appropriate for bridal gowns.

SUPPORTING THE DESIGN'S SILHOUETTE

The structural support for the silhouette of eveningwear design can be simply the lining, interfacing and backing that lend body to the fashion fabric. Or it can be an elaborately complex system of backings, interfacings, underskirts and underpinnings.

Various materials are used for backing and interfacing eveningwear. Some, including organza, silk muslin, chiffon, China silk and hair canvas, are also used on day dresses and suits. Others, such as horsehair braid, nylon crinoline and tulle, are generally reserved for eveningwear designs because they're stiffer and able to produce more dramatic silhouettes.

Deciding which backing material to use, whether to combine it with an interfacing and whether additional underskirts or underpinnings are needed involves some trial and error. There are no hard-and-fast rules, and each design will have different requirements from the next. For information on choosing backing and interfacing materials, see the sidebar on p. 53. For a discussion of working with backing materials, see p. 120 and p. 122.

USING A LINING TO CREATE SHAPE

Backings and interfacings are generally used to give a garment shape. Rarely do linings serve to shape a garment, but there are notable exceptions. Dresses with balloon, pouf or bubble skirts—also dubbed "harem dresses"—rely on a shortened lining to help give them shape. The fullness of these skirts can be controlled from the right or wrong side of the garment.

When a skirt's fullness is controlled on the right side, the skirt is generally narrow at the hemline and full above it, with the fullness gathered into a band at the hemline, as in the short evening dress designed by Yves Saint Laurent for Dior (shown at left on p. 188). The lining, which supports the skirt, is usually a simple tube that fits the body smoothly, and the fuller outer skirt is between 8 in. and 12 in. longer than the lining. When the skirt and lining are joined at the top and bottom, the outer skirt is forced to pouf out.

Designed by couturier Madame Grès in 1935 under the label Alix, this metallic evening coat is covered with an elaborate trapunto design in a leaf-and-bird motif on its front and sleeves. The back is quilted with machine-stitched channels. (Photo by Cathy Carver. Metropolitan Museum of Art. Gift of Miss Ellerbe Wood, 1940.)

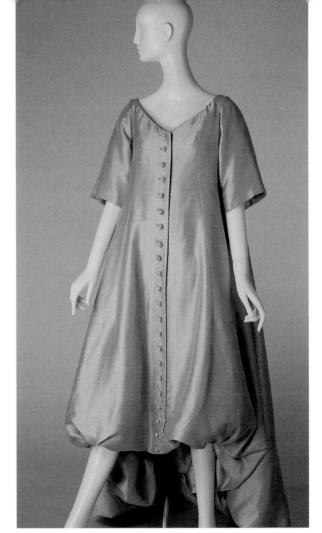

This short evening dress was designed by Yves Saint Laurent for Christian Dior in 1959. Sewn from silk faille, the pouffed harem skirt has combined support from the lining, two tulle underskirts and the skewed ruffles at the hemline (see p. 193 for a detail photo of the ruffles). The skirt's fullness is controlled on the right side with a band near the hem. (Photo by Susan Kahn. Metropolitan Museum of Art. Gift of Joyce von Bothmer, 1976.)

Designed by Yves Saint Laurent for Christian Dior's Fall 1959 collection and worn by the Baroness Philippe de Rothschild, this silk shantung coat-dress with 22 self-fabric buttons was dubbed 'Scheherazade.' The pouffed hemline of the skirt was created by gathering the fullness at the hem into the shorter lining. (Photo by Susan Kahn. Metropolitan Museum of Art. Gift of Baron Philippe de Rothschild, 1983.)

To create a dress or gown with a pouffed skirt controlled from the right side, begin by assembling the skirt and lining. Then baste them together at the waist and put them on a dress form or a hanger. Make a separate band of garment fabric, pin the bottom of the skirt to the lining, adjust the fullness to create the desired pouf and baste the band to the lower edge of the skirt. Then baste the skirt to the bodice for the fitting.

After the fitting and corrections are made and with right sides together, baste and stitch the skirt and band together. Press the seamline, wrap the band to the wrong side, and pin the band flat. Secure it permanently with a running stitch, then cover it with the lining and fell the lining permanently. If the skirt needs to be shortened after the band is sewn permanently, hand-sew a horizontal tuck in the lining, which will both shorten the lining and increase the size of the pouf.

The fullness of a pouf skirt can also be created and controlled entirely on the wrong side of the garment. In this case, the skirt hem wraps to the underside and is gathered to the lining, as in another design by Saint Laurent for Dior, shown above and top left, facing page. In this dress, the skirt is longer than the lining—from 4 in. in the front to 22 in. in the back—and is folded up to join the lining, with the seam joining the two, positioned above the folded hemline. When a skirt is short in front and long in back, like this one, the exposed section of the lining should be cut from self-fabric.

In this detail of the gown shown in full at right on the facing page, each front leg of the pantaloon was sewn to the front of the skirt so it moved with the wearer as she walked. (Photo by Susan Kahn. Metropolitan Museum of Art. Gift of Baron Philippe de Rothschild, 1983.)

The two underskirts on Christian Dior's 'Mexico,' shown in full on p. 192, contribute to the light, filmy quality of the design. One underskirt is sewn from silk muslin and the second from cotton tulle. (Photo by Susan Kahn. Metropolitan Museum of Art. Gift of Mrs. Henry Rogers Benjamin, 1965.)

Both of these techniques can be used on other garment sections, such as sleeves, and on garments other than eveningwear. For blouson blouses or puffed sleeves, the fullness is usually controlled on the right side since the blouse or sleeve needs to narrow at the waist or wrist. For coats and capes, this fullness is generally controlled on the inside since these garments usually remain wide at the bottom edge.

Whether controlled from the right or wrong side, a pouffed skirt can droop when worn. To prevent drooping, couturiers sometimes stuff the pouf with large balls of net. According to legend, Valentino once stuffed a dress with beautiful organza flowers. It was to be a secret between him and the client.

UNDERSKIRTS

One method of supporting a skirt's fullness is with one or more attached underskirts or separate petticoats. These undergarments range in shape from simple tubes that might be found below a slim or knife-pleated skirt to billowing, multi-layered and multi-tiered skirts lying beneath yards of satin on a wedding dress or ball gown. The design of the underskirt and the fabric it's sewn from are determined both by the garment's silhouette and by the drape, hand and weight of the fashion fabric.

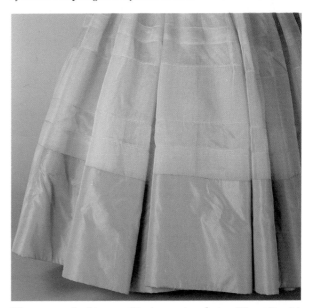

The two underskirts on Dior's evening design 'Compiègné,' shown in full on p. 191, are generously interfaced with horizontal rows of horsehair braid to support the gown's heavy skirt. The taffeta binding at the hem is cut on the crossgrain rather than the bias because the underskirt is rectangular and the hem straight. (Photo by Susan Kahn. Metropolitan Museum of Art. Gift of Mrs. Byron C. Foy, 1956.)

SPECIAL HEM FINISHES

Eveningwear designs sometimes need special hems. Two of these hems—weighted and arced hemlines—are especially useful for the home sewer. Weighted hems make the skirt on a long gown hang close to the feet instead of billowing in the wind—or they serve to prevent the back hem on evening pants or a long straight skirt from catching on the wearer's shoes. And a small arc built into the center-front hem of a floor-length ballgown keeps the wearer from tripping on her skirts.

WEIGHTED HEMS

Weights can be enclosed between the garment and hem allowance before a garment is hemmed or sewn to the outside of the completed hem, which allows for easy removal when the garment is cleaned. There are several different types of weights you can use: lightweight self-fabric and twill tape, separate round or square lead weights, gilded chains and weighted tapes, which have small lead pellets enclosed inside a cotton casing.

Self-fabric or twill tape is best suited to lightweight fashion fabric and works particularly well when applied only to the back hems of pants or long skirts. If the weights are to be concealed inside the hem, use individual lead weights, which can be hammered flat. The individual weights are used at vents, openings, corners of loose panels and at the ends of seamlines on medium-weight to heavyweight fabrics. Gilded chains are an attractive

means of keeping blouses and jackets from riding up, and weighted tapes are generally used when large sections of the hemline are to be weighted. Like lead drapery weights, the weighted tapes can be hammered flat.

When the weights are applied to a finished hem, gilded chains or decorative weights are most attractive. Since decorative weights are almost impossible to find, heavy, flat buttons can be substituted or lead weights can be sprayed with gilt paint or covered with fabric (see p. 80 and p. 82).

To add weights before hemming a design, first interface the hem with cotton flannel, hair canvas or muslin (see p. 68). Then, if you're adding a chain, baste it loosely to the interfacing at the hemline before completing the hem. If you're fastening individual weights, baste them just above the hemline at the garment openings and the ends of the seamlines. When the garment is cleaned, the dry cleaner should be advised of the weights in the hem if you haven't removed them beforehand to avoid press marks.

ARCED HEMLINES

Most women look beautiful in floor-length ball gowns—until they start walking. An arc at the center-front hem easily eliminates clumsy entanglement with billowing skirts and allows the wearer to move, and even dance, gracefully. The arc can be created by making the hemline shorter in front or by doubling the hem at center front. Doubling the hem is frequently

DOUBLE HEM

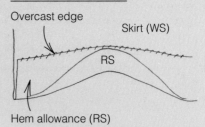

To create an arc, fold over hem allowance a second time, tapering ends.

preferable to making the hem shorter in front because it allows the sewer to control the curve and shape of the edge more easily.

When doubling the hem, you can raise it half the depth of the hemline. That is, if you start with a 4-in. hem allowance, you can raise the hem 2 in. A hem can be raised in front by as much as 5 in. without distortion, but that, of course, requires a 10-in. hem allowance. A more practical solution to raise a hem by 5 in. is to begin with a hemline that's already 2 in. to 3 in. shorter in front than in the back and double it.

To create an arc by doubling the hem, first finish the hem in the usual manner (see pp. 63-64). Then fold the hem under at center front and pin it, tapering each end to the finished hemline. Baste the hem and put the garment on a dress form or hanger to make sure the effect of the arc is pleasing. Then secure the hem permanently, remove the bastings and press the hem lightly.

Often sewn into the garment, underskirts can also be mounted on a separate slip base or waist cincher and are made from various fabrics such as cotton or nylon tulle, silk taffeta, nylon crinoline and soft plain-weave silks. In order to reduce bulk at the hips on a multi-tiered underskirt, each of its several layers is longer and sewn to the base foundation a little higher than the layer immediately beneath it. The shortest, bottom layer is sewn by hand to the foundation or slip base first; and the longest, uppermost layer, the one closest to the waist, is sewn last. The seam allowances joining these tiers to the foundation slip can be narrow and stitched toward the bodice, with the raw edges flattened against the slip with a catchstitch. Or the allowances can be wide and sewn with a buttressed seam.

Underskirts are often stiffened at the hem with horsehair braid sewn on by hand or machine. A single row of horsehair can be applied to one or more of the underskirts, or several rows can be sewn on each skirt one above the next. Horsehair braid is available in widths up to 6 in. and in soft and heavy weights. The heavyweight horsehair braid is available in wider widths than its softer counterpart and has a thread on one edge that can be gathered to shape the horsehair to fit a curve. Stiffer than the lightweight horsehair braid, it can support garments made from heavy silk, faille, taffeta, embroidered fabric and cotton pique, but it will, in turn, make the garment heavier.

Two Dior evening gowns, which the designer called "Compiègne" and "Mexico," shown at right and on p. 192, provide a wealth of information on underskirts, including the art of strategically stiffening them with horsehair braid. The two dresses are quite different. "Compiègne" is made of a heavy but soft silk satin patterned with velvet roses. Its floor-length skirt is enormous—7½ yd. at the hemline. "Mexico" is made of a lightweight, silk muslin similar to silk organza, but more opaque and softer. Its top skirt, cut on the crossgrain with the selvage at the hem, measures 7⅔ yd., not including the front drape. Its second circular skirt is pleated to a yoke and measures 5¼ yd. at the hem.

Both of the underskirts on "Compiègne" were stiffened with several widths of horsehair braid before being hand-sewn to a strapless tulle corselette. The outermost underskirt, made of lightweight silk, is darted and its edge is sewn flat against the corselette. It's stiffened with six horizontal rows of horsehair braid, ranging from 2 in. to 6 in. wide, that are machine-stitched at

Designed by Christian Dior for his 1954 Autumn/Winter Collection, this gown entitled 'Compiègne' is made of costly silk satin with cut velvet roses. The fabric was woven with extra silk warps that were cut by hand to make the roses 'bloom.' (Photo by Mike De Dulmen, courtesy of Christian Dior.)

the top and bottom. At the top of the underskirt just below the waistline there is a single row of ½-in. soft horsehair braid, applied with one row of machine stitching at the center. The straight edge at the bottom of the skirt is finished with a wide blue taffeta binding cut on the lengthwise grain, 11½ in. wide on the right side and 6¾ in. wide on the wrong side. The bottom underskirt begins about 2 in. below the first one. Also sewn flat against the foundation, it's stiffened with four strips of horsehair braid ranging from 2½ in. to 6 in.

The stiffening for Dior's "Mexico" is quite different. Since the fashion fabric is much lighter in weight, the underskirts have been designed to accentuate the diaphanous quality of this two-piece dress. The skirt

Made from delicate silk muslin printed with scallops, Christian Dior's 'Mexico' was created for his Spring/Summer 1953 collection. This two-piece dress has two overskirts, one cut on the crossgrain with the selvage at the hemline, and the second, a complete circle, finished with a more conventional hand-rolled hem. (Photo by Ito, courtesy of Christian Dior.)

SUPPORTING GATHERS AND RUFFLES

Seams can be used to support a given silhouette. A variation of the gathered seam (see pp. 48-49), the buttressed seam is cut with an extra-wide seam allowance, which forms a foundation under ruffles, flounces and gathered skirts and forces the fullness to stand away from the seamline (see, for example, the Balenciaga gown on p. 69 and the Givenchy design on the back cover). The width of the gathered section's seam allowance varies with the design, but it's generally from 1 in. to 5 in. and may not be the same as that on the section it joins.

To increase the buttressed effect when the design's fabric is unusually heavy or if you want an exaggerated effect, add a piece of crisp, lightweight interfacing at the top of the skirt on the gathered edge. Cut the interfacing on the bias to the desired width, which should be at least twice the width of the wider seam allowance on the gathered edge. Then before gathering the skirt, baste the interfacing to the wrong side.

To sew a buttressed seam on skirts or ruffles, fold the seam allowance of the gathered edge to the wrong side. Align the seamlines and matchpoints, with right sides up. Slipbaste or fell the sections together. Then machine stitch or hand sew the seam permanently, remove the bastings and press. Do not press over the seamline, but instead press each section separately to the seamline.

Another way to provide support for a gathered skirt is to sew a skewed ruffle on an underskirt. A skewed ruffle is made by folding the fabric lengthwise with the wrong sides together, and then shifting the top layer to one side. This ruffle can also be sewn to the outside of a garment and serve as pure decorative trim. On the detail of the dress shown on the facing page, skewed ruffles are sewn to the skirt itself, where they both look attractive and provide support for the fringed ruffles, which in turn prevent the skirt's pouf from dropping over the seamline.

The shifted top layer of skewed ruffles make them appear to be cut on a bias, even though they may actually be cut on the straight grain or crossgrain. They can be any width from a narrow 1 in. to a generous 12 in. When used to provide support, however, they're generally 3 to 6 in. wide.

consists of two overskirts cut from the design fabric, supported by two underskirts attached to a slim, silk crepe slip.

Made of silk muslin, the first underskirt has six tiers, each one about twice the fullness of the one above it. To give the underskirt some body, a strip of narrow, soft horsehair braid was applied to the hem edge and to the seamlines at the tops of the three lowest tiers. The second underskirt is made of cotton tulle. It's gathered into the seam at the top of the third tier. Two bands of horsehair braid are enclosed inside the hem.

It's possible that the underskirts were built up in several stages as the design's construction was worked out since cotton muslin would not behave the same as the fabrics used for the actual underskirts. This strategy may suggest an interesting plan of attack for the home sewer.

The two fringed ruffles in this detail of the evening dress shown in full on p. 188 are each supported by a skewed ruffle. The top fringed ruffle and the skewed ruffle supporting it are sewn to the skirt with buttressed seams. (Photo by Susan Kahn. Metropolitan Museum of Art. Gift of Joyce von Bothmer, 1976.)

SKEWED RUFFLE

Thread-traced seamline

Gather here.

1. Shift top layer of ruffle to one side (here shifted to right).

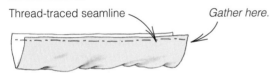

2. Tack folded edge to gathered seamline.

To make a skewed ruffle, begin by folding the ruffle lengthwise with wrong sides together and the folded edge toward you. Then shift the top layer of the ruffle to one side, match the thread-traced seamlines as shown above, and pin them together. The amount you can shift one layer increases with the width of the ruffle, but the more you shift that layer, the narrower the ruffle becomes. Adjust and repin the ruffle if you want to shift the layer more or less, baste the seamlines together and gather the ruffle.

To make the ruffle stand away from the skirt, baste the ruffle to the garment with a buttressed seam (see the facing page) and set it permanently with a short running stitch. For an even firmer ruffle, tack the folded edge of the ruffle to the seamline every 5 or 6 in.

UNDERPINNINGS TO SHAPE THE BODY

Some eveningwear designs are sewn with one or more custom-made underpinnings to support the garment's silhouette and hold the body in a smooth line underneath. Such underpinnings include a shaped waist stay, which hugs the waist and reduces stress on the fabric and fasteners at the waist; a corselette, or long-lined, boned brassiere that extends to the waist or below and gives the body a firm, smooth line; and a bust enhancer, which adds fullness to a small bust and roundness to a sagging bust.

SHAPED WAIST STAY

Because eveningwear usually fits more closely than daywear, the waist stays on evening gowns are generally wider and stiffer and control the body more than the waist stays on day dresses. Stays on eveningwear are usually darted to fit the body and are often boned so that they don't roll. Instead of the grosgrain ribbon used on waist stays for day dresses, eveningwear stays are made of stiffer support fabrics like petersham, faille, taffeta, girdle elastic or cotton corset fabric. If your planned gown has a fitted bodice and waist, you may want to consider adding a waist stay. (See pp. 49-50 and pp. 129-132 for more information on stays.)

To make a waist stay for eveningwear, cut the stay fabric 2 in. to 6 in. wide and 12 in. longer than the actual waist measurement. If the fabric isn't crisp enough to hold the body firmly, use two layers and machine-quilt them together. Next, pin the stay around the waistline of the dress form. Then pin out as many small darts in the stay as needed to make it fit the waist smoothly. Mark the waistline garment centers and side seam opening. Remove the stay from the dress form and re-pin the darts so they are on the inside of the stay, next to the body. Double-baste the darts and baste the stay to vertical seamlines on the inside of the garment for the fitting.

Fit the garment, pinning the stay together at the opening so that it fits snugly, and carefully mark the ends of the stay. After the fitting, remove the stay from the garment and stitch, press, and trim the darts. If the stay needs boning to keep it from rolling, sew the boning over the darts (see the sidebar on boning on p. 196). Additional boning can be added between the darts and the opening.

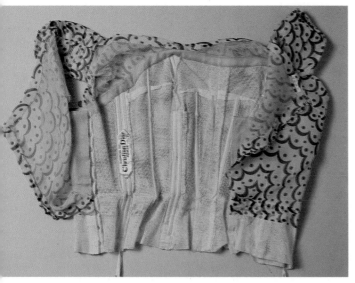

The cotton tulle corselette supporting Christian Dior's two-piece dress 'Mexico' (shown in full on p. 192) is cut double with a fold at the hemline, which extends about 4 in. below the waist. It's boned with 16 metal spiral stays of varying lengths, most extending to the hem and a few stopping at the waist, where the bodice is attached to the corselette. (Photo by Susan Kahn. Metropolitan Museum of Art. Gift of Mrs. Henry Rogers Benjamin, 1965.)

Finish the ends of the stay with hooks and eyes. To do this, fold the raw edge at each end to the wrong side and place a piece of plain-weave tape or selvage between the layers to reinforce the ends of the stay. Edgestitch the ends and stitch again ½ in. away. Then trim close to the second stitched line. To make the stay ends extra firm, stitch several rows in between the two rows of stitches you just sewed or insert a strip of boning.

If the garment has a back opening, sew the hooks to the end of the stay on the right back; if it has a side opening, sew them to the front section. Sew the eyes to the other end of the stay. To cover the hooks and eyes, cut a facing for each end of the stay out of 1-in. wide strips of lightweight silk or cotton tulle. Fold under the sides and edges of the facings so that the hooks and eyes will barely show. Baste the edges and fell the facing in place. Bind the long edges at the top and bottom of the stay with a lightweight bias or narrow tape. Then mark the waistline of the stay with catchstitches so when you sew the stay into the dress, you can match the waistline markings.

FINISHING ENDS OF A STAY

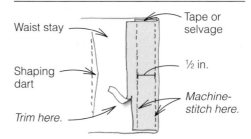

1. Reinforce ends with tape or selvage.

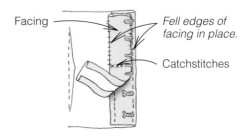

2. Attach facing and mark waistline with catchstitches.

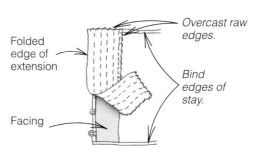

3. Make an extension to prevent hooks from rubbing.

On a couture garment, an extension is sometimes attached to the underlap of the stay to prevent the hooks from rubbing against the body. This underlap can be sewn from various fabrics, depending on your preference—velvet, faille, grosgrain, double-faced cotton flannel or cotton tulle. To make an extension, cut a piece of fabric that's 2 in. to 4 in. wide and the length of the placket opening on the stay. With the wrong sides together, fold the extension in half lengthwise, machine-stitch it ¼ in. from the raw edge, then overcast the edges together. Position the underlap under the eyes so that it covers the facing, and pin it in place. Sew it by hand to the back of the stay, placing a row of running stitches near the edge of the underlap and another row at the edge of the stay.

To fasten the stay permanently to the dress or gown, pin it to the wrong side of the garment at the waistline, matching the catchstitches on the stay and waistline markings. Beginning and ending about 1 in. from the ends, sew the stay to the waistline seam with a running stitch. On a design with no waistline seam, secure the stay with short French tacks (see p. 53) at seamlines and darts instead of sewing a row of running stitches.

CONSTRUCTING A CORSELETTE

Since a couturier wants to be sure the client doesn't wear the design over the wrong foundation or, heaven forbid, with no foundation at all, corselettes are built into many evening gowns. Reinforced with boning, the corselette is actually a long-line brassiere designed to fit the body like a second skin, lending a smooth and firm line to a woman's figure and at the same time supporting the garment.

A corselette can extend to the waistline or continue for several inches below it, depending on the design of the dress or gown and the figure of the woman wearing it. Traditionally a corselette is made of two layers of cotton tulle, but it can be made of linen, silk or power net (a girdle fabric with spandex). The cotton tulle, sometimes called English net or bobbinet, is lightweight, soft, cool to wear and doesn't ravel, but it's also expensive and difficult to find (see Sources of Supply on p. 215).

Many corselettes are simple, strapless designs, suitable for a variety of garments, but for backless designs and those with a décolleté or plunging V-neckline, the corselette will follow the lines of the bodice more closely. When made for such designs, the corselette is sometimes wired or stiffened with boning at the edges, and the bodice fabric is often applied directly to the corselette so that it's difficult to determine where the corselette ends and the bodice begins. Sewing the corselette into the garment and finishing the edges are done by hand, and even though it's a time-consuming, task, it's not particularly difficult.

The length of the corselette is determined by the design's silhouette. Although the corselette sometimes ends at the waist, it usually extends several inches below. For bouffant skirts, the corselette is often longer and serves as a base for attaching underskirts, which reduces bulk at the waistline. For close-fitting silhouettes and dropped waistlines, the corselette should be long enough to control the figure and maintain a smooth silhouette.

These directions for a tulle corselette can be adapted for other fabrics and foundation designs. In couture sewing, the corselette pattern is draped on the client's dress form. If you don't have a dress form, you'll need someone to fit the corselette on you.

Begin with a dress pattern for a simple princess-line sheath or shift. On the front and back garment sections of the paper pattern, measure and mark the bottom of the corselette no more than 7 in. below the waist and use the full pattern up to the shoulder. Once you've made and fit the pattern, you can cut the top to the height you want for the corselette.

Cut the corselette from two layers of tulle, one cut on the lengthwise grain and the other on the crossgrain, which together will strengthen the corselette and give it added flexibility. If you want even more control in the corselette, cut both layers with the lengthwise grain going around the body, with a foldline at the bottom. The foldline will help keep the bottom edge flat.

Spread the pattern on the tulle, allowing about 1 in. for seam allowances at all edges as well as at the garment centers. Thread-trace the seamlines, darts and garment centers and cut the tulle. Before pinning the tulle to the dress form, pin a linen tape from bust point to bust point, which will support the tulle between the breasts and allow you to smooth it out at center front. Pin the tulle to the dress form, beginning at the center front and working toward the side seams. Pin the corselette together so it fits smoothly and snugly. Release the tape at the bust so you can remove excess fullness, and shape the tulle between the breasts. Pin small darts from the center front to the bust points so it will fit like a second skin.

Examine the fit, checking to see whether another small dart at the waist or under the bust is needed. Then chalk-mark the seamlines and one or two matchpoints on each seamline. Then, using the garment pattern as a guide, mark the styleline (the upper edge of the corselette) at the top edge of the tulle and mark the hemline at the bottom. Pin a narrow plain-weave tape stay to the styleline to keep the edge from stretching, but don't trim away the excess tulle above the styleline until after the fitting.

Remove the tulle and double-baste the corselette for the fitting, including the taped stay at the styleline. Finish the opening according to the instructions given

BONING

The boning sewn into corselettes and shaped waist stays prevents horizontal wrinkles and supports the garment. Boning can also be used on skirts and underskirts to create unusual effects, like that in Charles James's "Four-Leaf Clover" design shown on p. 8.

Instead of the whalebone that was once used as boning, today's home sewers can choose among white or spiral steel, rigelene (woven polyester monofilament) and poly boning. Spiral steel bones are usually the best for corselettes and waist stays because they'll bend both sideways and back and forth. They're available in lengths of 2 in. to 14 in., and the ends are finished with metal tips (see Sources of Supply on p. 215). If you need shorter lengths, these metal stays can be cut with wire cutters and the ends covered

with new metal tips, which can be purchased separately. If you need longer lengths, use two stays and overlap the ends ¼ in.

Rigelene and poly boning are sold by the yard and are best used for support in hoop skirts and skirts like that on James's "Four-Leaf Clover" design. The arcs of the clover shape of this design were created with poly boning encased in cotton tape and sewn to the skirt's nylon crinoline backing.

The amount of boning used in a corselette or waist stay varies with the weight of the dress or gown. Most corselettes have 14 to 18 bones. The Dior gown shown on p. 191 has 16. When positioning the boning on a corselette or waist stay, begin with one length of boning on every seam or dart line. On corselettes, place another midway between the bust and underarm and at the center front. Then add

additional boning to create and maintain the desired shape and fit of your garment. Many couture workrooms extend the boning over the bust, and some never do because the support is more rigid.

Spiral boning can be sewn directly to the corselette with a catchstitched casing, but it's usually inserted into a casing ¼ in. to ½ in. longer than the boning and made of narrow plain-weave tape or, less frequently, ribbon or lightweight silk. To make the casing, center and pin a strip of plain-weave tape, ⅜ in. to ½ in. wide, over the seam or dart. Edgestitch the sides and bottom so that the boning will fit snugly inside the casing. Slip the boning into the casing and close the end securely with hand stitches. If the ends of the boning irritate the body, sew 1-in. squares of velvet or cotton flannel to the corselette over the ends of the casing.

BONING A WAIST STAY

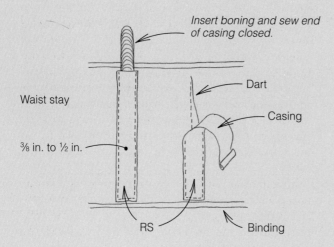

Insert boning and sew end of casing closed.

Waist stay

⅜ in. to ½ in.

Dart

Casing

RS

Binding

below. Since a corselette fits the body so closely, its placket should be finished before the first fitting, or a 20-in. zipper should be basted in temporarily. When setting the zipper, position the stop at the top of the zipper at the styleline of the corselette so the excess zipper hangs below the corselette's hem. If bust enhancers are needed, baste them in place for the fitting (see p. 199).

Fit the corselette on the figure without a bra. If you used a dress form to build the corselette, it may be too loose since the body is less rigid than a dress form. Pin out any excess until the corselette fits snugly and try to avoid ripping seams since you may have trouble repinning them on the figure. Remove the corselette, make any necessary adjustments and re-fit. This time, establish the locations for the boning as well (see the sidebar on boning on the facing page).

When you've perfected the fit, machine-stitch the seams permanently and press them open. Make the casings for the boning (see the sidebar on the facing page), and insert the boning. If necessary, trim the boning so it's ⅛ in. to ¼ in. shorter than the casing and does not extend into the seam allowance at the top. Then sew the stay permanently at the styleline and trim away the excess tulle above it. When needed, add a stay made from grosgrain or silk-covered elastic under the bust or at the waist to anchor the corselette and better define the bustline (see p. 129 for information on making a waist stay). Since there's no horizontal seamline, secure the stay with short French tacks, thread guides or a casing made from catchstitches. If you haven't cut

the corselette with a fold at the bottom, use hand-overcasting to finish the edge. Or, if the stay ends at the waist, finish the edge with a grosgrain stay.

Next, finish the edge of the styleline at the top of the corselette. The type of edge finish you choose depends upon the fabric and style of both the corselette and the garment. For example, the corselette on the red faille dress designed by Yves Saint Laurent for Dior (shown above) is finished separately with a bias binding cut from the dress fabric, which is less noticeable if the edge shows when the wearer moves. Applied by hand, the binding is 1 in. wide on the outside of the corselette and ⅝ in. wide on the inside.

On garments that will never reveal the top edge of the corselette, this edge is often finished with a silk bias facing or strip of tulle ½ in. to 1 in. wide. To face the top edge of the corselette with a bias binding, fold and baste the seam allowance to the wrong side and trim it to ½ in. or less, securing it with a catchstitch. Cover the raw edge with the bias strip and fell the strip in place. (For more information on attaching bias strips, see pp. 76-79.)

Corselettes can be fastened with hooks and eyes or with a zipper. Although the placket for the corselette on a couture garment is usually directly under the dress placket, it's sometimes offset about 1 in. to reduce bulk. The corselette placket can also be located at the side even though the garment opening is at the center front or back. For a hook-and-eye closure at a side opening, the ends lap front over back. For a center-back opening, the ends usually lap right over left like those on a shaped waist stay.

The placket for a corselette differs slightly from that on a shaped waist stay. Compared to the facings on the opening of a shaped waist stay, the facings on a corselette placket are generally sewn from cotton tulle and are slightly wider so the facing can be machine stitched into the placket to reinforce the edge and be used as an underlap. The facings can vary in width, but that for the underlap is generally a little wider than that for the overlap.

The directions given below are for finishing the ends with hooks and eyes. They can easily be adapted for a zipper placket. When sewing in a zipper, use an extra long one that will extend several inches below the corselette, so that you can easily step into your gown or dress.

Begin by cutting two pieces of plain-weave tape or selvage the same length as the corselette opening. Then cut the overlapping facing 4 in. wide and the underlapping facing 5 in. wide. Fold the overlapping facing in half lengthwise, enclose the reinforcing tape in the facing, aligning the raw edges, and baste the three layers together. Repeat for the underlapping facing.

Next, mark both sides of the corselette opening with thread tracing. With the corselette wrong side up, align the raw edges of the overlapping facing with the thread tracing on the overlapping side of the corselette opening. Fold and baste the seam allowance of the corselette over the raw edges of the facing and machine-stitch six to eight rows through all of the layers, spacing the rows 1/16 to 1/8 in. apart. Since the stitching both stiffens and reinforces the edge, the closer the rows are, the stiffer the edge will be. Repeat for the underlapping side of the opening.

Sew the hooks and eyes to the wrong side of the placket opening. Instead of spacing all of them evenly, you may want to cluster some of the hooks and eyes where the corselette opening will receive the most stress, for example, at the waist, top or bottom. Sew the hooks securely approximately 1/16 in. from the edge of the overlap. Then fold the facing over the eyelets so that only the hooks are exposed and fell the folded edge of the facing flat against the tulle.

FINISHING ENDS OF A CORSELETTE

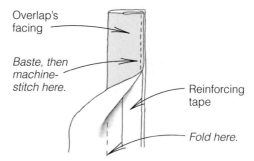

1. Enclose reinforcing tape in facing.

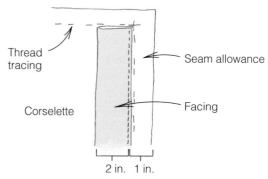

2. Sew facing to overlapping edge of corselette.

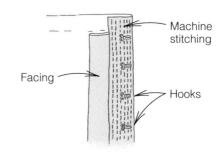

3. Fold seam allowance of corselette over facing and stitch six to eight rows through all layers. Then sew on hooks about 1/16 in. from edge.

Sew the eyes to the underlapping edge so that they extend almost 1/4 in. beyond it. Then fold the facing strip so it extends 1/2 in. beyond the eyes. Sew the layers together securely between the eyes and finish the top of the extension with overcasting stitches.

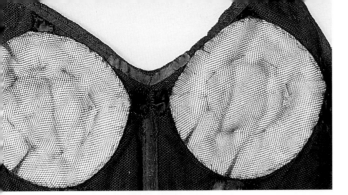

Small bust pads, called bust enhancers, are often used by couturiers to create a more pleasing silhouette. These full-circle pads were sewn into the silk charmeuse corselette of this lace gown and then covered with tulle. (Note the catchstitched elastic neckline stay.) (Photo by Susan Kahn. Author's collection.)

Bust enhancers

Used for both large-busted and small-busted figures to create a smoother, more attractive bustline, bust enhancers can be sewn into the garment or the corselette. These bust pads are made either as full or partial circles. Full-circle pads are placed at the crest of the bust to create a smooth look. Partial-circle pads are placed under the bust to lift it into a more flattering position or above the bust to fill in a hollow.

Sewn from lambswool or cotton batting, bust enhancers are constructed like shoulder pads. The following directions for circular bust enhancers can be adapted for partial circles or other shapes as needed.

Begin with five or six circles of padding in graduated sizes from 1 in. to 3 in. in diameter and stack them with the smallest circle on top. When working with cotton batting, use your fingers to feather the edges to prevent ridges. If you're working with lambswool, cut the edges. Sew the layers together with a loose stabstitch. To make a larger pad, cut more circles; the bottom layers can be larger than 3 in. or the pads can be more graduated. When making pads that are crescent-shaped, experiment with the arrangement of the stack until you get the shape you want. You can center the smaller sections as you would for a full pad or you can align one or more edges.

After you've made the pads, cover both sides with cotton tulle or lightweight silk before sewing them into the garment. Or you can attach the uncovered pads between the garment fabric and lining with a loose running stitch, or sew them in and cover them a single layer of cotton tulle or silk.

EMBELLISHMENTS

Many types of embellishments used on couture garments, like embroidery, beading and appliqué, are not executed in a couture house's own workrooms but rather are sent outside to small firms specializing in a particular ornamentation. The most important of these is the Parisian firm of Lesage, Master Embroider, which specializes in beading and embroidery. Begun about 1870 by the well-known embroiderer Michonet, who did work for both the House of Worth and Vionnet, the firm has a reputation for its creative use of materials and unusual designs. According to current owner François Lesage, one of the firm's most unusual designs was created in 1950 for a gown for couturier Jacques Fath's wife and featured real asparagus ferns. More recently, in the late 1980s, two richly encrusted jackets for Yves Saint Laurent were inspired by two Van Gogh paintings, *Irises* and *Sunflowers*.

Whether to be embellished in the couture house's workrooms or sent to a specialist, all garments are precisely fitted before any embellishment begins. The corrected muslin toile is used to make a paper pattern for designing the embellishment, which, like the garment itself, is proportioned for a particular garment and figure. For the home sewer, the easiest approach to embellishment is to use the corrected toile as a pattern, thread-trace each garment section on a rectangle of garment fabric and embellish the sections before cutting them out.

Preparing for embellishment

The ultimate success of your embellishment depends in part on the care with which you approach initial preparations like dressing the frame and transferring the embellishment design to the garment fabric. A frame is often recommended for appliqué, beading, embroidery, quilting and some passementerie because it holds the work taut and prevents the fabric from shifting and puckering. You'll need a rectangular quilting frame that's adjustable in size, which may be difficult to find. If you can't locate an adjustable frame, you can make one (for information on making a frame, see *Threads* magazine, No. 44, p. 52).

The first step is to use the corrected toile to cut out the garment fabric for all the sections being embellished. For each section, cut a fabric rectangle several inches wider and longer than the section itself. Then use the

Couture embellishments run the gamut from simple tucks, top-stitching and appliqué to elaborate beaded and embroidered designs. On this detail (above) of the lightweight silk faille appliquéd design by Mariska Karasz from the late 1920s (shown in full at right), the stitches are so fine and uniform that they form their own pattern on the inside of the unlined coat. Although most of the coat is made by hand, the dress is machine-stitched. (Photo by Cathy Carver. Metropolitan Museum of Art. Gift of Katherine J. Judson, in memory of Jeanne Wertheimer, 1977.)

toile to cut out a duplicate paper pattern of each section being embellished. Use a crisp paper, such as brown wrapping paper. Thread-trace all the stitching lines and grainlines onto the fabric section.

If you're fitting the garment itself instead of a toile, cut out the sections with at least 1½-in. wide seam and hem allowances. After fitting and correcting the garment, take it apart and make a duplicate paper pattern of the section being embellished. Then, whether you're working with the corrected toile or the fitted garment section, transfer all the stitching and grainlines to the paper pattern.

To transfer these lines, first place the pattern paper on a resilient surface like a cork table, felt table pad or piece of cardboard. Then place the toile or garment section on top of the paper, smoothing it and pinning it to the pattern with pushpins, working from the center out to the edges. Use a stiletto tracing wheel or a fine needle to transfer the lines to the paper pattern. Then draw or trace the embellishment design on the paper pattern, modifying the design as needed so that it fills the space attractively and does not extend into the seam allowances, hem or darts.

The design for the embellishment is usually transferred onto the fabric section before the fabric is mounted on the frame, but large designs may be easier to transfer with the fabric in place on a frame. There are several ways to transfer the design. On medium or dark fabrics, you can use white dressmaker's tracing carbon and a tracing wheel on the wrong side of the fabric. You can also thread-trace the design, but the most versatile method, and the one favored in couture workrooms, is "prick-and-pounce." This is done by dusting powder over the pattern paper perforated to duplicate the design.

For the prick-and-pounce method, you'll need a needle to prick the design into the paper; a pouncer, which you can either buy or make; and white or gray pouncing powder or cornstarch to mark the design through the pricked holes in the paper. Embroiderers use a special machine to prick out the outline of the design, but you can do this with a sewing machine set for 12 stitches per inch, with a large sewing needle or with a stiletto tracing wheel.

If you're making a pouncer, place the powder or cornstarch in the center of a 6-in. muslin square. Gather the muslin tightly around the powder and fasten it with a rubber band.

Perforate your paper pattern along both the lines of your design and the stitching and grainlines. If the design is symmetrical and is to be applied to two garment sections, neatly stack and pin together the two paper patterns you made, and perforate them as one. Remove the pins and separate the embellishment patterns without tearing them. Smooth the holes by rubbing them lightly with fine-grade sandpaper or place the patterns on the fabric with the rough side up.

The design can be transferred to the right or wrong side of the fabric, depending on which side you work to apply the embellishment. Most embellishments are worked from the right side of the fabric, but beading with a tambour hook is worked from the wrong side (see the photo at right and the instructions on p. 206).

To transfer the design to the fabric, place the embellishment pattern on the garment section, align the grainlines and stitching lines, and pin the edges together. Dip the pouncer in pouncing powder or cornstarch. Work carefully to avoid shifting the pattern, checking as you go to be sure the design is completely transferred, because, once you've removed the embellish-

Embroiderers in one atelier of the famed Parisian firm of Lesage, Master Embroiderer work with tambour hooks on the wrong side of the framed fabric to attach strings of beads held in the other hand below the fabric. (Photo courtesy of Lesage, Master Embroiderer.)

ment pattern, it's almost impossible to reposition precisely. When you've transferred the design, remove the pattern and connect the dots with white dressmaker's pencil or a sharp lead pencil (the embellishment will cover your marks). Then shake the fabric to remove the excess powder.

Thread tracing, the alternative method of transferring a design, is a good choice for marking net or lace, or for transferring the design to the other side of the fabric if you're incorporating different types of embellishment on the same piece. To thread-trace a design, begin with the right sides up, place the design pattern on the fabric, and smooth and baste the layers together. Then working from the center out, use a short basting stitch to trace the motifs, sewing through the tissue paper, and carefully tear away the paper pattern.

Once you've transferred your design to the fabric, the next step is to mount the fabric on the frame. If you're working with the fitted garment rather than the corrected toile, baste the center of each garment-fabric section being embellished to a large rectangle of muslin, anchoring the section with long stitches and a four-pointed to eight-pointed star. Using a short stitch, baste the seam allowances to the muslin. Turn the section over, remove the basted star at the center and carefully trim away the muslin in the area to be embellished.

To check the alignment of the framed section, compare the grainlines and stitching lines to the toile or pattern and make any necessary corrections before beginning the embellishment. Then, after you've finished the embellishment, check the garment section again against the toile or pattern. Embellishments usually cause the design area to shrink, and you'll probably have to relocate and thread-trace new seamlines.

Once the embellishment is finished, remove the garment section from the frame. Then remove any bastings on the design, leaving thread-tracings on the grainlines and stitching lines, and press the garment section. To avoid flattening the design, cover the pressing table with a thick towel and press lightly from the wrong side.

APPLIQUÉ

One of the simplest and most versatile embellishments, appliqué is formed by applying one layer of fabric—the appliqué—to the surface of another—the background, or ground, which is usually the garment section. Both the appliqué and ground can be made from a variety of fabrics. The appliqués on couture garments are usually bold and decorative, but they can also enhance the design more subtly, especially on printed fabrics.

There are several ways to sew an appliqué, but the hemmed and embroidered methods are used most often in haute couture. For hemmed appliqués like that on the Mariska Karasz design shown on p. 200, narrow seam allowances are left at all of the edges and are turned under and secured by tiny fell stitches. Embroidered appliqués like those on the Givenchy fur coat (above right) have decoratively cut edges finished with couched thread, which don't require seam allowances. Embroidered appliqués are always worked on a frame, as are large hemmed appliqués. Smaller hemmed appliqués, however, are sometimes worked in the hand on a flat surface.

On this fur coat designed in the late 1970s by Hubert de Givenchy, the edges of the suede appliqué are concealed with a couched cording. (Installation photo by Irving Solero from the exhibition 'Givenchy: 30 Years.' The National Museum of Fashion at the Fashion Institute of Technology, New York.)

To sew a hemmed appliqué, begin by transferring the design to the right side of the ground fabric. Generally speaking, the garment will drape better if the appliqués are cut on the same grain as the ground, particularly if they're large. Transfer the design motifs to the appliqué material. The traced line should be the finished edge of the motif, not the cutting line. Then cut out the motifs with ¼-in. seam allowances. For large motifs like those on the Karasz design, it's usually easier to handle and less likely to distort the appliqué if you baste it to the garment section before cutting around the motifs.

MAKING A HEMMED APPLIQUÉ

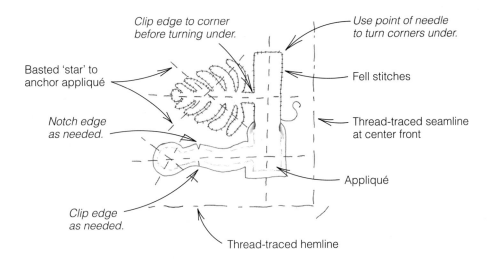

Clip edge to corner before turning under.

Use point of needle to turn corners under.

Basted 'star' to anchor appliqué

Fell stitches

Notch edge as needed.

Thread-traced seamline at center front

Appliqué

Clip edge as needed.

Thread-traced hemline

Working from the center toward the side seams, use fine needles to pin the appliqué to the ground, aligning the grainlines. Evaluate the design, and when necessary, rearrange the motifs. Baste the motif centers to the background with a four-pointed to eight-pointed star, depending on how large and complex the appliqué is, as shown above. Beginning with a small section, turn under the edge of the appliqué so that both the markings on the ground and appliqué are invisible, cutting the basting threads if necessary. Trim the seam allowances to ⅛ in. as needed around curves and points, and finger-press the edge. Secure the thread with a waste knot or backstitch and trim away the tail to avoid an unwanted shadow in the appliqué. Then, using fine silk or cotton thread in a color that matches the appliqué, secure permanently with a fell stitch, using the needle point to coax the seam allowances in place. On straight edges, make eight stitches per inch. On curves and angles, clip or notch as needed so the edges can be worked under neatly and space the stitches more closely together. The sharper the curve, the closer the stitches and clips will be. If the edge of the appliqué comes to a point, taper the seam allowance to the point and use your needle to work any stray threads under neatly.

When appliquéing a bias strip, it's sometimes easier to baste and/or press the seam allowances under before applying the strip to the ground. You must work carefully, though, to keep the finished width constant. To sew a bias strip, begin with a strip ½ in. wider than the finished appliqué and add ¼-in. seam allowances all around. Then, using a strip of cardboard as a pressing template, press the seam allowances under. Beginning with an outside edge, shape and pin a few inches of the bias strip to fit the traced design. Then work with two needles, one on each side of the strip, to attach it to the ground. First fell 2 in. to 4 in. of the outside edge of the strip with one needle, and fell the same distance on the inside edge with the second needle, repeating this process the full length of the strip. Sewing both sides of the strip at once prevents the inevitable rippling that would occur with a bias strip if you sewed it entirely along one side and then along the other side.

If your design includes turning a corner with the bias strip, anchor the tip of the corner on the outside edge first and then secure the inside edge, using the needle's point on both sides to shape the corner neatly. On unlined designs, space the stitches evenly so that the wrong side will also look attractive. (See pp. 45-46 for information on functional appliqué.)

PASSEMENTERIE

Passementerie is a form of embroidery using various trims and edgings such as braid, cord, fringe and ribbon to produce decorative patterns on a ground fabric. The trims can be sewn directly to the ground fabric, or they can be applied to a fabric band that is in turn appliquéd to the garment. Passementerie is worked with some of the basic techniques used in appliqué and can be applied to the garment with a variety of stitches, depending on the trim and desired finish. For inconspicuous applications, use fine silk or cotton thread in a color to match the trim.

You can apply passementerie by hand or by machine. If you're attaching flexible braids or cords to a garment by hand, use a running stitch secured with an occasional backstitch, which is easy and inconspicuous. For stiff braids and cords, use the slipstitch, fell stitch or couching stitch (see the drawing below), though the backstitch is the most secure. For a decorative finish, secure the trim with a couching stitch, using one or more contrasting threads. If you're applying passementerie by machine, use a cording or braiding foot (which is readily available at sewing-machine dealers) and a straight or zigzag stitch.

When you apply the trimming, work carefully to avoid twisting it. Corners should be sharp and curves should be smooth. If the trim is wide, keep it flat, miter the corners and secure both sides. Narrow trims can be stitched at the center or on one or both sides. Before pressing the embellished garment section, cover the pressing surface with a thick, soft pad or towel to avoid flattening the trim and place the garment section on it wrong side up. Press with a damp cloth and then press again until the fabric is smooth and dry.

For neat beginnings and endings on ribbons and wide trims, fold each end under, lay the ends flat against the fabric and fell them inconspicuously. If the trim is narrow, use an awl to make a small hole in the fabric and push the end of the trim through to the wrong side. If the end is frayed or soft, insert a thread loop from the wrong side, thread the end of the trim into the loop, and pull the loop and trim to the wrong side. Next, cut the trim end, leaving a tail about ½ in. long. Flatten the tail against the fabric so that it's aligned with the stitching along the trim and fasten it securely with a few hand stitches. Then trim the tail to ¼ in. When couching, secure the trim by sewing over it rather than through it.

The detail of this early 20th-century, princess-line dressing gown by an unknown designer is decorated with elaborate machine-stitched embroidery and braid passementerie in tree-like designs. At the coat's edges and seams, the passementerie was first applied to wide bands and then appliquéd to the fabric. (Photo by Susan Kahn. Metropolitan Museum of Art. Gift of Thomas Nichol, Jr., 1960.)

COUCHING STITCH

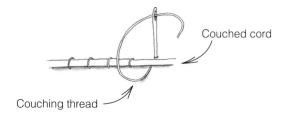

Couched cord

Couching thread

Beading

Beading is a form of embroidery that can sumptuously cover every thread of a garment or be limited to just a few motifs. Beaded embellishments are worked in everything from real gold, silver and cultured pearl beads to steel, glass and wooden beads, and even sequins. Apart from the expense of the beads themselves, the process is time-consuming and adds appreciably to the cost of a design.

In the beading workrooms in Paris and London, where most couture houses send their garments, beading is usually done with a tambour hook. This is a tool similar to a crochet hook that is held above the fabric (which is attached wrong side up to a frame) and passed through it to catch and anchor with a chainstitch a string of beads held in the other hand below the fabric (see the photo on p. 201). A few houses send their work to India or the Far East, where beading is generally done with a needle sewn through the individual beads to anchor them to the fabric.

Both methods have advantages and drawbacks. Since a tambour hook chainstitches around the thread holding the beads and doesn't pass through the beads themselves, very small beads can be used. However, if the thread holding the beads breaks, the chainstitches may unravel quickly and the beads will fall off the garment. By contrast, beading with a needle attaches the individual beads more securely but requires that the beads be large enough to enable a fine needle and thread to pass through the holes. Consequently the work is not as fine as that done with a tambour hook.

Regardless of the method you choose, use a large frame to hold the fabric taut. If you have a table that opens up to expand with a leaf, you can put the frame into the opening instead of the leaf, which is much more stable than propping the frame on the table or on sawhorses. Although limited space here permits only touching on a few basic beading techniques, they'll enable you to create many interesting designs.

Beads aren't always sewn directly onto the garment section. When I visited the firm of Lesage, Master Embroiderer, some of the workers were making separate beaded motifs on an organza backing that were to later be appliquéd to a garment. According to M. Lesage, this practice is not as unusual as it might seem. One

Beading and embroidery combine to create an elaborate design. (Photo courtesy of Lesage, Master Embroiderer.)

season Karl Lagerfeld, the couturier at Chanel, asked M. Lesage to bead a variety of classic Chanel motifs like lipsticks, double Cs, compacts and Chanel No. 5 bottles, working them as separate appliqués because he hadn't decided how he would use them.

There are at least two advantages to beading a separate appliqué rather than a garment section. First, the garment or toile doesn't have to be fitted before being beaded, and, second, the appliqué can be worked on a fabric that's especially suited for beading—for example, organza or the interfacing material Sewin' Sheer™, which home sewers will be familiar with.

Almost any sewing thread in cotton, silk, polyester or nylon can be used for beading. To strengthen the thread, pull a length of thread several times through a cake of beeswax. Then press the thread so the wax will penetrate it. If you're working with thread still on the spool, hold the thread between your thumb and index finger and pull it through to remove any excess wax. The thread color should generally match either the beads or the fabric, but, for a special effect, you can use a contrasting color.

For tambour work, you'll need a frame and tambour hook, which has a sharp point at the end and a notch above it. Tambour hooks are available in several sizes (see Sources of Supply on p. 215). To bead with a tambour hook, be sure you've transferred the design to the wrong side of the fabric and mounted the fabric wrong side up.

Beads can be purchased prestrung on lengths of thread or loose in vials or plastic bags. If you're working with prestrung beads and a tambour hook, you'll need to restring the beads since the thread they're strung on is probably fairly weak and may not be long enough to work with. Since you don't know how much thread you'll need, restring the beads onto a spool of thread rather than a cut length. To do this, first pierce the end of the spooled thread with the tambour hook or a needle. Pull the thread on which the beads are strung through this slit for several inches and then slide the beads from the old string to the new one. Pull out and discard the original string.

Making a chainstitch with a tambour hook and a string of beads is similar to crocheting a chainstitch with a crochet hook. Begin with one hand holding the tambour hook above the fabric and the other holding the restrung beads below the fabric. At the beginning of your design, pierce the fabric with the tambour hook, catch the spooled thread about 2 in. from the end of it and pull a thread loop through the fabric to the wrong side, without disturbing any of the beads. With the hook still in the loop you just made, secure the end of the thread by re-inserting the hook into the fabric behind where it first exited and pick up another loop. Pull the new loop up through the fabric and through the first loop, and then pull the first loop flat against the fabric.

BEADING WITH A TAMBOUR HOOK

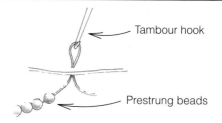

1. To begin beading, pierce fabric with hook and pull through loop of thread.

2. Reinsert hook through same loop, pull up second loop and pull first loop flat against fabric.

3. Once thread is anchored, chainstitch catching thread between beads to hold it against fabric.

Always keeping the hook in the last loop, insert it into the fabric again ahead of or to the side of where you just exited, as called for by your pattern. This time pick up the thread between the first two beads, and pull it through the fabric and the previous stitch so that the first bead is held tight against the right side of the fabric. Continue in this fashion, making the stitches the same length as the beads, until all the beads are applied to the fabric. (If you're beading sequins with a tambour hook, the sequins will stand on edge.)

To end the beading, insert the hook behind the last stitch, pick up the thread before the next bead, and pull it through the fabric and the loop on the hook. Break the thread, leaving a short tail.

VARIOUS WAYS OF BEADING WITH A NEEDLE

Beads applied with a running stitch

Beads, double sewn for security, applied with a running stitch

Beads applied with lazy stitch

Beads applied with couching stitch

Sequin, sewn with bead to secure it

Sequins sewn with backstitches

To bead with a needle you'll need beading or embroidery needles in a size appropriate for the beads or sequins. Begin with a medium-short length of thread and sew a waste knot and then two backstitches at the location for the first bead. Beads can be sewn quickly with a running stitch, but for more security, go through each bead a second time before sewing the next one. If the bead is too small for the needle to accommodate a second stitch, sew a backstitch in the fabric beneath the beads. You can sew several beads at one time by using a lazy stitch or by couching the strand of beads (see the drawing above).

To sew sequins or beads so that the stitches are invisible or to make the sequins stand on an edge, use a backstitch. You can also use a backstitch to sew sequins with a bead at the center or to create bead fringes. To end your bead work, make a figure-8 knot after the last bead and pull the knot through to the wrong side.

QUILTING

Quilting produces a surface that's either relatively flat or raised. Traditional pieced quilts are created by joining three layers—a top, filler and backing—and the thickness of their surface is fairly uniform. In trapunto quilting, sometimes called Italian or cord quilting, only two layers are joined—a top and a backing—but in between them, lengths of cording or small amounts of loose batting are inserted to create a raised design. Both types of quilted surfaces can be seen on the evening coat by Madame Grès for Alix on p. 186, and the Louis Féraud design below features corded trapunto.

Whether stitched by hand or machine, quilting can be applied to a variety of designs and fabrics. Heavy or thick fabrics are generally best avoided, however, since the quilting itself already adds weight to the garment. Because home sewers are generally familiar with flat quilting and there are many books on the subject, I want to focus here on trapunto. This raised quilting

Shown in Louis Féraud's Autumn/Winter 1991 Collection, both the red satin trenchcoat and bustier dress are richly embellished with corded trapunto quilting. (Photograph by Marc Martin, courtesy of Louis Féraud.)

works equally well to embellish large and small designs. The stuffing can be loose cotton or wool, silk batting, cords or yarn. If the garment is lined, the lining will cover the backing, and any utilitarian fabric like muslin, linen, woven interfacing, cheesecloth or lambswool can be used for the backing. If the garment is to be unlined, choose a fabric that complements the garment fabric.

To make trapunto, begin by transferring your design to the garment section, aligning the grainlines and basting the layers together at the seamline. Then mount the section on a frame. Quilt the design with a running stitch if you're going to stuff your design with cording or yarn and with a backstitch if you're working with thick or bulky stuffing or batting. In either case, make your stitches short and even, since trapunto highlights the quilting stitches. After you've finished quilting your design, take the work off the frame to stuff it.

If you're working with cording, it should be supple and soft enough so the twist doesn't show through the fabric. Although most yarns will not need to be preshrunk if the garment is to be dry-cleaned, cotton cords nonetheless do.

The best tools for threading the cord or yarn into the quilted channel are large tapestry needles and bodkins, which have blunt points and large eyes. In order to thread the needle with the cord, thread it first with a loop of regular thread. Then thread the cord into the thread loop and pull both the loop and the yarn through the needle's eye.

To insert the cord or yarn into the channel, begin at a corner or end of a channel. Make a hole in the backing with an awl by separating the threads and insert the needle without cutting the backing. Work the needle through the channel until you reach a corner or curve. Bring the needle out of the backing at this point and then reinsert it into the same hole to continue, leaving a ½-in. loop outside the lining. At the ends of the channels, cut the cord, leaving a 1-in. tail. When two channels cross, bring the second cord out and cut it, leaving a 1-in. tail; then reinsert the needle on the other side of the first cord. After all the channels have been padded, stretch the garment section gently in all directions. Many of the loops will disappear, and those that don't will be covered by the garment's lining. Cut the ends close to the backing.

TRAPUNTO

1. To thread needle with yarn or cord, insert yarn into thread loop passed through tapestry needle's eye. Then pull loop and cord through eye.

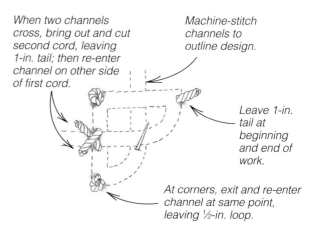

When two channels cross, bring out and cut second cord, leaving 1-in. tail; then re-enter channel on other side of first cord.

Machine-stitch channels to outline design.

Leave 1-in. tail at beginning and end of work.

At corners, exit and re-enter channel at same point, leaving ½-in. loop.

2. Insert cording into channels of design, leaving tail at beginning and end of work and loops at corners. When you're finished cording, gently stretch work in all directions to eliminate tails and loops.

If you're padding a design with a loose batting instead of cording, remove the garment section from the frame after stitching the quilted pattern. Cut a small slit in the backing with embroidery scissors in the first channel or area to be padded. Using an orange stick, gently push the batting in between the layers to fill the edges and corners of the design. If you make a small notch on the end of the orange stick, the batting will be easier to control. Work carefully to distribute the batting evenly and avoid lumps. After you've finished padding an area, close the slit with catchstitches, sewing into the batting for added security. Repeat this procedure, slitting, stuffing and catchstitching each area of quilting until the entire design is padded.

TOPSTITCHING

Topstitching can be used to create stunning embellishments, like that on the blouse shown at right. A popular embellishment in the 1960s and early 1970s, topstitching is appropriate for most fabrics and a variety of garments from sporty daywear to dressy evening designs. It's usually done with silk buttonhole twist, and less often with fine silk or cotton thread.

When applied to pockets and hemlines on couture garments, topstitching often looks more functional than it actually is. On ready-to-wear garments, topstitching is usually a construction element, holding facings or hems on details like pockets in place at edges.

In couture workrooms, topstitching is generally completed early in the construction process, before facings or linings are applied. The advantage of this early application is that without the facings and linings in place, there is less bulk and fewer layers to control, eliminating many of the problems that frustrate home sewers.

Since topstitching is generally done with the garment section right side up, be very careful when transferring the design to the garment section so that the markings don't show after the garment is topstitched. Before stitching the garment, make several samples on fabric scraps, experimenting with different threads, needles, stitch gauges, tension and even machine feet. Then, to topstitch the garment, begin with a new needle and plenty of thread on both the bobbin and spool. When the design is on the lengthwise grain, near the center of the garment, as it is on the Chanel blouse shown above, press a fold to mark the garment center. Then stitch from the center of the design out to the sides, completing the one side and then the other, which will prevent distorting the topstitching. When the design is parallel to an edge of the garment, use the thread tracing at the seamline or foldline as a guide, but try to avoid stitching over the thread tracings since they're almost impossible to pull out.

TUCKS

Used singly, clustered or sewn over an entire garment, tucks can range in size from tiny pintucks to wide, flat tucks. They can all be the same size or graduated, and they can be flat or stand up. They're usually sewn on the lengthwise grain, but they can be made on the crossgrain and bias as well as on curves. When sewn on the crossgrain or bias, they will not lie as flat or press as

Created in 1968 for an elegant Chanel cocktail suit, this blouse is decorated with topstitched 'stripes' from two to five rows wide. The neckline is trimmed with a separate, narrow, topstitched tube. (Photo by Irving Solero. The National Museum of Fashion at the Fashion Institute of Technology. Gift of Mrs. Lawrence Cowen.)

well as when sewn on the straight grain. Usually made by hand, tucks can be stitched completely from top to bottom or stitched partially and released.

Tucks require extra fabric, and designs like the Vionnet dress shown on p. 118 demand considerable planning. Simple parallel rows of tucks, like those in the Chanel blouse on p. 210 and in the blouse by Valentino on p. 28, are less complicated in design and planning.

When calculating the amount of extra fabric required for each tuck, remember that the minimum amount needed is twice the width of the tuck. As with most embellishments, there will also be additional shrinkage in the area of the garment section being tucked. The amount of shrinkage depends on the number of tucks in the area, and to compensate, you'll probably need additional fabric. As a ballpark estimate, plan on adding about 1/16 in. extra fabric for every tuck.

To mark the tucks, thread-trace the two stitching lines for each tuck, unless you're making very narrow 1/16-in. to 1/8-in. pintucks, in which case, thread-trace the foldline. With wrong sides together, fold and pin the fabric

Made entirely by hand, this elegant chiffon blouse was designed by Coco Chanel in 1937 for Diana Vreeland to accompany a black sequined trouser suit. It features tiny pintucks separated by strips of lace insertion, and ruffled chiffon that appears to be gathered at the neckline and center front but is actually made with short, released tucks. (Photograph by David Coffin, courtesy of the Board of Trustees of the Victoria & Albert Museum.)

so that the lines of thread tracing match, and baste them. Next, with a long, fine needle and very fine thread matching the fabric, use a short running stitch to sew the tuck permanently. Keep the stitches short and even, beginning and ending with two backstitches, and except for very long tucks, avoid breaking the thread in the center of a tuck. On curved tucks, since the underside is fuller than the right side, pull up the thread tracing before basting the tuck so that the fullness is distributed evenly. Then baste with the right side up so you can regulate the fullness.

THE BRIDAL GOWN

Traditionally, the finale of a couture collection is the bridal gown. From breathtakingly beautiful designs with yards of satin and lace to outlandish creations, bridal gowns are important to most couture houses because they're often the first, and sometimes the only, design a client will order. Of course, bridal gowns are also very important to home sewers, who may want to lavish more time than usual on labor-intensive couture techniques for this special garment.

For the home sewer, the success of the bridal gown depends as much on advance planning as on the amount of money spent. The design can be traditional or high-tech, but whatever its style, it should flatter the figure, hang perfectly without wrinkling and make the bride look as special as she feels. Making a toile for a wedding gown is crucial to be sure of a perfect fit and a flattering design (not to mention that it helps keep the gown much cleaner during its construction). And choosing the right backing and interfacing materials as well as making a corselette or appropriate underpinning will likewise be integral to the gown's success (see p. 53, p. 120 and p. 122 for information on backings and interfacings, and pp. 195-198 for information on making a corselette).

Among notable bridal gowns in this century was that of Princess Elizabeth for her 1947 wedding. The gown took 350 workers at the House of Hartnell in London seven weeks to make. Even though Great Britain still had major shortages and rationing because of the war, the satin dress and 15-yd. tulle train were richly embroidered with 10,000 imported pearls and crystals (the princess and her bridesmaids were allowed extra rationing coupons!). The train was attached at the shoulders with buttons and loops—a nice detail for modern brides.

By contrast, Princess Margaret's 1960 bridal gown, also designed by Hartnell, was a simple, V-neck princess-line design trimmed only with a narrow bias binding. Made of 30 yd. of diaphanous silk, its 12-gored skirt flared into an attractive bell shape and was supported by numerous layers of silk tulle and stiff nylon net. An inverted pleat at center back allowed the skirt to open for sitting and fall back into place when the princess stood, covering the wrinkles—another interesting design idea for home sewers.

Couture houses often tuck at least one good-luck charm into their bridal gowns. At Hartnell, the workers cover a small cardboard horseshoe with blue satin ribbon and sew it inside the hem. (Princess Diana's 1981 wedding gown, created by luxury ready-to-wear designers David and Elizabeth Emanuel, had a tiny gold horseshoe studded with diamonds and a small blue bow sewn in the hem.) At Hardy Amies, a married worker may sew a strand of her hair in the hem to wish the bride luck—or a single worker may tuck a strand in the hem in hopes of becoming the next bride.

Designed by Christian Dior for his 1949 Autumn/Winter Collection, 'Fidélité' is made of white satin and tulle. The skirt features a satin apron draped over an enormous skirt of tulle and tied loosely at the back, design elements that Dior varied in collections for several seasons. (Photo by Willy Maywald, courtesy of Christian Dior.)

SELECTED GLOSSARY OF TERMS

Applied-welt pocket: *See* Set-in pocket.

Armscye: Armhole.

Backing: Layer of support fabric applied to the wrong side of a garment section before the seam is sewn; called the underlining in home sewing.

Balance lines: Horizontal and vertical lines marked on the garment or muslin pattern to aid in fitting the garment.

Basting(s): Sewing temporary stitches into the garment for marking or holding fabric layers together until they're permanently stitched; also, the threads that are basted and generally removed before pressing.

Bespoke: English term describing a garment cut from a pattern custom-made for an individual client.

Bias: True bias refers to a hypothetical line at a 45° angle to the lengthwise grain of the fabric. Generally the term *bias* refers to any line that's off-grain but, in this book, is used to mean true bias.

Blind buttonhole: Decorative, non-functional buttonhole that can be either hand-worked (in which case the opening is not cut) or bound (in which case, the facing is not cut).

Bobbinet: Cotton tulle used for corselettes and sometimes called English net.

Bound pocket: *See* Set-in pocket.

Breakpoint: Beginning of the roll line on the front edge of the jacket.

Bridle: Roll line on a tailored jacket or coat; also the tape applied to roll line.

Canvas: Hair canvas interfacing; also, the inner structure of interfacings and backing of a tailored garment.

Catchstitch: Hand-sewn stitch that looks like the letter X and is used for sewing one edge or layer flat against another.

CB: Center back.

CF: Center front.

Chambre syndicale de la couture parisienne: Parisian High Fashion Syndicate, the organization governing the French haute couture industry.

Collar fall: Section of collar between the roll line and outer edge.

Collar linen: Crisp interfacing used in tailoring, sometimes called collar or French canvas.

Collar stand: Section of collar between the roll line and neckline.

Cording a buttonhole: Supporting and enhancing the appearance of a bound or hand-worked buttonhole with cord or several strands of thread inserted into the welts of a bound buttonhole or laid around the opening of a hand-worked buttonhole and covered with buttonhole stitches.

Couching: Embroidery technique for securing cords, threads or braids laid in decorative patterns on a fabric's surface by sewing over them with fine, inconspicuous or decorative thread.

Couturier: French term for a male or female designer at a couture house. (*Couturière* refers to a French seamstress or dressmaker, though it's occasionally used to describe a female couturier.)

Creaseline: Synonym for roll line.

Crossgrain: The weft yarns in fabric, which cross the vertical warp yarns and are at a right angle to the selvage.

Dart take-up: The fabric between the stitching lines of a dart, which is stitched out on finished garment.

Dauber: Small roll of muslin dipped in water and used to apply moisture to sections of a garment for pressing.

Domette: Synonym for lambswool.

Ease: To join two garment sections unequal in length, smoothly without gathers or pleats; also, a small amount of fabric fullness on one garment section, making it longer than the section it joins. Ease is used to provide shaping on the sleeve cap, back shoulder, bust and skirt waist.

Edgestitch: Row of stitching positioned about $\frac{1}{16}$ in. from an edge or seamline.

Face: Right side of the fabric or outside of the garment.

Fell: Inconspicuous stitch used for hemming, seaming and basting; also, to sew with a fell stitch, generally from the right side of the fabric.

Finger-press: Light pressing of the fabric with the fingertips after it has been pressed with steam.

Fitting: In couture, the term refers to the several sessions in which the client tries on the garment, whose fit is checked and adjusted as needed.

Flange: Pleat extending from the shoulder at the armscye.

Fulling: Adding fullness to the garment lining or backing so that the firmly woven lining or backing fabrics will not pull at the seams or restrict movement; also, the process of easing lapel facings to the jacket fronts or the collar to the undercollar to build shape into the garment.

Garment body: Garment front and back, excluding the sleeves.

Gorge line: Seamline that joins the collar and lapel.

Grainline: Direction of the yarns in the fabric's weave; the lengthwise, straight or vertical grain is that of the lengthwise warp threads; the crossgrain, or horizontal grain, is that of the crossing weft threads. Unless otherwise specified, grainline in this book refers to the lengthwise grain.

Grosgrain: A firmly woven ribbon with crossgrain ribs.

Ground: Background material for appliqué, embroidery and beading.

Holding short: Shaping the garment to fit the contours of the body by making the facing slightly smaller than the garment itself.

Hong Kong finish: Term used in home sewing to describe a bias-binding seam finish.

Hymo: Type of hair canvas, available in several weights.

Inseam pocket: *See* Set-in pocket.

Interfacing: Layer of support fabric between the garment and facing, generally applied at the garment edges to add body and stabilize the edge.

Lambswool: Soft, knitted fabric with a fleece on one side, used for interfacing and backing.

Matchpoints: Marked points on seamlines that are aligned when the garment is assembled. In home sewing, matchpoints are marked by notches on cutting edges and with circles or squares on seamlines.

Miter: Diagonal seamline at a corner; also, to join two edges at an angle.

Muslin: Inexpensive, plain-weave cotton fabric available in several weights and used for making toiles; also, the muslin toile itself.

Neckpoint: Point on the body at the base of the neck where the shoulder begins.

Notch: Angle formed where the collar joins the lapel.

Padstitch: Small diagonal stitches used in tailoring to sew two layers together to shape and/or add body to a garment section.

Petersham: Belting material similar to grosgrain but slightly heavier and crisper, used for interfacing, facings and stays.

Plain-weave silk: Silk such as China silk, silk muslin and silk organza with a plain weave, which is generally used for linings, backings, underpinnings, blouses and some dresses.

Press: To apply heat and sometimes moisture to flatten and/or permanently set a seam, hem or other part of a garment or garment section. In this book, the instruction "press the seam" generally means first to press it flat as sewn, then to press it open.

Rever: Lapel.

Roll line: Creaseline that separates a jacket front from the lapel.

Round corners: To trim and transform a square corner into one with a gentle curve.

Rucks: Upper ridges of gathers.

Première d'atelier: Head of a couture workroom, usually a woman (*premier* refers to a male head of a workroom, usually a tailoring atelier).

RS: Right side of the fabric, garment or garment section.

Running stitch: Permanent stitch used for seams, tucks, gathers and quilting, which can be even or uneven and long or short; sometimes called a forward stitch.

Seam slippage: Undesirable separation of fabric yarns at seamlines.

Set: Term used in fitting to describe how a garment sits on the body; also, a pressing term meaning to establish the permanent position of an edge or other part of a garment.

Set-in pocket: Bound, inseam or applied-welt pocket, which is set into a seam or slash in the garment body.

Shape: To shrink and/or stretch a garment section with heat and moisture.

Shell: Outside part of garment, not the lining.

Shell fabric: Garment fabric.

Shoulder point: Point on the body at the end of the shoulder.

Sleeve cap: Section of the sleeve above the underarm seam.

Sleeve head: Strip of wadding or interfacing used to support the sleeve cap.

Slipstitch: Stitch made from the right side of the fabric and used both for basting (and then called "slipbasting") and for permanently sewing seams that are intricately shaped or need to have patterns matched or be eased.

Sloper: Very fitted, basic muslin garment, used as a guide for adjusting the fit of other garments, for developing other designs and for padding a dress form; in French, referred to as a *toile de corps*.

Stay: Tape sewn to an edge or seam to prevent it from stretching; also, a small piece of interfacing used to reinforce an area like a pocket opening; also, a device like lingerie straps used to anchor a garment and prevent it from shifting unattractively when the body moves.

Styleline: The outside edge of a collar, cuff or lapel; the upper edge of a strapless garment; also, an unusual pocket opening, hemline or sleeve edge.

Tailor's tacks: Small thread tacks used in tailoring for marking seamlines and construction matchpoints on the fabric.

Thread tracing: A basting stitch used for marking seamlines and construction matchpoints on the fabric.

Toile: A fitting garment made of muslin for an individual client or a new design; also, the pattern this fitting garment produces.

Toile de corps: See Sloper.

Top-baste: To baste on the right side of the garment through all layers in order to hold a seam, dart or edge flat for sewing, pressing or fitting.

Topstitch: Row of stitching that shown on outside of garment.

Underlining: See Backing.

Underpinnings: Undergarments such as foundations, petticoats and corselettes that are necessary to support a design.

Utica linen: Closely woven linen used for interfacing.

Vent: Finished opening at one end of seam, used at the wrist edge of sleeves and at the hemline of some jackets and skirts.

Wadding: Cotton batting with a slick finish on one or both sides, used for making padding, shoulder pads and sleeve heads.

Wheel: To trace markings on cut or uncut fabric, the muslin toile or paper patterns with a dressmaker's tracing wheel.

Wigan: Cotton interfacing used in tailoring.

WS: Wrong side of the fabric, garment or garment section.

METRIC EQUIVALENCY CHART

One inch equals approximately 2.54 centimeters. To convert inches to centimeters, multiply the figure in inches by 2.54 and round off to the nearest half centimeter, or use the chart below, whose figures are rounded off (one centimeter equals ten millimeters).

⅛ in. = 3mm	9 in. = 23cm
¼ in. = 6mm	10 in. = 25.5cm
⅜ in. = 1cm	12 in. = 30.5cm
½ in. = 1.3cm	14 in. = 35.5cm
⅝ in. = 1.5cm	15 in. = 38cm
¾ in. = 2cm	16 in. = 40.5cm
⅞ in. = 2.2cm	18 in. = 45.5cm
1 in. = 2.5cm	20 in. = 51cm
2 in. = 5cm	21 in. = 53.5cm
3 in. = 7.5cm	22 in. = 56cm
4 in. = 10cm	24 in. = 61cm
5 in. = 12.5cm	25 in. = 63.5cm
6 in. = 15cm	36 in. = 92cm
7 in. = 18cm	45 in. = 114.5cm
8 in. = 20.5cm	60 in. = 152cm

SELECTED BIBLIOGRAPHY

*Out of print (check your library or see Sources of Supply on p. 215 for locating out-of-print books).

EMBELLISHMENTS

Bryant, Jan. "Tambour Beading." *Threads* 44 (December 1992) 50-53.

Caulfeild, S.F.A. and Blanche C. Saward. *Encyclopedia of Victorian Needlework*. New York: Dover Publications, 1972. (Good section on embroidery.)

de Dillmont, Thérèse. *The Complete Encyclopedia of Needlework*. Philadelphia: Running Press, 1978. (Good embroidery information; available from Lacis—see Sources of Supply.)

Jarratt, Maisie. *How to Bead: French Embroidery Beading*. Kenthurst, Australia: Kangaroo Press, 1991. (Available from Lacis—see Sources of Supply.)

Leffingwell, Jeanne. "A Thousand Points of Light." *Threads* 30 (August 1990) 38-41.

Morgan, Mary, and Dee Mosteller. *Trapunto and Other Forms of Raised Quilting*. New York: Charles Scribner's Sons, 1977.

Thompson, Angela. *Embroidery with Beads*. London: B.T. Batsford Ltd., 1987.

Yanagi, Amy, ed. *Stitchery and Needle Lace*. Newtown, Conn.: The Taunton Press, 1991.

FASHION HISTORY AND HAUTE COUTURE

Arch, Nigel, and Joanna Marschner. *The Royal Wedding Dresses*. London: Sidgwick & Jackson, 1990.

*Batterberry, Michael and Ariane. *Mirror, Mirror*. New York: Holt, Rinehart and Winston, 1977.

*Bertin, Célia. *Paris à la Mode*. London: Victor Gollancz Ltd., 1956.

*Boucher, François. *20,000 Years of Fashion*. New York: Harry N. Abrams, nd.

Charles, Regan. "La Creme de la Hem." *Avenue* 13, 6 (January 1989) 94-107.

*Coleman, Elizabeth Ann. *The Genius of Charles James*. Brooklyn: The Brooklyn Museum, 1982.

*Contini, Mila. *Fashion from Ancient Egypt to the Present Day*. New York: The Odyssey Press, 1965.

Cumming, Valerie. *Royal Dress*. New York: Holmes & Meier, 1989.

de Marly, Diana. *The History of Haute Couture 1850-1950*. London: B.T. Batsford Ltd., 1980.

*de Pietri, Stephen, and Melissa Leventon. *New Look to Now: French Haute Couture 1947-87*. San Francisco: The Fine Arts Museum of San Francisco, 1989.

Deslandres, Yvonne, and Florence Müller. *Histoire de la mode au XXe siècle*. Paris: Somogy, 1986.

*Dior, Christian. *Christian Dior and I*. New York: E.P. Dutton & Co., 1954.

Garfinkel, Stanley. *Completely Dior*. Cleveland: Telos Video Communications, 1987. Videotape.

——. Unpublished interview with Henriette Moon and Mrs. William Randolph Hearst.

Givenchy: 30 Years. New York: The Fashion Institute of Technology, 1982.

*Lambert, Eleanor. *World of Fashion: People, Places, Resources*. New York: R.R. Bowker, 1976.

Laver, James. *Costume*. New York: Hawthorn Books, 1963. Reprint. New York: Dover Publications.

*Lynam, Ruth, ed. *Couture*. New York: Doubleday and Company, 1972.

Man and the Horse. New York: Metropolitan Museum of Art, 1984.

Martin, Richard, and Harold Koda. *Flair: Fashion Collected by Tina Chow*. New York: Rizzoli International Publications, 1992.

Milbank, Caroline R. *Couture: The Great Designers*. New York: Stewart, Tabori & Chang, 1985.

Mulvagh, Jane. *The Vogue History of 20th-Century Fashion*. London: Viking, 1988.

O'Hara, Georgina. *The Encyclopaedia of Fashion*. London: Thames and Hudson, 1986.

*Penn, Irving, and Diana Vreeland. *Inventive Paris Clothes, 1909-1939*. New York: Viking Press, 1977.

*Picken, Mary Brooks, and Dora Loues Miller. *Dressmakers of France*. New York: Harper & Brothers, Publishers, 1956.

Steele, Valerie. *Paris Fashion: A Cultural History*. New York: Oxford University Press, 1988.

——. *Women of Fashion: Twentieth Century Designers*. New York: Rizzoli International Publications, 1991.

White, Palmer. *The Master Touch of Lesage*. Rungis, France: Chene, 1987.

Wilcox, Claire, and Valerie Mendes. *Modern Fashion in Detail*. London: Victoria & Albert Museum, 1991.

Yves Saint Laurent. New York: Metropolitan Museum of Art, 1983.

FITTING

Amaden-Crawford, Connie. *The Art of Fashion Draping*. New York: Fairchild Publications, 1989.

Bray, Natalie. *Dress Fitting*. London: Granada, 1978. (Distributed by Sheridan House, 145 Palisade St., Dobbs Ferry, NY 10522.)

Hilhouse, Marion S., and Evelyn A. Mansfield. *Dress Design: Draping and Flat Pattern Making*. Boston: Houghton Mifflin, 1948.

King, Judith E. *The Custom Dress Form*. Dayton, Ohio: Designing Lady Studio (325 Maysfield Rd.), 1989.

Kopp, Ernestine, et al. *How to Draft Basic Patterns*. New York: Fairchild Publications, 1991.

Liechty, Elizabeth L., et al. *Fitting & Pattern Alteration: A Multi-Method Approach*. New York: Fairchild Publications, 1986.

Stern, Suzanne Pierrette. "Padding a Dress Form." *Threads* 44 (December 1992) 35-37.

SEWING AND PRESSING TECHNIQUES

Cabrera, Roberto, and Patricia Flaherty Meyers. *Classic Tailoring Techniques: A Construction Guide for Women's Wear*. New York: Fairchild Publications, 1984.

Coffin, David. "Irons, Boards and Presses." *Threads* 10 (April 1987) 40-43.

di Bello, Angelina. *Haute Couture Techniques*. Montreal: Angelina di Bello, 1990.

Hopkins, J.C. *Edwardian Ladies' Tailoring: The Twentieth-Century System of Ladies' Garment Cutting.* 4th ed. Reprint, edited by R.L. Shep. Mendocino, Calif.: R.L. Shep, 1990. (Available from Lacis—*see* Sources of Supply.)

*Kennett, Frances. *Secrets of the Couturiers.* London: Orbis, 1982.

*Liberty, J.E. *Practical Tailoring.* New York: Pitman Publishing Corporation, 1955.

*Mansfield, Evelyn A. *Clothing Construction.* Boston: Houghton Mifflin Co., 1953.

*Mauck, Frances F. *Modern Tailoring for Women.* New York: The Macmillan Company, 1947.

*Picken, Mary Brooks. *The Language of Fashion.* New York: Funk & Wagnalls Company, 1939.

*Poulin, Clarence. *Tailoring Suits the Professional Way.* Peoria, Ill.: Chas. A. Bennett Co., 1953.

Reader's Digest. *Complete Guide to Sewing.* Pleasantville, N.Y.: The Reader's Digest Association, 1976.

Rhodes, Elizabeth A. "Charles Kleibacker." Unpublished manuscript.

Shaeffer, Claire B. *The Complete Book of Sewing Short Cuts.* New York: Sterling Publishing Co., 1981.

——. *Claire Shaeffer's Fabric Sewing Guide.* Radnor, Pa.: Chilton Book Co., 1989.

——. *Sew Any Patch Pocket.* Radnor, Pa.: Chilton Book Co., 1989.

——. *Sew Any Set-In Pocket.* Radnor, Pa.: Chilton Book Co., 1989.

Vogue Sewing. New York: Harper & Row, Publishers, 1980.

*Wilson, J. King. *The Art of Cutting and Fitting.* London: Crosby Lockwood & Son, Ltd., 1950.

Yanagi, Amy, ed. *Fit and Fabric.* Newtown, Conn.: The Taunton Press, 1991.

——. *Great Sewn Clothes.* Newtown, Conn.: The Taunton Press, 1991.

——. *Jackets, Coats and Suits.* Newtown, Conn.: The Taunton Press, 1993.

SOURCES OF SUPPLY

TAILORING SUPPLIES, INTERFACINGS, INDUSTRIAL IRONS AND PRESSING TOOLS, DRESS FORMS, THREAD

Atlanta Thread & Supply Co.
695 Red Oak Rd.
Stockbridge, GA 30281
(800) 847-1001
Catalog.

Banasch's
2810 Highland Ave.
Cincinnati, OH 45212
(800) 543-0355
Catalog. $50 minimum.

B. Black & Sons
548 S. Los Angeles St.
Los Angeles, CA 90013
(213) 624-9451
All supplies above except dress forms. Price list, interfacing samples. $20 minimum.

Greenberg & Hammer
24 W. 57th St.
New York, NY 10019
(800) 955-5135
Also has boning, weights and chains, horsehair braid and tracing paper. Catalog, swatches. $10 minimum.

Oregon Tailor Supply Co., Inc.
2123 S.E. Division St.
P.O. Box 42284
Portland, OR 07242
(503) 232-6191
Price list.

MISCELLANEOUS SUPPLIES

Britex
146 Geary St.
San Francisco, CA 94108
(415) 392-2910
Cotton tulle, interfacings, lambswool, cotton batting. $25 minimum.

G Street Fabrics
11854 Rockville Pike
Rockville, MD 20852
(800) 333-9191
Cotton tulle, boning, threads, weights and chains, petersham, books.

Lacis
2982 Adeline St.
Berkeley, CA 94703
(510) 843-7178
Books, needles, tambour hooks, threads, cotton tulle. Catalog.

The Sewing Emporium
P.O. Box 5049
1079 Third Ave.
Chula Vista, CA 92012
(619) 420-3490
Embroidery frames, professional irons. Catalog.

Things Japanese
9805 N.E. 116th St.
Kirkland, WA 98034
(800) 327-4222
Silk threads. Price list. Color chart.

TreadleArt
25834 Narbonne Ave.
Lomita, CA 90717
(310) 534-5122
DMC thread. Catalog, $3, refundable.

TSI
P.O. Box 9266
101 Nickerson St.
Seattle, WA 98109
(800) 426-9984
Beads and needles; tambour hooks special-ordered. Catalog. $25 minimum.

BOOKS AND OUT-OF-PRINT PUBLICATIONS

Books on Cloth
P.O. Box 2706
Fort Bragg, CA 95437
(707) 964-8662

Claire B. Shaeffer
P.O. Box 157
Palm Springs, CA 92263

Hard-to-Find Needlework Books
96 Roundwood Rd.
Newton, MA 02164
(617) 969-0942

Wooden Porch Books
Rt. 1, Box 262
Middlebourne, WV 26149
(304) 386-4434

INDEX

SENIOR EDITOR: Christine Timmons

PRELIMINARY EDITOR: Deborah Kops

DESIGNER/LAYOUT ARTIST: Catherine Cassidy

COPY/PRODUCTION EDITOR: Pam Purrone

PHOTOGRAPHER, EXCEPT WHERE NOTED: Susan Kahn

ILLUSTRATOR: Steve Buchanan

TYPEFACE: Goudy